Gertrud Kolmar

Dieter Kühn

Gertrud Kolmar

A Literary Life

Translated from the German by Linda Marianiello,

with poetry translated by Franz Vote

NORTHWESTERN UNIVERSITY PRESS
EVANSTON, ILLINOIS

Northwestern University Press
www.nupress.northwestern.edu

Printed in the United States of America

10 9 8 7 6 5 4 3 2 1

Library of Congress Cataloging-in-Publication Data

Kühn, Dieter, 1935–
    [Gertrud Kolmar. English]
    p. cm.
    Gertrud Kolmar : a literary life / Dieter Kuhn; translated from the German by Linda
Marianiello, with poetry translated by Franz Vote.
    "Originally published in German as Gertrud Kolmar. Leben und Werk. Zeit und Tod
in 2008 by S. Fischer Verlag GmbH, Frankfurt am Main 2008. \"
    ISBN 978-0-8101-2879-8 (cloth : alk. paper)
    1. Kolmar, Gertrud, 1894–1943? 2. Poets, German—20th century—Biography. I.
Marianiello, Linda. II. Vote, Franz. III. Title.
PT2605.H54Z747 2013
831.912—dc23

                                                                                          2012041526

∞ The paper used in this publication meets the minimum requirements of the American
National Standard for Information Sciences—Permanence of Paper for Printed Library
Materials, ANSI Z39.48–1992.

CONTENTS

Translator's Preface   vii

Gertrud Kolmar: A Literary Life   1

Afterword   361

Glossary   365

Index to Poetry Titles in English   367

Index to Poetry Titles in German   369

Writing for one of Germany's leading national newspapers, the *Frankfurter Allgemeine Zeitung,* Wolfgang Schneider said that "Dieter Kühn has reinvented the art of historical narrative." Kühn's German publisher, S. Fischer Verlag, had this to say about *Gertrud Kolmar: Leben und Werk, Zeit und Tod* [*Gertrud Kolmar: Life and Work, Times and Death*]: "Dieter Kühn's polyphonic biography tells the story of the great poet and her Jewish family, a family that was forced to emigrate to the four corners of the world. By way of documents, eyewitness reports, and letters, he presents a literary and political picture, a broad panorama of the period."

The English translation of Kühn's biography of the Berlin poet Gertrud Kolmar has been more than two years in the making. Some aspects of the work may initially strike you as foreign, because Gertrud Kolmar's world was rather far removed from our own. Yet when we look beyond superficial differences, Kolmar was not so different from you or me: she lived, she loved, and she created. And she did so in an era when women had many fewer rights and a murderous Nazi dictatorship decimated German culture.

Great care has been taken to ensure that the English translation, titled *Gertrud Kolmar: A Literary Life,* conveys the meaning of the original German text. Our special thanks to Dieter Kühn, whose generous, ongoing participation in the translation process helped us to remain faithful to his intentions. He is also responsible for the abridged version of the work on which the English translation is based. Our condensed biography of the poet thus includes those portions of the original work that he—and not we—considered essential.

Gertrud Kolmar: A Literary Life begins with an imaginary letter from Gertrud's father, Ludwig Chodziesner, to Gertrud's younger sister, Hilde. Dieter Kühn calls such letters "factitions." At the beginning of chapter 2, Kühn explains their purpose: "So as to clearly differentiate, I will identify letters that are not part of the written record as 'factition'—that is, fiction based on fact. Put another way, these interfamilial letters shall stay within sight of verifiable facts. They are meant to connect, form a bridge, create an atmosphere, and bring to mind the poet's symbiotic surroundings."

To differentiate between "factitions" and other, historical texts from which Dieter Kühn also quotes extensively, we have italicized the imaginary writings.

With regard to chapter 1, in particular, I believe that the following quotation from the opening "factition" will help you to understand why Kühn chose to open the work in this particular way: "Whoever wishes to understand her must first understand her father. For, in many respects, his eldest daughter followed in his footsteps." Throughout the work, Kühn capably demonstrates that the symbiotic relationship between Gertrud Kolmar and her father played a significant role in her life and career. On the positive side, this unusually close father-daughter relationship gave Kolmar the financial freedom to practice her craft.

We decided to use British spellings for Gertrud Kolmar's writings, for those of other family members and contemporaries, and for Kühn's "factitions." This gives their writing a more authentic flavor, while also transporting modern readers to another time and place. Gertrud Kolmar was proficient in many foreign languages, including English. She would most likely have known and used British English. On the other hand, Kühn's writings and all other portions of the biography, including the poetry translations, are written in U.S. English. This decision is very much in keeping with the polyphonic nature of the text: We can almost hear the voices of the various characters that make up the fabric of Kühn's newly created historical genre. In my view, this musical and theatrical element plays a major role in the effectiveness of his narrative.

My colleague Franz Vote translated the poetry in *Gertrud Kolmar: A Literary Life*. In addition to his expertise in the field of translation, Maestro Vote is a noted opera conductor. He consciously decided not to preserve the rhyme scheme of Kolmar's poetry, but to focus on rhythm, flow, and imagery instead. The poet-translator Jon Delcourt also served as poetry editor. Many thanks to both of them for their important contributions to the successful completion of this multifaceted project.

Finally, please refer to the glossary at the end of the book. We have tried to include footnotes in places where unfamiliar terms, facts, or names appear in the text. Some German keywords don't readily translate into English, so we've also added them to the glossary that you may revisit them at any time. These terms are not merely words, but the reflection of an entire cultural orientation and way of thinking. The word *Volk* is just one example of a word that was loaded with nationalistic and cultural significance in nineteenth- and twentieth-century Germany.

As translator, I feel that I've come to know Gertrud Kolmar and her family personally. My world has become larger in the process. Along with Dieter Kühn, I grieve when Gertrud and her father die at the hands of their Nazi persecutors. And I rejoice at her profound ability to write poetry for eternity, which was her express desire. For Gertrud Kolmar was one of Germany's greatest twentieth-century poets. She was also an intensely private person who lovingly served others. How lucky we are to be able to read her work today. If family members had not hidden her poems and other literary works during the Second World War, they would have been lost to us forever. I hope that you, too, will be deeply moved and inspired by the person and poetry of Gertrud Kolmar.

—*Linda Marianiello*

Gertrud Kolmar

Alive, you dead, you're alive; for I'm alive today.

You may well once have died, once been different.

But be now, and be this: for me.

—GERTRUD KOLMAR

In the future, someone will surely ask, "Who was the father of this great poet?" More precisely, what sort of person was this with whom Gertrud not only shared a home these many years but also collaborated so closely? I've planned to write down my recollections for quite some time. You just asked me about it again the other day. My response was more of a postponement, for I wasn't hedging the question. But the undertaking brooks no further delay.

I can assure you of one thing straightaway, dear Hilde: I won't be penning any memoirs. Particularly in view of Gertrud, I'd rather leave it to you to write our family chronicle. Insofar as work in chambers allows, I can merely do the preparatory work. You can do what you like with whatever I gradually submit to you.

So this letter will be a sort of script, a source document. You're already familiar with what I'm putting down here initially, but it's still worth mentioning. As a jurist, I must first come to terms with what is, for me, a new kind of written statement. However it may turn out, I'm saving you a bit of trouble in terms of what you have to ask about or track down. And I'll provide myself with a clear point of departure by starting with what's familiar, what's already known within our family.

I've given Gertrud the day off. A fair copy of my expert opinion can wait until tomorrow. She's making use of the nice weather to take a walk in the woods with the dog. Since that will drag on for another hour or two, I can think back a ways and bring to mind the roots of my life that are, and shall remain, closely entwined with those of your sisters and brother. As I said, it remains to be seen whether you will choose the same starting point. I am simply submitting a kind of "building material" to be freely exploited and utilised.

Now then, let us begin with the usual particulars! We Chodziesners got our name from the little town of Chodziez, north of present-day Poznan.

I must pause here, stop myself, for our name mustn't remain a mere, "bare" footnote, as it were. After all, Gertrud has done her part to ensure that it is known beyond the family circle. Up to now, I've spoken to you children about it only indirectly, so let me fill you in. For the record, I must add that neither you, your sister Margot, nor your brother Georg has ever really asked me about it. So I'll catch you *up without getting caught up in resentment—I am allowed this little pun and have spiced up my summations with similar asides in the past.**

Chodziez, the town that gave us our name, lies about one hundred kilometres north of Posen. As a brief reminder, the entire province was annexed and absorbed by Prussia during the First Partition of Poland in 1772. But our Chodziez is in the eastern half of the province, where the majority spoke Polish (and still do), so it kept its Polish name for a while. Until, approximately eighteen years after I was born, a district administrator by the name of von Colmar strongly favoured bringing the newly planned Posen-to-Schneidemühl railway line as close to Chodziez as possible. The town was thus connected to the railway, and not by a station way out in the steppe but reasonably close to the centre of our admittedly small city. To express our gratitude, the citizens decided to rename the city after the district administrator, with one tiny alteration: To differentiate ourselves from Colmar near Strasbourg, we replaced the C with a K. And that is how the city got the name which, in turn, became the name of a person. Or the nom de plume of our Gertrud, at any rate. The only thing to add is that, meanwhile, in compliance with the disgraceful Treaty of Versailles, Kolmar reverted to Chodziez and Posen to Poznan. Still, the area was Prussian for a century and a half. This had a significant impact on the appearance of the village-size town with a rectangular market square and prominently visible church.

We were actually supposed to schedule a family day in Chodziez so that a few of us could get together: your quartet of grown-up "children," plus my sister, my three brothers, and their families. Since I am one who longs for fresh air and exercise, which occasionally inspires you to ridicule, the first thing I'd have done would have been to take you to the town lake, Lake Miejskie, which is part of the Chodziez Lakeland. However, this means plenty of reeds, numerous footbridges, and dense borders of trees that mainly cause problems for fishermen. Oh, and the water lilies that grow in abundance along many shores, the ones that Gertrud loved so much. An altogether wonderful opportunity to swim, row, sail. Since there are hills in the vicinity, invariably called mountains by lowland residents, everything combines to justify the name "Switzerland of Chodziez."

I write this down in the hope—yea, the expectation—that you will insert these remarks in the chronicle. As a result, our rather rough, indeed unwieldy family name could finally acquire a bit of elegance, a certain aura.

On the other hand, my birthplace, Obersitzko, can hardly be written about in detail and is barely worth the effort. You could leave it at a simple mention. Like Posen, Obersitzko lies on the Warthe River and has about one and a half

---

* Ludwig Chodziesner was fond of puns and often inserted them in his legal summations. The pun involving *resentment* is not as effective in English as it was in the original German: *Nun, denn, ich trage nach ohne nachtragend zu sein.*

thousand residents. And it's identified with textiles, such as wool spinning and stocking manufacturing. So it's little wonder that my father, a dry goods dealer, had various products for sale that were linked to the processing of fabrics and cloth—with, in a word, sewing.

In the early days, his "store" may well have been a vendor's tray. Although it hasn't been explicitly recorded, my understanding of human nature and the world entitles me to this assumption.

You must picture my father, your Grandfather Julius, as a hardy man. A person like him was not only out and about in the bright sunshine; he set off in bad weather, too, accompanied by his dog. Otherwise, he'd have been badly out of pocket, and the family along with him. How many kilometres, how many miles must he have trekked through the province of Posen, within his own area or region, at any rate? I see him marching along, striding broadly, breathing freely, his face tanned by wind and weather. Even as I write this, I picture him on his way through the hinterlands of Obersitzko. Since he couldn't always return home, given the distances involved, I imagine he occasionally spent the night in barns, stalls, or little, sparsely furnished rooms. And he would set off again to each successive village with a box-shaped basket on his back. At the entrance to the village, he would stock and decorate the little vendor's tray in which he presented his buttons, buckles, needles, yarn, and twine. Going door-to-door, he would also occasionally offer toys that were made of wood, so that the weight didn't become burdensome.

In your eyes, I may be laying myself open to the charge of wanting to idealise a bit. But I certainly would not like to stand accused of that! So without any heckling or criticism from you, I asked myself whether Father ever had stones thrown at him or was chased by dogs on his trade routes? Whether, at the very least, people shouted spiteful things at him like "crooked-nosed, flat-footed Jew," and whether drunken village lads ever emptied his basket or dared to attack him? While he might have defended himself with his club, and the dog could have ensured that people kept a respectful distance, this might not have always done the trick. After all, a person was invariably attacked by a group in cases like this. But Father never spoke about incidents of this kind, so why should I, his son, make an issue of it?

Anyway, Father was mostly gone while I was growing up. So the chickens and ducks that ran around behind the house were all the more important to me as a child. Rabbits came with them, as well they should. Oh, and I mustn't forget the geese! Whenever I left the house via the back entrance, I passed through what amounted to a small zoo.

In the village, there was obviously a shortage of many things that we big-city folk seem to take for granted. Chief among these was medical care. There was a country doctor in town who often had to undertake long journeys in his horse and carriage. He also ran a little chemist's shop and pulled a tooth in a pinch—even our father, Julius, was not exempt from the latter. Yet there was no cure for his rheumatism. I know just how he felt at times, how much he needed a soothing remedy at the very least. There was no real protection from the dampness that affected his joints in the old familiar way on his long treks in the rain and sleet. If he ever limped as a result, it was more than likely that someone would call out to him, "Zydzie idz do Palestyny!" ("Jew, go back to Palestine!").

People have also said the same or similar things to me. But that wasn't the reason we finally left Obersitzko.

As they say here in Berlin, I was still a "young nipper" when my parents moved to Woldenberg. To simply mention the name of the town would not be helpful in this case either. We should begin with images or associations, at any rate. So I'd like to stress that Woldenberg explains my fondness for small types of settlements in close proximity to nature. Berlin is still the place where I am most professionally active. But I only feel truly at home in settlements of manageable size, perhaps with woods and water nearby.

Well then, Woldenberg is a railway stop on the Stettin-Posen line. This little city of no more than four and a half thousand residents is in the Deutsch Krone Lakeland, a region where lakes and rivers abound. Like Chodziez, the town lies directly on a lake, Woldenberg Lake. The Parish Church of Saint Mary, a Gothic brick structure, occupies the highest spot in this village of narrow lanes and little houses, though the town hall is magnificent. Linking the lakes is the Woldenberg Stream with its reeds, piers, and fishing platforms. A wooden bridge has been cut into the side of a hill above the railway line. Farther out of town, the natural surroundings are pristine and cannot be developed or cultivated because they are mostly swampy, at least at the edge of the softly flowing lakes and rivers. That's all I'll say about my second childhood home for the moment.

And the question arises as to why my parents moved there? Woldenberg is at the intersection of various trade routes. Most important, it lies on the road from Berlin to Königsberg. That's why quite a few businesspeople settled there, and cloth makers joined them. As far as that goes, it was the right environment for Chodziesner, the dry goods dealer. He gave up his vendor's tray and rented a shop. (Anyway, that's the order of events I've come up with.) In Switzerland, people would call it a haberdashery. Customers often came from afar. Whether shoulder pads or sewing needles, everything was on display, on offer. Business was good, and Father could put money aside. I was the eldest son, and this money came in handy for my education.

Speaking of education, we had one Evangelical and one Catholic school in town, and Jewish children went to the Evangelical school. Whether Evangelical or Catholic, the rod was the most important teaching aid in those days. It was quick to dance on the backs of smallholders' children, but spared the son of the goods inspector. Although most children spoke Polish, classes were conducted in German (also the official language, incidentally) by virtue of the directive from His

Imperial and Royal Majesty Wilhelm II. Wongrowitz and grammar school now follow in sequence. Here, too, it may sound pretty feeble to simply mention them, so do me a favour and elaborate a bit. I don't mean for you to embellish but to explain. Readers of our chronicle will surely not be made up of Wongrowitzers for the most part. So here are a few pointers, if you don't mind.

This small city of about forty-five hundred residents lies about fifty kilometres north of Posen. It has a Cistercian monastery, district court, and humanistic grammar school. Would you like further information in encyclopaedic style? Commerce in grain and pigs, if you please.

Now you'll probably burst out laughing, but Wongrowitz also lies on a lake! Lake Durowskie is its name. It's not a large pool or pond but a lake you can sail way out on, a lake with thick woodlands on the shore opposite the little town. A small river, the Welna, runs through town and connects this lake to other lakes. They call it Wongrowitz on the Welna. This basic constellation of little towns, lakes, and forests, precisely in that sequence, has shaped me to a fair degree. This should be brought out accordingly, emphasised as a portent of things to come or how I became who I am. And this, in turn, had consequences and repercussions for Gertrud. Whoever wishes to understand her must first understand her father. For, in many respects, his eldest daughter followed in his footsteps.

Now we can prepare for the leap to Berlin. The lake and forest lad became a student. You must remain cognizant of the fact that, in those days, it was only possible for a Jew to be upwardly mobile if he left the provinces—in my case, to study jurisprudence. In terms of jurisprudence, you need not hide the fact that I turned out to be an extremely successful, highly acclaimed lawyer. A saying just occurred to me that I cannot attribute to anyone in particular: "Only nobodies are modest." I need to hide my light under a bushel about as little as my talented if not quite so successful brothers, especially not in view of the many dark circumstances and developments in recent years.

How about a few bright splashes of colour to balance out the image of your father? I can call myself as a witness here. In a letter to my sister, Rebecca, I sketched myself as a young man in my late twenties with a head of very short hair, an elegant hat, and a smart walking stick. In those days, family members liked to emphasise the fact that I looked like Kaiser Wilhelm: similar build, hairstyle, and moustache. When I cycled through Grunewald, children saw me as the kaiser on a bicycle. If I went out riding, people called after me, "The kaiser, the kaiser!" And it wasn't only children who noticed the resemblance. There was a series about "Famous Lookalikes" in a magazine, which I'll look up for you sometime, and there we were, pictured side by side: Kaiser Wilhelm II and the renowned defence counsel Ludwig Chodziesner.

At the same time, I should emphasise how we differed. For as long he was emperor, Wilhelm II especially liked to be driven around in an automobile. But, as *you know, I look down on autos as parvenu vehicles. For me, the most beautiful form of rapid transport takes place on the back of a horse, provided I don't take the train. Just a passing remark.*

I am coming to the end of my comments for today. For thirty years, I was a partner in Max Wronker's local law practice. And, by the way, he is also from Posen. I may rightly report that I quickly made a name for myself as a powerful speaker in the courtroom.

The question immediately comes up as to why I became a lawyer and not a judge? Social conventions and circumstances were to blame. The legal system was already rife with antisemitism at the beginning of the century. I would call myself a Reform Jew or, more pointedly, an assimilated "holiday Jew." It is still typical for holiday Jews to appear in synagogue only on the High Holidays. Of course, people in Wilhelmine society hardly ever made subtle distinctions, such as "religious Jews" and "non-Aryan Christians." A Jew was a Jew and remained a Jew; baptized or not, the nose remained. To a great extent, Jews were barred from holding judicial office. So the only possibility open to me after studying law was to set myself up as a lawyer.

If I were you, I would stress an important distinction. Most jurists come from relatively well-to-do families, from a liberal, upper-middle-class milieu. The fact that the son of a Jewish small-business owner became an eminent lawyer, and the fact that my brothers also became lawyers, may allow us draw conclusions about how energetically we Chodziesners literally worked our way up.

This was finally acknowledged outwardly by the office of the joint practice and presented on the letterhead as follows: "Max Wronker, Lawyer and Notar;* Ludwig Chodziesner, Lawyer; Kaiser-Wilhelmstrasse 49, Corner Burg-Str." If you'll forgive me for saying so, we were soon considered the king and viceroy of criminal defence in Berlin.

| 2

We don't know for certain that Ludwig Chodziesner spoke and wrote in this manner, but the above letter is based on examination of his writing style in other documents. This also applies to his other writings and to those of Gertrud Kolmar's siblings.

As often and broadly as possible, I shall allow the poet to speak through her poems, prose, and letters. Everything that is quoted in her name corresponds to the editions; I haven't altered them one iota.

---

* A *Notar* is a lawyer who specializes in property law, corporate law, family law, or estate planning. There is no equivalent in the U.S. legal system.

So as to clearly differentiate, I will identify letters that are not part of the written record as "factition"—that is, fiction based on fact. Put another way, these interfamilial letters shall stay within sight of verifiable facts. They are meant to connect, form a bridge, create an atmosphere, and bring to mind the poet's symbiotic surroundings.

The documentation that follows will make my method clear. To begin with, here are two of her father's autobiographical papers.

Speaking of Woldenberg, he wrote, "We lived on the main street, which was called Richtstrasse. If you entered it from the train station, you'd soon be looking at the countryside on the far end. The little town was set up like a checkerboard with six longitudinal streets and about as many cross streets. One north-south side bordered on a large, beautiful lake; the other was bordered by a tree-covered hill. A high wall surrounded the entire town, even on the lake side."

Concerning Wongrowitz, he wrote:

In 1876, I entered grammar school in Wongrowitz at Eastertide . . . I lived in that little town for seven long years . . . The schoolrooms were part of a former Cistercian monastery that also housed the municipal court. The beautiful, old monastery church and presbytery rose directly beside the cloister.

My best subject was declamation. I received a special grade of "very good" on my report card, thereby sealing my fate as an orator. I remained a speaker and orator right up to my farewell speech as an Abiturient.* I'd already started much earlier at the town school, where I had to declaim in support of the capitulation of Strasbourg at a school function in 1870, as well as for the Sedan celebration† and on the kaiser's birthday. Mother always used to beat together an egg yolk and sugar, so that my voice would be clear and powerful. And my voice has remained strong throughout my forty years as a defence attorney and to this very day. I inherited this trait from my father who, whenever he spoke with a neighbour at the upper gate, could be clearly heard at the lower gate.

Here's another sketch of the dry goods dealer Julius Chodziesner from the autobiographical writings of Ludwig Chodziesner:

My father had a lively imagination, a wonderful memory, and a thirst for knowledge. A distinguished, lifelong post through learning and study

---

* An *Abiturient* is a pupil who is taking, or who has taken and passed, the *Abitur*—the final exam at the end of secondary education, usually after twelve or thirteen years of schooling.
　† The Sedan celebration, Sedantag, was a national holiday marking a German victory in the Franco-Prussian War in 1870.

was out of his reach, so he tried to achieve everything through his sons.
He saved every penny, tried to use each match twice, never smoked, and
never darkened the doorstep of any tavern. Those weeks in November 1903
were the high point of his life, his one and only "intoxication." For that was
when the name of his eldest son, his name and your name, was spoken and
celebrated on everyone's lips and in all the papers as the successful defender
of Countess Isabella Kwilecka, née Bininska. When people at the little
synagogue on Schulstrasse in Charlottenburg crowded around him, when
everyone congratulated him and wanted to shake his hand, then he felt, "I
haven't lived a lonely life, worked and gone without these many years for
nothing. I haven't lived in vain." He came home from the synagogue with a
glad heart, his head held high. There were tears of joy in his eyes, and he told
my dear, silent mother what good fortune had befallen him. She nodded,
she beamed, but didn't utter a word. She simply folded her hardworking
hands, covered in thick chalkstone, and said a prayer to God, "Praise be to
shem boruch hu!"*

A few remarks about Ludwig Chodziesner's mother: She "didn't have the
inspiration that shone in Father's dark eyes, nor his lively, truly passionate
temperament. Her gentle, blue eyes spoke of unshakable goodness and clear
perception that considered all things calmly. Her bent back testified to long
years of hard labour, to the many troubles and burdens she patiently bore on
behalf of her four sons and daughter. What determination, what energy were at
work in that frail body! So it was that our parents enabled their three sons to go
to university, even though they lived in a town that had no secondary school."
From his biographical notes and the beginnings of an autobiography:

In my writing desk are a number of manuscripts, quite a few newspaper
articles and printed sketches, albeit they offer more insight into the outer
course of my life than into my inner experience. You'll even find the
beginnings of a proper biography in a black patent leather notebook.
    My life's work has mainly consisted of facilitation, of disentangling other
people from the messes they've gotten caught up in. And I cannot speak
about them today or ever again. Like a father confessor, I must remain silent
about the insight I've gained into the depths or, more accurately, abysses of
the human soul.

A star attorney by contemporary standards, the celebrated lawyer occasionally wrote narrative texts, one of which was published in the 1904 *Berliner*

---

* "Praised be his name" (from the Hebrew).

Tageblatt, another in the magazine section of the *Berliner Morgen-Zeitung.* And legal matters played a role in each of them.

The Autopsy: A Reminiscence. Here is an excerpt from the opening section:

> It was twenty years ago in the autumn. Old Councillor Humbert sat in the office of the royal district court at Schwachenhagen at a long table with a green cloth thrown over it. Across from him sat his law clerk, who was still in the honeymoon phase of his probationary training period.
>
> It was already late afternoon when the bailiff entered the room and handed the councillor a thick communiqué from the office of the royal prosecutor. Court Emissary Wacker or "Herr Nuntius," as he liked to be called, wore a ginger-coloured wig and a warlike moustache of a similar colour.

Here is another excerpt, this time from the sketch *The Procurer.* The opening passage reads:

> Castellan (ret.) Wilhelm Biehl was once the most dapper and amusing noncommissioned officer in the Fourth Cavalry. But no one can see this from looking at him now. His head is bald, his black moustache has gone grey, his dark eyes peep out earnestly from beneath heavy brows. He's been a widower for many years. The same moment that gave him his one and only daughter also took his beloved wife from him.
>
> He sat in an old wicker chair, decorated with colourful beadwork, smoking a short pipe with an image of Kaiser Friedrich on its white porcelain bowl. Little Franz, his daughter's child, played at his feet and tried to catch the rays that the afternoon sun cast on the worn carpet through the white gauze curtains. But no matter how hard he tried, the little boy did not succeed in capturing one of the golden butterflies. Whenever he pounced on them, they settled on his hand, darted along his arm, disappeared, came back, and landed in his eyes so that he had to rub them with his little hands. Angrily, he fetched his grandfather's old soldier's cap from the mahogany bureau. But even beneath the cap, the shimmering butterflies wouldn't stay still. So he lost patience, abandoned the game, climbed onto grandfather's lap, and asked him to tell a story.

| 3

Factition: Anyone who is reading about your father in our family chronicle will surely want to learn a bit about your mother as well.

To begin with, whatever was all right with Grandfather Julius would have been fine with your Grandmother Hedwig. Their family also got its name from a town, Bad Schönfliess. Like your cousin Georg, you really ought to travel to this spa sometime and let yourself be inspired by the surroundings. In those days, Bad Schönfliess was in the rural district of Brandenburg, but it became Polish again after we lost the war. Trzcińsko-Zdrój, as it's called in Polish, lies about eighty kilometres south of Stettin, and you can get there by train with a change in Küstrin. This village of two thousand souls has a lovely old town hall and pleasant spa facilities, and is also situated on a lake, the Stadtsee. Here, too, the lake has a belt of reeds, bushes, and trees. And lots and lots of water lilies.

The Schoenflies family—scholars and businesspeople from time immemorial, which is to say, comfortably situated, well-off—came from this place. Your grandfather, Georg Schoenflies, was a member of the Berlin City Council and a representative on the committee of the Jewish Reform Community. City delegates in "official dress with golden chains" took part in his funeral, which must have made his rank and importance amply visible.

Your Grandmother Hedwig was highly adventurous. Even at around sixty years of age, when others had long since withdrawn from active life, she continually set off on tours to new places. These small groups were led by the Carl Stangen travel agency in Berlin. The company even offered a trip around the world, though it cost a fortune. (Someone could have built half a country estate with the same eleven thousand gold reichsmarks.) Although Hedwig could not afford to circle the globe, she still had enough for tours to Italy, Greece, and the Middle East. A relative, Gustav Hirschfeld, was the one who awakened her interest in archaeology. Hirschfeld led the excavations at Olympia on behalf of the government of the German Reich.

This quite elderly yet highly active woman could recount things that people like us, whose basic outlook is truly not provincial, can only read about. If you like, I will elaborate in our family chronicle on how your grandmother boarded a ship in Brindisi, how she looked down from the Acropolis on the dusty city, the bald mountain ranges, and the glistening sea.

The report could also include Grandmother Hedwig on the Mediterranean heading south, Grandmother Hedwig in Alexandria and Cairo, Grandmother Hedwig and her little group heading south again on a Nile steamship. When she sat on the deck of the ship, letting the shore with its many temples and pyramids glide by, she must have felt as if she were navigating the streams of centuries and millennia, heading upriver to finally reach the source of time itself. Yes, she travelled in a period when research yielded more and more discoveries going farther back in time, millennium by millennium by millennium.

So I finally see your grandmother in Karnak. The colossal dimensions of the temple complex make it the most astonishing edifice on earth. In my mind's eye,

I can still visualise what she recounted in her occasionally laconic, taciturn way: Hedwig standing in the middle of a half-collapsed structure, surrounded by columns of such height and breadth that the columns at Selinunte and Agrigento must have seemed dwarflike by comparison. Quite a few columns were lying around like outspread masses of stone. And Grandmother Hedwig—eyed with great suspicion by Herr Stange or his representative but no longer responding to shouts of warning—climbed up one of the recumbent giants, saw all of the rocky fissures, clefts, and crevices with grass, indeed entire bushes growing out of them, swaying in the desert breeze. This is roughly how she might have expressed it. She could afford the luxury of slipping away from her cabin, spending the night in the dead silence of the temple ruins in which she occasionally heard a lump of stone, a little chunk of stone, come loose from the giant columns. She almost felt as if the hieroglyphs all around her would break free of their cartouches and turn into sounds that only she was privileged to hear in the silence of the night. But the mystery did not reveal itself to her, and she returned to the ship, where she'd long since been expected. It sailed on that very night under starry skies to which she sang myriad hymns of praise. Even on clear winter nights, one can only dream of skies like this at our latitude. The stars were no mere points of light; they were like torches. In addition, the Southern Cross constellation sat just a few degrees above the desert horizon. Many stars were doubled on the surface of the water and, whenever she lowered her gaze, she had the feeling that she was no longer on earth and the ship was gliding through the Milky Way.

But her daughter, your mother Elise, never travelled as far as Egypt. And her first-born daughter, our Gertrud, travelled even less. She did go to France once. But Gertrud in Karnak is something I cannot imagine, much less Gertrud in front of the Sphinx that they say is even older than the pyramids right next to it.

But at least your mother travelled to Italy, which brings me to the topic of our honeymoon. Elise Schoenflies was twenty-one when I married her. She'd turned twenty-two in the meantime. We went to Rome, as was largely the custom, at least among the well-to-do. She wrote to my sister with great enthusiasm that I can only hint at off the top of my head—I'll dig out the letter for you when I get a chance. Here, so to speak, are a few offhand impressions: beautiful Rome, art that delights the human eye, the great allure of nature there, reminiscences of antiquity, panoramas of the entire city, southern plants and produce, an outing to Tivoli in the Sabine Hills, and the wide view of the campagna from there.

All in all, I'd like to keep this particular chapter in my life short. Otherwise, I'd have to grapple with Elise's occasional accusations that my standards were much too strict, that she couldn't really develop her own potential by my side. She complained, of course, that she hardly ever got to dance when she was young, because she always had to play dance music for others. Well, as far as our married life was concerned, we basically never went to the cinema and only made it to the theatre or the opera on rare occasions. But Elise played her Blüthner grand piano all the more to make up for it. You children must still have her Viennese waltzes, her melodies from Die Fledermaus and Die Csárdásfürstin in your ears. She could go on like that for hours, and you listened just as tirelessly.

Now you, Margot, or Georg might ask, "If Mama was so fond of these operettas, why didn't the two of you go to performances all the time?" For my part, I must confess that I couldn't write a brief in defence of operettas. The stories they dish up are truly outrageous! They're more entertaining than astonishing, not exactly amusing, but also not worrisome. I ask myself what strange characters were going through your mother's head, what kinds of stories and fairy tales she told you in her introductions to what are admittedly very stirring melodies at times? What worlds did she carry you off to in those early years, as if borne on Blüthner wings?*A variety show in Budapest, men in tails with hats and elegant walking sticks, a white camellia in their buttonholes, and shady women dancing the Csárdás. The men would love to see their lingerie, and not to merely look, since "women make the world go round." My ear still remembers it, for it just so happened that I was sometimes busy in the adjoining room and attended the performances. She seemed to be exhilarated by them.

As you know, I haven't always been sparing in my criticism, which sometimes annoyed Elise a little. But I certainly wouldn't and couldn't have dissuaded her from excursions to the realm of bats and swallows or from fantasising at her Blüthner. Perhaps you'll be able to see me as more than just a spoilsport, at least in retrospect, and may realise instead that I was not entirely wrong to withdraw, and find a proper way to express it. For I would sooner foster associations with ancient Roman writers in the firm belief that a Cicero or Caesar carries more weight than a Varescu or Prince Orlofsky.

But I shall cut it short for today. In conclusion, it will ultimately be up to you to describe your mother in a way that she liked to see herself, as a cheerful, sociable, loving, and musical person.

| 4

Daughter Hilde was, in fact, working on a Jewish family chronicle. The text was supposed to be divided into three sections: father's family, mother's family, and sister Gertrud.

This didn't happen until after the war though. She made changes to the drafts in a small ring binder with a now brittle red plastic overlay. So she assigned the

---

* *Flügel* in German means both "wings" and "grand pianos," a play on words that does not carry over into the English.

working title, "Gertrud's Ancestors," to the first section and "The Family" to the second. In a subsequent version, "Gertrud's, My and Walter's Ancestors," she tried including herself and cousin Walter Benjamin but ended up crossing it out.

However it was split up, she stuck to the task of the family chronicle. Begun in the 1930s, she took it up again in the 1960s, a period in which she also harbored literary ambitions of her own. She wrote short stories and journal articles under the pen name Marisa Marconi: "Her Name Was Anastasia," "The Cat House," "The Lost Soul," "Strolls Round Intragna's Church Tower," "On the Trail of the Old Zurich Judenschuol," and "Yvonne and the Kibbutz."

But she admitted to encountering certain problems in writing the chronicle: "I am at a loss when it comes to my father's forebears. There are no documents or family tree here, as there are for Moritz Schoenflies. Although I knew my paternal grandmother very well, the time when it would have been possible to find out anything from her is long past. And besides, she hardly ever spoke about herself."

Yet Hilde made a start. Here's what she wrote about Julius and Johanna Chodziesner in the province of Posen: "Our grandparents probably moved to Woldenberg shortly after Father was born, and they lived in a very modest little house. They ran a haberdashery out of the house, and residents of the surrounding area came there on Sundays to shop. Grandmother was actually a dressmaker by profession. Grandfather was a passionate bird lover and always kept a few songbirds in cages . . . Our father constantly told us that Grandfather never indulged in or treated himself to anything. He set money aside, groschen by groschen, so that he could enable his eldest son get a good education and study at university."

She even added, "I heard our father, who always spoke of his parents with the greatest respect and love, say over and over that 'Grandfather never saw the inside of a tavern.'"

Hilde, the family chronicler, had this to say about her grandmother: She "only comes to mind as a very old woman with a black scarf over her thin, parted hair. If her sons complained, she would say, 'Look at what's below you, my son, not at what's above.' Many things Grandmother said have accompanied me throughout my life. She has always been an example to me and my highest ideal. She was akin to our mother in her selfless goodness, though without mother's cheerful disposition."

The records are sporadic, of course, and occur spontaneously. Quotations must be placed in context, as here: "At this point, I would like to reemphasise what our father did for his siblings. He often told us that he went without food to enable his younger brothers to study. He paid for his only sister's trousseau and provided her dowry. His guiding principle was, 'Charity begins at home.'

After a hard course of study in Berlin, lodging in furnished rooms, he spent his probationary period in Frankfurt (Oder) and became an assessor for the famous lawyer Max Wronker, who subsequently made him his partner."

The Schoenflies family also kept a chronicle. Among other things, Great-Grandfather Moritz reported on his family origins, on overcoming various difficulties, particularly as a Jew. He gave an account of his six surviving children out of thirteen, one of whom was Georg, the father of Elise Chodziesner, née Schoenflies:

> Unlike today, when roads, railways, telegraphs, and financial institutions make it easier to expand and do business, I had to battle powerful competition and inconvenient transport links back then. Meanwhile, revolution and wars were also not advantageous but, thank God, I was able to overcome many difficulties. After being in business for thirty-one years, I was able to hand my tobacco and cigar factory over to my son, Georg, in 1868.
>
> Although my large family (with the exception of my wife) kept me very busy in many respects, and my office hours left me with very little extra time, I was not spared from community service. In addition to continuous terms as city councilman from 1851 to the present and serving as a board member of several associations, I've been treasurer of the Jewish congregation for several years since 1847, a representative for sixteen years, and chairman of the board for four. The only reason to mention it here is to identify the sudden changes in political and social legislation that have taken place from my apprenticeship up to the establishment of my business and beyond.

The rather cursory narrative about the life of Hilde and Gertrud's grandfather closed with the following remark: "Even if one concedes that many things in family portraits may seem less noteworthy for the moment, circumstances could still arise in which documents like these may prove useful." Which would actually come to pass . . .

| 5

Now we finally come to Gertrud! The first of four children, she was born in Berlin on December 10, 1894, "at four fifteen in the morning."

Georg Schoenflies had passed away barely one month earlier, and the painful loss of her beloved, highly esteemed father had lasting repercussions for Elise. Thus, she wrote to her sister-in-law Rebecca in mid-February 1895:

Today it is so bright and sunny outside, and I don't know why I have such a heavy heart. It really isn't my way to grumble or complain. But I am still completely unable to get used to the idea that my dear, good Papa is no more and I am fatherless. The more time passes, the more I yearn for him, so I seem to be the opposite of other people. I am, in fact, as happy and calm as before; my grieving disturbs no one. Yet I cannot rid myself of the thought, "If only Papa were still alive." Please don't be angry with me, dearest Rebecca, for receiving such a letter from me today.

The loss of her father was said to have shortened her pregnancy by several weeks, and Gertrud came into the world sooner than expected.

Elise also wrote to Rebecca at the end of January 1895:

If I've hesitated to send you a few heartfelt lines up to now, you mustn't hold it against me—Trudchen is to blame. Such a tiny creature rules the entire house, and since the nanny I have for her is fairly useless, I must to see to nearly everything myself. It gives me a great deal of pleasure, of course, but also takes a great deal of time . . . Just a few words about our little Trudchen, and then I'll close for today. I wish you could see her someday, our sweet pea. She already seems very sensible and smiles quite happily with her bright little eyes.

Gertrud was born on Poststrasse in the Saint Nicholas Quarter. Her father didn't have far to go from there to the office. Two years later, the family moved to Lessingstrasse near Bellevue Palace. A sister, Margot, was born at the new residence in 1897. After three years in Spreebogen, they moved to the West-end section of Charlottenburg. The family would reside there for the next two decades in a villa at the corner of Ahornalle and Platanenallee with a "spacious entrance hall, living room, salon, and men's smoking room." Georg was born in that house in 1900, and Hilde came into the world there a half decade later. The siblings' memories would become intertwined with the villa and spacious garden.

For their father, however, memories of this family home would be connected to reminiscing about the time of his greatest standing as a lawyer and defense counsel. Moreover, his success came at a time of growing prosperity. Share prices climbed, real interest rates rose, and industry boomed. The city also expanded to the north and east, where there were many industrial concerns and numerous tenement blocks. Both professional success and the occasionally delayed upturn in the economy had an impact on the lifestyle of the Chodziesners. Theirs was a privileged childhood that can be characterized as upper middle class, complete with a cook, maid, gardener, and gardener's wife.

* * *

The poet would later tell her little niece about her own childhood years:

> We liked playing outdoors best. There were three children next door, Johann, Peter, and Marion. They moved here from Hamburg. And since Hamburg is a port city, they knew more about seamanship than we did and always played "ship" with us. The ship was usually our jungle gym, complete with ladder, ropes, and bars. The children climbed around on it like sailors. Your mommy, who was still fairly little then, was the stewardess and had to take care of meals for the crew. The children's parents had been to Africa, and their gray parrot came from there. He had a red tail, was named Gascon, and could talk. Every spring, Marion happened to mention that this was the year their entire family would go to Lisbon, but they never did. The kids taught us Akree, a game from Hamburg. This was a kind of hide-and-seek. We played it in the long cellar corridor and in the many dark basement rooms beneath the house. But the "little forest" was an even nicer place to play in than the house or garden. This was a totally neglected and overgrown property, full of trees, weeds, and thickets. The people who owned it never set foot on the property, and when we went in for the first time, we had to cut and break up shrubbery, or we wouldn't have made any headway. In addition, there were useless old household effects lying all over the place: broken plates, saucepans with holes in them, and a slashed-open mattress with the stuffing bursting out of it. In the middle of the little forest stood a small wooden building that you couldn't see from the street. Perhaps it was really just a stable, but we children thought it was very strange and wonderful, and we called it the "witch's house." To us children, the most wonderful thing about the witch's house and little forest was that they were our sole province. Grown-ups never came in, because they didn't want to tear their clothes on the thorny bushes.

Famous neighbors in the Ahornalle included a professor, a painter, a sculptor, a bacteriologist, and an astronomer.

There was also a barracks nearby, however. Hilde reported that as children they often stood at the "little back gate" and watched the drills. Now and then, one of the instructors appears to have allowed himself a chat at the garden fence. Soon, we knew "them all by name: the officers, noncommissioned officers, and the sergeants." Hilde also reported that the siblings often marched alongside when "our soldiers" moved out with "bands playing."

At Christmas, even the girls got drums, sabers, uniforms, and "a very beautiful hussar uniform with spurs."

Memories have to be touched up and details verified. I'd long concluded from various remarks that the children could see at least part of the parade ground from the garden fence. In studying old Pharus city maps,* however, I could see that such a direct line of vision would have been impossible.

An old postcard shows the new barracks of the Königin Elisabeth Guard Grenadier Regiment No. 3 between the metropolitan railway line northward and the new construction site. The multistory, sprawling building conjures up associations with Prora, the several-hundred-meter-long holiday resort on the Island of Rugia. However, the barracks were more variously structured by comparison. Only a remnant, the officer's mess, was left after the air raids of World War II. In earlier years, there was a rectangular compound at the level of the Lietzensee, outside the barracks area of the parade ground. Bordering it to the south was the firing range, albeit on the other side of the train line. So it cannot have always been peaceful in this posh residential quarter.

Westend underwent rapid changes in the two decades that the family lived in this part of town. A city map from the 1920s shows that the parade ground had been developed in the meantime. So where did the drills take place? On the grounds of the barracks that were close to the family residence? But even then, there would have been no direct sight line and surely no chatting from across the garden fence, since Ahornallee and, parallel to it, Soorstrasse ran between the villa and the barracks. Even if very little new building went on there, the children would have had to walk a ways if they wanted to see how recruits were drilled.

And their father had to begin his route to the law practice, as well as to district court, on foot. He would have gotten on at the Westend station and changed trains later on. Beginning in 1908, he would certainly have had an easier time, because that was when they opened a new underground station, a branch line from the "Knee" at present-day Ernst Reuter Platz to Reichskanzlerplatz, now called Theodor-Heuss-Platz. His route to the train was just a hop and a skip from then on, as Ahornallee led directly to the square. An old photo shows a spacious park in the initial stages of planting. There's not a building to be seen to the south or west and nothing but the underground entrances on either side of the wide, completely empty street. A gigantic wooden sign with large lettering reads, BUILDING SITES FOR SALE. The broad expanse of Heerstrasse became a dirt road, and it still leads through the forest today.

Gertrud recalled those early years:

> Our childhood companions were always what mattered most to us. The first school friend who invited me to her house was named Tula Quittmann. Like the kaiser, she was born on January 27. That was a very nice arrangement,

---

* Pharus-Plan was the trademark of Pharos, a German publishing company specializing in maps of various German cities, including Berlin.

because we children dressed up in the morning and went to the kaiser's birthday celebration at school for just one hour. And since we didn't have any homework to do in the afternoon, we went to Tula's to celebrate her birthday. At lunchtime, there was vegetable soup (or "soup with everything in it," as we called it) with pancakes afterward. Because I was still very young then, I thought this was actually the kaiser's birthday meal, that it was served in every family and even to the kaiser himself. Well, there was something else I believed too. Some parents also came to the celebration at school, among them Herr von Kuczkowski, the colonel of our Westend Regiment. His three daughters went to our school. So the colonel, in a magnificent blue, red, and gold uniform, was given the place of honour among the various fathers and mothers. When we were leaving the assembly hall after the celebration, I curtsied very deeply in front of him as we passed by the parents. You see, I thought this high-ranking officer was the kaiser. He must have been awfully busy and must have had to cut himself up into lots of little pieces if he wanted to be present at every school celebration on his birthday! Anyway, this is what I thought, because I couldn't understand how someone could celebrate his birthday unless he was there in person . . . But here's what impressed me most of all that day: I was walking home alone at 8 P.M. As I came to Branitzplatz, a high silver pillar of light climbed into the dark night sky above a vacant lot. Today, I know they set off fireworks over an empty lot in honour of the occasion. But in those days, I'd never seen anything like it and took it for a heavenly apparition.

As a self-assured representative of the Wilhelmine era, Papa Ludwig was clearly king of his castle. This role had been sanctioned and canonized for decades. The head of the household decided what was done and what was not done. As a little kaiser in his own home, the father carried an authority that mirrored that of the kaiser in his palace, who, in turn, legitimized the father's role in the home by example.

The role of head of household did not have to be won by means of authoritarian, possibly aggressive conduct; it merely had to be filled. It is, therefore, difficult to distinguish between nature and nurture. "Papa" was patriarch and Padre Padrone [father and master]. His wife was duly submissive, and the children had to obey. This can only be touched on here but has been sufficiently described and analyzed in books about childhood in earlier times or the "history of private life." In the personality of someone like Ludwig Chodziesner, role and character interacted to form an amalgam.

One of the surviving photos from around 1900 shows him on his trusty steed in shiny riding boots, a white jacket and white hat, his massive head accentuated by a mustache.

What Hilde wrote about Grandfather Julius must also have also been true of her father: he "had a passionate temperament, but mellowed with age." This domineering yet passionate man set the tone of domestic life. As a result, "the children were not allowed to talk at table." After all, Father worked with great concentration and had to relax a bit at noontime, even more so in the evening.

It was Elise who provided balance and sociability to the extent possible. Here, too, there was an amalgam of character and role, the mother's equalizing kindness as a complement to the father's essential severity.

Berlin Childhood Around 1900 is the title of a work by Walter Benjamin. He was Gertrud's cousin, and his full name was Walter Bendix Schoenflies Benjamin. It was mainly Grandmother Hedwig who held the two branches of the family together. In one photo that is unfortunately not very clear, she stands proudly at the center in a black dress. Walter is standing to her right, leaning against her, in a white sailor suit and wide-brimmed hat. Also leaning against her on her left is Gertrud in a white dress and straw hat.

Their grandmother was not yet sixty at the time the photo was taken. Like any proper grandmother of the Wilhelmine Era, she appeared to command respect. In her wanderlust, however, she anticipated the lifestyle of today's grandmothers:

> If you visited the elderly lady by her carpeted bay window, decorated with a
> little balustrade that looked out onto Blumeshof, you could scarcely imagine
> how she went on great sea journeys, let alone excursions in the desert
> led by Stangen Travel, whose tours she joined every couple of years. She
> sent postcards from Madonna di Campiglio and Brindisi, Westerland and
> Athens, and wherever else she travelled. There was a whiff of Blumeshof in
> all of them. Her large, relaxed handwriting clouded up the sky or swirled
> around the bottom of the photos. They were so completely filled with my
> grandmother's presence that they became colonies of Blumeshof.

Several accounts of her journeys have survived, letters with exotic letterheads such as Khedivial Mail Steamship and Graving Dock Company Limited—and in Arabic script, no less. Or the Grandhôtel Huck, Smyrna, from that same period in April 1907, with a little steel engraving of the imposing edifice, signaling the luxurious travel arrangements, and Grandmother Hedwig's resolute pen strokes in black ink.

Here is a vignette of the voyage from Beirut to Smyrna: "The men in our group who had already made great sea journeys had never seen anything like it. I can still hear the sea booming and raging. Everything on the ship was flying to and fro, a bowl of ham here, a dish or a wine bottle there. People lay moaning on the stairs, in their beds, and the crew itself was probably most anxious of all."

For there were dangerous cliffs on which the ship would "inevitably" have been "smashed to pieces."

As original as her gifts were, her writing style was just as lively. Gertrud would later describe how the Christmas trees of her childhood were decorated. "Edible ornaments," "chocolate wreaths with white or colourful poppy seeds," "Russian confectionery," and "little quince sausages" were especially popular. But "the two cotton crocodiles that crawled over the fir branches every Christmas, zoological curiosities that Grandmamma Schoenflies gave us as presents," were not edible.

And there was another gift from her maternal grandma: "Among my 'treasures,' by the way, is a little, dingy-looking, inconspicuous stone, a small piece of marble from the Acropolis that Grandmamma Sch. brought me from her trip to the Orient, and I've stored it carefully in my jewellery box ever since."

In a letter to her niece, Sabine, whom I'll introduce later, Gertrud reminisced, "When we were children, we always went on holiday to the sea with our parents, your grandpa and grandma, that is. We took shovels and buckets to the beach, where we dug in the white sand and collected shells, pulled jellyfish and sometimes even little crabs out of the water. We also swam a lot, of course."

To go with the summer scene, here's a winter portrait with a big red cargo sled: "It was more like a coach than a sled. Two people hopped in and then sat across from each other. You pushed it from behind. An adult always had to do it, because it was much too heavy for a child to manage. A toboggan would have been more practical for us. But they didn't have them for children in those days, only for sportspeople."

I won't omit the obligatory report about Gertrud's school days but will keep it short. Childhood, youth, and school days often take up lots of space in autobiographies and memoirs. But the poet only jotted down a few, fragmentary memories, mainly in letters. So I'll just include two fragments here. The first concerns her time at the neighborhood elementary school:

> I still remember that each of us schoolkids had a large sketch pad, and I was s'posed to draw an Easter egg with black chalk on mine. But it didn't turn out well. I tried several times, and it always came out like a giant plum. As you can imagine, the art teacher was not at all happy with me. Even as a young adult, I tried repeatedly to sketch, draw, and paint. But I never really succeeded until, one day, I happened to cut little figures, animals, and landscapes out of black paper. I could do that. So I am not quite as "totally inept" at these art forms.

The second fragment is about her time at the upper girls' school in Charlottenburg: "Our school was pretty far away, and we always took the streetcar.

When it snowed heavily at night, there were still no snow sweepers around in the morning, the trains didn't run, and we had to walk. Needless to say, we arrived much too late at school and our boots were soaked for the most part. We took them off, placed them near the heater to dry, and all of us schoolgirls sat at our desks in our stocking feet."

The following anecdote [written by Gertrud] may portray Gertrud's character:

> As a child of eleven or twelve, I often went to a lake in the summertime. It was in the Charlottenburg palace garden, and they called it Kochsee [Cook Lake]. I have no idea why they gave it that name; it had nothing to do with cooking. There was a swimming pool with two female attendants, Miss Lenchen and Miss Hedwig. They always wore these enormous straw hats with enormous bows and taught the children to swim. They tied a belt with a long rope around us. We had to jump into the water straightaway, and the attendants held us up by the rope so we didn't sink.

Now a "funny thing" happened at that swimming pool:

> I lay on my back in the water and didn't move at all. I went slowly under, sank and sank, until I arrived at the bottom of the lake. Seeing as I'd swallowed enough water, I pushed off from the bottom with my feet and came back up. That was right beside the bridge railing, and many people were standing on the bridge, looking at me in total amazement. A child had actually seen me go under, believed I was drowning, and cried out so that people would come to save me. They came to pull me out of the water and were very surprised when I came back up on my own.

The rather small Kochsee between Westend and Charlottenburg had a swimming pool in those days. The lake was filled in a few years later, and the site was built on.

This scene entices one to paraphrase and play it out: Gertrud is unlikely to jump in, so she gets in the water (does it have a slightly marshy smell?) from the wooden jetty, sinks without the panicked movements of a drowning person— no splashing around, no gurgling sounds or shouting—and goes down quietly. Her disappearance attracts attention. A girl is missing—has she drowned? She's vanished, disappeared from the surface of the water at any rate. Must they start a rescue operation? Must brave men prepare to dive in? But the girl pushes off from the (musty?) bottom, comes up, and notices the gazes of the completely astonished onlookers. A child who supposedly drowned a moment ago now comes back up, gasps for air, and smiles as though nothing has happened.

Is there room for interpretation here? Lets herself sink, keeps out of sight, disappears, goes under, and comes back up . . .

Gertrud played a water lily. On a postcard, the poet again remembered her school days and the headmistress Miss Schmidt along with them:

> Whenever Miss Sch. had a birthday, we came to class nicely dressed with
> bouquets of flowers in hand. And when we were seated at our desks,
> a large plate with colourful little slices of cake was passed around . . .
> Presentations for invited parents also took place on occasion. I recall
> a little comedy of manners, *Les Fleurs,* in which each child carried the
> artificial flower that he or she was supposed to represent. It was in French,
> and I was *la nénuphare,* the water lily. I always loved this flower after that.
> It is full of mystery.

And what could the secret of the water lily be? Its large, supporting leaves spread out on the water. The flower of the *Nymphaea* rises up a little above the surface of the water, but the berrylike fruit ripens, nearly invisible below the watery expanse.

Here is another characterizing anecdote: "Even as a child, I'd gladly have been a Spartan and, in any case, I wanted to be a hero later on. I pressured Mommy into making Spartan black soup and was very fond of eating our lentil soup, because that's what Daddy said it was. One time, I held my hand over the open hearth in our kitchen so as to imitate Mucius Scaevola."

What solid proof of fearlessness! A city is besieged. Gaius Mucius Scaevola leaves it secretly and sneaks into the enemy camp with the intention of murdering King Porsenna. Scaevola is captured. He places one hand over a coal pan, possibly puts it in the flame, and shows no sign of pain. Porsenna is thus convinced of the besieged Romans' resolve and withdraws his troops.

| 6

Factition: Dear Hilde, I am growing restless. So I am doing the groundwork for you, this time by providing you with names as keywords to two of the cases that made me well known, even famous, in the years when Gertrud was a child and you were still a toddler.

The first name, Isabella Kwilecka, is that of my client from the Polish higher nobility. The dispute concerned an inheritance with a charge of "substitution of child." Together with Wronker, I defended Kwilecka brilliantly. You can confidently borrow the portion of my summation that was quoted in the Berliner Tageblatt [Berliner Daily Newssheet] of November 1903: "The truth, as sublime beauty, will not reveal her face to those who believe they can take hold of her through prejudice as written down in documents." You could also import my references to Martin Luther and Jan Hus. One may see a certain pathos in them, no doubt, but we can finally afford to indulge in it.

The second name, Philipp Fürst zu Eulenburg, is at least worth mentioning as well. A really famous client, this diplomat, an adviser and friend of the kaiser, got involved in a legal dispute that grew into a sensational case. The prince was accused of an offence against paragraph 175 of the Penal Code of the German Reich. I succeeded in preventing a conviction. The particular events could not be unequivocally proved and dated back a number of years. I pleaded the statute of limitations with a favourable outcome.

| 7

In addition to her father, Napoleon was another man the young girl admired while growing up. Gertrud grew up in the age of an eternally idealized and celebrated monarch, Kaiser Wilhelm II. And his legendary ancestor, Frederick the Great, was feted alongside him. Chronologically speaking, Caesar was also celebrated as his predecessor and Napoleon as his successor. This is how mutual idealization took place, its main purpose being to present the reigning (or rather, traveling) kaiser in the best light. At least in terms of propaganda, Kaiser Wilhelm and King Frederick, and Kaiser Wilhelm and Emperor Napoleon, stood virtually shoulder to shoulder.

So the schoolgirl Gertrud lionized the great Corsican and pinned up portraits of Napoleon in her room. Robespierre was another of the little girl's heroes. In an act of defiance, her female classmates called both of them criminals. This was certainly not based on historical knowledge but on the feeling that they'd done something to declare their independence from "crazy Trude." She could have come back with, "I'll see that justice is done to them both!" Was laughter their response? Did she beat a resolute retreat to her room with portraits of her heroes in it?

In any case, that's how her siblings remember it: She withdrew to her room with printed images of Napoleon. She'd apparently found sanctuary in the big house. The girl was especially nearsighted in the right eye and would put on her glasses only at home. In the outside world, Gertrud was afraid the other children would ridicule her, and she didn't want to be called "four eyes."

There was a box in her room in which she collected newspaper clippings. So she read, or at least looked through, newspapers after the paterfamilias had finished with them. What particularly caught her interest? What did she cut out? She probably wouldn't have passed on information about her special collection or the secret of her box.

Not only did Gertrud read and sift through newspapers; she was remembered as the eldest daughter who buried herself in a book in her room. And what else might she have read? Having just read historical accounts of the French Revolution, did she then read about Bonaparte's rise to power? Or did she read books that were age-appropriate for children and young people? The usual repertoire? None of the titles that were popular among children in those days should be named on mere suspicion. But the fact remains that Gertrud frequently disappeared into her room, where she sat and read. She didn't like to come out to play with her siblings and the neighborhood kids. Besides, she had very little interest in children's games.

An anecdote could provide us with clues about her early reading: "The Spartans made black soup," she said to her mother and immediately followed it with a question: "Why don't you make black soup?" As to whether her mother did any cooking with so many servants in the house, that's another matter. The reference to the Spartans could nevertheless be revealing. So Gertrud also read books that guided her to the ancient world. Perhaps she read Gustav Schwab's *Sagen des klassischen Altertums* [*Legends of Classical Antiquity*].

Napoleon's admirer studied at the upper girls' school in Charlottenburg. To simply mention the name of the school doesn't tell us anything, so we must dig deeper.

The completion of elementary school usually meant the end of a girl's education. If her education was to continue, it had to be privately initiated and financed. A successful lawyer like Chodziesner could afford to send his eldest daughter to one of the upper girls' schools, which were private schools licensed by the state. They weren't in school buildings but in multistory residential buildings, as was the case with the Auguste Weyrowitz Girls' School on what was then Berliner Strasse. There were six classes, mind you.

Institutions of this kind also conformed to predefined social norms. Girls were trained to become housewives and mothers. Female students were thus conditioned to play modest roles. Even Gertrud developed into an amalgam of role and character.

Any woman who wanted to get ahead after receiving her "school-leaving qualification" [secondary school certificate] had little choice and hardly any opportunities. Teachers' college offered the best prospects for women. After completing a two- or preferably three-year course of study, female graduates could then teach at an elementary or middle school. Beginning in 1905, women could also take the state exam for upper-level teaching posts, although it would be a long time before they were guaranteed a teaching position in public education.

Gertrud neither wanted to take this path nor should she have. After receiving her certificate in 1911, she pursued training for "girls of educated status" at the Arvedshof Country Women's School in Saxony.

The Jewish girl Chodziesner at a boarding school for home economics and agriculture? A highly unusual situation in those days! Jews hardly ever had farming in mind. This was not antisemitism; it was in keeping with Jewish self-awareness, the image Jews cultivated of themselves, and the problematic nature of same. In this case, Zionists in particular would have seen negative implications for their settlement policies. Palestine urgently needed farmers and agriculturalists, who were theoretically supposed to form the base of the population pyramid. But since most immigrants were businessmen, jurists, and self-employed persons, farmers were at the top of the pyramid. The balance had to be shifted here. Could Gertrud's presence at the country women's school possibly be seen from this angle?

The boarding school was founded half a decade earlier by Therese Rossbach. Her husband, Arved, had passed away four years prior to that, and she named the estate after him. The training center was affiliated with the Reifenstein Association for Women's Education in Farming and Home Economics. More than a dozen schools belonged to the association.

Arvedshof was near a small village. The school brochure, written by the headmistress, praised Arvedshof's idyllic setting in a landscape of gently rolling hills. Nearby was the "picturesque" village of Elbisbach with its "stately farmsteads, Old Saxon half-timbered houses, and high-lying church surrounded by cypresses." The facility itself was a modern school and country house beside a "cosy old estate, complete with outbuildings." Photos show it as an extremely typical, nearly villalike structure with decorative Fachwerk.* This was an establishment for upscale clientele, most of whom were daughters of estate owners and landed gentry. And the eldest of a Jewish lawyer's three daughters was now among them.

One photo in the advertising brochure shows a group of young ladies doing "hay work" in front of a wagon piled high with hay. Without exception, the ladies were in elegantly cut, ankle-length dresses, and one even wore a fashionable straw hat. The actual work was apparently being done by a giant man and two women in headscarves.

Two girls, or "maidens" as they were called, shared a rather large room with beds against the longest wall, two nightstands, and a desk right in front of the

---

* *Fachwerk* is a term that describes timber-framed buildings in general but may also refer to wall framing consisting of rectangular panels filled with brick, clay, or plaster.

window with a view of the countryside. Add to that a spacious dining room with a picture window overlooking the park, a music room with a grand piano, and an entrance hall with a fireplace and wood paneling.

The number of students at the boarding school was still small, around two dozen, thirty at most. The teaching staff was large. As for the teaching kitchen, there must have been assistants to heat up the large, freestanding underdraft oven in the early morning. The students didn't learn how to prepare *Bauern-schmaus* [farmer's feast] here, but rather a "hunter's meal for men's clubs," to cite one example. Great value was placed on perfect service etiquette.

There was a large washhouse. Did the women take over the soaking, pre-washing, lathering, and scrubbing on the washboard at the tub, or was this work left to the staff? The maidens certainly would have done the ironing, which was sweaty work, especially in the summertime. Tightly fitting pieces of heated steel were shoved into heavy irons that were heated in potbelly stoves until nearly red-hot.

Other facilities included a handicraft room, a "needlework room" for the *Damenflor,** and a loom. The students learned to make butter, produce *Quark†* and various other cheeses in the spacious, tiled teaching dairy that was out-fitted with the very latest equipment. In the hothouse, they picked heads of lettuce and cucumbers for the boarding school kitchen, as well as flowers to go in vases on the tables. The richly stocked chicken run, teeming with white hens, was surely important to Gertrud. In addition, there were vari-ous chores in the kitchen gardens and instruction (theoretical, at any rate) in fieldwork.

The school authorities set great store by "physical fitness and recreation," so there was a "large open-air and sunbathing area with gymnastics equipment." For inclement weather, the students also had a gymnasium for "modern calis-thenics." And there were spaces devoted to cultural activities. One student later reported, "We always danced after the evening meal, played lots of music, and read together." They practiced lieder in small groups.

So the question arises as to why the Chodziesners sent their daughter to this posh home economics and agricultural school. What did they have in mind for Gertrud? Wives of estate owners were being educated here, not homemakers or farmers' wives. So these were women who could expertly advise the staff in housework, gardening, and farming. Women who, no doubt, would follow their lord and master to farms in the colonies. The school brochure even emphasized this point: "It is precisely the opportunity to take driving lessons and riding

* *Damenflor,* literally "bevy of ladies," refers to a women's auxiliary or women's club, or the female guests of a men's organization.

† *Quark* is a soft cheese similar to cottage cheese.

instruction in astride and sidesaddle positions, as well as shooting classes, which makes this the right school for those who intend to go to the colonies."

Old postage stamps document the economic and political realities of the time—that is, the colonies of the German Reich. In leafing through my own father's album, I see German New Guinea, German East Africa, German South West Africa, Cameroon, the Caroline Islands, Kiauchow, the Mariana Islands, the Marshall Islands, Samoa, and Togo. No matter what the colonies were called, they all had identical subject matter on their stamps, a steamer puffing clouds of smoke like a warship.

Now can we imagine Gertrud as a little Wild West bride? Trude with a shooting iron, happy to be on the back of a horse like her father? It's more likely that her parents' wishes were influenced by Grandmother Hedwig's go-out-and-see-the-world lifestyle. Did Ludwig and Elise see their eldest daughter in Togo or South West Africa? Given his loyalty to the emperor, this would have perfectly fit the mentality of her judicial councillor father. Or was their daughter being trained in farming, riding, and shooting because, in the long term, they planned to emigrate to Palestine? Only a few Swabian families immigrated to Palestine in those days, and emigration would become an issue only during the period between the world wars. Although parents and daughter could never have known this prior to the First World War, these skills (with the exception of Gertrud's riding and shooting abilities) would later come in handy for their life together in a rather rural area. So what did they have in mind for her?

Gertrud doesn't provide us with an answer to this question. She later made rather incidental remarks about this period to her niece:

> I once went tobogganing in the Mulde Mountains at the age of seventeen. You needed about a quarter of an hour to get to the top of the mountain with your toboggan, and you were down at the bottom again in five minutes. In those days, I was on an estate with lots of other girls. There, we learned to cook, bake, sew, launder, and iron. But the sleigh rides in winter were best of all. To be precise, we had four or five great big genuine sleighs with horses harnessed to them. They wore little bells and colourful pom-poms on their harnesses. It sounded so pretty when the sleighs rode one behind the other, often for hours on end, through the immense fields they have there. Oddly enough, the coachman didn't sit on the box seat in front because there wasn't one. He sat behind us on a little raised seat without a back and held the reins above our heads.

As she also pointed out, "I always had a harmonica that I played rather well. I remember taking it along on wagon rides at Arvedshof and playing it by popular request."

| 8

The First World War! Even Gertrud's father, a proud likeness of the kaiser, was initially caught up in the nearly epidemic enthusiasm that generated patriotic statements about family, friends, and acquaintances.

In her preparatory work on the family chronicle, Hilde wrote, "I still remember a conversation at the garden fence; it may have been 1917. An old couple lived next door. All of their sons and sons-in-law, and there were a lot of them, were active officers. We used to play with their numerous grandchildren. 'They should just make peace, even if they have to hand over Alsace-Lorraine,' the good old soldiers' mother said to my father. 'How can you say such a thing?' my father cried. 'We can never hand over Alsace-Lorraine!'"

| 9

Gertrud met an officer named Karl Jodel. This meeting certainly didn't take place by a garden fence. In the socially acceptable fashion of the day, it more likely happened at one of the traditional receptions in one's own home or that of a prominent neighbor: Wealthy Jews, in particular, placed great value on introducing themselves and being introduced to prestigious guests.

The paths of young officers and respectable citizens would naturally have crossed. The socialization and status of young officers differed greatly from present-day career tracks. A cadet school education or a grammar school diploma with obligatory Latin study was a prerequisite for an officer's career. The kaiser himself would then assign a candidate to one of the regiments.

Young officers were held in high esteem, but the pay was terrible. A lieutenant had to come up with a monthly contribution, usually from his parents, of one hundred to two hundred reichsmarks for noonday and evening meals, billeting, and clothing allowance. (In terms of purchasing power, it would be several times that amount in euros today.) The greater the reputation of the regiment, the higher the expenditures.

For a lieutenant, marriage to a daughter from a well-to-do home was highly desirable.

Proof of adequate financial security was a prerequisite for granting a marriage certificate. For a young woman from a Jewish home, however, there was another problem: Officers were only allowed to marry Jewish women who were baptized. Was that part of the plan in the Chodziesner home?

Miss Chodziesner and Lieutenant Jodel: The renowned lawyer and his wife would have placed enormous value on the fact that the relationship complied with socially sanctioned norms. This sternly regimented society strictly observed the rules and did not welcome special arrangements, which could have spelled the premature end to a young officer's career. Gertrud, on the other hand, would not have expected her parents and neighbors to put up with conspicuous behavior. So we can safely assume that the lieutenant and the young woman were soon considered engaged. This was the only way that they could have appeared together in public or taken day trips on a barge, for example, as the following poem suggests. It is on excursions such as these that they most likely came into intimate contact, whether in the great outdoors, in a pension, or in a hotel. Anyway, the couple found a love nest, and Gertrud became pregnant.

I find myself in a biographical predicament at this point in Gertrud's life, for too little can be documented, and too much is open to speculation. So until further notice, I shall take back my resolution to refrain from classifying lines of poetry as autobiographical statements and jump ahead chronologically to cite a poem that was written between 1927 and 1932. It goes by the very nearly camouflaged title "Die Stickerin" ["The Embroiderer"], and I must single out certain lines. First, what is the embroiderer working on?

> I think they call it a macaw,
> the large parrot I'm embroidering in blue and yellow.
> He fans out, shrieking clearly on the bough.

The poet tells us the exact name of the parrot, *Ara ararauna,* a blue-and-gold macaw. This tall South American parrot has blue plumage on its wings and tail, a golden breast and belly, green to yellow coloring on the underside of its wings, and a black beak and throat. In the poem, the dominant blue and gold colors take on symbolic associations.

A link is thus established between the pronounced gold color of the gold-breasted macaw and gold of the *Spiegel* [meaning both mirror and collar patch] on the ends of the uniform jacket. People mostly spoke of collar embroidery in those days, although the term *Kragenspiegel* [collar patch] caught on later. The color of each insignia indicates the branch; here, lemon yellow is the color of the signal corps.

As the second half of the poem begins, the verse transitions from the gold of the bird's plumage to the gold of the collar patch. Gertrud also incorporates the blue of the *Ara ararauna* as a smooth segue into the memory of a steamboat trip they took—on the Havel River, perhaps?

> This breasted yellow is not enflamed enough;
> Green-gold, it seems to me a butterfly—

That's what I called the collar tabs on his gray coat
When, an officer, he went to war.

His blond hair. I loved it so . . .
It fluttered free: his hair so silver blond,
Trickling through my fingers like a sieve.
He didn't like that, used to scold me . . . So it went.

I think about the sailor. He wore no beard.
Thick around the steamer's prop, a maelstrom and a hiss.
He even gave me a white tasseled cap for the trip.
Behind us trailed the river streak like a long, gloomy fish.

For the parrot's wings, I choose a deep and shiny blue.
I always found him at my side when I slept;
But somewhere in France he lay in a wire nest
And every week he wrote me a nice letter.

I take these stanzas to be the poetic expression of a stage in her life. And I feel myself encouraged to do so by the poet herself, who left open, indeed offered, a portion of her poetry to be interpreted autobiographically or to be seen against the backdrop of her own life's story. I will substantiate this later on.

At the moment, however, her partner has evidently been assigned to the western front. This was no behind-the-lines assignment; he was dispatched "to the barbed wire entanglements" along the main front.

A signal corps took operations orders from the section of the front line behind them and passed on observations and measurements; for example, for "fire support." A person could thus get caught in the line of fire. In the long-drawn-out trench warfare involving monstrously heavy losses, intelligence officers seem to have been among the most numerous shell-shocked victims of modern mechanized warfare. They were often exposed to barrages for hours on end. Were they possibly subject to strikes in their immediate vicinity, and did they see comrades torn to pieces? What about the psychological cost of war? Today we speak and write about posttraumatic stress disorder, eating and sleeping disorders, and speech impairment. But there was still no effective treatment in those days, and the mentally wounded frequently remained invalids.

This was an extremely difficult chapter. The few available pieces of the mosaic don't fit together compellingly: officer, pregnancy, nervous breakdown, abortion, attempted suicide.

I must emphasize straightaway that the word "abortion" is not clearly spelled out in the written record. There is just one ornate choice of words that suggests an abortion. Hilde wrote about Gertrud's "strongly developed sense of duty and tradition-mindedness," and saw this as the "reason she could not bear an illegitimate child."

We also have no reliable knowledge of a suicide attempt. Here again, an independent conclusion has been widely sanctioned in the literature about Gertrud Kolmar. Even in the case of my first, purely makeshift string of mosaic tesserae, suggestive power notwithstanding, it does not lend itself to arrangement in a compelling sequence or chronological order. We can only speculate within the scope of probability.

The next clue is a sanatorium in Bad Königstein in the Taunus Mountains. The one and only relevant address here is Dr. Oscar Kohnstamm's sanatorium.

The Jewish neurologist started out modestly by taking in patients at his villa, San Marino, and his name got around. Word had it that spa visitors soon arrived from Ireland and even from New Zealand. Disorders treated included metabolic diseases, exhaustion, and "states of agitation." In the early 1930s, advertisements for Dr. Kohnstamm's sanatorium still alluded to "nervous disorders and mental disturbances." The sanatorium offered a diverse therapeutic regimen, ranging from naturopathy to hypnosis and "diet cures" to psychiatric treatment.

Kohnstamm built a small spa hotel that could accommodate about twenty guests. Since peace and quiet were also part of the therapy, it had double windows, double doors, and even double walls. An annex was opened in 1911.

Soon after the beginning of the First World War, the sanatorium was turned into a military hospital that mainly served combatants who were suffering from shell shock. Apparently, the institution could also accommodate a few private patients.

I've read that Gertrud met the officer here and that this could be where she had her (first?) sexual experience. But this is highly improbable, given the behavioral norms of the day. Gertrud was accompanied by her mother, after all. If they actually stayed at the sanatorium, they would have shared a double room, as was customary at the time. Daughter Gertrud was "under observation." And what's more, patients from the front had to follow a strictly regimented schedule, which Kohnstamm expected to have a stabilizing effect. So an intimate encounter in Bad Königstein was hardly conceivable. She could sooner have run into the painter Ernst Ludwig Kirchner, who had a mental breakdown after two months of basic training in Halle an der Saale and was declared unfit for military service.

There must have been a compelling reason why mother and daughter traveled such a long way from Berlin to the Taunus. And this was during the war, so were there compulsory transport shortages? If it was only a matter of Gertrud's recuperation, then there would have been enough choices in the area surrounding Berlin. The Mecklenburg Lakeland and even the Baltic were closer than the Taunus; why Königstein, of all places?

The scenario continues (for the time being): In Westend, the Chodziesners find out that Karl Jodel is staying in Königstein. Chodziesner may well have asked, "Does the man stand by his actions?" And some sort of mission might have ensued, in which Mother Elise was to "clarify" the matter. Or would he have said, "clear up"? So she travels with her pregnant daughter to Bad Königstein.

If this scenario isn't too far from what really happened—and I am treading on thin ice here, since it can't be documented—then the situation would not have been conducive to an amicable discussion between a distraught patient, pregnant daughter, and worried mother. Any hopes would have been dashed. The patient was suffering the effects of shell shock (perhaps even in the throes of a combat stress reaction?) and may have been incapable of communicating on the topic at hand. Since abortion was now the inevitable result, could this have caused the expectant mother's nervous breakdown?

As Hilde intimated, Gertrud wanted to spare her parents the disgrace, and perhaps herself as well. In the society of her day, the role of single mother hadn't even begun to take shape and remained taboo.

It must be added that, in the wake of the scandal, she could hardly expect lifelong support from her parents. As a young single mother with child, she would have had to be gainfully employed. Her training would have lent itself to teaching. But there was an extremely odd regulation called "Female Teacher Celibacy in the German Empire," a theme that has been taken up as "unwritten history" by women's history research. According to the *Zölibatsklausel* [celibacy clause] of 1892, married female teachers were not allowed to teach school, to say nothing of a woman with an illegitimate child. So the abortion was not only a sacrifice for her family but also a prerequisite for employment as a teacher.

Let me emphasize straightaway that the officer-pregnancy-abortion complex remains a Gordian knot. But we can safely assume that, for Gertrud, it was a traumatic experience. The theme of the unborn, wished-for child would be expressed time and again in her poetic work for years to come.

| 10

In 1915, Gertrud, now twenty-one, completed her traineeship in children's day care at the Gesellschaft zur Bekämpfung der Säuglingssterblichkeit [Society for the Prevention of Infant Mortality] in Berlin.

For a long time, I'd taken only fleeting notice of Gertrud Chodziesner's relationship with this institution, yet it may be biographically relevant. Perhaps the adviser at the Arvedshof Boarding School also suggested she pursue that occupation. During Gertrud's time at the school, the college was expanded to include a nursery facility. Was Gertrud involved or put to work there? And did this prepare her for subsequent work at the Gesellschaft in Berlin?

A 1904 issue of the *Zeitschrift für Ärztliche Fortbildung* [*Journal for Continuing Medical Education*] reported, "Last winter, a Society for the Prevention of Infant Mortality was formed here that mainly pursues the goal of making it possible for the great majority of people to purchase the most hygienically fresh, yet sufficiently inexpensive milk."

Just how relevant quality assurance for mother's milk was to Gertrud must remain an open question. The crucial point is that she did a practicum at this institution and, therefore, identified with the society's mission.

Several years later, the administration of the Poliklinik für Frauen und Kinder [Outpatient Clinic for Women and Children] issued the following reference: "Miss Gertrud Chodziesner worked at our child care center for an extended period in 1915. She always carried out her tasks with the greatest of sense of duty and also knew how to win the children's love to a great extent."

I interpret this as a compensatory gesture in response to the forced termination of her pregnancy. She may well have felt guilty, perhaps because she didn't put up enough resistance to her parents' demands, or perhaps because she hadn't broken free of family pressures and influence to spare the child. Did she long to keep the child?

Whatever her motives or what was behind them, Gertrud Chodziesner perfectly fulfilled the expectations of her era with regard to role and character. Here is what *Spemanns goldenes Buch der Sitte* [*Spemann's Golden Book of Customs*], a housekeeping and etiquette book published in 1913, had to say in the chapter about single young women: "The actual scope of work available to women, business management in foreign parts or children's education, offered enough opportunities to young women from better families."

She would work in children's education and business management, though she would later manage the business of her own family, first for her mother, then for her father. From an outside perspective, Gertrud looked very much like a well-behaved, modest, model daughter from a good home.

Gertrud characterized her role in children's education with the following anecdote:

> I recall an incident at the kindergarten where I was working in 1914 or
> '15. I'd given the children grey clay, and they were kneading away at it.

Each child shaped it without much instruction, got a kick out of it, and soon destroyed the shape again in order to form a new one, just as it occurred to him. Only one boy, who had recently come to us from the Pestalozzi-Fröbelhaus Centre, sat helplessly in front of his lump of clay. In response to my question, he said he wasn't used to doing anything without a model. At Pestalozzi-Fröbelhaus, they'd always had some sort of object to copy. So I put a water pitcher in front of him. All afternoon long, he tried very hard to copy it neatly and properly, and I nearly said, "by the sweat of his brow." The other children played and delighted in the process, whereas this boy toiled away and was only satisfied with his work when it was finished. There was a certain creativity in the sometimes barely recognizable shapes the others came up with. However, the perfectly formed pitcher was nothing but the work of a little imitator . . . At the other centre, the boy had completely lost his ability to portray things without models; hence my somewhat heretical views about kindergarten in general.

She continued with language study, which was clearly the next step at the time. *Spemann's Golden Book of Customs* also had this to say: "For the time being, the teaching profession remains the principal career option for the educated young woman. Here again, there is a palpable excess on the supply side and, having just passed her exams, a young woman often ends up bitterly disappointed, her hopes of finding a reasonably good job dashed. A two- or three-year course of study at teacher training college is the best means for female teachers to pursue an education. One must differentiate between exams for female teachers at the elementary and girls' secondary school levels."

In May 1916, the following certificate was provided for a course participant "of the Jewish faith": "At the behest of the Königliches Provinzial-Schulkollegium [Royal Provincial School Supervisory Board], her qualifications to teach the French language have been examined by the undersigned committee in accordance with the examination regulations of August 5, 1887. On the basis of her outstanding overall performance on the exam, we also hereby attest to the fact that she is qualified to teach French at girls' secondary schools, as well as at lyceums."

A half year later, a certificate with the same wording was issued in October, this time "regarding her qualifications for permission to teach the English language."

Gertrud also studied Russian with the help of a female friend: "I can speak and read this language rather well. . . . And I'd like to add that I have additional knowledge of Czech, Spanish, and Flemish, which makes it possible for me to read texts in these languages with the occasional aid of a dictionary."

| 11

Gertrud's first book, bearing the simple title *Gedichte* [*Poems*], appeared in December 1917. She wrote it under her pen name, Gertrud Kolmar. The volume was issued by a small publishing house, Egon Fleischel and Company, which also published Ina Seidel's poems. Seidel would later champion Kolmar, who was nine years her junior. As Hilde wrote, Papa Ludwig had "secretly" recommended his daughter's poems to Fritz Cohn, the owner of the company. There were forty poems on seventy-two pages.

Kolmar would later reject this volume of poetry. Yet it must be presented, since the history of her oeuvre always follows the course of her life story.

The volume starts off with a series of "mother and child" poems. "Mann und Weib" ["Man and Woman"] is the collective title of the second series, and it winds up with poems on the theme of "time and eternity."

The first sequence is the literary realization of what remained out of reach for the poet as a result of the abortion. The lyric *I* wishes to become a mother, plays the mother role through and through, portrays itself as the mother.

Here are the first three stanzas of "Meins" ["Mine"], the second poem in this volume, which evokes the wished-for child:

> I do not know when he will come,
> So I can touch him with my hands:
> With dark locks about his forehead
> And a red bow.
>
> I do not know if he will come,
> So that my eyes can see him:
> His feet, awkward and small,
> Not able to walk very fast.
>
> The road is long, very long:
> How would he dare such a hike?
> Yet surely my happiness, my great good fortune
> Are born in his tiny hands.

The lyric *I* in the second series of poems depicts the fulfillment of the maternal relationship. The title, "Aus Westend" ["From Westend"], apparently initiates a biographical link:

> The morning was so bright and cheerful—
> A wagon came from afar

And brought a load of straw
Leisurely to the barracks.

The mighty pile seemed a mountain to me;
It almost bumped into the sky.
And a soldier sat on top
Leading his white horse.

I thought: If you, instead of this warrior
Had taken a seat up there,
You would certainly have waved to me,
To come along for a bit.

Then, with a long line
We would lead the good white horse
And crawl deep into the straw,
So that no one could see us.

So that in this sky-high house
I were your only guest on Earth—
And I would think up beautiful names
For our two horses.

The little volume appeared as the third year of the Great War drew to a close. This suggests that the majority and probably all of the poems were written during World War I.

The dominant patriotism of the time had a profound influence on each and every person. Feelings of patriotic elation in the early stages of the war were replaced by calls for perseverance later on.

It was a time of intense peer pressure: You shall comment in accordance with the general consensus, show enthusiasm for how the war is going and proclaim its necessity, even in periods of defeat and increased suffering. People could hardly avoid being confronted with the predominant *Hurra-Patriotismus* [jingoism] or chauvinistic, militant utterings of the day, least of all in Berlin. And Gertrud?

There is not the slightest reflection of contemporary authoritarian or bellicose speech in her volume. And with a regiment barracks in the neighborhood, such talk would have hardly been surprising in conversation with high-ranking people in uniform. In addition, there was the influence of her autocratic father. Were there echoes, at least minor echoes, in his daughter? Several poem titles could, in fact, suggest patriotic resonance: "Trompeterlegende" ["Legend of the

Trumpeter"], "Marschlied" ["Marching Song"], "Soldatenmädchen" ["Soldier's Girl"], and "Die Fahne" ["The Flag"]. All the same, she did not abide by any expectations of a contemporary readership that was loyal to the kaiser. Amid the intensified battle cry of those years, the soft voice of the poet speaks in verses that do not drone along with *schimmernde Wehr* [gleaming weapons] but rather in lines that gesture toward disarmament. And in "Marschlied," of all things:

> A light blue ribbon flutters on my dress;
> Which, woe be to us, is a flag,
> Yes, woe be to us, is a flag!
>
> And if you have no helmet, I'll soon get you one:
> I'll forge it from flowers and rain.
> Take a branch from the forest as another weapon,
> So that the arms well suit you.
> Now we'll wander off, until the sun goes to sleep,
> And if the moon hides her light,
> Then we'll look deeply into our eyes,
> And they'll be our lanterns,
> Yes, they'll be our lanterns!

The last poem, "Ich weiss es" ["I Know"], is in a radically altered tone. Strongly suggestive stanzas articulate what has been witnessed and suffered here. These stanzas not only evoke the past but also anticipate the poet's later experiences in the form of a lament:

> Toil stands on the path I mean to take,
> Want stands on the path I mean to take,
> Death stands on the path I mean to take,
> Lamentation lies on the path I mean to take,
>
> And every milestone has a tongue,
> And all the little pebbles cry out,
> Crying woe—where a gasping girl fell, rattling,
> Fleeting, forsaken, tired and sick.
> Want stands on the path I mean to take,
> Death stands on the path I mean to take,
> And yet I will take it!
>
> Foolish girls in shame and torment:
> A thousand went before me.

A thousand will come after me.
I will be number one thousand and one.
My lips on a stranger's mouth:
And die a woman like a mangy dog—
You're not horrified? No.
My beating heart upon a stranger's breast:
Laugh, my eyes, before you have to cry!
And you won't cry alone.

Want stands on the path I mean to take,
Death stands on the path I mean to take,
Sorrow and lamentation, gloomy toil:
I know it, and yet I take it!

| 12

In November 1918, the soldiers' council of the Döberitz Prison Camp provided the poet with a reference:

> Miss Gertrud Chodziesner of Charlottenburg was employed from November 1, 1917, to November 30, 1918, as a French and English interpreter at the postal censor station of the Döberitz Prison Camp. Her job consisted of reading prisoners' ingoing and outgoing mail.
>
> We can testify to the fact that Miss Ch. carried out her work with very special enthusiasm and expertise. The closing down of the postal censor station has necessitated her dismissal.

In February 1927, "Max Wronker, *Justizrat** and *Notar* in the Prussian District Court of Appeals," provided written confirmation that the "above copy matches the original copy word for word."

Her job at the prison camp deserves more than a simple mention. To begin with, here are a few notes about the place where she worked. The enormous compound of the former proving ground in Döberitz lay southwest of Spandau and south of Falkensee. Wilhelm II was an initiator of the facility. The newly laid main thoroughfare leading out from Berlin to Döberitz is still called Heerstrasse [*Heer:* armed forces], and was called Aufmarschstrasse [*Aufmarsch:* parade, marching up] when it was built.

---

* *Justizrat* [counselor] is an honorific title granted to lawyers.

Even before the Great War, thousands of hectares of the originally forested area were cleared so as to create a steppe and desertlike topography. Rioting by natives of the area was put down.

The first military flight school opened prior to World War I in the northern section. This is where Flier Battalion 1 was stationed, a unit associated with the name Manfred von Richthofen, the Red Baron. The air base was moved, as another military airport, Gatow, was nearby.

So mail censor Chodziesner worked out in Döberitz on the edge of an artificial steppe, an actual created desert. The censor's office was probably in one of the larger garrison administration buildings that offered a wide view of the regular rows of barracks. After increasingly shorter periods of basic training, recruits were released and sent to the front. The barracks stood empty, and the garrison was turned into a detention and prison camp. By the end of Gertrud's employment, about thirty thousand prisoners from seven nations were penned up there.

The percentage of Russian prisoners was probably high at this camp near Berlin. So it may well be true that she acquired her knowledge of Russian here, as was reported within the family. She would mainly have inspected letters in Russian but may well have interpreted when the need arose. The letters were predominantly in French and English, however. Concerning her "time as an interpreter," she would later write that she hardly ever got to interpret at the postal censor station, where her knowledge of languages was required for reading "incoming and outgoing prisoner mail."

Can we describe her work in greater detail? We can only try, and attempts are fraught with questions. What guidelines was she required to follow? How much discretionary latitude did or could she allow herself? Were her inspections randomly checked by a superior? If a passage in a letter struck her as problematic, did she blacken or cut it out, or did she report it immediately?

Döberitz is connected to a surprising entry, which is to say, Bible reading: "I've read the Luther Bible for my entire life, and those who are able to judge have claimed that its language has very clearly influenced me as a poet. Indeed, I recall that a friend in Döberitz occasionally said, 'You speak like Martin Luther.' That was because I said, 'This towel is dirty beyond all measure.' By the way, I'm not as well versed in the New Testament."

This statement is doubly informative. For one thing, the Luther Bible influenced her poetic language. For another, one would sooner have expected a Jewish woman to prefer the Leopold Zunz translation of the Bible, which had been available since the 1830s. But the Zunz didn't appear to mean much to Gertrud Kolmar, who would ultimately own four Luther Bibles. Her most important edition was "an old Luther Bible from 1854 that Mother's mother (according to the inscription) received as a gift in 1855."

* * *

The war that was supposed to be over in a flash—or so people thought in their intoxicated anticipation of victory—dragged on.

Hilde wrote:

> The victory celebrations were less frequent, hunger was on the rise. My father, who permitted no smuggled goods in the house at first, ignored her when my mother asked him, "Do you really want the children to go hungry, then?" My teachers went to battle, and school was cancelled because of a coal shortage. My mother was out and about all day long to scrape together food for her large family. But since we didn't have any relatives in the countryside, it drove her to despair anyway. We had to slaughter our chickens, as we had no more feed for them. The time came when I asked for a piece of dry bread, and my mother shrugged her shoulders helplessly. There was no bread in the house and none to be had. My father was a rich man, but you couldn't eat money.

After the war, it would become clear where his overly correct attitude toward the black market had led. The siblings were malnourished. Thirteen-year-old Hilde had to be "sent to Switzerland by children's transport," where they spent two months putting the meat back on her bones. She would suffer the effects of nutritional deficiency for a long time to come. Did the eldest daughter at least get enough food in Döberitz?

November 1918 spelled the end of the war, the end of the German Empire, and the beginning of the revolution. To coin a familiar phrase, the whole world fell apart in the Chodziesner home. Hilde again, at the start of her family chronicle: "When I came down to the dining room, freshly washed and well rested, my father was standing at the window. 'Papa,' I asked, 'isn't it true that you still support the kaiser?' 'Support the kaiser? After he ran away and left us all in the lurch?'"

The esteemed, annually celebrated Kaiser Wilhelm had fled, had shirked his responsibility, had not held the fort, and had betrayed his country by becoming a refugee!

As Kaiser Wilhelm's double, this is how Papa Ludwig would have and must have thought, opined, and finally ruled on the matter. The fundamental conviction could also have taken root in him that a person didn't simply decamp, not even in a tight spot; he stayed in position and held the fort.

As a possible consequence Ludwig, the spitting image of the kaiser, may have wanted to prove he was superior to his long-standing role model in the most crucial respect and thus spurned any form of flight. Being someone's look-alike must not lead to self-betrayal! The kaiser was written off, Ludwig's own role established: One must persevere and stand firm!

| 13

"Spartacus is shooting again!" said "our gardener's wife," straining to hear the "distant rumble" from the east, coming over from the city.

Yet the property in Westend remained a *hortus conclusus* [an enclosed garden]. This was also true for Hilde. The fourteen-year-old made observations in child-like Sütterlin script,* arranged them in a book with silhouettes, and presented the book *Aus der Vogelwelt unseres Gartens* [*From the Bird World of Our Gardens*] to her parents on the occasion of their silver anniversary in March 1919.

Much of it sounds like a storybook tale: "In a big garden lived an old starling in an acacia tree with his mate and babies . . ." "Redtail's lodgings," the "black-bird family," and the little flycatcher were also observed and depicted.

Father's garden world evidently spurred sister Margot on to a later career as an ornithologist, and Hilde would have loved to be a zoologist.

| 14

In August 1919, the poet took up her first position as a private tutor in Berlin. Dr. Kurt Mühsam, director of the *National Zeitung* [*National Newspaper*], residing at Kurfürstendamm 281 in Berlin W 16, was responsible for hiring her.

These may be satisfactory, concise details, but what do they tell us? First, the name of the newspaper is confusing: This 1920s organ certainly had nothing in common with the radical right-wing paper of the same name published in Germany since 1951, and Gertrud's first private position was not in the home of a German nationalist.

Kurt Mühsam had married the historian Alice Freymark eight years earlier. They had three children: Ruth, Gerd, and Helmut. Gertrud must surely have regretted the fact that her employment ended in less than three months.

Frau Dr. Mühsam explained this in her reference: "From August 1 to October 25, 1919, Miss Gertrud Chodziesner worked in our home as a governess and language teacher to our three children, ages 7, 6, and 5. She earned the children's affection very quickly. Her calm, sensitive nature and thoughtful handling of the childish psyche make her the right sort for children, and one could

---

* Sütterlin script was a form of old German black-letter handwriting, based on medieval lettering, used in the first half of the 1900s.

not wish for a more suitable person. I am sincerely sorry that Miss Chodziesner is leaving our home. However, I am compelled to take my niece into our home, and she will also take over the supervision of the children.'"

In November of that same year, Gertrud set off on a trip to Ebermergen an der Wörnitz, which is between Nördlingen and Donauwörth on the present-day Romantic Road. For nearly nine months, she lived with Ella Dittmar, one of her former colleagues at the postal censor station in Döberitz.

This was more than just an extended visit with recurring strolls along the river. It either cropped up very quickly indeed or they had planned from the very beginning for Gertrud to help with the housekeeping and look after a child (or children).

An anecdote that was later recounted by Ella in a subsequent letter to Hilde shows how Gertrud dealt with the children:

> Now here you have a story about Trude that I associate with the word "lunch." Trude was visiting us in Elster. In a little Bavarian fit of rage, Willi threw a plate during lunch and broke it. Not slow to react, Trude threw the vegetable dish in the same direction. Horrified, Willi said, "You just broke Ella's tableware." To which Trude responded, "Maybe you shouldn't have done that because I thought this was a party on the eve of a wedding."* The curious thing about Trude was that she sometimes had a very dry sense of humour. In Ebermergen, she also wrote a poem à la Wilhelm Busch† to my father-in-law.

Gertrud came up with another funny poem, "Liebes Silberpaar!" ["Silver Lovebirds!"], though the date (Ebermergen, April 19, 1920) shows that it could not have been meant for her parents, who had already celebrated their silver wedding anniversary the year before. This poem was written for an aunt or uncle, whom she celebrated with a three-part poem, each beginning with the stanza: "Sitting here this peaceful evening / On the shady garden bench / Composing a song for a silver wedding, / seeking a rhyme for 'husband.'"‡

But something comes between each repetition of the stanza. In the first sequence, it's poultry that the rhymer apparently learned to put up with: "A black

---

* On the night before a wedding, according to a German custom called *Polterabend*, the guests break crockery to bring luck to the couple's marriage.

† Wilhelm Busch was a German caricaturist whose picture stories are considered forerunners of the comic strip.

‡ In the German original, the first and third and the second and fourth lines rhyme: "Sitze hier in Abendfried / Auf der Gartenbank im Schatten, / Dicht´ ein Silberhochzeitslied, / Suche einen Reim auf 'Gatten.'"

chicken runs over, / And picks at my boot buttons." And the next disruption comes straightaway: "Then a little white hen flies over, / How I should feed it." Finally, a gray couple, and they start cackling, too. The second part begins with:

> Sitting here this peaceful evening
> On the shady garden bench,
> Composing a song for a silver wedding,
> Seeking a rhyme for "husband."
>
> "Green was once the myrtle's branch,
> Where the couple exchanged rings"—
> Hey there, a buck rabbit
> Squeezes smoothly through the slats!
>
> Hey, whoops, here, there,
> Quick as an arrow he jumps on the lawn,
> Whoosh, now he's gone again!
> I'll catch me one of these rabbits!
>
> But only after lots of running around
> What luck, I grab him by the ear,
> But the writing————is over with:
> I'd sooner chop rocks!

In the third go-round of the third sequence, the woman receiving congratulations makes a fresh start, but the milk boils over, and she has to first clean the stove.

Her theatrically ill-fated silver wedding anniversary song was accompanied by a few lines in which Gertrud expressed thanks for the gift, a book "that I may not look at before I get home. For—'as depicted'—I don't get much reading done here." This is probably because she was more of a housekeeper than a guest at the time. In one photo, she is sitting at a little coffee table with Ella, another woman, and a child. Like the hostess, she is wearing a typical period apron dress and looks even smaller than her already diminutive size.

Gertrud had a chat with her friend Ella about the effect that women have on men. Looking back, Gertrud wrote:

> I certainly neither am nor was pretty, and yet . . . As a woman (not as a
> human being, apart from any affinity between the sexes, which actually
> happens rather often), it is not my manner or spiritual essence that has

made an impression on men, as one might think, but my face. Women, in particular, have often found this hard to imagine. Ella once told me in Ebermergen that she asked her husband during a train ride where, exactly, the effect I sometimes had on men came from, even though I actually wasn't pretty. While he by no means found me attractive, he thought it was my mouth and eyes that did it . . .

What the political scientist Hannah Arendt said about the writer Rahel Varnhagen in equally colloquial and pointed words can also be applied to Gertrud: "Nature didn't go to any trouble" over her.

Gertrud didn't compensate with fashionable clothes or elevate her small appearance by means of a charismatic, highly eloquent presence. But for all that, the dark luminosity of her eyes left a deep impression.

Recollections of Ebermergen was the working title of a project she mentioned years later that never came to fruition, "although I have the necessary 'material.'"

What sort of material could it have been? If she did manage her girlfriend's household in Ebermergen in exchange for room and board, and if she looked after, instructed, and entertained one or more children, then this material would have been of no particular interest and not even new. The same goes for charming scenery and flowing waters. So what was it that led her to stay in Ebermergen for three quarters of a year? Something must have happened that was worth remembering. A creative phase? A period of insight or clarity? A relationship with a man? Was it just a coincidence that she talked with her friend about her effect on men at the time? Did she provide a clue? It would certainly have been surprising for an extremely discreet woman like Gertrud to shed light on a love affair, of all things, in her autobiographical writings. Who could she have given or read these kinds of notes to? This remains an open question, a blank space.

Gertrud continued her journey from Ebermergen toward the Riesengebirge.* She apparently got to know a Czech border official rather well there. At any rate, she mentions a man with an extraordinarily thick head of hair, deep creases at the corners of his mouth, and a "brown carbine that smugglers hate" in a poem from that period. Thick hair, facial creases, and a hunting rifle with a short barrel do not allow us to glean more precise information about the relationship. Nevertheless, I have already stressed how dubious biographical information derived from poems is, as stylization inevitably takes place.

---

* The Riesengebirge is a mountain range in the present-day northern Czech Republic and southwestern Poland.

| 15

Even Ludwig Chodziesner, the lawyer, had invested a large part of his fortune in war bonds, money that was lost when Germany capitulated and the German Empire collapsed. Rapidly escalating inflation also set in.

A detailed account in a letter of July 1920, written in Westend, shows just how great the overall poverty and privation were in the aftermath of the war as a result of the collapsing mark. Hilde's father told her, "The first children's fete in six years took place yesterday on Haeselerstrasse with music, Bengal lights,* stands for playing dice, a torchlit procession, rockets, shooting, and other kinds of racket."

Gertrud continued the account:

In the last courtyard on Königin-Elisabethstrasse, they danced waltzes to the strains of the folk song "Es geht bei gedämpfter Trommel Klang" ["He Walks to the Sound of a Muffled Drum"]. Meaningful! There were cherry and ice cream cone tables, a wheel of fortune, and a bowling alley in the very same location. The wheel of fortune was operated by two individuals dressed half as Indians and half as Moors. The prizes consisted of paper flowers, little clay angels, glass and tin centrepieces, and other such treasures. The only true "valuable" always on hand was an entire loaf of bread, but that prize was meant exclusively for the organizer's relatives and friends.

Although her motives were charitable, the now twenty-six-year-old Gertrud had again taken refuge in her parents' home: "I continue to lead a peaceful life here, helping Mother insofar as I am able—and insofar as she allows herself to be helped!" Help was a crucial word in Gertrud's vocabulary.

The family could no longer afford the villa in Ahornallee. A baron purchased it at the end of 1920 or in early 1921.

Hilde, the chronicler, surely also spoke for her siblings when she wrote, "Prices went sky high, the money for the war loan was lost, and my father sold the house with the old garden, the home he'd lived in for nearly thirty years, the one in which I was born and grew up. When the garden gate slammed shut for the last time, I lost my true home. Once and for all, I was driven from my childhood paradise. I have never entirely gotten over the fact that strangers should live, laugh, and cry in rooms that belonged to us. I was not there for the move; I couldn't have borne it."

* Bengal lights are fireworks that burn with a steady, bright blue light.

The Chodziesners occupied one floor of a house at Kurfürstendamm 43. Hilde gave this account: "We found a big, beautiful, comfortable apartment in the city on a nice street. But it had no garden, no dog, no countryside, and no footpaths. It was a modern, big-city apartment like thousands of others. I finished school, went on to a higher girls' school, but I was not happy."

Gertrud found another position as a private tutor. Higher motives also played a role here, as she later articulated in comparing her sister Hilde's professional outlook and way of life as a bookseller with her own:

As for me, I am a very different sort and could presumably have devoted myself to being a homebody and raising children without missing much, and, believe you me, without becoming shallow or superficial as a result. Oh no! These simple, everyday things would have taken on a different, deeper meaning for me than for most women. My purpose has always lain within me, so to speak, and still does; what I am looking for is simply the right place in which I am able to devote myself to it.

Three references document her half decade of employment as a private tutor. We can tell quite a bit about her methods and conduct from them.
Mrs. Henny Zondek of Tauentzienstrasse wrote:

Miss Gertrud Chodziesner was with my children in the afternoons from October 20 to April 21. She knew in the most excellent way how to spend time with them and how to awaken their interest in the widest possible array of subjects. Miss Ch. has a calm, always consistently friendly manner in dealing with children, and so it is easy for her to earn their affection. If my health had not forced me to make changes in my household, I would have happily been able to keep Miss. Ch. with us for longer, as she was a most reliable caregiver for my children.

A half year later, Ludwig Schmoller of Janaerstrasse in Berlin-Wilmersdorf wrote the following reference, dated December 1, 1926:

I hereby confirm to you in writing that you were employed in my home as a language teacher for my two daughters from October 1, 1921, until this very day.
During this time, my children found you to be the very best tutor that we could have wished for, not only as a language teacher, but in every respect.
In the event that we now part ways after such a long time, it is only because the children are grown.

We wish you all the best in your future endeavours and hope that you will always keep in touch with our family.

And this was no mere cliché! In January 1929, Gertrud mentioned that "I was at the Schmollers yesterday."

Gertrud was not exclusively employed in the Schmoller home during that half decade but took on an additional assignment. Annie Schapski of Badensches-trasse also wrote a good letter of recommendation for the period "from December 1, 1923, to October 1, 1924," according to which Miss Gertrud Chodziesner was employed "in my home three mornings per week as a tutor to my two deaf-and-dumb children and to relieve the burden on me. In this brief period, she knew how to win the children's' love and complete trust. She looked after the children with great patience in the most inspiring way. But since I definitely must take a tutor into our home, I am unfortunately obliged to let Miss Chodziesner go."

Thus, Gertrud did not have her "lodgings" in the apartment or home of her female students, as was widely customary for tutors in those days; she went to each on an hourly basis. As ever, she lived with her parents.

| 16

It was around this time that Gertrud Chodziesner wrote four cycles of poems that were not published until after her death. More precise dating is barely possible. On average, records and research postulate that it was "circa 1920."

The cycle in which the lyric *I* is largely identified with the young Polish noblewoman Marie Walewska is a story in itself. Marie was Napoleon's great love, the woman he favored above all other mistresses for a long time. The poet was about twenty-five when she composed her theme and variations on love between the imperial general Napoleon and Marie.

Presenting a quotation from Benjamin Constant, the opening theme is already revealing: "All of my thoughts come from him / And go back to him. He is everything to me, my future / And my life." Many films have been made about this love story, and the most prominent actor to be cast as Walewska was Greta Garbo.

In the sequence of nineteen poems, the role of the young woman who submits to the great man is adopted. Two iconographic female poses were especially popular at the dawn of the nineteenth century: the woman kneeling or crouching at the man's feet, and the woman placing a wreath on the great man. The young poet observed this stereotype in her parents' home.

Here are two lines from one of the unconditionally intoned eulogies to the great man and conqueror: "And when he speaks, people must remain silent, / And when he is silent, then only God speaks."

The poem evokes the dream role of the female lover who is eclipsed in the presence of or, more likely, by her male counterpart. In greatly simplified form, the man is great, the woman ordinary; the man stands at the center, the woman on the periphery; the beloved hero blooms, and his female lover withers away. In that same vein, the three-stanza poem "Vergib" ["Forgive"] ends:

> I'll be a fleeting image at the page's edge
> Inside the eternal book of your deeds,
> I, a delicate, colorful finch,
> Flutter around an eagle's pinions
> Still shouting for joy as I sink dying
> While his wings glide sunward!

Three more early cycles have survived; most are texts in which the poet is still searching for her voice. But the approximately 150 printed pages in volume 1 of the complete edition allow for important discoveries.

One of the first poems, "Opfergang" ["Self-Sacrifice"], suggests that the lyric *I* and the poet herself are closely related and that autobiographical elements are being expressed:

> I knew that I, too, was born.
> There is a book, my name is in it.
>
> My own twenty years
> Wore heavily upon me, because I found the altar
>
> And shyly, upon its steps, placed my self
> For the sake of the Good Lord: given to you.
>
> And put my ego's bliss there, too
> And became rich because I had nothing left. Just you.

In "Mein Sohn" ["My Son"], the dominant theme appears once more, this time as the growing, longed-for child in fast-forward:

> Oh, I already know, that's how it's going to be:
> Breasts will bend to him, letting him drink,
> Give away his little smock soon;
> The long locks will be cut off,
> And with happy carefree footsteps
> He hops into his sixth year.

Oh, I already know, that's how it's going to be:
Pack up the books, hurry off to school.
Sharpen pencils. Money! and buy notebooks.
His dreams will have numbers and names,
Teacher's sayings, how the other boys talk
Pressing into my sweet's little head.

Oh, I already know, it will be
His father's strength and my weakness:
He scoffs, hard and defiant, when I speak,
Beating me with knowledge I never learned,
And I find within the apple of my eye
A cold light shining brighter every day.

Oh, I already know, that's how it's going to be:
Nights may glow, urging him, flickering,
He will blow up a red gate,
Make my blood flash in his veins—
But I, tired, will sit in vain
One evening and be all alone.

And then comes the untitled thirty-second poem in the third cycle:

Your gray scarf loses its color,
Your hair almost white and your eyes transparent,
But your face looks warm and burnt red,
From wine and the sun. Just so by a fence,
With barbed wire—because I think of the prisoners,
Who here, so bitterly blue and scarlet
Already in the autumn froze from winter—
And so you lean there.
Your smile flying over
The fencing, imprisoned by war and everything.

I again have the impression that intensity within the largely formulaic verses is most likely to build when the lyric *I* and the self of the poet begin to merge.

So I must be inconsistent once more and link a sequence of poems to a discussion of the poet's life. Could the allusion to a soldier behind barbed wire, a clearly trusted friend from the past, refer to Karl Jodel himself? In that case, he would have been sent back to the front after successful treatment (or treatment cut short on orders) and ended up in a prisoner-of-war camp.

The poem hardly creates the impression of an end to all affection for the man in the "gray scarf." We may provisionally conclude from this that the abortion did not put a strain on the relationship. But who else could she have blamed for it? The relationship with her father also appears to have been unencumbered, unspoiled. The relationship with her mother seems to have been rather difficult, however, with insinuations of a burdensome childhood. Did she, therefore, connect her mother with the forced termination of her pregnancy?

Now comes "Ende" ["End/Ending"], the last poem in the early "Cycle III." I could hardly breathe upon reading it for the first time! Here are the closing lines of the second verse:

> If I am seriously sad,
> I can no longer write verses;
> I sit silently in a boat
> And let it float me downstream.
> I will not find a rudder,
> I will not need a helm;
> If my love, my sorrow wants it so,
> I will capsize and sink.
>
> If I am in deep despair,
> I cannot moderately ponder:
> My cry is shrill and harried—
> Should I grab and restrain him?
> Nevermore shall my ragged thoughts
> be smooth, shiny lines;
> My heart is a bloody pulp,
> And I can neither shape nor polish anything.

| 17

The National Socialist German Workers' Party platform stated in 1920, "Only a *Volksgenosse* [fellow countryman] can be a citizen. Only someone who has German blood, irrespective of creed, can be a fellow countryman. That's why no Jew can be a fellow countryman."

Were such announcements, perhaps cited in the press, taken seriously by Jews at the time? They probably didn't see the statements as early warning signs but as guiding principles of a right-wing extremist splinter group.

* * *

Ilse Blumenthal-Weiss was a contemporary witness. Five years younger than Gertrud Chodziesner, she was born in Schöneberg. An orthopedist and physical education teacher, she was married to a dentist. She was twenty-nine when her first poems were published in Berlin newspapers, and she corresponded with Rainer Maria Rilke. Here is her contribution to oral history:

> I once saw an antisemitic demonstration that went along Potsdamer Strasse
> from Potsdamer Platz. I will never forget it. People were shouting, "Down
> with the Jews, out with the Jews, and . . ." This must have been around 1922.
> It came as a surprise to me that something like this could happen without
> anyone expressing opposition to it. To me, the existence of antisemitism
> was a foregone conclusion, a sad matter of course. Most Jews took the view,
> "We're doing really well, after all, so we'll put up with a little antisemitism."
> This was something that always made me terribly angry. There's no such
> thing as "a little antisemitism." Either there's antisemitism or there isn't.
> And if being a Jew meant I wasn't allowed to become a teacher, a university
> professor, or an officer, then that was enough antisemitism for me. Most
> people, including my parents, who were certainly doing well, thank God,
> did not feel the same way I did. My parents were so German that they
> were more German than the Germans. My father was a very distinguished
> resident of Schöneberg, had many non-Jewish friends, and was a member—
> you wouldn't know this—of the Central Association of German Citizens of
> the Jewish faith. I could never understand how they could be so German.
> I'm German, too. But if they didn't grant me the same rights . . . At any rate,
> all of this strengthened my belief in Zionism. It seemed to me back then that
> Zionism was a kind of solution to the Jewish question. This was a utopian
> vision, as we have unfortunately found out in the meantime.

The integration of Jews into twentieth-century Central European society can only be touched on here: to discuss this and other related topics would go beyond the scope of a biography. A Jewish renaissance was taking place at the same time. At any rate, we must point out that the search for Jewish roots on a grand scale not only was driven by developments after 1933, but also had already begun under pressure from growing antisemitism in the period of the Weimar Republic.

For most nominally Jewish citizens of that period, however, Judaism was "but a purely denominational appendage" in a secularized world. Sigmund Freud came up with the phrase "German citizens of Jewish unbelief." The Polish-born writer Isaac Deutscher introduced the idea of "non-Jewish Jews," and the German-born historian George Mosse spoke of "German Jews beyond Judaism."

Hilde, the family chronicler, wrote, "On June 25, 1922, I found the following entry in my diary, which otherwise contained rather personal, somewhat trivial matters, as I was still a young teenager then: 'They shot Rathenau yesterday. I don't know—there's such heaviness in the air. I'm afraid of something intangible. I'm scared that something terrible could happen. Hope I'm mistaken.'"

A note in her papers reads, "perhaps this is my Rathenau memento." We shall come back this shortly.

Walther Rathenau was an industrialist, chair of AEG,* a writer with six volumes of published works, and a politician who was foreign minister in the cabinet of Chancellor Joseph Wirth, as well as the initiator of the Treaty of Rapallo that improved relations between Germany and the Soviet Union. He was shot in the head by two right-wing extremists while driving in an open automobile. They murdered him because he was a Jew and because he fostered ties with Eastern [that is, Communist] Europe. In his eulogy before Parliament, Chancellor Wirth said, "A volcano threatens from the depths . . . And there is no doubt about it: This enemy is on the Right!"

Among the population, the murder was also frequently seen as a portent of things to come. Here's what Hilde wrote on the following day: "I believe I can say that, except for the revolution, no political event has shaken me so deeply as the death of Rathenau. I never saw him, never heard him speak, nothing of the sort, and yet . . . Strangely enough, I mourn him like a good friend. If I just think about it, I cannot stop crying. When I'm alone, I think about it over and over again.—Long live the republic!"

Did Gertrud also see signs of growing, nearly rampant antisemitism in the 1920s? In any event, her sister recorded an incident that took place in 1923:

> Yesterday, S. was here for the entire day. (He's an Indian, very dark-skinned, who once lived with us as a lodger and paid my mother four pounds per month for a comfortable room and full board!) We went for a stroll, when a couple of people passed us and said, "Freshly imported: Jews are from Palestine." "Swine," my cousin K. retorted, and two men pounced on him and started a brawl. (K. was just a boy of eighteen!) Amid repeated scolding, they finally dispersed. Why do things always have to be like this? We weren't bothering them at all. Why do they always have to start a fight? It upset me a lot.

She commented further on the subject that would eventually dominate her life as well: "Papa laughs when he hears people rail against the Jews or reads it in the papers. But it depresses me terribly, and I feel more alone than usual."

* AEG was a German maker of electrical equipment that existed until 1997.

| 18

An important change occurred in July 1923: The Chodziesner family left their apartment on Kurfürstendamm. After three years in the city center, their father could endure it no longer. He had to have space around him and needed to exercise in the open air. There is no record of what his wife thought of such a move.

I don't know how the lawyer financed a fresh start in that difficult, bustling, often chaotic period, particularly with galloping inflation! But the fact remains that it was of paramount importance for Gertrud's future. The counselor bought a house with a garden in Neu-Finkenkrug, the posh residential section of a village west of Spandau in the *jotwedee* (boondocks), as people in Berlin called it. But, on the other hand, it was a housing estate of similar character to that of the previous Westend residence!

Here, in the big garden and nearby forest, the counselor again found the coveted antidote to the constant pressures of the legal profession. In her ring binder, Hilde wrote:

In his spare time, our father was a skilled gardener who grafted roses. When the time for baby chicks came, he put them in his jacket pocket so as to bring the furry balls closer to the warm oven. A famous lawyer, he could just as well have been an estate owner or a forester and not have lacked a thing. In fact, he might have actually been happier. He had no need for company. Unlike Mother, he had no use for theatre and probably went along for her sake. He never went to the cinema in his entire life. "Life is enough cinema and theatre for me," he liked to say.

And here's another note that anticipates the evolution of domestic life in Finkenkrug: "What he needed were his brown-and-white spotted ducks (for whom he built a pond with his own hands), the wild garden, the old trees, the bird feeder on our veranda, his chickens and baby chicks, and, most of all, his dogs, two of which always inhabited our house and garden. He went for walks with them and one of us in the nearby woods."

Yet these were not rosy times. Hilde again in August 1923, this time written in a blue linen-bound journal with a fastener: "I went home earlier because of a general strike. Everything is so expensive. Women sit from one in the morning until who knows when and wait for butter. On every street corner, people whisper and murmur that shops sell the tiniest quantities of food at astronomical prices."

Her father continued to run to the offices in Charlottenburg and Central Berlin, but at least he was now a commuter. Hilde continued:

When Father came home from the city, we were already waiting for him at the train station so that we could immediately convert the money he brought along into merchandise, as we could have no longer gotten a piece of bread for it in the afternoon. We had only my friendship with the milkman to thank for the daily half litre. That was five years after the end of the war.

We sat in a single room to save on light in the afternoons. And because people were together so much, they became much more irritable than they would otherwise have been, and there were rows, ill humour, and anger over every little thing. No cosy togetherness, but constant, unnecessary outbursts. Everything is so unpleasant.

With regard to developments in her own life, she later wrote, "Since I had to earn a bit of money, I took up a position as an office helper at a small publishing house, having acquired the most basic skills in stenography and typing on my own."

And she became a bookseller "in an academic and, subsequently, in a literary (belletristic) bookshop. . . I hadn't originally chosen this profession; I wanted to be a gardener, but my father, who already had one daughter studying zoology, was opposed to this 'penniless' art. When I had to earn money later on, I accidentally came upon the book trade, which he was fond of. Once the choice was made, I became completely engrossed in the profession to a degree I would never have believed possible."

| 19

As a prologue to broadening the written perspective, I shall now introduce Walter Benjamin's brother.

Hilde had this to say about the Benjamin cousins:

In my childish ignorance, Walter struck me as strange and remote. And he really only took notice of Gertrud, who, apart from her poetic inclinations, was basically unlike him in terms of her downright unliterary manner and character. I know how disrespectfully we imitated our eldest cousin whenever he said, "Goodbye, Aunt Lise."

We showered all our affection on Georg, the second-oldest cousin. His calm, hospitable, cheerful ways and sincere nature most closely resembled Grandfather Schoenflies, whose given name he bore. He studied medicine and became a doctor to the poor in Wedding.

The relationship between the Benjamin and Chodziesner branches of the family was a close one. In a photo from 1906, all seven Benjamin and Chodziesner children were pictured together, as if to show that "we are *one* family!" The family may well have congregated again at Georg's wedding, in which case Ludwig and Gertrud would surely have been among the guests.

In a letter from early 1926, Walter Benjamin has this to say: "In a couple of days, my brother will marry a nice young girl, a friend of my sister." Seven years younger than Georg, Hilde Lange had passed the first state law exam at the time.

We need not go over Georg's early years at this point. Suffice it to say that he was a Communist by persuasion and, as one would say nowadays, "socially responsible." The previous year, he wrote a paper, Tuberculosis Mortality of Miners in the Ruhr Valley Before, During, and After the War. He worked on an essay, "Child Labour in Germany," and wrote an article, "Improving School Hygiene!" published in *Der Sozialistische Arzt* [*The Socialist Physician*]. He was associated with left-wing professional organizations, including the Workingmen's Samaritan Movement, the Proletarian Health Service, and later the Association of Socialist Physicians.*

What Georg and Walter would experience and suffer in the Third Reich is typical of the era in which their cousin, Gertrud, lived and wrote. It may be overly obvious to give priority to Walter Benjamin here. But, in any case, he will come up repeatedly as the poet's supporter. And there is a wealth of literature about him. Georg is an entirely different matter: As far as I can tell, there is just one biography about him, written decades after his death by his widow.

| 20

At the beginning of 1927, Gertrud moved to Hamburg for half a year. She was again employed as a private tutor, this time by the Alexander family in the upscale quarter of Harvestehude, and her lodgings were in their home.

What is written in the *Goldenen Buch* [*Spemann's Golden Book of Customs*] about the "treatment of private male tutors" in middle-class families, even after the historical turning point of 1918, would still have applied to how female tutors were handled as well. So I have changed nothing but the tutor's gender in the following quotation:

* The German titles of Georg's writings were "Die Tuberkulosesterblichkeit der Bergarbeiter im Ruhrgebiet vor, in und nach dem Kriege" ["Tuberculosis Mortality of Miners in the Ruhr Valley Before, During, and After the War"], "Die Kinderarbeit in Deutschland" ["Child Labour in Germany"], and "Ausbau der Schulhygiene!" ["Improving School Hygiene!"]. The professional organizations with which he was associated were the Arbeiter-Samariter-Bewegung [Workingmen's Samaritan Movement], the Proletarischer Gesundheitsdienst [Proletarian Health Service], and the Verein Sozialistischer Ärzte [Association of Socialist Physicians].

You should provide a nice, not-too-small room near the nursery so that she can always be close to her pupils. You should not give her the worst, most austere room in the house, nor the most rickety furniture, as still happens frequently in rural areas. Children will immediately notice that you have differentiated between their teacher and other members of the household. And if they even hear, "That is certainly good enough for the tutor," then they, too, will immediately think of her disdainfully. If the tutor takes a seat at the far end of the table with her pupils during meals, as well, then you must be careful to serve her before the children and not after them, as happens in many families, particularly among the aristocracy. If a tutor stays clear of all immodest claims, then she should rigorously insist on her rights in all matters that serve to erode her social standing with the children and place her on a par with domestic servants. When guests are invited, the tutor may not be compelled to take her meals by herself. If the children also stay away from the family table on such occasions, then the sensible-minded tutor will only consider it right to supervise the children. The tutor should be both a friend and an authority figure to the children. And parents to whom the upbringing of their children really matters should do their very best to support the tutor in her difficult and responsible position. Blessings will surely come to a child that grows up with "proper breeding."

One of the Alexanders' three sons later wrote:

Gertrud Chodziesner shared a large room with my sister, who was ten years old in 1927. From the windows, you looked out across a large balcony to our garden (willows, roses, almond trees, ferns, quince trees) and the gardens of other villas. My father was a top executive at the banking house of M. M. Warburg and Co., my mother a native of Vienna. Although one cannot judge this sort of thing very well as a child, I would like to believe— and hope very much in retrospect—that your sister felt comfortable in our home. My parents were interested in the arts, got along well with other people, and we were rather well off financially.

I know that my mother was particularly impressed with your sister's knowledge of languages. She once had a British tutor herself and was, therefore, quite at home in English. My father was educated at the *gymnase français* [French secondary school] in Berlin. He later worked in France for a year, so he loved the French language. Both were keen to see us learn foreign languages from childhood on. Gertrud Chodziesner was primarily supposed to look after my sister. We boys were a bit old for a female tutor: I was only thirteen, but my two brothers were already fifteen and seventeen.

This period presented a different picture from Gertrud's perspective, of course: "Back then, I had a governess position that I didn't much like. Yet I was happy to be there because I liked the city so much. . . .And I hardly ever think about the adverse, petty situation in that house."

H. G. Alexander wrote to Johanna Zeitler (Woltmann) about this matter in 1969 and mistook her for Hilde Chodziesner Wenzel, to whom he had written previously:

> As such, it pains me to now learn that your sister, a person of such extraordinary standing, did not feel happy in our home. Her verdict surprises me a little. To the extent that a thirteen-year-old can judge, an entirely cheerful atmosphere filled our home. My parents were interested in the arts, and it's not as if we were petit bourgeois. It crossed my mind that your sister may not have especially like playing the role of "nanny," as people used to call it, which was hardly commensurate with her abilities. So her displeasure could have carried over to the entire household.

Concerning her years as a tutor, Gertrud could rightly claim in retrospect that, despite occasional differences of opinion with the parents of her pupils, "all the references in my possession are outstanding. Since it may occur to some that, despite these good references, I held several positions for only a short time, I would like to make the following comments: During the war and in the post-war period, there was a lot of anxiety and many kinds of changes took place within families. And some of these positions were considered short-term from the outset."

"Because I liked the city so much . . ." The Alexander home was a convenient place from which to go exploring. Upon reflection, H. G. Alexander wrote, "Yes, we lived right near the Alster River in the elegant district of Harvestehude. The house we rented was at Frauental 13. From there, you could get to the Alster and, in fact, to Fernsicht in less than ten minutes, where you could enjoy a famously beautiful view of the Aussenalster Lake. From Fernsicht, you could take a steamer to Lombardsbrücke and Jungfernstieg. You could also walk along Harvestehuder Way, which ran along the banks of the Aussenalster."

This is where Gertrud went to her very own *Schule des Sehens* [School of Seeing]:*

---

* The original "School of Seeing" was a painting school founded by the Austrian artist Oskar Kokoschka in Hohensalzburg Fortress in 1953. Its purpose was to "revive and cultivate humanist ideals, particularly among young people, in the aftermath of World War II."

Like a silhouette artist, I once saw everything in terms of outlines, in silhouettes alone. I first learned to see things pictorially in Hamburg's ring of landscapes around the Alster Basin. When evening conjured up a mauve sky over the water and the first lights went on, the Uhlenhorst ferry-house on the far bank looked like an enchanted castle. Swans drifted slowly by, looking for a place to rest . . . Do you know Runge's *Morning**—perhaps from the blue book *Der stille Garten?*† Like the marvellous paintings of Caspar David Friedrich, it hangs in the Hamburg Art Gallery. After having seen it quite often, I observed it on a grey day and was delighted. In that gloom, it shone on me with an entirely distinct, indescribable lustre. In unnameably sweet colours . . . I remember it to this day . . . Back then, I had a governess position that I didn't much like. Yet I was happy to be there, because I liked the city so much. I remember one evening at the Stintfang: The *Cap Polonio* was there with its red-capped smokestacks . . . The canal, the golden spire of St. Katherine's Church, and the green patina of the Petriturm . . . The City Park, Botanical Garden, the lawns of the mansion gardens in Harvestehude with heaps of squill and crocuses in the early spring . . . And the gulls at Jungfernstieg . . . All of this and much more has been saved in my memory, as in a beautiful picture gallery. And I hardly ever think about the adverse, petty situation in that house.

After a total of eight years as a "nanny," Gertrud wanted to make a fresh start. She applied to the Language Services Division of the Foreign Office as an interpreter and translator. Her application was turned down flat—"rejected," as they would probably have put it in officialese.

A copy of the politely buffered rejection letter, dated June 11, 1927, has survived: "After reviewing your translation test, I would like to inform you that, should the need arise, you would be entrusted with French-to-German and English-to-German translations. This could only happen, however, if our official translators were especially overburdened with a workload that seemed to justify the enlistment of unofficial personnel."

What the "Head of Language Services" either dictated or wrote here closed the door to future prospects. So did Gertrud want to improve her starting position before making another try? If she couldn't get a permanent position as an "official translator," then could she at least get assignments on the free market? Gertrud wanted to improve her prospects for success and her chances of employment; she didn't give up and resumed her education immediately.

---

* Philipp Otto Runge was a German romantic painter whose painting *Morning* depicted a landscape at dawn with religious figures.

† *Der stille Garten* [*The Quiet Garden*] was a lavishly illustrated art book featuring German painters of the first half of the 1800s.

Apparently accompanied by a friend of about the same age, Susanne Jung, Gertrud traveled to Dijon in late summer to participate in a holiday language course for foreigners. Susanne was a teacher at a girls' high school and, after the war, became a senior secondary school teacher in Düsseldorf.

This would be her first and only trip abroad. Gertrud observed:

> Apart from the fact that I am no "traveller" by any means, if I were to arrive in a country where I didn't know the language, I would invariably feel something akin to "forlorn." To someone who speaks few or absolutely no foreign languages, it might not matter at all what country he lands in from a linguistic standpoint. I, on the other hand, never had a feeling of foreignness in Dijon or Paris back then, yet would be somewhat afraid of my own presumed helplessness in Rome or Venice. (Although one could surely "get by" with German, French, or English, this would always remain a stopgap solution.)

Her performance in the French language course shows why she felt nearly at home in France in her second language. According to the *Certificat complémentaire* [supplementary certification], she attained the maximum of twenty points in nearly every section, thereby receiving, "the *best* certificate that the University of Dijon awarded to a foreign student in 1927," as stated in the addendum to a copy of the certificate that was issued on October 12. And her fresh start as a poet came just two days later.

| 21

The turning point in France! We shouldn't simply stick with the phrase "turning point" in this case; the decisive moment must be accentuated and elaborated on. Colloquially speaking, the poet was barely recognizable in the texts that postdate her sojourn in Dijon, Beaune, and Paris. A liberation, a veritable transformation had taken place. Only now, after many enjoyable and several very intense poems, did she develop what could be called an individual style. From now on, we'll be able to identify Kolmar's poems even if her name is not attached to them.

In a 1934 letter to Walter Benjamin, she would express herself in surprising depth concerning her models, impulses, and affinities. I am taking this letter out of chronological order, for it is within this context that its true place lies:

> Rilke and Werfel are German poets who have, perhaps, influenced me; that is, particular aspects of their works in both cases. With Rilke, I am particularly drawn to the "plasticity" of the later poems; he got it from the Frenchman Rodin. And, speaking of myself, I would like to say that I have

also presumably been influenced by the French now and again, seeing as no artist is an entity unto himself and does not spring like Athena from the head of Zeus. In 1927, after a long, sterile period, I found my way back to poetry upon returning from Dijon. My giant elk on the "Wappen von Allenburg" ["Allenburg Coat of Arms"] is, indeed, no synthetic imitation but probably (may zoologists forgive me!) the natural offspring of Leconte de Lisle's powerful bird in "Le Sommeil du Condor" ["The Sleep of the Condor"] (from *Poèmes barbares*). I know that I am greatly indebted to Leconte de Lisle. Yet surely he brought out what already lay within and did not impose something intrinsically foreign on me. Whatever I've read of the latest French poetry must have disturbed me very little because I am not able to recall anything of the sort at the moment. My "latest" is Paul Valéry, some of whose poems strike me as very strange, especially the short ones. But I admire and love some of the longer ones and by no means consider them highly abstruse. I can no longer pass by a young, rather sinuous beech tree in the woods without thinking of the verse, ". . . *et ce hêtre formé de quatre jeunes femmes . . .*" [and this beech formed by four young women], from "Au Platane" ["Of a Plane Tree"], without seeing the four young women who hold up the crown, although sometimes there are only three. To me, "La Fileuse" ["The Spinner"] from the *Album de vers anciens* [*Album of Ancient Verse*] is among the most beautiful of all poems. I am like you when it comes to poetry: It often happens that I don't like a poet's oeuvre in its entirety, yet there are particular poems that I can read again and again. That's how I feel about Rimbaud, who disgusts me more than attracts me as a person. I once ran across his "Le Dormeur du Val" ["The Sleeper in the Valley"] and have never found it again. An old beggar used to come to our house a few years ago. He looked totally smashed, but I always gave him something because, to me, his face could have been that of Verlaine's twin brother.—And then there is Milton's *Paradise Lost*. (Whenever I read it, I get angry about Klopstock's unhappy Messiah, who certainly made biblical epics unpalatable to many Germans.) Do you know this work? I think it's splendid, especially the portrayal of Hell and Pandemonium.

Now please don't take my letter for a poetic creed or a profound discourse that aims to be of value, but simply for what it is: a chat that your last letter enticed me into writing.

A poem written in Beaune, one of the few that is dated in the manuscript, starts a new chapter in the history of her work and marks a new beginning for the poet: "Beaune, Côte d'Or—October 14, 1927." And this date pointed the way forward!

Kolmar would later incorporate this poem into the cycle "Weibliches Bildnis" ["Female Portrait"]. Serialized self-portrayal does not dominate here, and there are no variations on a self-portrait. What takes place here is an interplay of disguise and exposure or, less pointedly, stylization and self-portrayal. The old theme of the long-awaited child is present but in a new style.

In anticipation, I shall emphasize three lines from "Die Irre" ["Astray"], lines in the grand style of the poet: "I'd like to fill all of the land with my gaudy gladiolas, / And rip my heart into carnations, to strew over the globe, / Over all of France, over all of Germany, over all of Belgium, over all of Poland!"

I sip vermouth with puckered lips.
Soot and tar drip from my nostrils.
My eyes are fixed on fields, cultivated with gloom,
And that's why I have neither sight nor tears.
My child lives all alone in the garden
Under a hard, massive stone.

Oh see! See! What a head I must uphold!
Red and yellow, half sulfur, half clay.
Mine was smashed and chopped off
By a guillotine from the Great Revolution.
Evil hounded me through the entire zodiac,
     Leo, Aries,
And Cancer attached a she-devil to my head.

Hunters and thugs, henchmen,
Oh gendarmes of the world, furious!
Yet my ugly head does no evil;
And look here! My hands are good.
Decorated like a grave, so lovely with flowers,
As his grave.
I picked all of them from the park beds and gravestone wreaths.

I'd like to fill all of the land with my gaudy gladiolas,
And rip my heart into carnations, to strew over the globe,
Over all of France, over all of Germany, over all of Belgium,
     over all of Poland!
And this I do for my son; it will make him happy.
He returned from the war with a wild, shaggy beard,
They were afraid of him and put him in a shallow grave.

The city keeps getting larger, the farther I walk,
It stretches out, crazed, so that I might never reach my goal.
When I stand at the cemetery gate in the evening,
It is swept away from me again with each dawning day.
I sit myself in front of the schoolhouse, nodding to the little ones
    with my red lobster skin full of scabs;
For wherever I sit: I always go to my child.

| 22

Let's play make-believe. If Gertrud had remained in France, what effect might this have had on her life and work?*

A subject could come up that might otherwise remain a mere name in Kolmar's circle: Susanne Jung, the cousin who took part in the language course with Gertrud in Dijon. The two young women would have traveled on to Paris together, where they would have shared a hotel room.

A preliminary decision about choice of hotel could already have been made. Given their small travel budget, would they have taken a cheap hotel so they could stay longer? Extended their stay for as long as possible: "What are we missing in Düsseldorf and Berlin anyway?" And Susanne might have added, "Why else have we expanded our knowledge of the national language?"

Gertrud might have responded noncommittally, but we won't go into that here: in this book, she will only come up with reference to the written record. On the other hand, Susanne could have sounded her out: "But there is no one waiting for you. All right, your parents, but you have two sisters in Berlin who can help in a pinch. As far as finances go, we don't need to worry right now. Perhaps we'll find work . . ."

Gertrud's careful questioning could have elicited a response such as this: "Language instruction! Whether you teach French in Peine or German here in Paris, it really amounts to the same thing. Apart from that, Paris has a bit more to offer than Peine! Your beloved Valéry lives here, after all! Perhaps we can pay our respects to him sometime . . . Oh, don't be so timid. It could easily happen. Valéry might well appear at a lecture or a reading, and we'd speak with him afterward, place one of his books in front of him, ask him to please sign it. He might even ask where we're from. Surely he'd be pleased to hear that people in Germany not only read his poems but also know one or two of them almost

---

* In real life, Gertrud and Susanne returned to Germany in autumn 1927 after their study trip to France.

by heart . . . Why should the cat get your tongue in the process? Just say yes, and then we'll see."

In the following narrative, the German writer Helga Cazas could serve as the model for a sketch of the poet's alternative life. Cazas would immigrate to Paris several years after Kolmar's visit and would later write a book about her years in France. She experienced what Kolmar might have under similar circumstances but in a different way.

In searching, you'll first discover a little hotel room in the Latin Quarter on Rue Laplace. The alley is so narrow that you could stretch a clothesline from the mullion and transom to a window in the opposite row of houses. And the room has a big bed, wardrobe, chair, washbasin, bowl, and jug. The toilet, a Turkish toilet,* is on the mezzanine floor. You would eat breakfast and dinner in the little room: cheese and baguette, coffee or tea, a little soup on occasion. Oh, you could make semolina pudding on Sundays as well. What is semolina called in French? Let's see . . . *gravelle,* that's right—but where can you buy it around here? Where can we get an answer to our question about *gravelle*? "The French don't eat semolina pudding. They do bake a cake called *gâteau de semoule* from semolina."

What about excursions? We don't need to list any famous buildings, as the following will do: In the evening, you walk to the square at Jardin du Luxembourg. For a visual perspective, picture "the Rue Soufflot, at the end of the Panthéon, glowing white and perfectly formed; to the left of it, the little church dedicated to Sainte Genevieve."

In our ongoing attempt at a sketch of Gertrud's alternative life, we see Susanne and Gertrud reading the daily paper to improve their French, but mainly for the classified ads. *Et voilá,* here's someone looking for a female tutor and language instructor. Go introduce yourself! No, don't think about it for long—grab the bull by the horns!

Gertrud could actually have been accepted, could well have been hired. Having met with the family's approval, she would soon be loved by their eight-year-old daughter, then recommended to others. And Susanne might have found something she liked, perhaps her first translator position.

Because she has a guilty conscience, Gertrud sends several postcards to her parents. Looking ahead, Susanne now gets a pack of additional postcards with Parisian motifs. She also buys postage stamps straightaway and cannot simply toss them. And what about Helga Cazas? Her hotel room becomes rather cramped; she wants to rent a small apartment. She gets a helpful tip about an apartment on Avenue de Corbéra that has just become available: "A Spanish

---

* A Turkish toilet is a squat toilet with no bowl.

architect built the blocks of flats. They were all alike, and the facades were painted pink." An elevator made of grillwork, a telephone box that takes *jetons* [tokens] . . . And if you get a call, the concierge shouts your name in the courtyard and the sound booms all the way up to the fifth floor! You could even hear it in the corridor with your door closed.

Cazas continued:

> The bathroom was on the left, tiny, but there was a bathtub next to the washbasin. And a proper toilet, a normal one, not a Turkish one. Then came the kitchen, also tiny, and barely more than one person could fit into it. Then two rooms, the larger one used as a living and dining room. A door at the end of the corridor that opens to a storage room . . .
>
> And there was neighbourly assistance. People rustled up a coil spring mattress that you set on a block of wood, a wardrobe, although the door had to be clamped shut with a strip of cardboard, a slightly wobbly table, and two chairs, even if they were worn out. But you could nail a wooden board to them and place a cushion on top. Plus pillows, covers, a little rug, so the room looked cosier.

Another attempt at a sketch for her alternative life shows Gertrud continually giving language instruction. She soon finds her way around by Métro [subway], and her network grows. Mademoiselle Jung's work situation also improves. The little pack of Paris postcards dwindles. Papa Ludwig writes back, Mother sends greetings, even if they are a bit sullen. One would rather see Trudchen back in Germany, but she is over thirty now, and one cannot tell her what to do after all. And who knows? Maybe she will finally meet the right man for her in Paris. The brother of a good man, whose daughter she was teaching, educating . . .

And she is not only influenced by Rimbaud, Valéry, and Verlaine; a new relationship will set her language free. No more complaints about the child she couldn't have. Listen, Trude, that was twelve years ago, so what about a Parisian child? You mustn't be miffed. One can allow himself a bit of humor now and then.

The domicile almost became homey when Gertrud's parents sent the wished-for commode by rail to be picked up at the customs office. And one of the drawers was reserved for manuscripts of new poems.

(End of the sketch and back to Berlin!)

| 23

The poet had found a new voice! And in that same year (1927), she would show just how many registers she was capable of.

Apparently, she was in a genial mood during this poetic fresh start, this year of inner liberation; she alternated between major and minor keys and wrote several poems that can be categorized as "occasional and jesting poems." Surprising facets appeared! This ability to alter tone and subject matter within a short time would again become apparent a half-dozen years later. In this regard as well, Gertrud Kolmar was an exception among her male and female contemporaries. A note about the writing style: The jesting poems were obviously written down rapidly in impromptu form. She was sparing with punctuation in the process, so we should not just silently add it back in:

> It's strange how people
> conclude things
> That yesterday, or today
> They always sing the same tune
>
> About a little girl
> And beautiful sunshine
> About wine and the Rhine
> Nothing but such rhymes.
>
> I've never lost my heart in Heidelberg
> And never drank wine on the Rhine
> I was born in Stralau-Rummelsburg
> And have a beer joint at Friedrichshain.

We can verify the names of city districts. Even the made-up-sounding name, Stralau-Rummelsburg. During my years in Berlin, I occasionally rode my bike from Kreuzberg to Stralau, a peninsula on the River Spree. From there, I glanced southward to Plänterwald and northward to Rummelsberg with its old prison behind some poplar trees. The former East German head of state Erich Honecker was locked up there for a time.

Contrast is the focus of my little presentation on poems from those years. I do not consider it appropriate in this case to line up poems on a systematic basis, that is, somber poems first, then poems in sunny keys. This is not how our poet should be portrayed; simultaneity and synchronicity of opposites were much more typical of her style. In the period following her return from France, she wrote both serious and humorous poems. This deserves more than mere mention: it must be discernible. We're certainly not talking about the variety of texts but about measuring their spectrum. So as part of our contrasting cycle, here is the poem "Die Tänzerin 2" ["The Dancer 2"]:

Where did happiness go? Mine's gone,
A penny, rolled under a cabinet;
But I hurl a scimitar into the Moor's dance
Along with my mind of gold.
My pitch is so long, and the jump so wild,
That I forget what I am:
More than a strangely animated image
And less than a sorceress.

Oh, desolate brown Saracen!
Oh, dance of Tyrian Baal!
These are borrowed masks,
I'm always the pain during the dance,
I dance the father, who, lame and soon blind,
Crouches at the courtyard window, painting the spring,
I dance the little feverish child
And the rent, unpaid.

Tell me, what can I be? A doll?
To the right, to the left, back on track.
Call it the rounds begging for soup,
Sarcastically that means: the cries for bread.
Why am I dressed like a colorful bouquet?
You sit around, you men—ah, less close!—
Undress me in your mind,
And I, I do not hinder you.

Do you think even juice that's bitter
will intoxicate your mouth?
I want to attach my limbs to you,
Where I can't attach my gaze.
If my nails claw for money,
Lust glides shamelessly from my hand;
Far away I lie in the lonely field
And see this body on fire.

A blue-green feathered courtesan,
Who blinks her circular eyes and conceals her foot,
I am in an old faded Pavane,
Trembling and languishing from my own haughtiness.
But into my dazzlingly bejeweled dress he thrusts

A greedy hand! How sad!
And if just one torn feather falls off,
My blood splatters from the quill.

And we go immediately to a second Berlin poem, "Der Einheitsschein" ["Single Ticket"]. The occasion was the introduction of single-fare tickets by the Berliner Verkehrsbetriebe [Berlin Public Transportation Authority], or so I have read in the commentary to the newly edited poems from her estate:

Vera with the slim calves
And shaped like a mannequin
Makes her home in Lichtenrade!
And I live in Grunewald.

Previously I had to drive a car
Yet my wallet was empty
And over the years I thought
You should just get rid of this luxury.

Today you go from Panke
All the way out to Krumme Lanke
Up, down, in and out
And all for a single ticket.

Through all of Berlin for twenty pfennig
From Rummelsburg to Tauentzien
From Pichelsdorf to a new world
All for one price.

My little Liselotte
Asks me night and day
My dear Otto please be nice
And give me a Hanomag locomotive

I press her relishing the moment
Just two groschen in your hand,
Sweetie, what do you need a car for
What you need is just plain reason

For today you go by . . .

Every class of subway
ABOAG omnibuses* and trams
With the tiniest of tills
Over the entire Pharusplan map.

And it's all about saving, saving,
And that's not at all difficult today
If you have a lot of driving around to do
You'll be a millionaire for sure.

Today, you can take the U1 from Kreuzberg directly to the end of the line at Krumme Lanke, a little lake in Zehlendorf. All of this is consistent with what the cheerful poet is rhyming about here!

And now, another decisive, indeed drastic change of key in "Die Erzieherin" ["The Governess"]:

Going through this life is not difficult.
But it's certainly difficult to exist in this life;
For I always walk secretly with the deer
Into deep, wild, unknown forests.

Into unrecognized forests. Where danger
Sings of adventure
And a star, not subject to any ornithology
Perches crimson crowned on cobalt blue talons.

Two delicate children cradle their little crowns with fruit,
With the mute air of infinite harps
And shield me from all others on the run,
That I must educate, pamper, punish, but not love.

Oh dear child. How my wings would have covered you,
Before lengthy knitting, the dust from spinning took their power
    and glow,
Yet, full of envy, your mother hid your joy from me,
Because of their duty, the orphans came begging to me.

---

* ABOAG (Allgemeinen Berliner Omnibus Aktien Gesellschaft) buses provided public transportation in Berlin in the first half of the 1900s.

I fill their outstretched hands, as I like.
It's not their own . . . The day, standing without a head, tepid and flat
Is like laundry and homework
During the everyday stroll to the canal.

It's been a long while, since I questioned a book;
Because in books I always spoke to myself . . .
Sometimes, brought into the room by someone, I find
An old print, an image of man and animal.

A girl dispatches the very sun with her ball,
A movie princess playing in the sand dune,
Casually our budding dancer caresses
A poor little monkey with the rings on her hand.

And there's gold and the pleasure of travel, wine and hunting
Strawberry lace and her velvety skin;
I scour the plate and board: a maid,
Silent and paltry. Yet she's exuberantly loud.

Maybe they don't have my dream forest in view
With its leaves that oh-so-slowly turn a tired color,
Nor the bare street,
Where I wander daily dying.

| 24

The poet had a soft spot for "character dance," as it was called in those days, or modern dance, as it is known today. In her surviving letters to Hilde, she mentioned five world-famous or widely known female dancers.

First on the list was Anna Pavlova, the Russian ballet star who was especially acclaimed in Paris. "The Dying Swan" is the role most closely associated with her.

Mary Wigman was also famous, though her aura was very different from Pavlova's. Eight years older than Gertrud, she enjoyed her greatest fame as an expressionist dancer in the 1920s. She developed dance forms and choreography in a "new, free dance" style that did not exist up to this point.

The third, Charlotte Bara, was called "Santa Ballerina" or "hallowed dancer" and, in the eyes of the painter Heinrich Vogeler of the Worpswede artist colony, danced more "like a mad nun." She particularly loved to appear in dance scenarios based on sacred themes, which she called "Gothic art." So it was fitting that this Jewish woman would convert to Catholicism. Some of the titles of her dance evenings: "The Passion," "Angel of the Annunciation," "Mary in Sorrow," and "Veronica's Veil." Amid all this solemnity, an occasionally grotesque title, such as "The Happy Jumping Jack," would pop up. Bara toured Europe time and again, so it's possible that our poet could have even seen the star in Berlin.

Grete Wiesenthal also enjoyed renown, though prior to the First World War. This solo dancer of the Vienna Court Opera ballet had especially great success with Viennese waltzes. Along with her sister Elsa, she developed original dance forms and a new style. She was a dancer, "who I admittedly know only from photos and descriptions."

Lucy Kieselhausen was one her students, "and I have seen her more than once." Kieselhausen developed several scenarios; for example, Salambo, based on Gustave Flaubert's novel. Gertrud Kolmar must have seen her in the first half of the 1920s, for she died tragically when "a burning jet of flame from a petrol explosion in her bathroom" killed her in 1926. Like Charlotte Bara, she also appeared in grotesque dance performances.

Apparently, Gertrud Kolmar held what we now call experimental dance theater in high regard. She saved program booklets and flyers from dance evenings, perhaps in her "brown painted starch box" that accompanied her through all her the years of family life.

In addition, there were program booklets and playbills from the Reinhardt theater. I assume that Hilde, the family chronicler, did not randomly mention the name Reinhardt. We may also conclude from this that Gertrud went at least on occasion to the Deutsches Theater, which was for some years headed up and shaped by Austrian-born actor and director Max Reinhardt. According to the sisters' accounts, performances at the Reinhardt theater made such a deep impression on Gertrud that she would speak and rave about them for weeks.

Sadly, only two works, *Danton* by Romain Rolland and *Dantons Tod* [*Danton's Death*] by Georg Büchner, are mentioned. In 1916, Max Reinhardt staged *Danton's Death* in what the German theater critic Herbert Ihering called "the definitive stage adaptation of a poem." But there is no such thing as a definitive interpretation in the theater, and so the work was newly staged at the same theater by Erich Engel in 1924 with Fritz Kortner as Danton. As a resident of Berlin, Gertrud Kolmar could have seen both stagings. She supposedly then quoted, perhaps even recited, entire scenes at home.

| 25

In the 1928 Easter supplement to *Literarische Welt* [*Literary World*], Walter Benjamin introduced two of his cousin's poems, accompanied by this note:

"Only one volume by the author has been published to date: *Gedichte*—by the Berlin publishing house of Egon Fleischel in 1917. I am publishing the following verses not so much to call attention to these early attempts but rather to place sounds not heard in German women's poetry since Annette von Droste in readers' ears."

The titles of the poems are "Das grosse Feuerwerk" ["The Great Fireworks"] and "Wappen von Zinna" ["Zinna's Coat of Arms"]. The latter is one of the poems that were written mainly after 1917 and published posthumously. Thus, these poems stem from the period between the first little volume and the 1934 *Gedichtheft* [*Poetry Notebook*]. A gap of seventeen years between the two publications was an enormous stretch of time for this prolific poet! Did external barriers impede her progress? Prior to 1933, there ought to have been one or two publishers in Berlin whose catalogs could have accommodated a volume of Kolmar's poetry. But did she write to the publishers, send them texts? Or did she not even try in all those years? Did she have no further interest in doing so? She apparently had her father's initiative to thank for the first volume, and publication of her second book took place after Ina Seidel intervened.

Between 1917 and 1934, only three poems were published singly, two of which were promoted by her cousin. And Anton Kippenberg, the head of Insel Verlag, included two poems in a 1930 almanac. A total of seven poems published in seventeen years has to be a first! Writing poetry was important to her, vital to her life. But what was done with the poems afterward seems to have been of secondary importance to her.

It's conceivable that the presentation of the two poems was preceded by (additional?) discussion between the cousins and that the question came up as to whether Gertrud should try to become an independent writer.

I do not mean to suggest here that a particularly intense relationship, anything more than a familial connection, existed between Walter and Gertrud. Rather, it was a matter of mutual respect, and they were occasionally in touch. The following sketch therefore remains within the realm of probability because in 1928 Walter Benjamin spent most of his time in Berlin.

So it's not unlikely that an argument—with the word "writer" at the forefront—developed during a gathering of close family members. Gertrud saw herself strictly as a poet; she had no intention of becoming a writer. She didn't want to write for "today" but for "eternity." This type of thinking was common in those days: Osip Mandelstam and Marina Tsvetaeva would also stress the fact that they were poets, not writers.

Yet Walter Benjamin would not have given up so easily. Publishing poetry could not provide an even modest standard of living. If Gertrud wanted to do well as an independent poet, she would have to work for the German radio network or in the feuilleton* department of a newspaper. This was the only way she could earn enough to keep her head above water as a self-employed person. In any case, she had to get a move on! She had an urgent need to broaden her range! Even so, her income would be meager. She had to know it and go on that assumption.

No matter how Walter Benjamin may have spoken to Gertrud about this matter, she was more put off than encouraged. At any rate, there is no record of her having written for radio or a feuilleton. Since she had not yet written a story, novel, or play, and she continued her focus on poetry, a career as a writer was inconceivable at that point.

So why not become a language teacher at a girls' high school? But with two foreign languages and lots of papers to mark, she would hardly ever get around to writing poetry! Then why not continue to work as a private tutor? If she'd already worked and lived in a private household, then why couldn't she do the same thing in the Chodziesner home? As an au pair, so to speak, in her own family. Couldn't she get room and board and earn her keep by working in the house and garden?

| 26

Gertrud, soon to be in her mid-thirties, still lived in her parents' home in 1928. Her mother, Elise, needed help, and it seemed that neither Helene, the reliable housekeeper, nor any of the three siblings could or was prepared to provide it. So Trude stepped into the breach: "My mother's serious illness forced me to devote myself entirely to her care and to the housework."

She would not always dedicate herself to nursing during the next two years. At any rate, she would later write, "Apart from that, I was busy in Finkenkrug with *housekeeping, gardening,* and *Kleintierzucht.*"†

The third keyword, *Kleintierzucht,* was a theme taken up by Gertrud herself. As previously in Westend, the family kept poultry in Finkenkrug. So, as I mentioned before, it's hardly a coincidence that Margot became an ornithologist. She was already listed as a member of the German Ornithological Society in 1924. And what was her main field of research? Chickens!

Margot's special knowledge would be of direct help later on and would save her from the Nazis. But, in the years before emigration, did the two

---

* The feuilleton department of a newspaper is a literary and arts section.

† *Kleintierzucht* is the raising of small farm animals.

sisters occasionally engage in shoptalk? Discuss the optimal layout of the open-air enclosure when poultry was kept outdoors year-round? Or the species-appropriate construction of the chicken coop, particularly in consideration of the constant threat from martens? And what about feeding the birds potatoes?

I don't want to further develop this scenario, though I will subsequently refer to Margot's publication on the topic of chickens. But before I do, we should at least mention the ducks on the property. Hooded ranger ducks and mallards in the little pond that their father designed, complete with a little duck coop—did they ever breed little ducks in it?

Better quickly change the subject to rabbits that hopped around in that garden enclosure. They were part of the work world at Finkenkrug, too, and thus part of Gertrud's linguistic milieu. Was there shoptalk with other rabbit keepers in Finkenkrug? About the wrong kind of green fodder and swollen bellies? Only don't give them any cabbage, and don't dare give them any potatoes. But carrots, more carrots, and carrot greens—they can't get enough of them, can really get hooked on them. Oh yes, and so-called busy food, branches that they're supposed to nibble on so their teeth don't get too long, which could significantly hinder food intake, even to the point of death. And what to do when rabbits fight tooth and nail? Leave them alone or at most intervene the minute you see blood? Should you castrate bucks as early as possible? And have you also noticed that, when in danger, they duck as low to the ground as possible, lay their ears back, and remain in that position until it's all over with? You can reenact it in your mind, can't you? But, for now, peace and tranquillity reigned in Finkenkrug.

"Scientific Results of Applied Poultry Breeding" was the topic of a lecture that Margot Chodziesner gave at a meeting of the German Ornithological Society in September 1929. By October of that same year, the paper was published in the *Journal of Ornithology*.

Her sentimental feeling for keeping and breeding poultry was most certainly awakened in the garden at Westend and nurtured further in Finkenkrug. So Papa Ludwig had pointed the way for his two daughters, and Margot had turned a hobby into a profession.

She would have already seen at least some of the things in the kitchen gardens of both upscale residential enclaves that she would later observe at the Berlin Zoo and on the grounds of the Zoological Institute in Dahlem. Margot and Gertrud would surely have exchanged views on these matters. Margot may also have possibly reported on her paper, either in advance or in summary. With this in mind, I shall use quotations and excerpts, taking little excursions to a lexical "field" that Gertrud also tilled.

The year 1928 was the year of the rooster, and 1929 was the year of the hen:

As a result of an abnormally cold winter, hatching time began extraordinarily late this year . . . Ducks are very shy and sensitive to any type of disturbance . . . During excessively dry hatching, the shell becomes so dry and brittle that the chicks are no longer strong enough to completely break open their shells . . . If young hens are kept without any roosters at all, as generally happens with large flocks, then at around 6–8 months of age and, within a few weeks of having laid, they are exceptionally in need of mating . . .

Margot reported on some of her research:

I have measured many breeds of chickens by first weighing them, then making cardboard outlines of their outstretched wings, cutting them out, weighing them, and converting the results to square centimetres. If I use the same grade of cardboard for all measurements, then the values produced— that is, the number of square centimetres of wing surface as compared to an animal's body weight—can be compared across all breeds. These measurements actually show that lightweight breeds have larger wings, and dwarf breeds have the biggest of all. As a result, the lightweight breeds are, in point of fact, exceptionally quick and rather good flyers, while the heavier breeds fly very little or no longer fly at all.

And here's another experience that Gertrud was able to share with Margot: "Since there's still lots of spare time in the hatchery when hatching first begins, and one always feels happiest about the arrival of the first chicks, we're in the habit of sitting almost continuously in the coop with the firstborns on the first day. Each and every time, the result is that they don't want to be left alone at night and make such a commotion that there's no other solution than to sit with them until they are fast asleep." A little report on the mood at hatching time . . .

Another heading is rose cultivation. And this hobby was also introduced by their father.

The writer Jacob Picard refers to it. He was one of very few colleagues with whom Gertrud Kolmar kept in touch, possibly through her father, since Picard was also a lawyer and headed up an office in Berlin. Picard was from Wangen on the Bodensee. He wrote: "Father [Chodziesner] . . . was a gardener in his spare time. Above all, he planted roses and was always surrounded by dogs that accompanied him on his walks through the nearby woods."

Ludwig Chodziesner opened new linguistic vistas to his daughter: The realm of legal language and the vocabulary of a *Notar;* the linguistic vistas of a man to whom horses were as important as dogs, animals as important as flowers.

And, most important, the linguistic expanses of a rose cultivator. Here, I shall design a little border as a field of words: rose beds, ground-cover roses, bush roses, dog roses, climbing roses, crinkled buds, tapered blossoms, rambling blossoms, roses like pom-poms. Prior to 1930, hybrid musk roses with large stems and densely compact flowers were cultivated by an English vicar. The type known as the Peace rose before the Second World War was given the name Gloria Dei rose after the war began.

By way of an addendum, let me say that Gertrud particularly loved copper tips also known as *Crocosmia,* montbretia, or falling stars. Walter Benjamin's wife, Hilde, vouched for it: "Trudchen showed me delicately blooming copper tips, some of her favourite flowers, and seeing them always reminds me of her."

I'd also like to have these flowers in front of me, so I get some photos up on my computer screen. A single, proud plant doesn't appear, for copper tips grow in groups, in veritable bushels. The stalks can be up to a meter long, the leaves lanceolate and shaped like swords, and the little flowers are spiked. The spiked flowers come in different colors, depending on the variety. Some are apricot-colored, lemon-yellow or golden, while others are blood-red or bright red. The spiked flowers unfold more modestly than rose blossoms. Is that why Gertrud liked them so much?

| 27

Through the symbiotic relationship between father and daughter, Gertrud also became a rose enthusiast. A "rose bed sonnet" came into being, and among the titles are hybrid roses Mulatto Rose, Captain Harvey-Cant, Ville de Paris, Hadley, Madame Ravary, Angèle Pernet, Etoile de Hollande, Madame Caroline Testout, and Hugh Dickson:

> *The beautiful miracles of the seven kingdoms,*
> Soon to be brimstone butterflies, appearing large on stalks,
> Soon lesser flamingos, which fell into the bushes,
> Soon to be shells, are made of magically tranquil pools.
>
> O my roses. Hearts, may you fade,
> Limp and exhausted from playing in the white sun,
> Consumed with your own exuberance, all of it just too much;
> Carry on singing to the grave, sweet corpses!

I won't separate you from your sweet branch,
Nor study you inside narrow, warm glass,
Lengthening your short blossoming span.

Oh well: burn up your immeasurable brilliance,
Instead of being swept away by the hot earth,
While wishing for a long, boring life.

Regina Nörtemann found out that all of the roses named and celebrated by the poet in 1926 were listed in a sales catalog for the Kordes rose nursery in Holstein with descriptions of the rose varieties and a price list. Of course, the poet did not consider herself obliged to provide descriptions; keywords set poetic connections in motion—for example, in the case of her poem named after a new variety introduced by Wilhelm Kordes, "Die Rose des Kondors" ["The Rose of the Condor"]:

No, it's not a rose: it's the shreds,
Of wattles, fiery, wild and naked,
Of a fabulous bird, that plops down jagged
With metallic black treasures

While in front of gawkers' curiosity and horror
The vulture crams and chops hideous carrion,
While grabbing the rock, an artificial mountain,
With awkward force, brought between the matrix
broken and jam-packed by people.

Oh, if he could only spread his huge coat wide,
He would turn away from you in disgust

And float away down the ages without a word.
And from the edges of his weary wings
Dropping gray, the snows of the Cordillera dry up.

A rose, a prima donna takes the form of a beastly plant associated with vultures that reads like an act of revenge on the beauty of roses. The following description of this variety appeared in the Kordes catalog: "This is the most beautiful rose that has been brought onto the market up to now. Among all the beautiful colours, none can equal this marvellous novelty. The flowers are full, most noble in form and manner, and stand atop beautiful, firm stems. They are cappuccino brown on a golden ground, remain golden as they fade, and are most rewardingly vivid."

| 28

Das preussische Wappenbuch [*The Prussian Coat of Arms Book*] is a cycle of poems that took shape during the winter of 1927–28. Something astoundingly banal triggered these poems: Collector's stamps from the firm of Kaffee Hag that you pasted into booklets. The little stamplike images with city emblems had been placed in packaged coffee since 1913. And this advertising campaign continued up to the Second World War, unchanged over the course of a quarter century!

Königswalde is one example of the imagery, and the following details appear above the city emblem: "Königswalde in the Neumark. Free State of Prussia/ Province of Brandenburg/Administrative District Frankfurt (Oder)." This information is on the reverse side: "Königswalde in the Neumark. City of 1,311 residents (1925). Coat of arms: An adolescent damsel with flowing, golden hair, clothed in silver except for her gold crown, holding a green fir tree in each hand." And a small box reads, "KAFFEE HAG / caffeine-free ground coffee."

Brother Georg collected these stamps and gave his sister access to his album. Between sightings of collector's stamps and the genesis of poems are creative outflows upon which biographical narratives shed no light.

One example contained in the bundle of documents is "Wappen von Lassan" ["Lassan Coat of Arms"], Pomerania. The image reads, "An ascending, silver fish on a blue, star strewn ground." And yet another Kolmar prominence:*

Women stride over the pools without shoes.
How can women walk over water?
They carry light-braided netting in their hands
And tower powerfully when they hurl it up into the sky,
Curved arms standing on the flowing mirror of water.

For fish are floating in the blue expanse.
Where do fish thrash about with night owls and stone curlews?
Their fins sounding silvery as they rise.
Sometimes they rest up there on the maple branches;
They chased the shimmering star in its zenith, until it fell down.

The silver fish sing on land and sea.
When did you ever catch fish, who were not silent?
Orfe and loach keep silent. But they, without a name,

---

* This is a reference to a *solar prominence*—a tonguelike cloud of flaming gas rising from the sun's surface.

Scatter trickling seed over all their sounds,
Filling the globe like the glittering buzz of bees.

Sitting one hour each evening near you at the window.
Who hasn't wished for the remaining hour in vain?
And now it comes and shares the simple food from your table,
And perhaps teaches you the song of the singing fish.
Yes, it comes: once. Not often.

Apparently convinced of his cousin's stature as a poet, Walter Benjamin gave this poem in 1929 to a journal, *Neue Schweizer Rundschau* [*New Swiss Review*], published by Max Rychner.

| 29

In the spring of 1930, Gertrud's mother died after a long, serious illness that, even today, is a euphemism for cancer. She had been "faithfully cared for by Gertrud."

Hilde, the family chronicler, wrote further: "If she had lived longer, many things would probably have turned out differently. Given her practical, life-affirming ways, she would probably have been able to get the entire family to leave Germany in timely fashion at the dawn of the Hitler regime."

Elise Chodziesner was buried in Stahnsdorf. And where is Stahnsdorf? A glance at the city map shows Stahnsdorf at the same latitude as Potsdam, to the east near Teltow. Back then, it was a town outside the Berlin city limits. Why wasn't Elise Chodziesner buried in the Jewish cemetery in Charlottenburg or Heerstrasse? Both areas would have been on the direct line from Finkenkrug and easy to reach. Getting to Stahnsdorf, on the other hand, meant riding to Westkreuz, traveling on to the station at Wannsee, and taking the *Friedhofsbahn* (also called the "widow's train" or "funeral train") to the Southwest Cemetery. Stahnsdorf was the largest cemetery of the Evangelical Church community. Jews were generally buried in Jewish cemeteries; Evangelical and Catholic cemeteries didn't allow the interment of Jews. But in the huge area of the forested cemetery grounds, some exceptions were permitted, and Jews could also find their final resting place there.

Why Ludwig Chodziesner allowed his wife to be buried in the cemetery of the German Evangelical Synod remains an open question. Because it was the largest forest cemetery in Europe? Because Elise's grave lay in a vast park? Or because that's where the burial places of industrialists like Ernst Werner von

Siemens, composers like Engelbert Humperdinck, illustrators like Heinrich Zille, film directors like F. W. Murnau, clairvoyant performers like Erik Jan Hanussen, and painters like Lovis Corinth lay?

The answer to this question can most likely be traced to Ludwig Chodziesner's assimilated position in German society. His Jewish wife should not be buried in a Jewish cemetery. In the event of sympathetic inquiries from outsiders as to where his wife was buried, he probably wanted to have an innocuous response at the ready. And the most likely and expected response would have been, "Oh, I see, in Stahnsdorf."

And Gertrud stayed on in Finkenkrug. Hilde offered a revealing interpretation: "So our aging father could no longer muster any determination after the loss of his beloved partner, and Gertrud was the only sibling who stayed with the old man, which she considered to be her duty as his child."

Their "aging father" was sixty-nine at the time. He was, in fact, suffering from rheumatism, especially in his arms, but was otherwise in good shape and certainly not an invalid! And with his sturdy constitution, that was not to be expected in the near future. Even without his daughter, he would have been looked after. Helene Köpp, the cook and housekeeper, was still in the family home and would stay on. Wally, the maid, was at her side. In addition, a typist, an office worker, even a secretary could easily be found in those days of high unemployment. So, in truth, this was no emergency situation that would have forced a decision on the part of his daughter. Rather, she took up this post of her own free will and entered into a promising and fulfilling set of circumstances. The father's strength and his daughter's weakness were like yin and yang, at least within the family. Gertrud did not take a strong stand and risk leaving home; for example, by virtually demanding her own apartment in Charlottenburg. The advancement of her literary work was apparently more important to her than personal growth. The villa and gardens in Finkenkrug seemed to provide favorable conditions, so she stayed. In the process, she decided in favor of a life of renunciation and dependency. Better to work as a secretary to a high-ranking solicitor than to try to distinguish herself in the literary field and possibly make a living from her writing. She might not have been able to withstand the pressures of internal and external expectations. To the extent that she knew herself or believed to know herself, she made her decision with a long-term perspective in mind.

| 30

By mid-August 1930, Gertrud had begun to write a novel, *The Jewish Mother*. She finished the work on February 1, 1931.

To briefly summarize, Martha Wolg is an animal photographer and single mother. Her little five-year-old daughter has been abused in a community garden. The mother finds her half-dead child and brings her to the nearest hospital. The child's internal injuries are so massive that "Ursa" has little chance of survival. She dies at the hospital. Not until just before the end of the novel does Martha confess that she euthanized her child.

She is appalled that child abusers often receive light sentences in the court system, so she tries to find a man who will hunt down and kill the perpetrator. She offers herself in payment. A willing man turns up, the reward is paid in advance, and they sleep together. The return favor is on hold, but the reward is paid again anyway. The man is dismayed at her coldness, other than in bed, and backs off. Martha realizes too late that more than mere business had been transacted. Sex in return for a murder that does not take place and, what's more, she is developing a taste for it. The man leaves for good, and Martha is again completely alone. She walks into the Spree River.

A deeply stirring melodrama with many late expressionist gestures: "She sobbed, choking. She buried her burning head in her lap." There are also late expressionist gestures regarding nature: "At the window, November elm boughs reached upward in supplication like naked, emaciated arms of beggars." An exaggerated description of a peacock butterfly: "Melancholy and weeping calm welled up in its velvety eyes."

I could cite additional sequences in similar keys but would rather emphasize her precise descriptions of the surroundings that Kolmar lived in before moving to Finkenkrug, the ambience of the former northwest city limits, the brightly splotched transition from urban development to open country. She must have keenly observed the areas bordering town on walks and excursions.

The novel opens with: "It was the evening of August nineteenth. Autumn had arrived. The scanty trees lining the street had turned golden and shivered. The storm rolled in like a giant, long-legged bird with powerful, grayish-black wings, driving the rain down in sheets between the rows of dirty, oldish houses." In this case, the poet was creating art.

And then there is the streetcar ride:

> To the right of the car, the hospital fortress stretched out expansively along
> the roadway: red walls and iron gates, little towers and walls armoured with
> wild grapes, and a clock face with gilded numbers. To the left, the gardens
> of the residential area came to an end. There were old Franconian gardens
> with wild bushes and trees, ridiculously southern, pillar-bedecked Italian
> structures with flat roofs, and others in the style of Scottish castles with
> stepped gables and battlements. Deeply saffron-yellow roses glistened above
> easy-care lawns, many drooping and laden with raindrops. And now that

the streetcar departed the hospital, a suburban world of leafy terrain and allotment gardens arose with nameplates like PLEASANT SUNDAY COLONY and GREEN FIELDS. Yet between isolated settlements, barren stretches opened up, sparsely covered in field growth and scantily sheltered by low, densely topped pines that, under blue skies, might well simulate umbrella pines in Campagna but that spoke only of northwest Charlottenburg in the windswept, cloudy gloom.

A streetcar stop:

She went a few steps back up the street she'd just come from and turned onto an unpaved path that ran between the settler's land and the Rosskaempf farm. And there were narrow quads on the right-hand side with vegetable and strawberry patches and bunches of purple and red dahlias ruffling around the foliage. On the left side of the lane was a wildly overgrown garden adjoining the Rosskaempfer home, a little, crumbling wooden house with VILLA GRAZIETTA in fuzzy lettering beneath the sloping roof . . . The courtyard was also made of unsurfaced sand, now filled with mud puddles. It was shaded by two maple trees that also darkened the windows across from the entrance of the grey, unadorned, multi-storey house. The Grazietta garden area consisted of one courtyard elbow, the shorter arm of which enclosed it. The front wall ran at an angle beyond the other, narrow end, with the leafy eyes of an enchanted park peeping over it.

Other sequences in the novel also match the exactitude of her previous descriptions. One of them leads into the woods, showing Kolmar's passion for walking in the woods. Here is yet another portrayal of her Berlin surroundings:

Those few who got off with them had scattered behind the train station and were now making a pilgrimage to two or three underused outdoor cafés, the last of which was called Blitter's Eden. The café was behind a little grey, one-storey house, had no fence, a worn-out lawn with old linden trees, and a skittle alley in back. Two, small weather-beaten flags, one red-and-white, the other blue-and-yellow, fluttered above the tavern sign; they hung down like dismally withered, faded little leaves on winter branches. Then came rusty brown mesh, now-deserted summer estates with silent, wooden foliage, empty fruit trees, raspberry bushes, garden beds like streusel cake tins filled with heavy, black, sopping wet crumbs, and a last surviving alder trunk in the corners. This abandoned countryside looked very cheerless and desolate beneath the cold heavens. The pallid grey sky shivered wearily, as if it would soon snow, not in soft delicate flakes, but raining down hailstones. And it

had been a beautiful morning . . . Then came the forest, a mixed woodland
of fierce, furrowed twilight red oaks, mournfully red glimmering pines,
elephant-skin beech trees. Meandering undergrowth. The path was wide,
but filled in. Deposits of rotten foliage slipped, squeaked and crackled under
foot. But the grass was green, and little dollops of snow lay here and there, as
if dribbled from a spoon.

And Kolmar sounds an alarm. Martha Wolg visits the man she hopes will help
her. She has to wait for him and leafs through a magazine lying on the table:

The cover reads: "Hugin—the German Weapon—the Paper for Nationalist
Thought." And between the headings, a raven holds a swastika badge in
its claws. She leafed through it a bit and found just what she was looking
for: ". . . Judah has underhandedly made the yoke for German necks."
"The true enemy . . . goes past you day in, day out, flat-footed, potbellied,
crooked-nosed, filthy." "The sons and daughters of Israel . . . parasitic
plants on German stock . . ." She lowered her head and read on: ". . . and
we still don't get it. Jewish arrogance . . ." She thought, "Arrogance? We are
not arrogant, I'm afraid not, though we could be. We probably ought to be
arrogant. We survived Rome, saw Byzantium in ruins, and even this enemy
can only kill us if we become corrupt ourselves. We must simply be strong
and brave enough to sink below the surface again, to endure . . . We must
merely withdraw into ourselves again; no one can persecute us there. Israel
is like the dust of the earth: everyone treads on it, but the dust survives all."

By writing this novel, did Kolmar wish to become a self-supporting author?
Once again, the question arises as to whether she submitted the typescript to a
single publisher. There is no written reference to it. The book would not appear
in print for the next four decades.

| 31

And she wrote about her life. More than ever, she wished to help her father in
the office and also took part in a continuing education course. Then again, was
this really necessary?
   The successful lawyer had apparently come into money again after sustain-
ing financial losses through war loans and inflation. In addition to the house in
Finkenkrug, he owned a piece of land with a house in Berlin-Steglitz. The total
value of the property was nearly one hundred thousand reichsmarks, which,
by the standards of the day, was a large—indeed, a huge fortune! And a new

piece of land in Finkenkrug was also mentioned, although it didn't show up in subsequent asset statements. Two, if not three, properties—not bad! He could certainly have afforded a secretary to take dictation and type for him. Yet his daughter felt called, even obligated, to provide her father with extensive help, not only in his capacity as a lawyer but also as a *Notar.*

She would write in a subsequent CV: "For as long as my father was a *Notar* in Finkenkrug, a rural community, I was his sole office helper and, to educate myself in becoming a *Notar*'s assistant, participated in a course given by the Berlin lawyer Dr. Bähren."

| 32

Factition: My Dear Hilde, Assuming that you are really interested in writing a chronicle of our family with Gertrud in mind, then it could well make sense to at least point out that, as a renowned lawyer and defence attorney, I have also been a Notar and will remain so until further notice. This combination is rare today and only possible in the regions. Not being a lawyer, here are a few keywords in case you need them. A lawyer can draft contracts; a Notar is authorised to certify them. My law and Notar's office is a very sought-after place of employment because it also makes for good earnings.

The reason I continue to work at my advanced age does not appear to be completely clear to you children. There are still no old-age pensions for lawyers. As self-employed persons, we must either save for old age or continue to work. While it's true that I am one of the top earners in the legal profession and was able to build up reserves, inflation wiped out most of my savings. And my ongoing financial burdens are rather large. But I can't complain.

So that there are no misunderstandings that awaken longing for the "good old days," at least in retrospect, you should mention in passing that I may be an exception with respect to earnings. The situation was and is not favourable in my profession. There were and are too many lawyers: the bar association tried in vain to put entry barriers in place. The worldwide economic crisis had a lasting and profound effect on judicial administration as well. Around one-quarter to one-third of regional lawyers could not live on what they earned. I was not among them, however, or I would hardly have been able to afford to buy real estate. But those purchases have largely exhausted my financial resources, so I must (and want to!) continue working. And I am no exception in that regard. Recently, I noted a revealing statistic: more than 90 percent of lawyers over sixty-five continue to practise their profession. With regard to proper portrayal of my person, you should at least mention that I am among those human beings who are entirely able to enjoy peace and quiet at home, in the garden and woods. It is not only character traits that shape and typify a person but also circumstances to a large extent as well. That's the reason for my notes, and I leave it to you to use them as you see fit.

Concerning your sister, who always helps me out so selflessly, in the office as well ... You should mention that our poet had to learn a new language, not a very poetic one, and not just in her law office course. She's had to make room in her head for new words, specialised vocabulary and new phrasing, even though the latter is fairly standard to a large extent.

I think that we should not limit ourselves to a blanket comment, for this would not do justice to my daughter, your sister. Trude now moved in two linguistic universes, one in the ground floor office, the other in her corner room upstairs. Your portrayal should make this clear. In addition, I'll permit myself to offer several formulations, as they will be unfamiliar to you.

Should you take up my offer, I will provide a proper frame of reference for the following formulations, which are taken out of context. Please understand the following as nothing more than a provisional offering of subject matter: "Requires authorisation of ... the natural persons concerned are ... represented by a competent third party, the certifying official can ... changes or additions require a specific form ... if authentication involves an inspection or the performance of other duties, then ... if there are serious interests that warrant protection ... the ... to be cancelled; legal basis for the transfer of ownership."

Your sister also knows and uses terms such as these. Because of this, it must be noted that many—indeed, most—people see her as a mere "office worker," the secretary to a Notar, and not primarily as the poet who assists me. Whereby I must immediately add: A poet who never shows any outward appearance as such, may well not wish to come out of obscurity. Otherwise, I wouldn't have had to exert a certain amount of pressure at the time when her first volume of poetry was published—albeit this was made easier and fostered by the fact that our friend, Fleischel, had me to thank in several points of law. As the Latin saying goes, Manus manum lavat [one hand washes the other]. This is just a note in the margin and should not be entered into the family chronicle you are penning.

| 33

By the middle of the nineteenth century, Finkenkrug in East Havelland was already a popular day-trip destination for Berliners. It had been a train stop on the route to Nauen since 1850. A postcard from 1903 shows the half-timber structure of the old train station.

The train station was a starting point for hikes, especially in the Brieselang Forest. Those who didn't want to hike could go swimming in the idyllic Lindenweiher [Linden Pond], site of an "active bathing life" in the 1920s and '30s.

Thus, Finkenkrug was doubly attractive as a day-trip destination and a "summer resort in the countryside." Chodziesner could have followed recommended tips, but it's more likely that he got to know the little town as a day-tripper.

The house he bought was and still is in Neufinkenkrug. As previously mentioned, it was a posh residential area on the edge of the little village. The building of vacation and country houses in Neufinkenkrug was limited to a maximum height of two stories. The streets were paved with rustic cobblestones or, as of the period in which I was working on this book, were still sandy tracks. Sidewalks were either sandy paths or paved with small cobblestones. Meanwhile, the roots of trees along the avenue have frequently caused the paving to buckle. There were around six hundred residents in Chodziesner's time.

Anyone who settled in Neufinkenkrug wanted peace and quiet—and found it. A retirement spot, old age pensioners, retired folks, final resting place, retirement, period of rest, refuge, fortified castle refuges . . . There was no more action, no more throbbing or stirring in those parts. People there lived as if cut off or set apart. The streets, neighbors, trees, flowers . . . People there were safe from new impressions; this was the kingdom of the "constantly recurring." Walks in the housing estate, walks in the outdoors, walks with the dog, walks without the dog, hedge trimming, and watering the flowers. Out there in Neufinkenkrug, people got away from everything, both positive and negative, that made up the life of a metropolis. Out there in Neufinkenkrug, East Havelland, Gertrud also lived a sheltered life—for the time being.

Even during a second drive to Finkenkrug, the posh part of town was not easy to locate within the residential areas. Falkenhagen and Falkenhain, Falkensee and Seegefelt: everything merges into everything else.

Upon inspecting the locale for a second time, I am seething again! Not a single property in Neufinkenkrug has fallen prey to such brutal deforestation as Feuerbachstrasse 10. Only three old trees have been left standing, a huge linden among them; the remaining plot of land has been leveled for a sports complex, including a ball court with standard high wire-mesh cages, a running track for long jumping, and a playground with tires suspended above sand. Couldn't people in the German Democratic Republic have celebrated the author whose poems expressed vehement opposition to Nazi terror as an "antifascist" and treated her house and property with care? And couldn't the Bundesvermögensstelle [National Property Agency] or the educational authority that took over this branch of the Lessing School after German reunification have shown a little more respect for the house in which one of the greats of German poetry lived and wrote?

The house and property are closed on weekends. In addition, unauthorized entry is forbidden by a sign on which is written a word I learned for the first time: *Hortsport* [after-school care center sports]. The house and property as part of the East Lessing Grammar School and After-School Day Care Center? In a subsequent telephone conversation with a kindergarten teacher, I hear the chirping of little children's voices in the background. Lots of children in the house would surely have pleased Gertrud Kolmar!

An alley goes from this mixed ensemble to the Finkenkrug village center, that is, to the train station. Waldstrasse, Breitscheid-Strasse with trees, gardens, villas; the train tracks and overhead cable are already visible. Not much more to it, though. The train station with its imposing facade was torn down in 1995 and replaced by a train stop, just two platforms with ticket machines and schedule boards. The railroad track is dead straight on the local line, travel time to Berlin-Charlottenburg about 25 minutes. Back then, it took the same amount of time from Lehrter Station.

A couple of stately houses are near the train stop; a decaying villa with an unlit, fifties-style neon sign marked LIBRARY. In a side section, a faded, weathered sign for the BUTCHER'S SHOP, which had been part of the consumer chain in GDR times.* The fenced-in building now awaits an investor and will go moldy until then (or so it was in 2003).

Returning to the posh residential area, it looks far bigger than the old village of Finkenkrug. On a map, the village looks more like an appendage. The street curves in toward the underpass beneath the tracks and leads directly into the woods. Since the time of Theodor Fontane, strollers really didn't have far to go before they were surrounded by green pines: Eichkätzchenallee to the north, the forty-meter-high Piepenberge to the west, Bredow Forest, Brieselang Forest, the Heimische Heide [moorland], and Old Finkenkrug is further north, where Nauener Chaussee bumps into another Finkenkruger Strasse in Brieselang. Sandy soil, pines, pines, pines . . . and on a summer's day, it almost feels like the Mediterranean, calm, calm, calm.

We again come to the quarter with streets named after famous painters. From the poet's brutally misappropriated house and on to Lindenweiher with a nearby street to the right, another to the left. A narrow, reed-filled stretch of water along a row of tall trees, and then comes the round pond beyond a little earthen strip. The water had been silted up, filthy, trashed for decades, but a citizens' initiative launched the restoration. They had to do a lot of dredging. Displays behind glass show the before and after, as well as a photo from 1940 with four young women on a footbridge above the pond's offshoot. The display case glass was shattered.

But with the sun out, a gentle breeze, rustling leaves, here a few reeds, there a little island of water lilies, and several ducks paddling around, we get a snapshot

---

* The German Democratic Republic (GDR) was a socialist state established in 1949 in the Soviet-occupied zone of Germany. It existed until 1990.

of the little world to which father and daughter had retreated. Gertrud also went swimming here. I allowed the stillness grounded in rustling reeds and leaves to sink in. May the impression last for as long as possible, strengthening my response to this woman's poetry.

Just how short on excitement, stimulation, and happenings life in the Finken-krug housing estate of retirees and weekend visitors was became evident in the first year. In a December letter, Hilde learned that an earpiece to Gertrud's eye-glasses had broken off, "and I am no longer used to writing without glasses." In other news, they gave their cook, Helene, "a pair of slip-on winter pants" for her birthday. In those days, such items of clothing went by the name of "passion killers."

Gertrud continued: "Dot, dash.—Do you know what I saw yesterday? I was putting my bedding in a side window to air out, and while I was doing so, there came a crackling and banging from the top of a pine tree right in front of me. And there sat a large beast, a really large brute, a Eurasian buzzard, completely calm and secure! He stayed a while, then flew over to the Grieshabers. I shall close on this note."

Gertrud Kolmar actually conformed to contemporary expectations. For exam-ple, a poet lived as secluded a life as possible, preferably in the country, where he or she turned out work from his or her "innermost" resources and developed inner riches. Social goings-on, vibrant environments were most likely inimical to the development of literary works of art.

All a bunch of clichés! In modified form, they nevertheless describe the poet's exceptional lifestyle. She hardly got involved in any of life's adventures. As far as we know, just one little excursion with a long-standing correspond-ent took place several years later. But the only adventure she got involved in unreservedly was her relationship to language. In this case, we are the fortunate heirs of a woman who largely renounced personal fulfillment and in its place put something approaching contentment. But perhaps this was true happiness in her eyes—happiness in a quiet corner?

In the warm months, life in Finkenkrug largely meant living and working in the vegetable and ornamental gardens as well as the little park area of the sprawling property: "Raking, digging, and chopping . . . sweeping the street in front of our front door . . ." and taking care of the chickens, ducks, and rabbits.

And we must add the keyword, "dog." Gertrud gave Hilde Benjamin the gift of a little book by Wilhelm Schmidtbonn, published in 1927, *Die Flucht zu den Hilflosen—die Geschichte dreier Hunde* [*Flight to Dereliction: The Story of Three Dogs*]. The recipient wrote, "She gave it to me as one of her favourite books." I was able to get hold of the book and pick out a few quotations that fit our context plus shed light on this aspect of her personality, which is to say, her love of animals. But not even the love of dogs was unique to the father-daughter symbiosis at Finkenkrug: He had his German shepherd (or two, at least on occasion); she had a greyhound and a borzoi.

These dogs of Russian origin were apparently popular at that time. *Borzoi* means "swift, agile." Borzois were bred in Czarist Russia for rabbit, fox, and wolf hunting. In photos of that period, you sometimes see borzois with hunters on horseback.

When I do an online search for "borzoi," selected examples of breeding show up on the screen for me to admire, primarily portrait photos taken after "wins in beauty and performance." And decorative, sketched and painted borzoi images, a porcelain figure of "Madame and Borzoi," a young, naked woman . . . the inner world of breeders specializing in borzois. I don't know whether Gertrud's Flora had a studbook number or if her exact date of birth was written down. Male borzois frequently have names in their papers that sound as if they'd been concocted by a con artist: Odin of the Russian Empire, Dashkoff of Comté de Gruyère, etc.

After I've looked at quite a number of photographic images, I see my first live borzoi and, while consulting with the dog handler, am sniffed at in little Köln-Mülheim Park. A borzoi is not big but "tall," if you please. And this one here "has a full set of teeth and everything he ought to." He's registered in the studbook. His nearly streamlined head is shaped as though built for extreme speed. His eyes are actually almond shaped. I find that he has a good temperament, is easy to keep in an apartment, simply needs his corner, never barks, at most growls softly a couple of times when playing with another dog. He's very suitable for families with children, also a pleasant companion for older folks, and needs no muzzle since his game hunting instinct has been bred out.

I'd barely developed a sharp eye for borzois when I discovered another one, and there's nothing easier than striking up a conversation with a dog owner. Yes, the slim, narrow head is fairly round at birth, of course; but then it lengthens, and a little bony protrusion shows the growth pattern. When you train a borzoi for the racetrack, it can easily reach almost forty-four miles per hour. Yet there's a danger that, once it has reached a velocity such as this, it may no longer come back.

I then saw a completely white borzoi in Berlin on the Kurfürstedamm. This is no large, lumbering dog: the slim, long-legged animal with an almost coquettishly prancing gait moves more like a prima donna of the dog world. The white ones are indeed rare, extremely so: borzois are usually "covered all over" in black and white. Yes, that's what they call it: covered all over. Black on the back and flanks with white areas shaped like islands on top. Spotted coats are definitely the rule. Naturally, white borzois are more delicate. "But isn't he a beautiful boy?"

| 34

I bought the *Insel Almanach auf das Jahr 1930* [*Insel Almanac of the Year 1930*]* from an antiquarian bookseller. In it are printed two of Kolmar's poems under her pen name.

The second poem, "Die Entführte" ["Abducted"], seems weak but revealing to me. It conjures up an idyll: A woman wearing an apron is hoeing in the garden while her child "sleeps peacefully." The child's father is a "simple man" who "doesn't like to write and reads very little" and seems to be a partner rather than a husband. Key here are: "tanned child" by day, "a man's shoulder" by night. In the case of this poem, any attempt to establish a connection between text and life is doomed to fail.

The middle verses of the first poem, "Die Gauklerin" ["The Clown"], are particularly important. I shall quote the entire poem because its publication marks the beginning of a biographical development:

> The yellow birds are never anxious,
> When I go to grab them,
> Like fluffy balls
> They quit their handiwork;
> Who also knows the green glass harmonica,
> That don't break when falling,
> Or the silver ring, which fell ringing,
> gliding unerringly?
>
> Surely what I did while smiling,
> Deserves a laugh;
> There's certainly nothing so elfinlike,
> Insignificant and done without so easily.
> A cup, shy of violets
> Carried the lesson I drank,
> Taking delicate flight from its coarse wood,
> And adventure from mere stone.

---

* The *Insel Almanach* [*Island Almanac*] was a literary journal produced by the German publishing company Insel Verlag and used to promote its writers and publications.

Art, that for no reason and for a short while,
Cares for a ball of soap,
Colorful ribbons of falling water,
The spill of a rainbow,
Which silently mixes and quickly blurs
A puzzle that he writes,
Is extinguished forever, if you like
And, if you wish, remains so forever.

Spurning the less skilled world,
Wherein my being lives,
Have pity on the circular money,
That stubbornly sticks to my finger:
And yet, when barren space
Once hit painfully lame,
My childhood dream elates you
And you have your fill.

No wonder people sat up and listened! Ina Seidel and Elisabeth Langgässer praised both poems, as did Karl Josef Keller, a young chemist who wrote and published poems. He wrote to the poet. An exchange of letters ensued that would be followed by their meeting years later.

| 35

In Finkenkrug, the image of a nondescript, indeed emphatically nondescript person was firmly established. As a child, Gertrud had placed little value on pretty clothes, something her mother occasionally complained about. She wore the most modest, old-fashioned-looking raiment. The poet hid, as it were, behind the little woman who, upon seeing her, would more likely remind you of the nice auntie next door than a lyricist who wrote world-class poetry, sister to an Achmatova or Tsvetaeva.

Only a few photos of Gertrud have survived, and she's most likely to be seen with family members or at the coffee table with a girlfriend. She is seated in one, standing to the side in another.

I am astonished each time I look at one of these photos. This inconspicuous woman wrote such magnificent poems? They provide a catalyst for further reflection on creativity and phenotype. Should we consider a person's creativity and, in this case, true genius? Must a person's appearance be in keeping with what her work represents? In Gertrud Kolmar's case, we could speak of concealed, practically camouflaged creativity. In no way did she show off, behave conspicuously, or place herself in the limelight. She didn't make herself into an interesting person so as to awaken interest in her work or draw attention to herself, and she was not interested in any kind of public role. She acted inconspicuously, spoke softly, if at all. Any sort of self-emphasis was foreign to her; she didn't even want to promote herself as an artist in any way. Not even in her wildest dreams did this dance enthusiast see herself striding down the staircase in a musical revue.

Fade into the background, be modest, make herself look small. This is legible in the most literal sense, and no knowledge of graphology is necessary to discern it. In all of her letters in the Marbach Archive, it strikes you that Kolmar's handwriting was diminutive, even prior to the period in which people had to use paper sparingly. Her signature was sometimes even smaller than the running text, almost to the point of disappearing. Her sister Margot's signature was certainly five times larger by comparison. The poet's lettering, on the other hand, approached the limit of readability.

"Invisibility cap" is an obvious theme that Hilde introduced in an attempt to portray her sister: "With her, there was no outward extravagance, no showing off or drawing attention to herself. In fact, it often seemed as if she had donned a camouflage cap so as to make her actions completely invisible."

She especially wanted to make herself invisible as a poet. Please don't discuss literature or poetry, not even among close family members. It's best to take no further notice of her and leave her to her quiet, modest ways. People rarely got news of what was being written in that corner room. Did she ever read a new poem to her father who, after all, had acted as mediator for the first volume of poetry and certainly not done so blindly? She also read to her youngest sister, Hilde, from time to time, but this was practically under the guise of a conspiracy. That was because writing ought not to become a topic within the family and most certainly not among relatives or acquaintances. She was mortified if the family doctor asked the habitual question, "Well, Miss Trudchen, how's the poetry coming along?" As they say in such instances, she dearly wished the earth would open up and swallow her. In the first place, she wrote poetry for herself, wanted to be the judge of her own poems, and notoriety wasn't that important to her. "In the end, it may strike you as strange," she later wrote to her sister, "if I admit to the fact that, as gratifying as it is that my work gives something to others, this doesn't give me as much pleasure as the work itself." Writing poetry was primary; appearing or taking the stage as a poet, secondary.

Yes, creativity can apparently seal itself off, emitting very little and hardly manifesting outwardly. She did not look like someone to whom you would ascribe exceptional artistic achievement, nor did her quasi-bohemian lifestyle create such an impression. Even upon longer acquaintance with her, indications of anything extraordinary are not in evidence. This petite woman did not reveal anything of her true greatness and was constantly underrated as a result.

Even among close friends, for example, the family of their friend and associate in the firm, *Justizrat* Wronker, people apparently didn't know that Gertrud wrote poetry. A prime example surfaces when Gertrud later reported on a social gathering in which an opera singer shone and a famous actor was present: "'Nothing but famous people, artistic talents,' said Frau Counselor Wronker's cousin, who was seated next to me. 'We're the only two nobodies and no-talents.' I listened without batting an eyelash. Another time, however, she commented that I looked as if I wrote poetry. I did not answer her . . ."

In *The Story of Just Casper* and *Fair Annie,* Clemens Brentano developed a more solid explanatory model:

> It is really a dubious matter to be a poet by profession, rather than just on the side. You could easily say to him, "Sir, just as every human has a brain, heart, stomach, spleen, liver, and the like, he also has poetry in him. But anyone who overfeeds one of these parts, feeds or fattens it like an animal, and engages in it above and beyond all others, indeed makes it into an occupation, must feel shame in the face of all other human beings. Someone who earns a living from poetry has lost his sense of balance. And however good an oversize goose liver may taste, it still presupposes a sick goose."

This model was a precursor to Freud's popular theory of sublimation, which has been brilliantly refuted in the meantime by the appearance of figures like Picasso. So I would like to politely reduce Brentano's drastic analogy as follows: Creativity is like a capsule, frequently hidden in outward appearances that permit no conclusions whatsoever about genius. Rather, creativity seems to be a special part of a human being, the appearance of which need not correspond in any way to the extraordinary quality of what she produces.

With Kolmar, creativity was surrounded by homeliness. Hardly anyone in the Feuerbachstrasse neighborhood would have ever imagined that the petite woman with Papa and Flora was among our greatest German-language poets. She differed fundamentally from Else Lasker-Schüler, whose exotic dress, for example, eccentric behavior, and passionate lifestyle alone attracted attention, which then by design also included her work. The poet Kolmar, however, retreated behind the person of Chodziesner, making her even smaller than her diminutive figure. She was an especially clear example of creativity that shone inward but did not radiate outward. Gertrud Kolmar went about creating her work and not making much of her appearance.

In the case of this East Havelland poet, you could almost imagine she had spun a fairy-tale cocoon for herself and created a homogeneous inner world. Yet, of all people, this woman gave rise in her works to astounding breaks with the past and great leaps forward. She often emerged powerfully from her inner world, decisively expanding her linguistic spectrum.

Two oft-cited phrases by Hermann Broch must be repeated with Gertrud Kolmar in mind, the first of which is: "If I had to write an autobiography, I would have all sorts of problems owing to a lack of material."

And the second: "At any rate, something I share with Kafka and Musil is that all three of us have no real life story. We lived and wrote, and that's the whole story."

The latter comment did not prevent any biographies from being written about Franz Kafka or Robert von Musil, or even about Broch.

But the first phrase and keyword, "autobiography," could easily be applied to Gertrud Kolmar. She did not make the slightest effort to write autobiographical material with literary aspirations in mind.

| 36

The circumstances in Neufinkenkrug and its rural setting ought not to determine the orientation of this book, because messages from family members continued to reach father and daughter in Feuerbachstrasse.

Hilde Benjamin, admitted to practice law since 1929, and Georg, a district council member in Wedding and editor at the journal *Der oppositionelle Arbeiter-Samariter* [*The Worker's Samaritan Opposition*], had a wake-up call, a particularly close encounter with the transition from the Weimar Republic to the Nazi dictatorship.

In looking briefly at the years after 1930, the Great Depression also resulted in budget cuts that affected the health care system. The title of a critical piece by Benjamin was "Cutbacks! Cutbacks! Cutbacks!" Hospitals were to be closed, hospital care restricted, health insurance benefits reduced; and doctors were to prescribe the most inexpensive medications. Benjamin vehemently protested these impending developments. Growing unemployment and increasing poverty were accompanied by scabies and lice, rickets and tuberculosis. And "skin diseases are increasing at the same rate as unemployment and poor living conditions."

Having opened his own practice, Georg Benjamin had an awful lot to do. And because most medications produced by the pharmaceutical industry were too expensive, he made his own formulas.

Dr. Benjamin also treated victims of growing terror by the Sturmabteilung (SA),* one patient with lacerations to the head, resulting from frequently used brass knuckles; another with extensive bruises on his skull and shoulders, welts on his back and buttocks; and yet another with a bruised right eye and four teeth knocked out.

| 37

In a bundle of poems written in the half decade since her fresh start in 1927, the subject of "the child" continues to play a dominant role. The same is true of animal-related themes and the mistreatment that humans often inflicted on dogs and horses. The third set of topics was female portraits.

There are numerous indirect and nearly direct invocations of "longing for a child in the flesh." It has already been sufficiently emphasized that poetic quotations should not be taken as autobiographical statements. Yet in the opening poem of the third volume, Gertrud Kolmar invites, even exhorts us to do so!

First, a sequence from the poem with the nearly programmatic title, "Fruchtlos" ["Fruitless"]:

> I see. I feel:
> Through the locked door without a sound
> Comes a child.
> The one thing, given to me, that I did not bear.
> Not born for my sins; God is just.
> I remain silent, and do not complain,
> I carry and cover
>   my head, so that I can locate it
> Many an evening.

Would it be too simplistic to associate "sins" with her consent to the abortion, even if she was forced into it? Would it be too bold to interpret the "murder" in the poem "Die Kranke" ["The Invalid"] as another expression of the term "abortion"? "The ax lies in my womb" is one of the poet's more radical formulations. I quote the third through final stanzas:

> I turn my head like the head of a doll;
> My neck creaks, turning hard.

* The Sturmabteilung (SA) was the military wing of the Nazi Party.

My keeper brings me mollycoddled soup,
Placing a thin slice of bread next to me,
Which is angular and colorless.
I also ate the round, brown,
sturdy bread of the healthy?
Even with effort I cannot empty the plate.

There are children singing. So unspeakably . . .
Stay calm . . . it's going away.
It was a piece of fluff, very fine and delicate,
In a few hours it withered.
It kept germinating my disease within my heart,
A mother's suffering, the punishing switch.
Which struck at it and carried out the murder.

I don't want to ponder it anymore.
For what I think about,
Whisks my brain into a sticky foam,
And a spider running over my skull tingles,
And before my eyes space distorts,
Once, just once I close them both:
Then out of one grows a weeping willow
And from the other the tree of life.

"For what I think about, / Whisks my brain into a sticky foam . . ." The poem "Die Gesegnete" ["The Blessed"] may also fit into this context and closes with a suicide fantasy:

It is night. And a thing called shame.
I may not give birth to you.
I know the express train, which tears up the forest.

Then I go over to its bare tracks
And become weary and go happily to bed
Across two flat bars of iron.

It's difficult to break free of or ward off the idea of a train line cutting through the forest leading to and passing through Finkenkrug.

Four poems in their entirety shall close this chapter in the history of her work, beginning with "Spaziergang" ["Stroll"]:

Come, let's go under trees,
Hanging full of shiny rubber balls,
To shrubs crowded with switches
Where red blossoms spin like tops.

Come, let's go into the garden,
Where little toy animals graze,
Lots of dolls, silky yellow and lilac,
Standing slim upon finely raked beds.

Blue chickens, which don't exist, really,
Silver-combed, seeking your hands,
Taking bread crumbs and bits of offered grain.
Fearlessly grateful, because of the child she loves.

Out of the dune, which rises from the sea,
Crawl a bucket, cake pan and shovel,
Conch shell, showing the untrained lip
Its most beautiful songs.

Railways stomping out their rhymes,
Wave merrily with disheveled hair.
Want to go to the brown cliff?
Every journey takes you home again.

For granate wine springs from the rocks,
Showers of raspberry and lemon water;
Green woodruff leaves fill barrels,
And honey rolls swell on the stone.

Come, dear heart, and let us go,
Light lamps, fry eggs,
Stuffing your stockings and discuss,
Everything we've seen together.

An imagined idyll with child. And then come recollections of her own childhood, this one in a room inside Grandmother Schoenflies's apartment. That's
where the child saw dolls, wondrous figures, and the glass-encased model of a
mine in which little figures of workers could be moved into stereotypical action
sequences. The poem is titled "Grossmutter" ["Grandmother"]:

I have not set foot there for a long while.
With its silver stovepipe,
Shiny, dark green satin wallpaper—
In front of the sofa cushions the little blackamoor,

Who played with the children when they came by,
Wearing turban and purple harem pants:
His crooked dagger, which they eagerly took,
From the blue sash with gold fringe . . .

There he sits, limp, so thoughtful in the corner,
Gloomy as the diamond on his Arabian shoes,
And next to him on a crocheted white blanket,
Atop a round ornamental table, the elephant sleeps,

Who, often and easily, by a thin magic key
Is coaxed and stimulated out of his fixed dream
And who, while pounding his trunk,
actually lifts a black wooden ring.

The colorful mine, which they so enjoyed,
Waits crumbling and dusty under the glass dome:
The tiny workmen standing idle,
This or that one's hammer already plundered.

And oh, if they entered the green living room,
Their first glances shy and full of awe,
Asking for the delicate plaything,
Which was always wonderful and new!

Now they look to distant, wild lands,
That are stranger than my mine,
And see the Moors without blue ribbons.
And yet each was sweet, each a child

And had fresh eyes, ready for miracles,
That sprang all spring and flowers from the fabric.
This, today, is all just tomfoolery,
The miner's cage, the light in the cave passageway.

When I powered it up for the last time,
Listening at the wall of ore
The little man bowed, remaining thus
Standing and listening forever. Like my heart.

These poems were written prior to 1933, poems from the final phase of the Weimar Republic. Hardly a poet of her generation had as wide a range of expression as Gertrud Kolmar, and this allows us to expand the chapters on the history of her work. And yet only certain features can be singled out. "Die Verworfene" ["The Castaway"] is an example pointing to the subject of alienation, even in the familiar atmosphere of the home:

In my room I'm completely lost.
All of the things say they do not know me.
The heater with its coiled, whitewashed pipes
Twitches in my hand and wants to burn it.

The chair, painfully shy, pulls my coat down.
In the glass cabinet small cups whisper rattling.
Blue lilacs look at me from a narrow vase
Indulgently, as if I caused them to fade.

I had no idea, that this is: Conscience.
The dead hostility of these things that I grasp,
The sofa cushion with a firmly brocaded look,
The tall chair, deliberately stiff.

How does a table learn, what's never sanctioned by people
And never scolded—and never experienced,
The mirror negates, what I agreed to,
And, hating, lies through the shining of my hair?

My big woolen skein jumped from the windowsill,
Anxiously hopping like a purple rat;
I must have thought that I had thrown it,
And then realized that it was rejecting me.

We shall close with a contrasting text, "Die Unerschlossene" ["Undeveloped"]. She portrayed herself as a woman who was still not really seen and could not fully be seen by others. This poem clearly represents another change of key:

I, too, am a part of the world.
I have never reached mountains,
have left bushland unpenetrated,
Pond bays, river deltas, salt-licking coastal promontories,
Caves, wherein huge dark green reptiles flash,
Inland seas, flaunting orange jellyfish.

My breast buds are not washed by the rain,
No stream tore them open: These gardens are remote.
No adventurer has yet conquered my golden sandy desert valleys
And the snows, lying virginal at barren heights.

Bare red rock monsters strangle condors with clawed fingers,
Splaying their feathers in the air, knowing nothing of their conquerors.
Are they eagles? Primeval eagles, too—who listened, when one screamed?—
But my big vultures are more powerful still and stranger than them.

What I conceal no longer breaks out of earth already closed;
Because no alpha snake leads flocks of rigidly writhing vipers there,
No toads light the way for themselves at night with the carnelian in their head.
The secrets of the copper chalice have long been gathered from the
    defensive moss.

And above me there are often skies with black stars, colorful thunderstorms,
In me there are lobed, jagged craters, trembling from the compelling glow;
But a pure and icy spring is there too, and the bellflower, which drinks it:
I am a continent that one day sinks, mute into the sea.

| 38

The *Machtübernahme* [takeover of power] on January 30, 1933, was a historical turning point. With the blessing of President of the Reich Paul von Hindenburg, Adolf Hitler became chancellor of a coalition government consisting of Nazi and German National People's Party representatives. Nazi propaganda also happily made use of the terms *Machtergreifung* [seizure of power] and *Machtantritt* [accession to power]. This language was meant to suggest that a dynamic, revolutionary sweep to power had taken place. But the change of government was legitimized by elections. No sooner was Hitler *Reichskanzler* [chancellor of the Reich], however, than democratic parties and institutions were liquidated.

Unfortunately, Ludwig Chodziesner did not speak about his experiences in the early years of Nazi rule in written form. But we can call on the notes of his Berlin colleagues, such as Fritz Ball, who was also a Jew. What Chodziesner may have learned within his circle of colleagues and what his daughter may have heard about him in turn should assume greater immediacy in the process of drawing analogies:

In the late afternoon of January 30, 1933, a client brought a special edition of the "late edition" to the office.

One of my employees barged into my office. Doctor, sir, Hitler is chancellor of the Reich. Hindenburg has made Hitler chancellor of the Reich.

The agitation in the office was indescribable, and work was unthinkable that day. But everything remained calm in the days that followed. In the lawyers' room of the Higher Regional Court in Berlin, you suddenly encountered colleagues in SA uniforms, people you would have never known were Nazis. I could keep on going to court and carry on with my courses for the first state examination at the Higher Regional Court. I admittedly saw some of my fellow students in brown uniforms and sometimes noticed hostile looks. But everything went on as usual, and the predominant feeling was that those who saw Hitler's antisemitism as nothing more than a political weapon in the battle for power were proven right. As soon as he was a statesman rather than a party leader, he would be more moderate and behave more discreetly. Joseph Goebbels as minister of state, impossible!

But we soon heard about colleagues being arrested and secretly disappeared. At first, it was the Nazis' political opponents. But we quickly heard that businesspeople, doctors, and lawyers had been arrested, people who, to our knowledge, had never worked in opposition to the Nazis. Terrible rumours about basement atrocities emerged.

In those days, a lead article in the *Jüdische Rundschau** said, "As Jews, we've come face-to-face with the fact that a power hostile to us has taken over the reins of government in Germany."

The board of the Central Association of German Citizens of the Jewish Faith issued the following statement: "We obviously regard a ministry in which National Socialists occupy influential positions with the greatest mistrust, even if we have no other choice under the present circumstances than to wait and see what actions it will take. . . . We are convinced that no one would dare infringe on our constitutional rights. Every harmful attempt will find us in good form

---

* The *Jüdische Rundschau* [*Jewish Review*] was a German-language Jewish weekly.

and decisively on the defensive. Apart from that, the watchword 'Remain calm' particularly applies today!"

On February 2, however, the lead article in the association's journal said:

> German Jews look to the future gravely and anxiously. It makes no sense to delude oneself about the dangers inherent in the fact that the leading men of a party which has written the battle against the Jews on its flag now dominates German politics.
>
> The question many Jews have been asking is: Will Nazi antisemitism become state doctrine? Will Jewish citizens be declared enemies of the state? Will they carry out what they have only threatened to do up to now, such as: "Sweep them out with an iron broom . . . Handle them with dog whips and boot heels . . . Beat the enemy to a pulp . . ."

The Central Association issued reassuring watchwords, one of which, "Wait and see," struck a favorable chord among Jews. What rowdy antisemites had bellowed and printed couldn't, wouldn't be adopted by a civilized Central European nation, would it?

Yet Arnold Zweig's telling phrase, "the invasion of public life by force," was conspicuous and unmistakable. Zweig soon found himself forced to flee Germany, to live in exile.

The monthly issues of the Central Association's journal stopped with the January/February 1933 edition, which is indicative of the prevailing situation. The editorial staff said good-bye in a fairly long article titled "Mass Hysteria" and subtitled, "A Chapter in Human Failure."

The article pointed to "witch hunts and persecution of heretics" in ages past. But "we don't need to go far back in history at all to gather material that illustrates the topic of mass hysteria." The key word, "antisemitism," comes to mind. What may be typical in this case is that people "considered the victim guilty and that the injustice done to him was regarded as just punishment."

The Reichstag [parliament building] is burning! On February 27, 1933, barely a month after the *Machtübernahme,* a fire broke out in the Reichstag. Even today it is not clear whether the rumor that spread swiftly was true: the Nazis had set the building on fire themselves, and the alleged arsonist, Marinus van der Lubbe—a pro-Communist Dutch anarchist—was nothing more than a sacrificial pawn. Regardless of who set the fire, the Nazis, with Hermann Göring leading the way, quickly turned the opportunity into a second, now total *Machtergreifung.* The very next day, they pushed through an emergency decree "for the protection of the people and state," giving the government full discretionary powers.

It must have been immediately clear to the lawyer Chodziesner that the Weimar constitution had been repealed and the constitutional state had been liquidated. Reports of the immediate onset of hunting down Communists (and others) even reached Finkenkrug. The SA was now fully unleashed, and there were beatings, looting, torture, and executions.

| 39

With the change of government and the takeover of power, a period of demeaning experiences began for father and daughter, even in the apparent seclusion of Finkenkrug. What had been a freely chosen symbiosis became a *Zwangsgemeinschaft* [forced association], a word used frequently in that period, especially among Jews. The all-inclusive, racist term "Jew" was imposed on German citizens of every stripe. "Jew" applied to members of the Verband nationaldeutscher Juden [Association of National-German Jews], who strove for complete assimilation, but every bit as much to Zionists, who would rather have spoken Yiddish or Hebrew than German and had formulated contrary ideas besides.

The rapid transition from coalition government to Nazi dictatorship, definitively completed in June 1933, had such a powerful effect on the lives of the poet and her father that it had inevitable repercussions for this book. Now more than ever, the poet's biography would become a dual biography of father and daughter.

Once again, Gertrud had lived with her father in Finkenkrug for half a decade, and the fact that she had done so of her own free will cannot be stated emphatically enough. But unless she decided to emigrate without her father— that is, to flee the country—she would have to stay from now on. There were quite a few writers, such as Alfred Döblin and Heinrich Mann, who had already left the country in February and March, shrewdly.

All steps that were now taken against lawyers directly would indirectly affect the poet as well. In the end, she carried on with her work in the law office, which would continue to operate for another half decade. So she must have noticed what was being directed at members of her father's profession, what he found out in his line of work. Insofar as specialist materials entered the house and probably landed on her desk first off, she would have read and at least taken note of them. So she surely noticed the pseudo-legislation of repression in the *Reichgesetzblatt* [*Legislative Bulletin of the German Reich*] to which every lawyer subscribed. It's conceivable that she pointed out brand-new implementing regulations, ordinances, and statutes to her father, or that he came into the anteroom from his office, saying indignantly, "Just look at this!"

I can also imagine that Gertrud would have provisionally sorted incoming mail, would have taken dictation, would have converted pleadings into fair copies, and would have taken care of correspondence. And she could well have been present when visitors and clients reported on their own experiences or those of others. She thus followed and experienced the rapid reduction of a constitutional state to a state in which the law was extensively defined by those in power and replaced by decrees. And so, for the time being, it was primarily the official language of the rulers that had an impact on the house in Feuerbachstrasse.

To make a long story short, she learned directly and indirectly from her father just how swiftly and brutally society would be transformed. This, too, was symbiotic. The way it affected her father's profession must therefore be made clear again.

| 40

By the second month of the Nazi regime, Jews had already become victims of violence. "Doomsday scenarios from all over the Reich," said a review in the *Israelitisches Familienblatt* [*Israelite Family Newssheet*] from the second week of March. "In the past week, there were incidents in nearly every corner of the Reich that led to threats against and, quite often, to assaults on Jewish persons and to the closing down of Jewish businesses by irresponsible elements. Given the unfortunate profusion of such instances, it is virtually impossible to go into elaborate detail and perhaps not absolutely necessary, because there are notable similarities between many of them."

In the Chodziesner home, attacks on jurists were the most likely topics. Were there phone conversations, emergency calls?

During one incident, garbage trucks drove up to the *Oberlandesgericht* [higher regional court] on Reichenspergerplatz in Cologne. These electric pickup trucks were normally used to transport trash cans from courtyards to the street. Jewish judges, lawyers, and public prosecutors were hauled from official chambers and offices, berated, beaten, and dragged through hallways. But something else happened. Several "Aryan" *Referendare* [law students] steered Jewish colleagues out through the back entrance. Anyone who did not escape was chased to the forecourt of the building and forced to climb onto the small loading areas. Since the screens on the garbage trucks were low, the jurists had to hold onto one another when the convoy of vehicles set off on parade through the city.

Inauspicious details were reported by Fritz Ball, a lawyer colleague from Berlin: "Two SA guards had to stand in front of every Jewish business, every house of a Jewish lawyer or doctor and prevent customers, patients, and clients from entering. Many decent German men and women were more determined than ever to seek out their Jewish lawyers or doctors, although they knew that they could not help them. But they wanted to express their support and sympathy for those affected, either by visiting them or making purchases at a Jewish business that very day."

Ball was also waylaid at his office and driven to the SA barracks in General Pape Strasse:

> They dragged me into a corner. I saw a large *sjambok* [animal hide whip]. They bent me over, but did not strike me. They just lifted me and let me fall into a chair. They tied my arms behind my back. They yelled as if dead drunk. Among them were many intelligent faces. I believe I even recognized some of them. All were young guys between the ages of eighteen and twenty-five. They called to me, asked questions, cracked jokes, shouted one another down. Then one of them stood in front of me and said,
> "You'll be shot dead at 6 A.M."
> I answered, "I don't think so. I know that I'll be released tomorrow morning. You wouldn't shoot an innocent man."
> Suddenly a hullabaloo. They brought gigantic scissors and then got going. They tugged at and cut my rather long hair. They tried to cut a swastika into my head. They wounded me, and I bled. They pushed and shoved one another to see better. The noise, the yelling got worse and worse.

At night, the SA put Ball into a crowded cell. A man who had been tortured lay on the floor, spitting blood: "An SA man guarded the door from the inside and kept it locked." He wanted to prevent particularly brutal colleagues from forcing their way in and resuming the assaults. Things calmed down in the barracks. Ball continued:

> Then, suddenly, music was coming from somewhere in the building. They were playing hymns on accordions and concertinas. The music sounded faint in the closed-off cellar, but I could distinctly hear every note and knew straightaway which instruments were being played. The music had a bewildering effect. How did hymns come to be played in this barracks at three in the morning? In between, you could hear very faint, indistinct, yet clearly terrible screaming sounds. An eerily tense mood prevailed in our room. Everyone listened with horrified expressions on their faces. The young man next to me and I still didn't know what was going on. But we were soon to be enlightened. When they were beating a man to death upstairs, they played hymns to drown out his screams.

Horror gripped me. This music, these hymns, were the most horrific thing I had experienced up to now. I could no longer lie down. I stood up, looked dirty. My coat was a filthy mess and wet straw hung all over me. Someone made room for me, and I sat down on the bench. A gall bladder attack caused intense pain and nausea.

He was released the next day. As he left the building, he feared he would be shot "in the process of fleeing." But he was able to return home:

My father was sitting in the office, along with a woman who had been our Jewish chief clerk for many years. All other employees were on leave. A twenty-two-year-old female stenographer who had worked in my office for six years was arrested shortly after me. She was so upset by my arrest that she said something. Our apprentice, a girl of sixteen, reported her, and they were in our office again an hour later. It was the same SA, and they took her away amidst cheering . . .

I sat in our dining room with my wife, my father, and our chief clerk. I looked so different with my hair chopped off. I had turned grey overnight.

Our cook came in and didn't recognize me. When my wife told her who the gentleman was, she began to cry. So we knew that we could trust her.

| 41

The Act on the Restoration of the Professional Civil Service went into effect just a week after the boycott,* as did the Act on the Admission to the Legal Profession, a pseudolegal measure to "weed out" Jewish lawyers:

The admission of lawyers, who within the meaning of the Act on the Restoration of the Professional Civil Service of April 7, 1933 (*Reich Law Gazette* I, p. 175) are not of Aryan descent, can be revoked up to September 30.

The word "can" was apparently of critical importance. Unlike the Professional Civil Service Act, the Legal Profession Act was formulated as a discretionary provision, which meant that it left room for circumspection. In most cases, however, the provision was rigorously enforced.

And a form letter with the following wording would also arrive at the Feuerbachstrasse residence in Falkensee-Finkenkrug: "The admission of the lawyer

* The boycott refers to the Nazi boycott of Jewish businesses on April 1, 1933.

Ludwig Chodziesner to the legal profession at the local and regional court in Berlin has been revoked pursuant to Section 1, para. 1 of the Act on the Admission to the Legal Profession, because he is not of Aryan descent.'"

A subsequent article in the *Juristische Wochenschrift* [*Weekly Law Review*] said the following: "The Act on the Admission to the Legal Profession of April 7, 1933, was the first measure for keeping Jews out of the legal profession. Insofar as they were not frontline soldiers or had been admitted after August 1, 1914, Section 1 of the act permitted the admission of non-Aryan lawyers to be revoked. The measure was successful in that 1,500 non-Aryan lawyers had been removed by the end of 1933, but there were still around 2,900 Jews in the legal profession."

One of the exemptions applied to Ludwig Chodziesner: he came under the category of *Altanwälte* [long-standing lawyers].

Even he had to file a petition to be allowed to carry on in the law office, and he had to undergo examination. The petition was generally worded as follows: "On the basis of the local decree of April 6, 1933, I ask to be reinstated as a lawyer and *Notar*. I am not politically active and have never belonged to a Marxist party. I unreservedly acknowledge as legally binding on me the situation now established for me on the basis of the well-known agreement."

Examination by Nazi authorities followed such a declaration. This investigation could drag on for weeks, and a lawyer was not allowed to attend to or represent clients during that time.

In Chodziesner's case, they apparently found no incriminating evidence in regard to his way of life or in the exercise of his profession. He was, therefore, able to continue practicing in both capacities for the time being.

| 42

Factition: I must write down, spontaneously, what I could also tell you if you were visiting out here, which unfortunately may not be for a while. So I will begin a sequel to my letter. Despite the turbulence of the last days and weeks, we should not lose sight of the goal we've sworn several times to achieve; that is, to write a family chronicle that takes your elder sister especially into account. But you must no more take a backseat than your husband, who, as you know, I think a great deal of, and rightly so.

These days, the telephone lines have been burning up, as it were. Gertrud had to keep calling me into the house. I was busy with, or rather, busied myself with preparing for the planting season. At the same time, I was trying to work off my rage and grief with the spade.

"*Poland*" *seemed entirely lost at first, but then phone calls and visits very gradually clarified the situation. A surprising number of colleagues have successfully
used the optional provision of the illegal law, invoking their time at the front or
referring to the fact that their legal careers began prior to the cutoff date. For the
time being, the latter also ensures the continued existence of my practice. I reckon
that three-quarters of jurists of Jewish origin remain (primarily as judges) in office
(even if not in positions of authority), or continue to work as Notars or lawyers, as
in my case. You must take a deep breath and catch your breath at the same time,
provided I may put it that way.*

*But I don't want to gloss over the situation by any means. Besides good news,
I receive calls for help, direct and indirect, that are becoming worrisome of late:
"Admission cancelled . . . Pensioned off with retirement pay . . . Membership on
the Judicial Examination Board revoked . . . Transfer to a lower-ranking position
. . . On behalf of the Prussian minister of justice, assuming you are in agreement, I
relieve you from the performance of your duties until further notice . . ."*

*As a soldier, I would say that the exploding shells are coming ever closer. But
only distant rumblings can be heard on the eastern horizon here in Finkenkrug.
I'm not always listening, am primarily concerned with reorienting and reorgan-
izing my office. Despite all the restrictions, I must create and retain a certain room
for manoeuvring.*

*Now you will ask, "And what field of activity is still open to you?" I have
tried to answer this question myself by designing an ad that I could, perhaps,
place in the Central Verein Zeitung.* The wording would go something like this:
"Counsellor Dr. Chodziesner (followed, of course, by the address) will handle the
proper and speedy implementation of your emigration: Tax and foreign exchange
advice inclusive of capital transfer tax and Reich Flight Tax . . . Processing at
all offices, such as emigrant advice centres, foreign exchange offices, the Reichs-
bank, the Palestine Office . . . Liquidation and optimum realisation of assets,
management and utilisation of blocked balances, items to barter . . . transfer
questions . . ."*

*So how does that read? Do you think this is how I should go about it? What's
certain, in any case, is that I will primarily represent clients in tax and foreign
exchange matters. Legal advice regarding foreign exchange issues is becoming
increasingly important. And the pseudolegal "Aryanization" of Jewish property
will take up more and more of my time, and Trude's along with it, as will transfer
and sale of real estate, execution of wills, receivership, and trusteeship.*

*Moreover, payments in kind are likely to increase through emigration and pro-
fessional obsolescence: we Jews, in particular, will no longer be allowed to train a*

* The *Central Verein Zeitung* or *C.V. Zeitung* [*Central Association Newspaper*] was the weekly newspaper of the Central Association of German Citizens of the Jewish Faith.

new generation of lawyers. So my desk will hardly be empty. Visits and calls from Berlin show that I still enjoy a distinguished reputation going back to my heyday, which works in my favour. So Trude will have to prepare many pleadings, draw up many records of proceedings, and prepare many handouts. The fact that we speak the same language, and not just legally, proves to be a further advantage.

I can also speak with Trude about feelings of extreme anxiety. There are repeated, private reports of assaults, indeed torture, sometimes even with fatal consequences. In addition, our brave Hilde Benjamin tells of truly monstrous things. Clients pass on horrific stories from their circle of friends and acquaintances, and occasionally from their own families. One truly has the feeling that Hitler and his followers have opened Pandora's box. What else may be in store for us?

Come what may and whatever the future may hold, I will stand by the motto I've adopted from Goethe: "In face of all forces maintaining defiance."

| 43

Measures were even taken against literature! As early as April 29, the entire board of the German Publishers and Booksellers Association passed an Immediate Program for the German Book Trade. Point 10 stated: "With regard to the Jewish question, the board entrusts itself to the guidance of the Reich government. The board will carry out government directives on behalf of its own sphere of influence without reservation."

A working committee from the Ministry of Propaganda drew up a "list of undesirable literature." Here alone, twenty-four authors and sixty-four titles of S. Fischer Verlag* were listed. Negotiations resulted in the exclusion of several names and titles, but the committee stuck to its overall demand. The publisher was to delete ten authors and a total of fifty titles from its list. Chief Editor Oskar Loerke wrote in his journal, "Books by new authors came back in bales," as if sales had "suddenly stopped."

That same year, 1933, Ina Seidel was preparing a selected edition of poems for her colleague. They planned to call it *Die Frau und die Tiere* [*The Woman and the Beasts*], poetry by Gertrud Kolmar. The typescript was submitted to S. Fischer Verlag, which rejected it.

Nevertheless, the potential volume is part of the history of her oeuvre, and the titles of the selected poems have been handed down. The poet accepted what her editor had compiled. I can just imagine this particular book project.

---

* S. Fischer Verlag is a leading German publishing house.

Here are two verses from one poem, "Schwarzwild" ["Wild Boar"], that Ina Seidel chose for the planned volume. This is a poem in which, for the sake of poetry, Gertrud Kolmar forgot her mission to love animals:

> Mild the day, laden with fruit,
> Bread in sheaves, pain, and thanksgiving,
> Everything that from tangled paths
> Sank into the golden pannier:
> A sickle strikes about the branches,
> You stride, man and reaper,
> Bearing away the deliciously heavy load,
> To the dark blue houses.
>
> White clouds of cloth blow freely,
> A loose corner throws out a band;
> Colorful apple, red rose
> Dance on the basket's rim
> In the walls, in the rubbish,
> In the forested cove,
> Floating on sunken puddles,
> Yellow rose, colorful fruit.

The second set of closely related topics is the voice of the child whom Gertrud Kolmar was never able to call "My child." But this is the collective title of a half-dozen, very different poems that were chosen for the volume. These are the last two verses of "Eisvogel" ["Kingfisher"], a poem with a sublime, Kolmar ending:

> Oh, I know him well, the spirit-bird,
> Who sharply stabs a twitching something at me,
> Breaking out of billowing gray chambers
> And tearing into the sky.
>
> Above, crystal laws crack,
> Torrents let loose, limitlessly hot and quiet,
> And flames lower a golden net
> Over a cherry tree in April.

Now we come to an example, "Die Fahrende" ["The Traveler"] from the cycle *Weibliches Bildnis* [*Female Portrait*]. With Walter Benjamin's help, it appeared in the *Neue Schweizer Rundschau* [*New Swiss Review*] in 1929 and was reprinted in 1933 in the anthology *Herz zum Hafen* [*Heart as Harbor*], "present-day

women's poetry edited by Elisabeth Langgässer in collaboration with Ina Seidel." Considering Kolmar's modest expectations, it was a success and, as these
lines show, it was well deserved:

> All railways steam into my hands,
> All large harbors toss ships about for me,
> All hiking trails plummet into the grounds,
> Taking their leave here; because at the other end,
> Greeting them cheerfully, I stand smiling.
>
> If I could only just grab a corner of this world,
> I would also find the other three, would knot the cloth,
> Hang it on a fastener and wear on my neck,
> Flushed cheeks, inside the globe,
> The brown seeds and smell of Calvilles.
>
> Heavy iron grating clatters out my name for a distance,
> My spying steps lurk about a hunchbacked house;
> Long-lost pictures turn back into their frames,
> Blind desire and wishes of the lame
> Ladle into my travel mug, which I thirstily drink dry.
>
> Naked, fighting arms I plow through deep lakes,
> I pull the sky into my shining eyes.
> At some point it's time to stand still on the path,
> And look at the meager stocks, while, hesitatingly going home,
> No income but the sand in my shoes.

This is evocative role-playing, considering that Gertrud Kolmar herself was certainly not a traveler in East Havelland. And so it again becomes necessary to
place her life's story and oeuvre on parallel tracks.

| 44

Before I begin to discuss Georg Benjamin again, I must reveal my main source
of information about him. It comes from the biography *Georg Benjamin* by
Hilde Benjamin. She got to know the Chodziesners through Walter and Georg:
"I have photos in which the children of both families are pictured together."

Hilde, née Lange, rode out to Finkenkrug for the first time "on a late summer's day ... This visit may have been in connexion with my law office, but

could also have taken place after my husband's first arrest. As I recall, it had mainly to do with Father C., who had sent me my first clients for my law practice. But I ended up in the garden with Trudchen, and three images pop up in my memory: the big garden that seemed to merge with the forest, a large dog ... and delicately blooming red crocuses. At this time, a conversation also took place between Georg and Walter Benjamin in which the brothers spoke about poems by Trudchen that Georg and I didn't know."

Hilde Benjamin on "Uncle Ludwig's" daughter: "If I should try to explain Gertrud's nature, I would put it this way: The wall behind which Gertrud lived was not only one of inconspicuousness and peculiarity. She gave off an aura of both great calm and inner disquiet. She seemed dark, but not gloomy. Dark, warm colours are what appeared to surround her. She was tart, full of mild bitterness. She made a cool, but never cold, impression."

After the war, the woman who wrote these reminiscences of Gertrud Kolmar was vice president of the Supreme Court of the German Democratic Republic. She was minister of justice from 1953 to 1967. Due to her harsh sentences, including two death sentences, she was referred to as "bloody, red Hilde" and even "The Red Guillotine." The chairman of the State Council, Walter Ulbricht, dismissed her for rigorousness that was no longer in keeping with the times. But she got a professorship and subsequently wrote the book during retirement. It is harsh. As a writer, she was mainly interested in the organizational methods of former leftist associations like the Association of Socialist Doctors. Playing down my aversion to the author and filtering out the ideological parts, I have already consulted the book and shall continue to do so.

Ten days after his brother Walter had left Germany, Georg received a letter of dismissal from the state commissioner for business transactions of the borough mayor. He had meanwhile become an intern at the Infant Welfare Station in Neukölln.

On April 12, a form letter also arrived from the chief of police, signed "on behalf of" same. It said, "Under Section 1 of the Decree of the Reich President for the Protection of the People and the State I hereby order that, in the interest of public safety, you be taken into custody until further notice."

Georg was picked up by policemen, who behaved properly. They delivered him to the municipal prison at police headquarters on Alexanderplatz. He was admitted to the Berlin-Plötzensee Prison at the end of April. The "Plötze" was run by the police and Gestapo, so raids or attacks by SA detachments were nearly impossible. His wife was allowed to visit him.

In May 1933, they searched her apartment and law office: "Approx. seventy-five pounds of books and eleven folders" were seized on receipt. The Nazis defined them as incriminating evidence. She was a lawyer who had chiefly undertaken the defense of workers and Communists. The most spectacular case with the slipperiest consequences was her defense of the landlady who rented a room to Horst Wessel,* the Third Reich's highly celebrated "martyr." He was especially known for the "Horst Wessel Song" ("The SA marches, ranks tightly closed"), which became a second national anthem that was sung at nearly every event. The SA *Sturmführer* and his girlfriend lived as lodgers in the home of Elisabeth Salm. Wessel refused to pay rent for his girlfriend. At a local pub, the landlady asked members of the German Communist Party for help. The men saw the matter differently than the landlady had envisaged, and several of them accompanied her. Hated for his brutality, Wessel was gunned down and died six weeks later. Wessel's apotheosis and martyrdom were soon taken up on behalf of the "movement."

In the 1930 trial against the Communist perpetrator, Salm, Hilde Benjamin argued for her acquittal. After all, Salm could not have foreseen the result of her appeal for help. The lawyer, in turn, could have not foreseen the consequences that would arise three years later from this case. They accused her of "defending Communists and accepting fees for their defence from the Rote Hilfe,"† and she would make a further donation to their cause: she would be forced to close down her office before the end of May.

Georg was shut out of the Berlin Association of Statutory Health Insurance Physicians: "Grounds for your employment as a health insurance physician: *Bezirksverordnete* [district assemblyman] of the Communist Party." In addition, the decree of April 22 said, "The employment of health insurance physicians of non-Aryan origin, and the employment of health insurance physicians who have been active in the Communist sense, shall be terminated."

Georg Benjamin was transferred to the Sonnenburg Concentration Camp in late summer. His family now feared the worst! In June, Walter Benjamin wrote, "My brother is in a concentration camp. God only knows what he will have to go through there."

| 45

After the first quarter of 1933, there were no more professional options for Gertrud Chodziesner. What "Aryan" family would have taken a Jewish tutor into

---

* Horst Wessel, a Nazi storm trooper, wrote the lyrics to the "Horst Wessel Song" in 1929 and was shot to death in 1930. Nazi propaganda chief Joseph Goebbels claimed Wessel had been murdered by Communists and turned him into a martyr of the Nazi movement. The song became the official song of the Nazi Party and later a national anthem of Germany.

† The Rote Hilfe [Red Aid] was a leftist prisoner support group.

their home or apartment at that point? With very few exceptions, Jewish families were already under increasing pressure and couldn't afford a tutor. Gertrud was now entirely dependent upon her father. She therefore continued to do household chores and office work.

The familiar life in Finkenkrug now became a kind of camouflage, the most inconspicuous life they could possibly lead. But social control in neatly arranged settlements, such as villages and posh residential areas, was much tighter than on the streets of a large city. The future thus depended a great deal on the neighbors' attitudes. If people didn't consciously watch, did they keep a constant eye on them as instructed? What could they have possibly noticed even so? The old man walked a German shepherd or two . . . The little woman worked in the garden . . . Father and daughter with a greyhound . . .

Yet sister Hilde attests to the fact that they were afraid: "We didn't dare laugh out loud in my father's garden anymore. . . . People turned around on the street, and you slowly felt like a hunted creature. . . . My father, who was the only Jew in the suburb, once asked a woman he knew well not to visit or be seen with him so often because she might get into serious trouble."

Were the Chodziesners also in danger of being attacked? Or did a remnant of respect shield them for the time being? The successful lawyer with an aura of someone who exuded authority . . . The little, unprepossessing daughter that people probably knew little about, just that she looked after the house and garden in an exemplary manner. Her book of poems certainly wasn't on display at the Finkenkrug stationery shop, and there could hardly have been a bookstore in town. So the daughter touchingly took care of her father and attracted attention only when she took the white, buoyantly strutting borzoi for a walk.

What was daily life in Finkenkrug like for father and daughter? Gertrud saw herself as both a homemaker and a domestic servant. So she took over most of the shopping in stores at the train station. And did she ever walk, cycle, or ride to Falkensee, which was somewhat bigger and had more for sale? Or did the cook and housekeeper Helene Köpp do the shopping? Or Wally, the maid? Would she have been reproached with: How can you shop for Jews? How can you houseclean for Jews? How can you wash their dirty clothes for them?

If Gertrud went shopping, what must she have heard and felt? Did they push her back or shove her aside? And did they ever weigh her purchases extra well? Did a woman put something in her shopping bag while going by? And finally, did she walk through the village with her head held high or with her head lowered, seeing nothing so as not to be seen?

In considering their social circle in Finkenkrug, I would imagine and am almost certain that father and daughter had very few contacts. That's how they both wanted it. Family came first, and there were still visitors from Berlin. Was there anyone else? Did Papa Ludwig always go for walks alone with the German shepherd, which may also have been for protection? Did another pensioner join him? Or did even close acquaintances keep their distance?

Here's a version based on known patterns of behavior: "Please understand, Counsellor Chodziesner, that it is purely a formality and in no way detracts from our deep respect for you and your daughter. But in my prominent position, I simply cannot afford to show up here too often . . ." Another possible scenario: "We've known each other long enough, esteemed colleague, and of this you can be sure: nothing can diminish my respect for you and your dear daughter. But circumstances unfortunately prevent our lovely chats from continuing as usual in your home . . ." If they met people on the street or came within sight of others, did people avoid the Chodziesners, steer clear of them, want nothing more to do with them on the face of it? After all, it was well known that even a greeting could get a person in trouble if someone reported him or her.

Letters addressed to father or daughter were doubtless monitored: "Concerning surveillance of Jewish mail: The president of the Reich Post Office Administration in Berlin has instructed post office directors, insofar as they consider it necessary, to submit all suspicious postal items that come from Jews or are addressed to Jews to their local Gestapo office or police administration to be checked. Post office directors should first get in touch with their local Gestapo or police office concerning the enforcement of this measure. I ask that post office directors also be contacted locally and arrangements be made in keeping with the local situation. In general, it will suffice for suspicious international mail to be inspected."

We must therefore bear this in mind when reading Kolmar's letters. From the approximately 165 printed pages of the present edition of her letters, those from the period prior to 1933 take up just five pages or so. Most of the letters are addressed to her sister, Hilde, who immigrated to Switzerland in 1938. This means that, even in the Chodziesner home, international letters were written mainly with an eye to the censors. This must have had repercussions. Gertrud's letters were entirely apolitical as a result. Needless to say, her letters didn't give an account of what she heard or learned about the fate of other Jews. She wrote only about family matters, the garden, dogs, and woods.

On this score, Kolmar's letters furnish a historical perspective: "German classical writers like Goethe, though not Schiller, lived through the French Revolution, Napoleon, and the Napoleonic Wars. Yet there is very little about the events of the day in their works. Current events are sort of like impressionist paintings: if you look at them close up, all you see is a jumble of brushstrokes, dots and spots that only turn into a recognizable whole when you see them from a distance."

* * *

Even if Gertrud Kolmar didn't mention the book burning of May 10, 1933, or, in any event, we don't find any mention of a book burning in the surviving texts, this turning point must be emphasized. The events have been described so often, of course, that we need not repeat them here.

The book burning did not affect Gertrud Kolmar anyway. Very limited circulation is what protected her first little volume of poems from the actions of Nazi students. And such fragile protection could be revoked.

That same year, she arranged for a small publisher to issue a second selection of poems that she compiled herself. And she did so in darkly foreboding times.

| 46

Something completely unexpected happened in August, September, and October 1933: despite her extremely isolated life, Kolmar wrote poems in which she brought charges against Nazi terror.

As previously mentioned, her cousin Georg was placed in the Sonnenburg Concentration Camp in late summer, and this may have been the trigger. Hilde Benjamin could have reported on it during one of her visits. She may have told Gertrud what prisoners in concentration camps like Sonnenburg and Dachau had to endure. This may have provided the spark for several poems in the cycle *Das Wort der Stummen* [*The Word of the Voiceless*], a "humane document."

In 1978, *Das Wort der Stummen* appeared in East Berlin as a "licensed edition for the German Democratic Republic." The quarto edition was bound in posh linen, bore the subtitle *Posthumous Poems,* and included "Remembrances of Gertrud Kolmar" by Hilde Benjamin.

Jumping ahead chronologically in terms of our biography, Hilde later wrote: "Shortly after Uncle Ludwig's death, she gave me a little parcel of manuscript pages and said, 'Take it.' I took the pages, unread, as a bequest. As with my husband's letters and papers, I hardly dared look at them. They were wrapped up, hidden, and stored in a safe place."

Hilde Benjamin would take the little bundle of documents with her to Steglitz, where she lived with her son in her parents' home. Steglitz was a Nazi stronghold (!), and several of the poems she'd hidden there could have easily cost her life had they been discovered during a house search. So she buried these highly explosive texts in the garden. I read the following in one of Benjamin's letters from 1946: "When I took the little volume of poetry out of my garden." She was referring to the "little parcel" of manuscript pages she'd "moved" there for safekeeping.

The poems in this cycle also show Gertrud Kolmar as a peerless example. The poet's spontaneous, powerful responses to events in her country may well be unique. There is an existential difference between what exiles articulated from a relatively safe distance and what she wrote in a country that persecuted Jews! If the poem "Der Misshandelte" ["The Abused"] had been found in Finkenkrug by anyone in uniform, she would have found herself defenseless, in so-called protective custody, and open to assault:

> In my cell, the light burns all night.
> I stand by the wall daring not to sleep;
>
> For every ten minutes a guard comes to look at me.
> I keep watch at the wall. His shirt is brown.
>
> The others come back, talking among themselves
> They laugh at my cries and moans,
>
> They stretch my arms forcefully, calling it sport.
> My knees give out . . . finally they leave.
>
> I did not see trees, sun—are there any really?
> Or a place where a poor child still loves his father?
>
> Not a sign, no letter—yet I still have a wife!
> They said: "You're red; we'll beat you black and blue."
>
> They used rods of steel for whipping, and my body was just . . .
> Oh God! Oh God! No, no! I am not religious,
>
> I've never prayed in the field, in the hospital,
> Just evenings as a young boy, with Mother sitting on the bed.
>
> The earth is the crypt of a prison, the sky a blue hole.
> Do you hear me, I deny you! My God . . . ah, help me anyway!
>
> You are not: for if you were, you'd have taken pity on me.
> Jesus suffered for all of you; I suffer for myself alone.
>
> I stand, caving in, with water and some bread
> For hours and hours. How good, how good death is!
>
> Lying down . . . enclosed in a deep, dark shaft.
> No glaring lights. Just sleep. Just silence. Night . . .

"Anno Domini 1933" is a ballad about the murder of an Eastern Jew. I must emphasize this point, because the foreignness of Eastern Jews had become a considerable problem for the Jewish community, and Eastern Jews were frequently confronted with rejection. So an act of solidarity, let alone identification, was the exception:

> He stopped at a street corner.
> Soon hedged in by a crowd of people.
>
> His beard was black, his hair smooth.
> A large eastern face,
>
> Yet hard and weary from suffering.
> A long-forgotten hair shirt.
>
> He spoke and a child, moved by his hand
> Stood poor and icy:
>
> "It makes you sick, makes you pale,
> Like leprosy adorning your hate,
>
> Teaching you to stammer your curses,
> Turning its head into a flag,
>
> Eating away its heart with your plague,
> So that it leaves the small sky—"
>
> Then a bare fist reaches for words:
> "Swallow your own roaring filth!
>
> You dress up like Jesus Christ
> And are a Jew and Communist.
>
> Your curved nose, Levi, Saul,
> Here, take your blood's due and shut up."
>
> The shock threw him, the beating broke him.
> The people went along with it. He remained.
>
> In the hospital toward evening
> a doctor came to his bed. It was already over.—

A gallows, a crown of thorns
In the distant dust of the East.

A kicking boot, the strike of a club
In the third, Christian-German Reich.

Several questions come to mind: For what purpose and, above all, for whom did Gertrud Kolmar write these poems? So that they would disappear into a hole the minute she put them on paper? As a sign for posterity?

She would hardly have written these poems to present or read to her father. The old man would have been appalled: "For heaven's sake, Trude, you'll get us into a hell of a mess!" He could have reacted like this or in similar fashion. She herself realized the danger, indeed the mortal danger: "If they find this sheet of paper, they will grab me . . . by my bloody shock of hair and grind me through the darkest holes!"

But critically discerning poems like these will out, must go public, no matter how small the audience. Kolmar could only recite or present them to an inner circle—for example, her siblings—in which she was absolutely safe from denunciation. Afterward, she must have hidden the poems in the house or garden until she handed them over to Hilde Benjamin in 1942. So she stored these explosive verses in Finkenkrug for nine years, and they could have blown up in her face at any time!

We must put things into perspective. The quotations and poems in our commentary could create a stringent, uncompromising impression if we were to group them thematically around buzzwords like "Jew" and "concentration camp." Presented as blocks of text, they could certainly appear almost monolithic. And it's possible to draw conclusions that fulfill readers' expectations; for example, that would logically move us toward but would actually lead us away from uniting Kolmar's life and work. To get a differentiated portrait of the poet in this phase of her life, we must include the poetic context of such politically involved and morally accusatory poems.

For the first time since 1927, Kolmar jotted down the dates on which the poems were written. I have thus been able to draw up a chronological list for August, September, and October 1933. All twenty-two poems were written within this three-month period. The poems on Jewish and concentration camp themes induce a powerful, lasting effect. But Kolmar concurrently wrote poems on the themes of the lost child, gardens, and Robespierre. The following titles indicate the breadth of their thematic and linguistic spectrum:

On August 18, apparently as an addition to her rose cycle, she wrote "Die gelbe Rose" ["The Yellow Rose"], and "Robespierre" the very next day. On

August 20, she took a detour into Greek mythology with "Die Mutter der Grac-
chen" ["Mother of the Gracchi"]. Three days later, she jumped to a phase of
contemporary history that was part of her own life's story in "Der 9. November
18" ["November 9, 1918"]. Three days after that came "Heimweh" ["Homesick"]
on August 26, followed by "Milton" on August 27. The first in a series of poems
with a radical, new approach that arouses admiration, accompanied by awe,
came in September: "Wir Juden" ["We Jews"] on September 15 and "Im Lager"
["In the Camp"] two days later. She put the sketch for the latter aside. "Ewiger
Jude" ["Wandering Jew"] appeared three days thereafter, and "Lied der Schlange"
["Song of the Serpent"] on September 21. On the following day, "Die Gefangenen" ["The Prisoners"] changed themes again. "Garten" ["Garden"] came two
days later, and "An die Gefangenen" ["For the Prisoners"] the following week.

The sequence in which the collection was written continues although, strictly
speaking, it is not a cycle. Yet the previous compendium already makes it difficult
to establish connections between actual biographical situations and the origin
of the texts. Isolated poetic events seem to manifest without continuity. In one
poem, torturers stand accused, and the next day a murderer like Robespierre is
feted. Politics of the day are next, followed by a celebration of mythology on the
day after that. Is it possible to take a basic substance that we might call "linguistic protoplasm" and crystallize the most diverse, contrasting forms of poetry out
of it?

| 47

Expounding on current affairs and their transformation into poetry . . . In the
epilogue to her commentary, Regina Nörtemann quoted from an article, "Im
Konzentrationslager" ["In the Concentration Camp"], pseudo reportage by an
English columnist about the Sonnenburg Concentration Camp that appeared
in the September 17, 1933, edition of the *Berliner Tageblatt*.* More or less con-
temporaneous pseudo reportage on Reich Radio about a visit to a concentration
camp near Berlin said everything was legal and in order . . . They asked an old
Communist whether he was satisfied with the provisions and generally happy.
He always answered in a single syllable, "*jau*" ["yes"]. And that was the end of it.

The following quotation is from the print version:

During my visit, there were several hundred people in a large courtyard.
Several of them marched to a song, while another group was enjoying a

---

* The *Berliner Tageblatt* [*Berlin Daily Newssheet*] was one of the most important liberal newspapers
in Germany.

game. All were involved in things they appeared to really love. "What is your name?" I asked one of them. "Von Ossietzky." The commandant told me that this man was the former publisher of *Die Weltbühne.** "I am not a Communist," the prisoner explained to me. "I am a Social Democrat and haven't changed my mind." But many other prisoners admitted that their previous Communist ideas were entirely wrong and that, if they were to be released, they would have nothing more to do with politics.

In addition to this entire pack of lies, the article praised the "friendly tone amongst guards and prisoners . . . Yes, there was severe discipline. But no fear, no terror tactics."

This portrayal, most certainly coordinated with the Ministry of Propaganda, culminated in the claim "that all these rumours of terror tactics in the concentration camps are empty talk."

That same day, Gertrud Kolmar drafted her poem "Im Lager" ["In the Camp"]. We must respect the fact that the poet set the sketch aside, so I shall only include the first few lines:

> Those walking about here are just bodies
> They no longer have souls,
> Just names in a clerk's book,
> Prisoners: Men. Boys. Women.
> Their eyes staring blankly

Here are several more phrases from the sketch: "Strangled, trampled, blinded . . . No heart, no more heart to affront! . . . . Only fear, only horror on their faces, / When a bullet takes a victim in the night . . ."

Assuming the Chodziesners even subscribed to the *Berliner Tageblatt,* read this particular edition, or heard the pseudo reportage on the radio, the propagandistic whitewashing could hardly have touched off a draft of such dark intensity. If Kolmar actually took note of newspaper articles or radio reports, then her sketch for this poem can only be interpreted as a decisive countergesture of emphatic proportions.

I have derived this attempt at an explanation from the following example in which text and context can be more easily aligned. Kolmar added a note to the title of her poem "An die Gefangenen" ["For the Prisoners"]: *At Harvest Festival on October 1, 1933.* We must now envision what was reported in the Nazi press, on Reich Radio, and fresh in the poet's mind.

---

* *Die Weltbühne* [*The World Stage*] was a German weekly covering politics, art, and business.

This was the date set for the Third Reich's first Harvest Festival to take place at Bückeberg bei Hameln. Nazi architect Albert Speer designed the layout on the slope, which included platforms for leading party figures, flagpoles by the hundreds, and so on. The press set the mood in the words of a pastor, no less: "Leadership of a man sent to us by God . . . In addition to blood and race on native soil . . . The God-given and natural foundation for a people . . ." This was no simple gathering but a mass of half a million farmers and their wives. They cleared a pathway, the Führerweg, through the huge crowd. To heighten suspense, Hitler intentionally arrived late, strode along the planned route . . . to the sounds of the "Badenweiler March"* and frenetic cheering. Hitler, the "people's chancellor," accepting flowers, clasping hands. The six-hundred-meter "way through the people" took him three-quarters of an hour, his ascent to the summit both direct and symbolic.

One participant's account:

> It got dark early. Powerful floodlights illuminated Bückeberg. The military band began to play "Now Thank We All Our God," and the prayer of thanksgiving intoned by hundreds of thousands of voices rang out across the square, hill, and wide plain. It was 7 o'clock. The führer's voice came out of the darkness of the night, amplified a thousandfold by the huge loudspeaker. Indeed, it was not only the world's greatest but also the most thrilling rally of this sort ever organized in honour of the peasantry. A roar, a veritable storm of jubilation rang out across the square, interrupted only by the "Horst Wessel Song."

This was pretty much the image of the event that was conveyed to the public. The poet's pseudo-dedication reveals a new facet of her work. She becomes sarcastic and responds to the rhetoric of power with an opposing gesture.

"An die Gefangenen" ["For the Prisoners"] has a powerful prelude, expresses highly dramatic solidarity with the victims of the regime, and voices certainty that the mere discovery of this poetic manuscript could bring about the very experiences she has accusingly brought to mind. And the closing verse has the tenor of a baroque *vanitas:*†

> Oh, I want to sing you a song, created by the earth itself,
> The mountain's black firs flutter wildly,
> The sea foam is swept up like refuse
> The fleeing clouds tearing—O God, we humans are dwarfs.

---

* The "Badenweiler March" is a Bavarian military march.
† A *vanitas* is a painting that serves as a reminder of the inevitability of death.

Thoughtfully, I brought three wise words together
Instead of sounds squirting like hot blood from the heart,
That race along, like an alarm bell screaming at midnight,
When apocalyptic riders sit upon maned horses.

And I should put my fist down within your torments,
That it may be consumed, cracked by licking flames,
Oh, along with you, convulsing, beaten, hungry,
I, too, should crawl over a weeping stone, bound in iron.

That will come, yes, that will come; make no mistake about it!
For if they find this sheet, they will arrest me.
Lord, grant that I, fully awake, may place myself before your great,
    holy court,
At the moment they drag my bloody shocks through dark holes!

You, girl of seventeen, whose locks they tear to pieces,
You, poor young man whose ribs they cruelly break,
I want to despair, want to cry out, wretched, injured,
And like a bird, sing to the needle piercing an eye!

What is life? A dunghill, where white narcissus bloom.
What's a body? It was beautiful, yet soon must end.
What is the soul? Just sparks, merely a little glow,
And they cover it up, cover it with quiet, powerful hands!

| 48

Diaries give us the best sense of the atmosphere in the early months of the "Thousand Year Reich." The widely known diaries of the journalist Viktor Klemperer are a prime example. But I prefer to go exploring. The historian Willy Cohn's extensive diary, *Kein Recht, nirgends* [*No Justice, Nowhere*], was also published in 2006.

Cohn kept his given name, Wilhelm, because his parents revered the kaiser. Like the Chodziesners, the Cohns were from the province of Posen. In World War I, Wilhelm was a soldier in a field artillery ammunition supply train. He studied history after the war and dreamed of pursuing a career in academia. But antisemitic prejudice in the university system impeded and, in fact, prevented him from doing so. He therefore decided to become a teacher. Cohn taught history, German, and geography at a multidenominational grammar school.

He conducted historical research on the side, mainly on the Normans, so they occasionally addressed him as "Norman Cohn." He had two sons from a first marriage. His second marriage was to Gertrud (Trudi), who was twelve years his junior. They had two daughters. Cohn was forty-four years old in 1933, a popular pedagogue, a published historian, and a broker of "positive Judaism," what he called "my Zionist persuasion." And they had already dismissed him from teaching in 1933 because he was considered a "leftist." In August of that year, the couple were staying in Hohndorf so they could track developments from a reasonably safe distance:

Since they muzzle all free expression of opinion everywhere, a person can only write about what he thinks of this society in his diary. Even so, one must brace himself for all sorts of terror tactics. One of the two people who was taken into custody for the murder of the student, Steinfeld, has been let go. What does the life of a Jewish student matter! There is no more justice in Germany! Nowhere . . .

Göring supposedly gave a speech against the Jews on the radio that was full of the most dreadful vituperations. A direct invitation to commit murder! The passions of the masses have been whipped into a frenzy. Just like the Middle Ages! Worse in some ways! One would gladly not think about all of this, but it's not possible!

Nonetheless, it is very difficult to totally banish the love of Germany from one's heart! Yet one really must! Never before has a campaign been conducted that was so full of spiteful slander! And they call themselves a civilized race! . . .

Yesterday, SA hordes forced their way into the court, shouting "Out with the Jews," and beat the lawyer Maximilian Weiss to a pulp. The day before yesterday, they dragged the general manager Barnay into the Ostwitz Forest and struck him down with truncheons and dog whips. That is the Third Reich. . . .

All Jewish judges and public prosecutors in Breslau have been let go, even the baptized ones, albeit I took a certain delight in the misfortune of the latter. Lawyers have been told not to go to court, not even to their offices. These are the circumstances under which we live. At the same time, one has the feeling that he's been cut off from the world altogether, because the newspapers don't say anything about it. . . .

Perle told me that the lawyer Jonny Schneider was beaten with a dog whip in front of everyone in his office and let go from his position as legal adviser to the Oder boatmen. That is how this society debases human dignity. A civilian and seventeen brownshirts showed up at his office! This affected me deeply! And people now call this the building of a nation! . . .

All sorts of things have been happening again lately. People have been dragged into "brown houses" and beaten horribly. What I consider much worse than these violent clashes is the destruction of livelihood, the ban on kosher slaughtering, sacking people! How many people are left with nothing overnight? How many people have nervous breakdowns from the daily anguish? Everything is strained to the breaking point. The hardest hit, of course, are those who never thought about the shake-up of their bourgeois existence....

I am rather depressed today. Whenever I take up the subject of escape in the diaries, it's not entirely successful. There's no longer any point in considering diversion of any sort outside of the home. I won't and can't think about the future at the moment. One simply has to put everything on hold! If German Jews would only take a lesson from this, finally stop trying to assimilate, and live their own Jewishness! . . .

Deep down, I am getting more and more used to the idea of emigrating. I believe that, in the long run, people will find it difficult to bear things. Acts of terror are on the rise, and foreign policy problems are increasing along with them. Of course, both interact with each other: mousetrap! Thus, reading the paper every day is quite agonizing, although necessary in the end!

| 49

Returning to Kolmar, she wrote a poem titled "Die jüdische Mutter" ["The Jewish Mother"]. It joins together the theme of persecution of the Jews and the theme of the imagined child:

> I have only this child, born in need,
> Am a poor widow, a dressmaker.
> My little child is human, has a nose, mouth, and ears,
> And beautiful dark eyes that always shine at me.
>
> He wants to learn, to count, read, write,
> Doesn't throw the pen down and keeps his notebook polished,
> Wants to share his little efforts with all the others.
> The teacher seats him apart on a bench for Jews . . .
>
> Because he's just one, the others are the majority;
> They tease him and splash ink onto his clothes.
> He often likes to play with his little girlfriend in the courtyard,
> But they all drive him away and refuse him.

If a door gets smeared, a glass picture frame smashed,
A latch bolt loosened: The Jew did it.
I may not cry, my heart alone sobs angry and bitter—
My child, my child bears the sins of their world,

Envy, spite, cowardly rage, all their disgrace,
Upon shoulders that still cover the child's blue angel wings.
You, so deluded by your own creations,
Do you think, when you awaken my silent tears,

Do you think it righteous to pray together in churches,
Accepting what the pastor says in your comfort,
And then going and kicking this soul like an animal?
Oh, even the respectable don't do that to animals!

From within your ranks you throw sharp pebbles at him,
You make him stand in the corner, shy and alone,
You want to tear his colorful new apron from him,
You paint a swastika into his book.

You! You! Oh noble men of honor, worse than rabble!
I may not curse you, who are wasting and withering;
For the stern judgment of God still stares from within this grim house.
Get up, my child, and accuse them with your youthful words!—

He sleeps. Please God, in his dreams
Don't allow worries to germinate, the bitter seeds that you sow.
I'll turn to my lamp, hem skirts again,
Just a poor Jewess, who sews your clothing for money.

| 50

At the end of 1934 and the beginning of 1935, Gertrud Kolmar let a Jewish man
be heard in her first theater piece. She set it back in time to the final phase of the
French Revolution and the Reign of Terror, yet it was also timeless and exemplary. He spoke about problems that twentieth-century Jews must also have
experienced. The very first instance proved applicable: "Aryans" refused to pay
outstanding debts to their Jewish business partners. This soon became something people took for granted:

I am an old Jew. Many years ago, I was a young Jew. And I wanted to earn my
doctorate, become a learned man like Maimonides, but nothing came of it.
I had to become a tradesman like my father, and I had to bargain all my life.
Then came a decree, then another decree, a restriction, then another restriction,
after that a prohibition and another prohibition, and trading wasn't worth it
anymore. I'd saved a little money, and I lent it at interest. You call it usury! What
was I supposed to do? If someone is hungry and has no bread, he scrapes the
last dregs from the bottom of the barrel. I'd have gladly engaged in another
trade if I could have. But when the due date came, not a single debtor paid.

Wherever he went to collect on his loans, people presented him with receipts
with false signatures on them, and they were from the exact same judge to
whom he turned for help. There, he was told, "The slips are genuine. These are
honourable folk. Christians. But you are a Jew and a swindler. You will apolo-
gise and pay a penalty right now."

That ruined him. In a small room of the Tuileries "that served as the official
chambers of the security committee," the old Jew told fellow prisoners about the
history of Jewish persecution:

A person went walking, stick in hand. Guard dogs barked away at us and
people cursed us continually. If an epidemic hit a town, a Jew had poisoned
the well. And if a child did not show up, then a Jew had cut it to pieces. There
are the gallows. There is the rope they used to pull us up. There is the wheel
they broke us on, there are the block and the rack! They strangled us with
swords in Poland, beat us with truncheons in Germany. In Spain, they lit piles
of wood and burned us alive. The destroyers ran after us with flails, shovels,
and axes. Holy books were torn to shreds, rooms stripped bare, children were
torn from their mothers, and mothers . . . were destroyed. They squeezed,
crushed, and trampled us like grapes. Our blood flowed like wine. A good
wine, a strong wine . . . and now we are grey ashes. We trembled, wailed, and
wept, but God did not bury us with Ashur and Babel . . . Israel is like the dust
of the earth: everyone treads on it underfoot, but the dust survives all!

A stage direction follows: "He raised his voice to such a degree in uttering the
final words that one of the two gendarmes woke from his slumber and shouted,
'Shut up, Jew!'"

| 51

So what types of texts did the Third Reich celebrate? With what kinds of material must Gertrud Kolmar have been confronted? In what type of atmosphere

was she writing? What seeped in, what rolled over her in waves via press and radio?

She wrote poetry in a linguistic environment contaminated with Nazi jargon. It would be easy to quickly assemble an anthology with a selection of former poetry collections, but I will focus on just one figure in the Nazi literary scene.

As "state poet," Gerhard Schumann (1911–95), was feted from the very start. He was what we might call a trendsetter today, a leading voice in the literary establishment of those years. The poetry of this SA *Sturmbannführer* and head of the SA *Hochschulamt* [Office of Higher Education] enjoyed widespread circulation, at least according to how he listed it later on: twenty thousand copies for one volume of poetry, fifty thousand for another, up to seventy thousand. Did he round up belatedly? Anyway, Schumann was among the elite guard of Nazi poets.

Lines from a martial hymn to the führer, such as those that people like to cite in studies and documents about literature in the Third Reich, need not be recycled here, as they don't lead anywhere. We will therefore examine only one published volume of Schumann's poetry, *Schau und Tat* [*Vision and Action*].

The volume opens with an initial *Sonettenkranz*,* an elaborately constructed literary form from the past. The formally correct concoction becomes problematic by way of content. There is no overt or hidden propaganda: in fact, the content is absolutely apolitical. It creates a heroic, momentous impression on a solemnly dramatic keynote with murmurings of so-called death and the life to come. Of course, it gets transposed and embellished with clichés, linguistic obfuscations, and empty formulas.

I've marked the following in pencil: "Star above those hours . . . united through blood . . . found the core of being . . . blue night benediction . . . brought deep sorrow . . . dark power . . . fire of souls . . . choose the boundless tempest of sounds . . . devote oneself to the word in the dark peal of bells . . . deep boundlessness . . . blazingly sweet desire in the womb of woman . . . devout vision . . . shivers of illumined understanding . . . gentle waves of a woman's love . . . rich, dewy melodies . . . effervescent stirring up of juices . . . sighing souls joining together . . . the deepest . . . consecration . . . quiet tears . . . longing for a purer completeness . . . shyness in the loins . . . but they always rattle at the last doors."

And everything "becoming round and complete." Now I know what a closed system is. New experiences and new wording are out of the question. The opening and closing garland of sonnets was formulated to stand the test of time, to generate conviction and lasting value. A monumental impression was to be imparted, marble and bronze were to be allied. But this more

---

* A *Sonettenkranz* [crown of sonnets] is a sequence of connected sonnets.

closely resembles applying an antique finish to a row of columns* than the balcony of a half-timber house with a bull's-eye window and flower boxes for geraniums.

Just how innovative Kolmar was in a period of highly celebrated epigonism thus becomes clear. The exceptional quality of her poetry becomes even more obvious against the background of what was then conventional and would soon become habitual. While so many joined the call of linguistic dictators, she preserved her own unique voice. She was resistant to slogans, as she had already shown in the First World War.

In a time and place where Schumann was among those who controlled the literary scene, Gertrud Kolmar would hardly have stood a chance, not even as an "Aryan" poet. She might have been able to publish one or two poems in *Das Innere Reich* [*The Inner Reich*]. But publishing a book would have been rather unlikely because the men who controlled the book trade would have had little use for her texts. Political awakening was, indeed, frequently celebrated in that highly conservative atmosphere. Yet these high and mighty men were incapable of a newly articulated awakening amid altered parameters: the little lady in Finkenkrug succeeded where they failed. She hardly ever adopted the conventions that were celebrated back then. Even if she wrote sonnets, they were not about heroes but roses. Apart from that, she was not tied to traditional forms, such as odes or elegies. To the extent that he didn't already fete himself, a Schumann was celebrated precisely because of such attachments to traditional forms. Whereas he celebrated closed forms, Kolmar produced free verse, most decisively in the late cycle *Welten* [*Worlds*]. A Schumann, on the other hand, subjugated himself to a pseudo-classical tone and expected his readership to also be subservient to this type of narrative: poetry as a symbol of power, a superstructure built upon old pedestals and foundations, a sermon in secularized "Canaan tone."† A Schumann was always the same. He would surely have preferred to hear, "He remained true to himself." People remained true to their convictions, and oaths of loyalty were among the rituals of the period.

None of this elicited a response from the poet. She wrote her poems single-mindedly and unswervingly in the roaring echo chamber of that time. The poetry she wrote in her best, most intense texts lies well outside the mainstream; that is, the pseudo-lyrical idiom of the day.

---

* The reference to an antique finish on a row of columns may refer to Schumann's use of classical poetic forms, such as sonnets and odes.

† The reference to "a sermon in secularized 'Canaan tone'" may mean that the poetry had a biblical tone or hinted at connections to the Promised Land.

| 52

I get the distinct impression that, prior to the 1930s, the fact that Gertrud Chodziesner was Jewish played hardly any role in her conscious awareness. What the Jewish scholar Gershom Scholem said about Walter Benjamin could also apply to her: "His almost total ignorance of things Jewish."

The Chodziesners also had no "attachment to Jewishness." The siblings had almost no religious upbringing, neither at home nor in school. As people often used to say back then, they came from a "nonreligious home." Judaism was still a nonissue for the Chodziesners.

The same was true of other families. In *Bilanz der deutschen Judenheit 1933* [*Balance Sheet of German Jewry in 1933*], Arnold Zweig noted, "As far as they were aware, nine-tenths of German Jews were nothing more than Germans with an element of Jewishness that they felt vis-à-vis religion, roots and family, and that could easily be housed within their sense of home[land]." There were families that went to church on Christian feast days and to synagogue on Jewish High Holidays. But the number of Jews for whom Judaism was of no further importance was considerably larger. A Berlin lawyer and *Notar* named Bollert made a typical remark: ". . . my wife is considered Jewish, although she's had nothing to do with Judaism for so much as one hour of her life."

In 1933, however, the topic of Judaism became relevant, indeed highly charged. "Say Yes to Judaism" became a slogan, particularly in Zionist publications of the period. Many secular Jews would even ask themselves, "What is Judaism anyway?" They could read the following in the *Philo-Lexicon*, put out by the German-Jewish publishing house of the same name: "Judaism is a spiritual-religious basis of membership in a community that, as a result of the absence of dogma in its belief system, is difficult to grasp and goes back to divine revelation based on common understanding among all Jewish schools of thought."

| 53

It was the middle of 1934. Here is an excerpt from an "overview of the political situation" in a report from one of the main Gestapo offices: "As cited in the previous progress report, whereas a portion of the Jewish population behaves quite modestly, another portion presents a rather arrogant demeanour. Some Jews cherish the hope that things will turn in their favour. This is supported by the fact that, as of late, many a letter sent from abroad to Jews here in Germany contains remarks like 'Stick it out: things will soon change in Germany! We know more here than you do there,' and 'Remain calm, there will be an end to it soon. It won't take as long as it has up to now!'"

"Harmful Equanimity" was the heading of a commentary in the *Central Verein Zeitung*:

> The other day, an English Jew who visited me before his return to his homeland said: "During my visit to Germany, nothing got my attention more than the remark made by some German Jews, 'It will be all right.' Our community thus denies the existence of severe problems with a single, short phrase and what one might call careless equanimity. One gets used to the idea and prefers to remain free of other people's worries.
>
> 'It will be all right!' People cannot revise fate to their advantage! Is that how Jews feel? . . . Judaism has taught us differently. Anyone who says, 'It will be all right' and leaves it at that, because he thinks he cannot have a say in his fate, is not a Jew. Resignation leads to ruin. The will to contend our fate shall preserve us."

Repatriation began. People who emigrated in 1933 experienced things that were worse than expected, whereas it appeared as though the situation in Germany had not gotten as bad as anticipated. Emigrants found little welcome in other countries for many reasons, including high unemployment in European countries; the ongoing effects of the Great Depression; admiration for Hitler in many cases; very little empathy for people who fled their country; pigheaded authorities; unfriendly, downright hostile inhabitants of foreign countries; and widespread antisemitism.

So many turned their backs on their host countries and, in the end, put their hopes in tolerable conditions in their country of origin. According to a report in the *Central Verein Zeitung*, about one-third of Jewish refugees returned.

Most emigrants had sought greener pastures in France. But in February 1934, hatred against Jews was running high in that country.

| 54

And here is an entry about Gertrud's brother, Georg. All that was known about him until now is that he was a qualified engineer. Otherwise, there wasn't much to say about him. Hilde's vain attempt was characteristic: "I'd like to say a few words about my brother, Georg, who, like his Benjamin cousin, was named after Mother's beloved father." Thereafter, the page in her little ring binder remained blank.

But Georg should not take second place to his sisters, especially not in the scheme of this "chronicle of a Jewish family" within the larger context of that era. The family offered to help me.

Wolfgang, Georg and Dorothea's only son, lives in Australia. He now goes by Ben and was formerly in a leading position in the oil industry. A heartening, fruitful email correspondence developed between us. And this included scanned documents, transmitted in a jiffy!

At twenty-three, Georg began working for one of the market leaders, C. Lorenz AG in the Tempelhof district of Berlin. The company specialized in "telephone and telegraph plants, and train signal building." In 1931, the company issued a reference that provided information about his fields of work:

> For the first two-and-one-half years, Mr. Chodziesner worked in the construction office, where he was mainly engaged in the development of circuitry for telephone and signal facilities. For the next five years, Mr. Chodziesner worked in various laboratories . . . For the three-month period before his departure from the firm, Mr. Chodziesner worked in the patent department where, in addition to his laboratory work, he was employed continuously from February 1930 on. Mr. Chodziesner particularly handled patent applications in the fields of telegraphy, wireless telegraphy, and telephony, including phototelegraphy.
>
> Mr. Chodziesner always completed the work assigned to him to our complete satisfaction.
>
> As a result of the takeover by the Gesellschaft für Telephon- und Telegraphenbeteiligungen m.b.H. [Telephone and Telegraphy Company, Ltd.] in Berlin W 56, Mr. Chodziesner has retired from our service and will take on a position with the company.

He was a highly rated specialist. A later reference, issued in Australia, allows us to deduce how greatly he was valued at the Lorenz firm. Chodziesner was most emphatically recommended as a very experienced, intelligent, reliable employee who was never sick and led a disciplined life.

He probably already lived this way at Dorothea's side. She was the daughter of the Rabbi Dr. Julius Galliner. Georg and "Thea" apparently met at a gymnastics club they belonged to and got to know each other better during canoe excursions, which were popular water outings in the vicinity of Berlin even then.

A later "certificate of employment" from the main patent office of the Gesellschaft für Telephon- und Telegraphenbeteiligungen, also in Berlin, attests to his resumption of work in 1931:

> Mr. Georg Chodziesner, a qualified engineer, has been employed as a patent engineer for the entire telecommunications area in our main patent office since May 1, 1931, following the takeover of the patent department

of C. Lorenz AG. He dealt with all matters of industrial property rights; namely, the drafting and handling of patent applications for German and foreign companies linked to the International Telephone and Telegraph Corporation, as well as the translation of documents written in English that arrived from overseas. . . .

Antenna construction, wireless navigation, telegraphy, and telex technology are among his areas of specialization. . . .

Furthermore, he was frequently called in to clarify points of law that, among other things, came up during patent litigation.

| 55

A child was born at the beginning of November in that fateful year of 1933. Gertrud lovingly watched and guided her progress. Her name was Sabine, the little daughter of Hilde and Peter Wenzel. In Nazi terms, she was the child of a "mixed marriage."

Her father originally worked in agriculture. Consequently, there is a reference issued by a baroness: "I hereby certify that Peter Wenzel was previously employed in my large agricultural concern." What's more important, however, is that he ended up as a bookseller.

In the rush toward obedience, the bookstore in which he worked had already fired him by 1933. He was likewise expelled from the Reich Literature Chamber.* Even booksellers had to join the chamber, and membership was compulsory. "Objectionable character" was the reason for his dismissal. This "Aryan" was "related to Jews" through marriage. One of his grandmothers also didn't conform to the guidelines of National Socialist racism. A surprising definition of his status reached me from South America: according to Peter K. Wenzel of Rio de Janeiro, his son from a second marriage, Peter Wenzel was classified as a "mestizo." The Wenzels temporarily left their little Berlin apartment and retired to Finkenkrug for about six months. So Sabine was present in the home of Counselor Chodziesner and his eldest daughter before she was even born.

Sabine quickly became the darling of the family, though less so in her mother's case. I will not disclose the full extent of what the daughter, who now goes by Sabina and lives in a beautiful coastal area of Brazil, wrote to me: a single word, "burdens," will suffice. The child found that Finkenkrug provided balance.

* The Reich Literature Chamber [*Reichsschrifttumskammer* or RSK] was a professional organization of writers under Propaganda Minister Joseph Goebbels that denied membership to non-Aryan authors and blocked publication of their works.

Sabina Wenzel sent me a sketch of her life and gave me permission to quote from it: "My grandfather was the most important role model in my early childhood years. He went for walks with me in his big garden in Finkenkrug, and we usually found goodies on a tree that we brought home to share. I was proud of being allowed to play on my grandfather's ivory chessboard, apparently a very special privilege, and also pleased that I slipped into my aunt's bed in the morning, and she read or told me stories. I even remember the stuffed animals on the bed in my room."

Hers was a childhood idyll in a time of growing pressures and threats, although they did talk about whether they should emigrate and start a new life in a foreign country. Hilde later wrote: "However, my father thought we could possibly starve abroad. And they wouldn't be able to harm my husband. Surely things were never as bad as they seemed, and not much would change in our business lives."

So the Wenzels started their own business in 1934, set up a bookstore with a second-hand section and lending library near Kurfürstendamm. They worked hard to build a new life and brought the baby to Finkenkrug many times.

For a while, Gertrud became a substitute mother. She looked forward to these visits for days in advance, while also dreading each and every good-bye. Looking back, she would write in a letter to Hilde in 1938: "Frankly speaking, in years gone by I sometimes positively dreaded it when the child was supposed to come stay with us for a longer period. It wasn't about the extra work, not at all. Rather, it was because her presence reminded me so powerfully and painfully of what I did not have."

Factition: My Dear Hilde, After the most recent, hearteningly numerous conversations in house and garden, it's about time for your father to pipe up again in writing. Naturally, those are the places where we talk about obvious things and up-to-the-minute news. For my part, I speak about the constant work at the law office, excursions with the dogs, Gertrud's enormous workload, my beloved granddaughter who, as I can attest, is in the best of hands with Trude, and about your work in the bookshop, of course.

This is where I shall make up for whatever I am loath to express at Gertrud's lovingly set coffee table: How I admire your and Peter's courage, your persistence, and the optimism that goes with them. All I can say or write in response to the fact that you and Peter have set up a bookstore in the hope of attracting more than just a Jewish clientele is, "My hat is off to you!" The two of you are so vulnerable! When I lie awake at night, I imagine a notice in a storm trooper showcase: "Jewess and husband related to her by marriage had the audacity to open a new bookstore in the heart of Berlin." I truly don't wish to paint a portrait of doom here. After all, you know what bravery you've mustered and what ultimately single-minded belief in a brighter future into the bargain. This has to be said loudly and clearly at some point, at least in written form.

And I must add immediately that no praise is too high for Peter's plan to collect and place typescript copies of Gertrud's poems in safekeeping. Our brave Hilde Benjamin has admittedly declared herself ready to do her share in protecting them. By virtue of being a bookseller, however, your husband will sooner be in a position to judge the value and importance of the works than Hilde in Stre-litz. Insofar as it is within my power, I will stand at Peter's side in this matter to advise and act, wherein it may well be better to ask for my advice and leave the action to my esteemed son-in-law. If he is prepared to make such a commit-ment, he must be firmly convinced of the importance of the maturing oeuvre. My nephew Walter may strongly confirm his assessment in turn. But since he is currently in exile, he can hardly arrange for individual publications, which makes the task your husband has set for himself all the more pressing. Despite many a well-nigh apocalyptic image, also fuelled by your fears of another war, there remains hope in a future where it will be easier for Trude to meet with a proper response to her work. As a jurist, I admittedly don't always find it easy to relate to her language (insofar as Trude allows me to take part in her work at all). And that is why Walter's and Peter's involvement provides me with exhilarat-ing proof of the importance of her poetic craft. If Peter's plan is successful, then this will also become a chapter, indeed a momentous one, in our family's little chronicle, a chronicle that will become increasingly necessary, the farther the fam-ily begins to scatter across the globe or intends to do so. Whereby I in turn feel justified and motivated to draw up this brief account of events, conveying submis-sions and offerings for the deferred and, hopefully, never to be repealed chronicle of a Jewish family. (I don't know if I've emphasised this sufficiently already: It can, of course, only deal with the history or histories of our present-day family, including the grandparents. We should not go further back into the past—leave that to the Aryans, who must establish their identity down to the umpteenth generation.)

I don't want to write about my present office activities and the growing prob-lems associated with them in this context, and one or two keywords will surely crop up in connexion with them anyway. Lately, another, decidedly more weighty keyword has come threateningly to the fore: war!

In view of an impending war, Peter's intention to place Trude's poetic oeuvre in safekeeping takes on a new urgency. And it is advisable to place several carbon copies in safekeeping at good distances from one another, rather than just a single typewritten copy of each.

In this case, I am thinking beyond the borders of Germany, a country I am in no way inclined to leave, just to state this clearly once again. As a German lawyer and Notar, I have done more than carry out my duty. Even in a time of persistently confused thinking, this must finally be recognised. And so be it if this recognition only results in people leaving me and mine in peace. Would that be asking too much? In this regard, the Reich leadership would do well to take a look at Italy, where hostility toward and hatred of Jews are not part of Fascist doctrine.

And so, having removed many of the objectionable parts, I shall end my notes for today and devote myself emphatically to gardening, which is one of the best antidotes to this uprooted, poisonous time in which we live. Many things have admittedly been built on and planted in sand here. But we shall yet obtain the needed humus so that nature may strengthen us in vital optimism.

In this spirit, Your Father

| 56

And now an interim report on Karl Josef Keller, with whom Gertrud Kolmar corresponded. (All of their letters went missing, were lost or destroyed.) She would later meet him in Hamburg for a brief journey they took together.

I shall borrow a sketch of Keller from Johanna Woltmann:

> He was born in 1902, lost his mother when he was six. A self-educated person, he learned to appreciate poetry in his youth but was obliged to do laboratory work for IG Farben in Ludwigshafen. Time and again, he went on big hikes and trips to escape the restrictions of everyday life. He traveled on board fishing vessels in the Atlantic, the North Sea, and the Mediterranean; lived with fishermen and sailors, and surrounded himself with a sailor's and "eternal hobgoblin's" mystique. A poet and adventurer, who espoused "wide open spaces, sea and waves." He was small in stature, had a lively temperament, liked to laugh.

Keller wrote four volumes of poetry, two of them published in 1933 and 1934. I have here the second one, *Gesänge an Deutschland* [*Songs to Germany*], which is more like a booklet of poems than a volume: thirty-two pages; that is, two printed sheets that fold down, paperback.

The titles of the first poems, together with each of the opening lines, set the tone: "Germany, O Mother"... "Germany, O Heart of Europe" ... Character-istic passages include: "For you, my country, are eternal youth among nations ... You are the jubilant awakening of all that lives ... Once you soar on starry flight, rushing upwards from most fertile native soil ... Turn homeward, oh people, silent in your increasing suffering, to the borders of your very own sacred realm . . . You rise from the depths of night, holy and born of mother . . . Safeguard, dragon conquerors, safeguard your radiant head!"

Final quotation and then that's enough (for me): "My people: / in blackest night / the fire of conflagration / was given to you." And so the world would be set ablaze five years hence.

In that same year of 1934, Gertrud Kolmar's book of poetry *Preussische Wappen* was published by Rabenpresse, a publishing house founded by Victor Otto Stomps. It contained selected poems from the unpublished *Das preussische Wappenbuch*, written in 1927–28.

Even this publication required compliance with regulations. Before printing a new work, every publisher was required to file an application at the *Reichsschrifttumskammer* (RSK) on Hardenbergstrasse in the Charlottenburg district of Berlin: "We address the following inquiry to you as to whether there are any reservations concerning the person N.N." Publication was only possible upon receipt of an *Unbedenklichkeits-Bescheinigung* [Certificate of Harmlessness] that, one hoped, did not involve any subsequent measures. In Kolmar's case, no such certificate has been documented. But chances are that such a procedure was followed, and publishers had to plan on long waiting periods. Could this also explain why the project, begun in 1933, would only be completed a year later?

We must add here that only RSK members could publish their work. The official terms were *Zwangsmitgliedschaft* [compulsory membership] and *Eingliederungspflicht* [obligatory affiliation]. Jewish authors were also obliged to join the RSK, which is just one of the Nazi administration's many inconsistencies.

However, it is highly unlikely that Gertrud Kolmar would have been accepted into the Reich Literature Chamber. She hadn't published enough to meet the admission requirements. One of the requirements read: "Anyone who engages in writing on a very limited basis, but has no principal occupation," shall be "released from obligatory affiliation with the RSK if activity is" limited to "12 small publications per year at most."

A few remarks about the small "Aryan" publishing house and its publisher: V. O. Stomps, known as "VeeO," was three years younger than Kolmar and came out with his first book of poems in 1920. Six years later, he self-published a second volume. Stomps did the typesetting and saw to the printing.

And how did the publishing house get its name? Stomps and his partner, Hans Gebser, didn't get along well at first with the used handpress that they bought: "We consoled ourselves with a bottle—the machine stood in the darkened corner and, with each additional schnapps, its contours reminded us more of a spooky raven, the hand lever of a wing raised to strike." In the end, they printed shortish texts with this machine, and these were in print runs of three hundred copies on average.

In the 1920s, the publishing house came out with the literary journal *Der Fischzug* [*The Catch*], "pages for art and poetry in the New Germany." This was followed by *Der weisse Rabe* [*The White Raven*] in the 1930s. A random sampling of authors of articles, other writings, and books: Gottfried Benn, Bert Brecht, Albert Ehrenstein, Max Herrmann-Neisse, Peter Huchel, Hermann Kasack, Oskar Loerke, and Paul Zech.

We have reports of chance meetings with the poet that confirm publication of the little poetry volume. The writer Horst Lange noted: "I ran into Kolmar two or three times at the Stallschreiberstr. office of V. O. Stomps in Berlin around the time that he published her *Preussische Wappen*. She gave the impression of being rather absentminded, unfocused, yet passionate. From a distance, she resembled Lasker-Schüler,* but was less hysterical, less carried away by fits of rage (than that one!). She was always calm and quiet instead, as though she were listening in on something. Her eyes were the most beautiful thing about her."

Oda Schaefer† also met her colleague Gertrud at the publisher's office: "Shy and unprepossessing, hidden within herself, she kept her distance from our Bohemian world."

Here are two more comments that Johanna Woltmann uncovered, the first from Jacob (or Jakob) Picard, Gertrud's writer colleague and a solicitor colleague of her father's: "Outwardly, she was rather plain, ran the household for her father. But she must have been attractive once, and one cannot forget her large, warm eyes."

The final statement came from Karl Escher, author of entertaining novellas, theater critic of the *Berliner Morgenpost*,‡ and writer of poetry that the actor Erna Leonhard-Feld incorporated into her recitations: "She didn't look like a poet at all: small, unattractive, far removed from any sort of female vanity. If you didn't know who she was, you would have to take her for some sort of minor character in a gentle, bourgeois novel, a governess or a poor relation. She spoke very little to friends and, even with respect to acquaintances, subjected them to extraordinary modesty. Only when her large, golden-brown eyes lit up in conversation, when she overcame her strange shyness about revealing herself, did you sense the uniqueness of her spirit."

* * *

* Else Lasker-Schüler was a German poet who wrote on Jewish themes in a romantic or expressionist style.

† Oda Schaefer was a German writer and journalist who became one of Germany's best-known poets in the 1950s.

‡ The *Berliner Morgenpost* was the morning newspaper of Berlin.

And how did she see herself? The way she dealt with her name points the way to some extent. In this case, she had several problems.

She never used her second given name, Käthe. She didn't entirely approve of Gertrud or "Trude" and liked "Trudchen" least of all. Actually, Trude sounds homely and hardly fits a poet draped in such linguistic finery. She would have preferred a different first name: Esther and Judith were desirable names, and she used both as titles of poems. These two names stood for strong women who became rescuers of imperiled Jews, whereas Judith, meaning "she who is blessed," is more iconographically rich for her beheading of Holofernes.

And Gertrud's surname? Hard to remember. And how was it pronounced? Gertrud supposedly pronounced her Polish surname softly, melodiously, and with a gentle resonance. Once she became a public figure, a poet's name was not insignificant. Customers who wanted to ask for one of her poetry volumes in a bookstore might have felt slightly uncomfortable in mentioning the name "Tschot-zies-ner" or "Kott-zies-ner." How did you know if you'd made a fool of yourself in front of a knowledgeable retail bookseller?

We've gotten used to the name Kolmar. She apparently never quite embraced it herself. I assume that her father had the first poetry volume published under the name Kolmar so that Gertrud wouldn't immediately be pigeonholed as the daughter of the famous jurist but as a person in her own right who had to first make a name for herself. Maybe Stomps also suggested that they stick with Kolmar in lieu of the unwieldy, Polish-Jewish name Chodziesner. She was also listed as Gertrud Kolmar in the *Insel Almanach*. A few of her poems were printed under the name Chodziesner, and the actor Leonhard-Feld identified them as such at her events. Gertrud never signed her letters with the name Kolmar, not even those to her colleague Picard, for example. He, in turn, sang the praises of "Gertrud Chodziesner's extraordinary verses" in public.

And today? Within the framework of equality, German texts call her Kolmar. Period. They occasionally add her first name. I prefer to use both names, but sometimes write, "die Kolmar" [the Kolmar]. This is not meant to sound disparaging or condescending but as a sign of respect.

And yet we must remain conscious of the fact that Gertrud Chodziesner would not have approved of persistently being called Gertrud Kolmar. Nevertheless, that's how it turned out, which is not to say that we may take it for granted.

In a detailed letter of October 1934, Kolmar reported to cousin Walter on the newly published volume of poetry. But, first of all, she mentioned a change of address: "Our street has been renamed and renumbered." Streets in the posh residential area were and still are named after painters. According to a circular from the Reich Interior Ministry, all streets that were named after Jews or

*Mischlinge** of the first degree had to be renamed. So the name Feuerbach was eliminated, although this measure was rescinded after the war. She wrote from the new address in Manteuffelstrasse:

> Dear Walter, I was so happy to see your handwriting again and, above all, to hear that you feel comfortable where you are now living. Aunt Clara told me at one point—a long time ago—that you were in Denmark, but couldn't furnish any particulars. Otherwise, I would have sent you The Prussian Coat of Arms even sooner, especially since I have you to thank for the inclusion of "The Lassan Coat of Arms" in the Neue Schweizer Rundschau and your contribution to that little piece of work was certain. With this letter, you shall now receive a little booklet that was published as a collection in a similar little poetry volume that includes about twenty coats of arms from my larger book of heraldry. I had already negotiated the release and even concluded the contract with the publisher at the beginning of 1933. But events were such that publication of the little book dragged on for such a long time. On one of the first pages, you will find the dates on which the verses were written. I wanted to establish that I wrote the "Lassan" when patriotic poetry was not all the rage. . . .
>
> Nothing new to report here: our reclusive life in Finkenkrug continues as before. My father was happy to receive your greetings and sends his to you as well.
>   As a "little encore," it also occurred to me that I could send you one of my more recent poems, "Robespierre," which I especially love. Of course, I have no idea whether you will like it as much as I do.

Benjamin would hardly have liked this eulogy, this hymn to a state-sponsored terrorist. Here are several, typical lines:

> I want to touch you with my hands,
> I want to dig you out of your tomb.
> Climb up! You may, you may not end . . .
> . . .
> Oh, that I wash every stain away,
> That spoiled your face so! . . .
> . . .
> You, more than human. You, not just a shadow:
> Cast by some deity.

---

* *Mischlinge* (mixed breeds) was the term that the Nazis used to describe people of partly Jewish and partly Aryan ancestry. A *Mischling* of the first degree was a person with two Jewish grandparents.

The lyric *I* wants to wash every blemish from the face of Robespierre. He, of all people, as the embodiment of justice, as the shadow cast by a deity! The poet again proves to be a sister of Proteus: in the same year that her magnificent heraldry poems were published, she wrote this adoration, this apotheosis of a despotic ruler!

| 57

Once again, I must emphasize that the gap of seventeen years between publication of her little poetry volume in 1917 and the booklet of poetry in 1934 is an enormous interval for the continuously productive poet! Prior to 1933, there ought to have been one or two publishers in Berlin whose list could have accommodated an additional volume of Kolmar's poetry. But did she even write to publishers or send poems to journals? Or did she not so much as try in that decade and a half? She apparently had her father's initiative to thank for the first volume, and publication of the second book took place after Ina Seidel intervened.

Between 1917 and 1934, only three poems were published singly, and two of them were launched by her cousin. Only seven poems were published in seventeen years, which may have been a first! So I conclude with some reservations that writing poetry was important, indeed vital to Kolmar, and what happened to the poems afterward struck her as secondary.

The cycle of poems *Das preussische Wappenbuch* took shape during the winter of 1927–28. What Stomps published in 1934 was a limited selection of what are admittedly high-caliber poems.

The first of these Prussian coats of arms is the "Wappen von Brüssow" ["Brüssow Coat of Arms"]: "A silver castle in front of a red background upon a green base, a red ladder standing in its tower vault." And the text makes a quantum leap to a higher dimension:

> If you always have your room,
> If you always have rye bread,
> That is plenty and is misery,
> That is everything and is plight.
>
> Hear padding in the narrow passage
> Like the dull circling of a mole,
> Greedily scraping, wickedly snatching,
> Lecherous joke and stale prize.

Choose dimensions, think of color,
Violate your quietest hours,
Lay them gently into old topsoil,
Take the bouquet, visit yourself.

And immediately lock the door
Outside help, the neighbor's ax!
Your ax, reflecting sun-red,
And the spider lends her rope.

Now comes planing, now hammering;
Heartbeat and dream suffice,
And added to the long twilight you see
Colorful shoots.

The moonlit night advises you, keep working.
The cuckoo calls seven times,
Yet you lift the purple ladder
At the brightest rays of dawn.

In this instance, efforts to draw connections between life and work must surely fail. What can be presented biographically doesn't even suffice for an anecdote. The collector's stamps serve more as an indirect trigger for poetic projections shooting out into the free space of linguistic expression. I can no longer get many a line out of my head: "And added to the long twilight you see / Colorful shoots . . ."

"Wappen von Friedland" ["Friedland Coat of Arms"] is another highlight from the slim volume of poetry. The visual image: "A silver castle with two towers on a red ground, on whose open gate a golden hedgehog stands."

The most beautiful things pickle at night
As in a preserving jar;
You must screw on the lid:
There they smell, they grow,
They undulate, they dance
And they taste sweet like grapes.

The little child, who goes to his pillows,
The mother, who turns the covers down,
You'd be well advised:

You know what the moon meant,
That appears yellow as an orange tree,
And how the stars implored.

The blueberry takes its course,
And black flowers break open
Made of white ceramic stove tile,
A dwarf hedgehog stands and flashes,
Where rock crystal is carved into a castle,
With its golden spike.

And all flee the glass prison,
And each glows like blackberry juice
In dripping globs.
The dew-domed castle blurs,
The hedgehog's golden cloud glows
On account of the shelled island.

And when the child awakens to the game,
He'll still find the glittery quill,
Shorn from the hedgehog's fur.
It delights him so, it's hardly any use to him,
It's as useless as his dream
And soon gets lost.

And last but not least, "Wappen von Zechlin" ["Zechlin Coat of Arms"], Margraviate of Brandenburg: "Silver: on reed-filled water, a red boat in which a fisherman in blue costume pulls up his net." Here, too, are closing lines that could become a catchy tune: "A fish made of dew is motionless / and you'll never see it."

The sun quietly rows westward,
A strawberry-colored swan.
Because I want to fish for silence,
I follow my rowboat.

A little sorrow rises in the east
Made of faded gray,
Evanescent like a summer dress
A woman, long beclouded.

The pond frog whines, laughs and glugs
Hardworking and out of sorts,
Until he swallows earth and green slime
And his orbit blurs.

Daily drudgery, hardship:
Whatever remains,
Is an empty snail shell,
Driven by the waves.

A strayed golden oriole hovers,
Is the crescent moon whirring?
"If the mesh lies hollow and slack,
The catch has been worthwhile."

"Lift your heavy net and see,
Maybe you're pulling nothing at all;
A fish made of dew is motionless,
And you'll never see it."

| 58

Once again, Kolmar deals with Maximilien Robespierre, a name in written history that stands for state-sanctioned, licensed terror: the Reign of Terror.

A sketch from late fall 1933, "Das Bildnis Robespierres" ["A Portrait of Robespierre"], documents her turn toward Robespierre for the first time. This is Kolmar's only surviving essayistic work. A special occasion actually set it off: "I was pleased that his bust was supposed to be unveiled this morning in the town hall at Arras." That took place on October 15, 1933, perhaps in anticipation of the 140th anniversary of his death the following year.

The author's question sets the stage: "How could a portrait of Robespierre that created party hatred and showed a narrow-minded, pushy individual, a cowardly, cruel hypocrite, how could this portrait remain indestructible?"

There are no further quotations or comments, just a report. A bundle of poems, "Robespierre," followed the essay. Gertrud Kolmar apparently wrote these poems in connection with the essay, probably in late fall 1934 for the most part. There is a compendium of forty-five poems, around eighty printed pages, about people and events from the period of the French Revolution.

Not all the poems center around Robespierre, and he sometimes just haunts a text like a ghost. Several poems bring to mind companions of the central figure, such as the equally handsome and cruel Louis Antoine de Saint-Just, whom many have characterized as the angel of death. Then come Georges Danton and Jean-Paul Marat, whose chiefly dark features are supposed to accentuate the shining light of Robespierre.

The lyric *I* idolizes him, as in the poem "Die Kerze" ["The Candle"]. They called Robespierre "La Chandelle d'Arras" ["The Candle of Arras"]. Typical lines of adoration once again:

> Look, I'm alone, I'm weak and mortal,
> Yet I live, go about talking,
> Wander about, to become your servant,
> Gently into your long-lost sanctuary
>
> . . .
>
> Wanting to place you, oh candle, at the center
> A new face looking out,
> To moisten my mouth with your flame,
> That the sound of his song of your pure light
> Might linger.

In a second candle poem, "Ein Gleiches" ["The Same"], the "lyric *I*" stylizes Robespierre as a role model: "I want you to put you in my place: appear! . . . I want to be your chalice . . . Now drip, constant light, redeeming into me . . ."

Again, philology insists that the lyric *I* and the self of the poet must be systematically regarded as separate. But in the case of literati, there would be no proper point of departure if there were not connections, however methodically impure, between the literary and actual selves. Something like visual contact often seems to exist in this case. By invoking the nearly metaphysical light of Arras, the essence of the poet seems to shine through. The restriction of the *I* to the point of self-effacement, the basic pattern of a woman who subordinates and subjugates herself to, and seeks shelter beneath, a domineering male figure. The accompanying ideal is the purifying wax candle of Robespierre that drips salvifically onto the passionate enthusiast.

How can we maintain biographical composure here? Kolmar places me in a truly awkward position with her unconditional, almost blind adoration, indeed worship of the dark figure that becomes totally transfigured into a shining light. In an era of two dictators of unprecedented historical dimension, she continues her monomaniacal efforts to idealize a dictatorial ruler, to even bestow a halo on him. To praise an exterminator, a liquidator in a period of unconditional personality cult in the "Greater German Reich" and the Soviet Union alike!

In the Kolmar exegesis, people have made pretzel-shaped, roundabout attempts to confer ultimately positive value on poetic texts like these and to cover them in a delicate web of interpretation. But the elegies to Robespierre cannot be upgraded in this way. In many cases, they are dramatically crafty poems in which Kolmar made up her own formulas.

What happened here? An act of unbridled identification has taken place with a person who punished every form of exuberance for life with instant death. What has taken place is the canonization of an ascetic, who had everyone beheaded if they didn't conform to his standards and didn't accept his dogma.

Kolmar doesn't seem to notice any of this: historical facts and circumstances float behind seven veils of rapture. This leads to an embarrassing situation that well-meaning interpretation can hardly cancel out. Thus, she makes the child in the title, "Maximilian," into her wished-for child: "You child. I dreamed you . . . You child. My child. You lived for me . . ."

Between November 24, 1934, and March 14 of the following year, Gertrud Kolmar wrote *Cécile Renault,* "a play in four acts."

Her dealings with Robespierre developed into a complex with a double meaning. Following the essay and bundle of poems, we now get Robespierre for a third time. I have considerable difficulty with this work as well. To neatly say what my respect for the poet must endure, I think the play is a flop and embarrassing besides. Others apparently see it that way, too. It has never been performed, although the script has been available since 1997. One can tell all too easily that the play was not checked by a dramaturge, be it at an agency or a theater. If it had been checked, suggestions for revising it would surely have ensued.

A brief account of the piece. The little royalist Aimée Cécile summons all her courage and visits Robespierre at home in the evening, which could have led to misunderstandings that, in light of her purity and innocence, would have quickly blown over. After initial difficulties in attempting to speak, adoration follows: "She fell down before him" and implored him: "Give us our daily bread. And forgive us our trespasses. And deliver us from evil. For thine is the kingdom and the power and the glory. Forever and ever. Amen."

After this secularized version of the Our Father, Robespierre gently admonishes her to behave moderately: "Please stand. One respects citizen Maximilian Robespierre but does not kneel before him." After briefly attempting to resist such idolatry, he quickly relents.

The question asked by someone named Julien is decisive: "What can become of you other than the crown of olive leaves and fruits?"

Robespierre (quietly): "The crown of thorns."

Then Julien kneels before him: "Messiah."

And Cécile, in a biblical tone: "Lord, I know that I am not worthy to dwell beneath thy roof. But only say the word, and thy maiden shall be healed."

This is followed by the stage direction: "Long silence. Little Julien and Cécile Renault kneel with hands folded."

| 59

In November or December 1934, Gertrud Kolmar traveled to Hamburg to meet Karl Josef Keller, the man with whom she'd exchanged letters. Was it his idea? He was apparently disappointed with her appearance. You can tell this from the last sentence of a subsequent, polite account: "She was a petite little person with a pale face, dark hair, didn't look like a typical Jewess. She was a rather unobtrusive figure and made no more of herself that what she really was. She was pleasant and modest. You had to have a picture of her inner life to be able to appreciate her."

In Hamburg, they toured the harbor and visited the art gallery. They went on to Lübeck. She apparently didn't have the courage to go into Buddenbrook House.* In Lübeck, they also saw the Seamen's Guild House that she wrote a poem about. They traveled back to Hamburg and parted after three days together.

Gertrud Kolmar observed strict secrecy with regard to this relationship. At any rate, we can conclude this from the ample silence of the written record. She apparently never revealed the name of her first partner beyond her closest circle of confidantes, and that also seems to have been the case with her new relationship. So do I have the right to mention more than just the initials of his name?

We can and are allowed to know his name because her partner from 1934 got in touch with Hilde Wenzel after the war and made his identity known:

> You will surely be surprised at these lines from the hand of a stranger. I
> had a terrible shock the other day, because I just happened to find your
> sister's poetry volume, *Leben,* in a bookstore, and got hold of your address,
> because I simply had to write to you.—I cannot believe that your sister
> is purportedly dead. Mind you, I saw her for the last time at Christmas
> 1939, for she looked me up in Ludwigshafen. And I warned her. She was
> optimistic. My God, we were very close, and I once had all of her verses
> before everything I owned was destroyed. Some of the poems in *Leben* were
> written after we were together in Hamburg. I was with her in Lübeck. As I
> say, I still cannot believe all of this.

A question and answer in a letter from Gertrud to Hilde may indicate how close they were, or at least felt: "Do you know when I have most fervently prayed? Not because I felt unhappy, but because I was happy, infinitely happy ... I heard the breathing of a slumberer in the night. I stretched out my hand without touching him and, on the ceiling of the room, saw the blue-black heavens with stars dancing in them. And I sat up in my bed and prayed ..."

---

* Buddenbrook House is a museum devoted to the German author Thomas Mann.

* * *

Several poems were dedicated to "K. J." Johanna Woltmann championed the hypothesis that K. J. stood for the officer, Karl Jodel, with whom Gertrud had a relationship during the First World War. Woltmann cited Hilde Wenzel's tip, which is weighty testimony. But does that make it the last word?

I consider it highly unlikely that, at a time when she devoted herself to a new partner, she would dedicate poems to a man to whom she had been close nearly two decades earlier. At the same time, she still suffered from the aftereffects of that relationship and the forced termination of her pregnancy. I am certain that the poems were dedicated to Karl Josef!

There are also motivic connections. Looking back, Gertrud wrote: "My last— and most beautiful—trip was to Hamburg, Lübeck (in Buddenbrook's footsteps) and Travemünde, and the most indelible impression was one winter night on a lonely seashore. My travel diary is made up of seven poems . . . more poetry than truth—and yet truth as well."

This cycle is biographically puzzling. Gertrud concealed the poems about the trip as the work of an English poet. The heading of the typescript reads: "SEVEN POEMS from German Sea by Helen Lodgers. From the English."

Now and again, the English is threadbare. An English poet would certainly not have written "On the Alster" if "Along the Alster" was meant. I suspect that we can find other blunders in the homespun English, but they are unimportant. The important thing is: how are we to interpret this literary smoke screen? Hermann Kasack, chief editor of S. Fischer Verlag in the early years after the war, wrote on the cover sheet of the little collection: "Presumably not translations, but original poems. The translation was probably only fabricated by Kolmar in the thirties for political reasons!"

Peter Wenzel, who decisively championed the publication of her unpublished works, said something similar. He would also submit this cycle to the publisher Peter Suhrkamp, accompanied by the following note: "The information about a foreign author may be fictitious or, better still, a disguise that would have made publication possible during the Nazi era."

But such a publication (undercover, so to speak) could have become tricky. Rowohlt got into problems because his publishing house put out texts by Jewish authors who wrote under pseudonyms. The problem would have actually been twice as big with the publication of the cycle. Not only would the granting authority—that is, the censorship board—have asked about the English author, but it would have inquired about the translator as well. It would hardly have been feasible for the Jewish translator to also produce a pseudonym. Tiered disguises on the part of two "straw women" at once? . . .

We don't know when the camouflage took place. Was it shortly after the cycle was written or not until years later? This is an important point with regard to the disguise theorem. If the disguise took place in the period when the poems were written, which was around 1935, then hardly a plausible reason can be found for it because the poet would officially publish another poetry volume three years later under her own name. So what purpose would a fictitious Helen Lodgers have served? Kolmar could have published the entirely apolitical poems under her own name in one of the remaining Jewish periodicals.

If she didn't attempt to disguise the cycle until later, after the third poetry volume, after the war began, then the question also arises: For what purpose? Was she planning to publish the little cycle in a journal? And what periodical would have been open to a Helen Lodgers from the land of the "archenemy Albion"? Or should one see the camouflage as a sign that a fourth volume of poetry was being planned? Then why seven poems and not seventy straightaway? Why would anyone write these ideologically harmless poems under a pseudonym in the first place?

In short, I cannot imagine that she disguised the poetically transformed travel diary for potential publication. The more likely scenario is this: The disguise was to hide it from her continuously domineering father. She had lived in close quarters with the aging gentleman for a half dozen years, and he'd gotten readily accustomed to it. His "Trudchen" gave him a hand in the office. Trudchen took care of his creature comforts. Trudchen took walks with him. Trudchen told him, the intermediary for her first poetry volume, at least cursorily, what she was working on or had been working on. Trudchen remained devoted to him in every respect, had everything she needed to live and write poetry in the house and garden, didn't she? And now a trip? A trip on which she was meeting a man! And the man who sent her letters on and off for years was now in close physical proximity in Hamburg, Lübeck, Travemünde, on sightseeing tours, as well as walks along the beach and, possibly, in pensions or hotels. Was it not possible that fear of losing his daughter or something akin to jealousy stirred in the aging man? What would have happened if, upon discovering the poems, Papa Ludwig had indirectly found out about the relationship? A sudden change in the domestic climate?

The symbiotic relationship with her father was far-reaching, extremely so. Letters written by both of them jointly show this. Even after she wrote a confidential letter to Hilde, "Papa" wrote to his "dear little bee," "little doll," or "little monster" on the reverse side of the letter paper. This sort of thing went on as "writing to," which is to say, adding a note, writing something in at the bottom.

So where were the limits of privacy in this case? Can we rule out that he ever asked as a matter of form whether he was allowed to glance at the earlier part of the letter? Would she have been able to say no? So was it tacitly assumed that he at least glanced at the small, indeed tiny script prior to adding his own long strokes? Only on rare occasions did she prevent such united correspondence: "Papa would surely love to write to you as well, but I would prefer not to show him this letter. And so I greet you on my own, but warmly, Your sister Trude."

This type of safeguarding was the exception. They usually wrote and signed as a team: "Papa and Trude." Since they were so joined at the hip, can the idea that he looked at her poetry manuscripts be ruled out? Was that the reason for writing under the guise of Helen Lodgers?

Without the translation, however, would she have been able to prevent her father from possibly looking at the little cycle by hiding it in the painted brown starch box? He would hardly have searched there. On the other hand, she also stored letters in the box. Would he have ever looked up something because he wanted to refer to an earlier text? And as chance would have it?

Poems should never become an instrument for making statements about biographical details. However, poems within the biography of a poet can show how such details were stylized.

As we shall see, Gertrud Kolmar encourages us to read a volume of poetry like a book of life. At the same time, she makes it more difficult through the intensity of her articulation, which is particularly impressive in several poems that concern or may concern the lovers' trip.

How does she transform their brief sojourn on the wintry sea? Into summertime poems! "Meerwunder" ["Sea Miracle"], the seventh poem in the transposed "travel diary," shall serve as an example. The connection between life and poetry is very tenuous here. And it again proves the necessity of separating her life story and the history of her oeuvre from each other by chapter, of placing them on parallel tracks and not presenting them as a continuum:

> When I conceived the child with starry green eyes,
> Your delicate, beautiful child,
> Salty water sloshed in cisterns,
> Saint Elmo's fire sparkled from courtyard lanterns,
> And the night wore a ring of coral.
>
> And a mane of algae wafted at your chest
> So green, so green and silently melodious.
> Waves lapped very gently about barges,
> Large swans sang within dreamy black reeds,
> And only the two of us heard them.

You emerged from the seas at midnight
Your body icy, cool and dripping.
And wave-cradle spoke to wave-cradle
Of our gentle lying together,
Of your arms around a woman.

Unseen dancing lifted up the mermaids,
And wild harps rang out darkly,
And the moon shed its silvery twinkle
On fish scales, all lucent and mother-of-pearl;
My linens smelled of the sea.

And shepherds again watched over their sheep
Like once . . . when an unnamed star gleamed.
And ships that sleep on foreign coasts,
Trembling softly, dreamed of port
Of home, now so small and distant.

The pollen flowers opened and fanned out,
Scattered from your hand into my lap;
Eagle rays fluttered about my feet,
Triton and olive snails crawled
On my hip, white sand.

And your pale beryl eyes frightened
The crowned snakes back to their homes in rocky shafts,
But shimmering salmon leapt in the wetness,
Blue light sprayed on crests of waves
As night does from raven-black hair.

Oh you! . . . just you! . . . I felt your limbs
And wooed and tingled and frothed over you.
And all the winds kissed my eyelids,
And all the woods tumbled down on me,
And all the streams flowed into me.

The attempt to couple sequences of poems like these with traceable autobiographical situations that can be dated may appear almost nonsensical. These are magnificent projections of speech that shoot out into the open space of poetic expression.

Nevertheless, the poet puts in markers that point to experiences that correspond to the poems, such as dedications to "K. J." Motivic connections to the man by the sea turn up. One of the poems "dedicated to K. J." is "Der Wal" ["The Whale"]. The beginning is passionate: "You. I wanted to claw you from the sky, / pull you down deep into my life."

And "Fischkönig (An K. J.)" ["Fish King (To K. J.)"], a poem with a grand opening: "Where are the names that I knew? / A scream tore them to pieces." "Die Verlassene" ["The Abandoned"] is surely the most intense of her poems "to K. J.":

> You're wrong, if you believe that you're far away
> That I thirst and can no longer find you?
> I fix my eyes on you,
> With these eyes, both of them dark stars.
>
> I pull you under my eyelid
> Shut it and all of you is inside there.
> How will you get out of my senses,
> The hunter's web from which game never escapes?
>
> You'll never let me fall from your hand
> Like a withered bouquet,
> That blows down the street, outside the house
> Trodden by all into dust.
>
> I loved you. So much.
> I've cried so . . . in fervent supplication . . .
> And love you even more for I suffered because of you,
> When your pen refused to write any more letters to me.
>
> Friend and master and lighthouse keeper
> On the narrow strip of island,
> Is what I named you, gardener of my fruit orchard,
> And though there were a thousand wiser, none was more just.
>
> I hardly felt that I broke harbor,
> Which held my youth—and little suns,
> Or that they dripped away, trickling into sand.
> I stood and gazed after you.

Your passing remained all my days,
Hanging like a sweet smell in a dress,
That it does not recognize, doesn't count, only receives
Carrying it always.

We come to the transformed "travel diary" once more. In this case, biographical connections are barely detectable. The "Haus der Schiffergesellschaft" ["Seamen's Guild House"] is an example of a poem that is apparently connected to the short trip yet remains uncoupled from autobiographical events.

We again come closer to a possible biographical spark in the poem "Wacht" ["Watch"], also from the North Sea cycle. It is one of the great love poems in the German language!

A song sounding in her beloved's slumber!
When everything is collected, calls, conversations and commentaries
And evenings, like children's toys, get stored in a closet,
The black mother, silent in veils and crowned

Strides down the staircase of a high tower,
A storehouse brushed in veiled moonlight,
The silver lamp; when she weeps silently
Preparing a restorative made of poppies and asphodel:

Then I hear your breathing.
You sing. I look for you, yet may never reach you.
Oh, everyone tells me that you sneaked away—
For how long? Where? I cannot see you any longer.

You're far away, separated, so far from my soul.
If your body, too, remained close to mine;
I touch your shoulder: you. I love you . . .
And feel the words which I conceal in shame during the day,

And yet this face, bent over yours,
Never awakening the sleeper, just wanting to watch praying,
So that this room doesn't fall into a cave of gray dragons,
Once eyed in the tangle of a boy's anxious dream.

And yet this heart, split by the chiming hours, knows
That you turned from it, and will never return.
Oh star, gleaming above me in the warm darkness,
When will I shiver, alone, before the snowy morrow?

You do not know. And yet in the end you're ready
To flee from me without haste along your strange pathways—
I like to lie quietly at your shoulder where I place my temple,
My hands on my heart, which cries out for mercy.

| 60

We presume it was likely that literary discourse did not take place in the home from which these kinds of high-caliber texts emerged. Gertrud would have found it strange to monopolize the conversation: her father would have been the family spokesman. One gets the increasing impression that they were more likely to have spoken about warning signs in the legal sphere than problems of the literary establishment. Her father probably shared more about his world with her than the other way around, and domestic conversations likely consisted more of legal jargon than poetics. Even from this point of view, legal language cannot be ignored in the biography, as there were two linguistic worlds residing under one roof: logical, legal discourse and nonlinear, liberated speech.

So here are a number of concepts from the realm of the *Notar*: Negotiations about an amicable settlement . . . reasonable easements and land charges . . . in a form that could be entered in the Land Registry . . . for an adjustment proceeding . . . charges on real property . . . initiate an invalidation procedure . . . record a marriage contract as a declaration of intent . . . only during the lifetime of the depositor may the instruction . . .

Factition: Dear Hilde, We shouldn't negotiate the chronicle project in writing alone: the compilation will at least require the occasional consultation and verbal agreement. To that end, I offer my written documents for future use. Verbal exchanges alone seem too error-prone, and points repeatedly come up whereby memory has an altering effect. So let's continue with our largely habitual written statements.

On account of the turmoil of these horrible times and their effect on the family, it seems to me that it is increasingly necessary to continue work on the family chronicle. As emphasised once before, we are both conscious of the fact that the chronicle can only cover three generations. We don't have to participate in the obligatory people's sport of genealogy; don't need to do that at all, seeing as we're already branded anyhow.

To put it concretely again, the chronicle must start with my parents in Posen and your grandparents in Neumark. The dry goods dealer Julius Chodziesner and the world traveller Hedwig Schönflies ought to lead off our story.

In addition to my papers, you will certainly ask your oldest sister about the family during one of your visits, which I hope will take place again soon. Yet I can only attest to what you have known for a long time anyway. You won't get much out of asking your sister. Upon being asked to tell you about her life, she will respond with no more than subterfuge. She won't speak at all about experiences that have had a lasting effect on her, such as her relationship with that officer whose name I can no longer remember. Her inner connexion to the man from the signal corps seems definitively cut off. Trude conceals and guards this secret. She has firmly sealed it within herself, and nothing will be able to break the seal.

You'll probably not even find a way to approach the matter of Gertrud's long-standing assistance in the family law office. With regard to this, you should at least mention in passing that it is nothing unusual, much less a situation that distinguishes me as a person. The combination of office and living space under one roof is widely accepted.

Since I work closely with Trude in the law office on weekdays, I must undertake to write about her job. And I do so with the expectation, yea, the request that my groundwork may also have an effect on your larger task. If we leave out the office-work aspect of her life, then only a distorted view of Gertrud will emerge. I would like to, indeed must, bring out the true picture, which is not even incidentally about me, as I can assure you in good conscience.

Instead of presenting samples of legal terminology, you should give preference to reporting on one or two cases that we've handled on behalf of our clients.

I'll indicate them by means of headlines: Pro-Jewish attitude as grounds for dismissal . . . Termination because of interracial marriage . . . Termination of a Jewish employee . . . This case here I'll cite as an example.

A Jewish employee worked for seven years, lastly as a buyer at a textile company in the Köpenick district of Berlin. The company let her go as of the end of 1934, the reason being that they received a letter from the Nazi district committee that said, among other things, "We are no longer in the position to continue being your customer, as we can no longer expect party members and members of our organisation to make purchases in future at a company that still has Jewish employees working for it. If you are not willing to draw the obvious conclusions about your Jewish employees, then we are obliged to take the appropriate steps for the protection of our party members." The employee, who had to care for a seventy-one-year-old father and a disabled veteran brother, considered the termination unlawful and called upon the company advisory board to intervene, but they refused. The employee then sued to be reinstated, referring to the termination as illegal and unethical. After all, she had been employed as a buyer for years, was the only non-Aryan among the hundred or so company employees, and, moreover, never came in contact with the public.

The suit was dismissed on the grounds that the company had wanted to avoid the threatened countermeasures. Since the termination had ensued to avoid serious harm to the business, the grounds for dismissal were neither illegal nor unethical. Quoting from the statement of reasons: "It is well recognised under the law that a termination can be unethical and void on account of its motives. But in this case, the termination occurred for business reasons to avoid the threat of serious detriment to the business. Such a termination on the basis of sound considerations is not unethical. The notion of a sense of decency on the part of fair-minded and right-thinking fellow Germans depends on a transformation to which the National Socialist worldview should attach great importance."

The client wanted to challenge the decision and was referred to us by an acquaintance. I immediately saw a new approach. It's best for me to quote from a fair copy of my pleading, which Trude took down and typed up: "It must be generally assumed that, even under the altered view that the German State and the German Volk have adopted towards the Jews, the proposition that every employee of non-Aryan descent can be dismissed without notice cannot be recognised in the sphere of economic activity."

A clear opinion, don't you think? I followed it up with these reasons: "The laws and ordinances enacted by the Reich government regarding employment of non-Aryan persons apply to career civil servants, employees and workers at public firms, lawyers, patent lawyers, doctors, dentists and dental technicians, commercial judges, lay judges, jurors, labour court judges, tax advisers and the like, and thus to all people who are in public service and enjoy public trust. Corresponding measures of a legal nature with regard to employees of private enterprises do not exist, so their employment is not inherently subject to any impediment."

Nevertheless, I must concede that "the new attitude of the German people toward the Jews, grounded in the rise of nationalism, is so fundamentally different from the previous one that, even in the area of private contract law, its consequences can in no way be missed."

So much for examples of various cases that occupy Trude and me in the law office. We see your sister in the less magical light of harsh, workaday life.

| 61

Which newspaper did they read in the Chodziesner home that actually shaped opinion and, in turn, perhaps influenced decisions?

The *Jüdische Rundschau* [*Jewish Review*] that came out twice a week? This publication had already proved to be a mouthpiece for Zionism, so it is highly unlikely that the Chodziesner household subscribed to or read such a paper.

A subscription to the *Central Verein Zeitung*, the "paper for Germans and Jews," was much more likely, indeed almost certain, as a later remark referred to it. The paper was a liberal-conservative periodical published by the Central Association of German Citizens of the Jewish Faith.

The association paper, which came out twice a week, gave the impression of authority, suggested an aura of sophisticated elegance, and was addressed to educated readers. Several headlines from leading articles included: "Mission, Guilt and Destiny . . . The Pillars of Our Future . . . The Communal Path . . . Assimilation or Synthesis: On the Fundamentals of German-Jewish Existence. . ."

What significance did the term "assimilation" have in the Chodziesner home? Neither father nor mother was baptized, nor did the parents have their son or daughters baptized—and baptism generally counted as the first stage of assimilation. Baptism was frequently followed by a name change, so a person named Rebecca could become Regine. When girls and women married, they could finally change their family name; that is, become Aryanized. Aryanization could also facilitate standing and advancement in German society.

Of course, Ludwig Chodziesner made a name for himself without such concessions. Yet he played the role of a Prussian and Wilhelmine lawyer most convincingly. He did so not only through his marked resemblance to the kaiser but also by means of his clients, through whom he indirectly represented the kaiser in the Eulenburg and Adlon proceedings.

Nevertheless, Gertrud Kolmar later expressed a critical opinion of Jews who "seemed assimilated in a bad, purely superficial way, some of whom could hardly come to terms with being Jews after not being so for decades."

Now, Hannah Arendt had thought through the logical outcome of the prevalent approach to the interpretation of assimilation. According to that approach, strictly implemented assimilation led to "the radical obliteration of one's own identity." Collectively, assimilation ended in the "disappearance of Jews in non-Jewish societies."

Looking rigorously ahead, Arendt wrote, "If one really wants to assimilate, then he cannot pick and choose from outside what he would like to assimilate into, what pleases him and what he doesn't like, in which case he may no more leave out contemporary antisemitism than Christianity. . . . In an overwhelmingly antisemitic society—and that means every country in which Jews have lived up to this century—a person can only assimilate if he assimilates into antisemitism."

So this would be the most radical outcome: A Jew who wanted to fully assimilate would have to precariously turn against himself and prove to be an antisemite, if need be.

If we think about it from this endpoint, it becomes clear that Gertrud Kolmar was not one to assimilate. Over a longer period, she came to identify with her status as a Jewish woman. First, she took part in a widespread turn to Judaism that was driven by social developments. In those days, people characterized this behavioral pattern as "initially just a naively indefinite response to cataclysmic events."

A return to Judaism thus took place as a widespread reaction to the pressures of radical social change. Gertrud also participated in this trend but took her own path in the process. She embraced Judaism without taking part in the Jewish religion. At any rate, it wasn't reported, mentioned, or intimated anywhere that she went to a synagogue. She certainly made fun of it when her father set foot in a house of God again after a long hiatus.

She embraced the history of Judaism, integrated it into her own life story, documented it in a number of poems, and already did so plainly in a 1933 title, "Wir Juden" ["We Jews"]. She said so right away in the first line: "I love you, I love you, my people." She recognized that her personal history had already begun centuries before her birth. So it is only logical that she wished for a Jewish first name like Esther or Judith. By incorporating Jewish history into her own personal history, from the destruction of Jerusalem and the Diaspora impelled by Roman military power, she not only emphasized her place in society but also showed a willingness to allow Jewish destiny to affect her personal fate.

Born into a nominally Jewish family, she became an avowed Jew, at least in her own eyes. She apparently stood alone in her clarity and resoluteness. This is how Hilde may have come to wrongly conclude that her eldest sister was a Zionist. Gertrud's decisive, if delayed, identification with Judaism and the Jewish people was apparently foreign to someone like Hilde.

| 62

Factition: Strict Papa, Dear Daddy! You will almost guess what's going on with me today: that cursed subject of emigration. I've already tried to speak to you about it several times, but in your (pardon me) occasionally imperious way, you have advised me that, "Hilde, now is not the right time!" And then you either had to take the dogs out, tidy up several plants, answer a letter, or you simply wanted to keep a clear head. My sister and brother had similar experiences when they broached the subject, and you certainly can't speak of "women's fears" in Georg's case. Nevertheless, it was the same with him: "Now is not the right time!" I have learned from such experiences, am consequently writing down what I've already told you recently. And you can freely choose the right moment in which you are inclined to answer my letter.

Now you may ask, "Why doesn't Hilde turn directly to Gertrud in this matter?" I've tried that, too, of course: it's not as if we only talk about Sabinchen and new books. But Trude tends to avoid the topic or seems to persistently opine that people exaggerate a lot, and all of this will somehow sort itself out. In short, she doesn't want to hear a thing about emigration or, to put it bluntly, about fleeing the country. She doesn't actually say so explicitly, but the right time never comes for her to discuss the subject.

So I am turning directly to you. Quite frankly, I'd like to take advantage of your influence with Trude, something we siblings have complained about occasionally. She's more likely to listen to you than to us younger siblings. After working with her for so many years, you will know how to find the right moment in which to speak to her about this pressing problem. We also respect the fact that, to be able to write poetry, Trude must keep a certain frame of mind in spite of all the immediate and peripheral troubles. You know that Peter and I greatly admire her work, that Peter will do everything possible to protect it, whatever may be in store for us—which any fool can plainly see, I'm afraid. So why are Margot and I, and why is Georg probably planning to emigrate? We have a heightened sense of what is going on around us. Our Benjamin cousins alone make that clear, indeed all too clear: Walter in France and Georg in a camp. Is Walter perhaps an adventurer, who was simply waiting for the first cue to get permission to lead an interesting life abroad? Is Georg possibly a fanatic, who wanted to take it upon himself to become a martyr by making needless statements at the wrong time? Doesn't all that Georg's Hilde tells you mean anything to the two of you?

But there it is, and there your statement stands like a stern doorkeeper: "Now is not the right time!" And you emphatically change the subject, stand up abruptly from the coffee table, or reproachfully say nothing. And what about Trude? She has to explain something to Flora, must discuss something with Helene in the kitchen, or has to make another fair copy of a business letter. I cannot see how all of this should be more important than considering the fastest way that one can get out of and farthest away from this country of brownshirts. This point must be at the top of the agenda, even for you in Finkenkrug. With all due respect, it won't do for you two to hide out there. You surely receive bad news from the family, and there are a number of reports from legal circles, as well as from clients. But the shock waves have already petered out by the time they reach you in East Havelland. On the other hand, things are really heating up here in the "capital of the Reich." Peter and I are much more directly aware of what's going on. I am already making my own preparations. Your brothers have begun to tie up loose ends, and so has your sister. I can just hear you saying, "Wild horses couldn't drag me to South America!" Fine. It doesn't have to be Uruguay, but what about England?

The way we siblings see it, England would certainly be the closest and best bet for the two of you. After all, Gertrud has taken her English language exam, as well as the French one, so she could give French language classes in England. And translation work would also be a possibility. If she didn't gain entry there, Trude wouldn't think she was too good to do household chores for a family. Or she could do agricultural work: she acquired the necessary skills for that in Arvedshof. So these are favourable preconditions for residing abroad. And for you, as well.

Yes, that's right: it reads, "And for you, as well." In England, you would hardly be "condemned to idleness," as you are wont to put it. Of course, you couldn't work as an attorney in a foreign legal system. But you could become a senior partner or a consultant to one of their lawyers specialising in immigration of German expatriates.

Alternatively, you could fall back on something that used to be a natural for you: you could write for newspapers and journals on a freelance basis. The major papers would certainly remain closed to you, but there are less prominent, entirely respectable forums, such as Senior's Watch. We got a copy of it the other day. You could contribute sketches to such a paper, as you did to the local press in the old days; in this case, sketches of everyday life in Nazi Germany. You've sufficiently demonstrated that you can write, both in family circles and beyond.

So you'd write sketches of daily life under the swastika, and Trude would translate them. In any case, we can safely assume there would be interest in contributions of this sort. The long tradition of isolationism admittedly continues to influence people, but they are beginning to wake up. There are indications here and there on the publishing horizon. Most notably, Bodley Head is publishing books that report on Hitler's Germany, contraband that we smuggle into our store. For your sake, I'll mention just one title, Behind the Scenes of German Justice. You could also provide a glance behind the scenes, because you have access to a wealth of information.

As far as your personal lives are concerned, very sought-after contributions such as these could help establish new contacts in England. And a lot would have to go wrong before there wouldn't be a senior in the neighbourhood who also devoted himself to rose cultivation. They also keep a great many dogs in England. You could take over dog-walking duties, and people would soon be ready to do you a favour in return. In short, to bring the subject to a close, you would by no means have to remain as hopelessly isolated as you are wont to rather morosely picture it.

Now please take time to study this written statement in depth, rather than simply skim over it. If our mother were still alive, I am absolutely certain that she would plead the case for emigration along the same lines as I, as we are doing. Trude won't be the one to say it's time to go. The signal will have to come from you, all the more so in this case. Then Trude wouldn't make any more excuses, would follow you, obliged to you as ever. And that, in turn, places the responsibility on your shoulders.

I think those were good closing words. In the meantime, I've nearly typed my fingertips sore on this old Remington—an English typewriter, practically an omen! Tomorrow will again be a tough day, but I wanted to use this Sunday afternoon to implore you to stay on the topic of England! Set an example!

Factition: Dear Hilde, Unfortunately, I see that I am forced to deal once again with the disagreeable argument that accompanied a deceptively relaxed chapter in your visit. I mean the discussion of the all-too-well-known question as to why I don't go to England with Trude in tow, etc., etc., ad lib.

In conjunction with the debate over change of location, I must point out something that confirms my position, even if I haven't properly put forth an argument up to now, and that is the financial aspect. In other words, my nearly zero desire to get involved at this level with a country of robbers and murderers.

By not aligning myself with the often hurried flight of numerous Israelites, it turns out that I have saved myself from running into an open trap.

While this word may not apply literally to the facts of the case, it still concerns the openly functioning machinery of looting. The Nazis are after our money, to state and write it in reasonably casual terms. They want to get rid of us, but they want to rob us first with their "property confiscation legislation," along with all the usurped vocabulary of the law that has been superseded by the dictates of despotic measures. One could almost come up with this motto: they want to delete us from the ledger and enter us in the debt register.

The Reich Flight Tax serves as the primary instrument. Chancellor Heinrich Brüning actually introduced it to stop the flight of capital to foreign countries. But the Nazis have eagerly seized upon this instrument, for example, have given it more teeth by decreasing the tax-exempt amounts.

A total 25 percent of assets shall be taken away, twenty-five in one fell swoop! They'll put the screws to anyone who doesn't pay punctually. For each commenced half month of outstanding debt, 5 percent of the total must be paid! One quickly arrives at a murderous interest rate this way. In addition, under Section 9 of the Ordinance on Reich Flight Tax, a fine can be assessed in an unlimited amount.

Now I could have said, "Fine. I'll just give the money to you siblings who remain at least for now before Gertrud and I leave the country, as I am being incessantly prompted to do." But they would have taken action against such a gift as tax evasion. The gifts would have been allocated to the assets again, and that would besee above.

As for me personally, I do not want to grant so-called rights to the police state in any way. As soon as someone extends a little finger to them, they tear off his hand posthaste. Assuming I'd paid my tribute to the tax man, I would not be protected from follow-up by the Gestapo, which could reproach me for some earlier case or accept the unproven allegation that I was a leftist or the like. They could have applied Section 2 of the Expatriation Act to me already, and the partial expropriation by means of the Reich Flight Tax would have been followed by full expropriation using the declaration of forfeiture of the assets.

To make the procedure clearer to you, I will pick up on what Szanto, director of the Finance Department, recently outlined in a report on "economic assistance" for Jews: A German citizen of Jewish or Mosaic faith wants to emigrate. To settle the formalities, he enters a room in which ten or twelve desks are lined up. A Gestapo officer sits behind each desk. He goes from desk to desk or queues in front of each one. They extort fees and various emigration taxes from him every time. Finally, he is nothing more than a beggar with an emigration pass.

I wanted to spare myself and you along with me from these kinds of degrading procedures. You should remember me as an upright person who held his head high despite all odds.

| 63

In March 1935, the émigré Gershom Scholem in Palestine reported to Walter Benjamin, who had immigrated to France, that his brother had been taken into preventive detention: "There's no trace of him since that time. No doubt he's been taken to some concentration camp or other." And he asked if Walter's brother was still in Germany.

The émigré Benjamin responded from Paris to Scholem in Jerusalem: "My brother is still in Germany, where his wife has a well-paid position with the Soviet trade mission in Berlin. After his release from the concentration camp, he went abroad once, but only as a holiday traveller. He has one son who, according to the photos I've seen, is very good-looking. Quite wretched that your brother's situation is so sad. But whose field of vision is not filled with such images?"

By Christmas 1933, Georg Benjamin had been released from the Sonnenburg Concentration Camp. The Nazi state was not entirely well organized at that time. The man with the double enemy profile of Jew and Communist was able to travel to Switzerland with his wife on vacation in 1934. He could sign up for lectures, at least within the framework of continuing education courses for Jewish doctors as organized by the health administration of the Jewish community. He got a driver's license in 1935. He borrowed medical books from the German Doctors Library. The seemingly monolithic state structure had holes and recesses, and Georg Benjamin took advantage of them. He actually continued his illegal activities (employment?) with the forbidden KPD.* Not even his wife learned what he did there, nor was she able to find out later on.

But in October 1936, Walter Benjamin had to tell his friend in Jerusalem that Georg had been arrested again.

He was temporarily admitted to Columbia Haus, an old military penitentiary at Tempelhof Field, one of the early concentration camps, and he could write a letter to his wife from there: "Dear Hilde, you must now try to find a way to lead a completely independent life with our son, and with friends and relatives who will help you. We must reckon that this will be a very long, drawn-out matter. You must and should make all decisions in future without taking me decisively into consideration. My son, our Mischa, will have to gradually forget me for the

---

* The KPD [Kommunistische Partei Deutschlands] was the German Communist Party.

time being. I hope that it will happen rather quickly for him. Or do you want to send him something now and then from Georg, who is away? Do what you think is right."(Georg, "who is away," was a code word that one learned to use so that the censors did not black out words and sentences, so that letters were not confiscated.)

After one week at the concentration camp, he was sent to the Moabit Prison as a prisoner awaiting trial. It was possible for family to visit him there. The criminal division of the Berlin Court of Appeals sentenced Benjamin to six years in prison. Quoting from the statement of reasons: "The accused continuously translated articles from foreign—English, French, and Russian newspapers— that involved Germany and conditions in Germany, although some articles were about political developments in Spain and France as well, to facilitate their dissemination in Communist circles, i.e., for propaganda purposes."

He was admitted to the Brandenburg-Görden Penitentiary. It was designed in 1927 as a model penal institution for "humane enforcement of sentences." The motto posted at the entrance read: "Work, discipline and goodness / ease a hard spirit, blot out the past, / take one back to the parental home." The new building was finished in 1935; Brandenburg-Görden was considered the "most modern penal institution in Europe." There were four buildings: Political prisoners were held in solitary confinement in Buildings I and II. Criminals and "those in preventive detention" were in the other buildings. There were eighteen hundred prisoners in all, and the number would more than double over the course of the war. Georg Benjamin was in one of the single cells on the third floor of Building I, Station C. They were so small that prisoners referred to them as "beehives." Benjamin was moved now and then, once to a cell with a view of the courtyard, another time to a cell with a view of the forest. Forced labor "consisted of separating string remnants into their constituent parts and—prior to that—loosening countless knots with the help of a large nail. New string was made from the raw fibre, or so I think." Cellophane bags of "every imaginable type from shirt to coffee bags to the smallest little bags for lipsticks and the like" were glued together before Christmas. Outdoor work, "a very welcome change," included building levees on the Elbe and working on a floating crane. There was time to read (Tolstoy) and to play chess, which he especially loved. He recommended chess moves to his son ("My dear Mischa-Master") by letter. What allowed Benjamin that kind of personal space during his imprisonment was the fact that there were very few Jews among the prisoners, so there were no antisemitic measures or actions. The worst of all possibilities didn't always materialize in that dark era. Benjamin actually cherished the hope of being able to emigrate after his release: "What is my attitude about a response on a questionnaire for the USA or Bolivia with regard to the criminal offence? As far as I know, there is a so-called 'revised certificate of good conduct' for emigration purposes."

| 64

In April 1936, the *Central Verein Zeitung* published a little anthology of poems by Jewish authors. The person responsible for it was Kurt Pinthus,* best known for editing the anthology *Menschheitsdämmerung* [*Dawn of Humanity*], which was published in 1920 with the subtitle, *Symphonie jüngster Dichtung* [*Symphony of Recent Poetry*]. *Dawn of Humanity* consisted mainly of expressionist poetry.

Pinthus accompanied his compilation with an extensive commentary, according to which the poems selected were sent to the editorial staff unsolicited. I assume that Kolmar was a member of that group. However, she was presented under her birth name.

We can discern Kolmar's exceptional status in comparison to the other texts. From among twenty contributions, there is only one other poem of distinction by Nelly Sachs. A considerable number of texts awaken associations with poems from the previous journal, *Die Gartenlaube* [*The Arbor*]: "Roses, radiant over the desk . . ." Idyllic texts indeed predominate: "The child walks his sunny path / Along the bright, long way." Only a single contributor, Willy Blumenthal, seems to have responded to the contemporary situation in "Gedichten von Abschied und Aufbruch" ["Poems of Farewell and Departure"]. But even in his case I must read the following: "God gave the sons a new heroism: / They smile at their old mothers / And conjure their tearful, woebegone mouths / Creasing in this hour of separation." Another example? Paul Mayer: "Who dares be lonely, / Dull from torture? / Wind caresses towers and city / With cool, comforting hands."

Further citations would be superfluous. The ambience of Gertrud Chodziesner's poem has already been sufficiently characterized. Was the poem she chose a profession of loyalty? The title, "Die Tochter" ["The Daughter"], is hardly coincidental. It's the only poem in the anthology to contain a dedication, *Meinem Vater* [To My Father]. He would have read and given his blessing to the poem:

> Even if I'm still carrying, forming in my hands
> A flicker, which escapes every attempt at shaping,
> Yet, like a basket on a scales
> Moves downward deeply and oh so carefully,
> Even if, with calibrated words, I measure
> What sometimes seems immeasurable,

---

* Kurt Pinthus was a German writer and literary critic who emigrated in 1933 to escape Nazi persecution. He taught theater history at Columbia University in New York from 1947 to 1961.

No molten ore like a forge,
And not flaunting violence like an enemy?

This is just fragrance in a room,
The scent of flowers never glanced at;
It weathered, and I never protected it;
Because it returns with the sound of a bird:
A titmouse's chirp at the window,
The black starling on the cornice, a gift,
And in some unknown way
It's back around me, as it was.

Isn't that the gold-crowned calf calling to us,
That moves the poor girl's heart,
Leading her to a wonderful bark
And then puts its hands over her eyes,
Because it tosses and binds the woman to the man?
Lingering and wandering between child and father
It's just a voice, sinking and disappearing,
And a hem quietly dragging.

Conversations meander, dull, everyday,
Far from the wild, bloodcurdling scream,
That rises up and states the unspeakable;
God's sun does not break us apart . . .
Oh, how should I frame the comparison,
What I can hardly picture myself?
A love without a name,
Often languishing—and silent. Yet lasting forever.

There is truly a higher level of linguistic intensity! Pinthus also emphasized the poet's special status: "And standing apart from all others, she who is richest in fantasy and expressiveness, the very gifted Gertrud Chodziesner: more than a talent—a dream walker."

It is worthwhile to briefly follow the editor's additional, generally subdued remarks. He offers an explanation for the glossing over of facts in many poems, for the largely conventional attitude and style, as well as for the dilettantism: "The stormy year of 1933 must have stirred the hearts of Jews in Germany to the depths, where old Jewish sorrow slept. But this painful experience did not immediately or directly become the poetic word. Great historical events almost never spontaneously bring forth great artistic achievement. The unfolding of disturbing events always seems to have crushed poetic creativity."

Pinthus could not have known that Kolmar would write accusatory poems in "immediate and direct" response to contemporary events.

We come back to the question of her name. Why was the poem published under her family name? In this case, the answer may lie in the dedication. The dedicatee was supposed to remain publicly recognizable. So we can assume that, even two decades after the period of her father's spectacular success and high standing, the name Chodziesner would have evoked a response in Berlin. Beyond the dedication, the family name signified togetherness and common interest.

As a result, acceptance of the poet's name would have been easy. Editor and poet would have known or at least seen each other at one or the other evening recitation, and she would have hardly been surprised at the publication of the poem. Thus, she would basically have been able to write to or tell Kurt Pinthus she was pleased that he was going to present one of her poems, but would he please do so under her nom de plume? A publication here and there under her family name would probably cause confusion because she wasn't so well known that people would see the names Chodziesner and Kolmar as identical. Such a request would surely have been granted but most certainly would never have been made. But was that only because of the dedication?

The question arises across the board whether her poems were presented under her maiden name at recitations. On such occasions, she could have said to the nearly befriended speaker, either formally or informally, "Erna, please be so kind as to announce my poems under the name Kolmar." This apparently did not happen.

Thus, a little-known name in the literary establishment had an even less-known name added to it, which could have only adversely affected the poet's renown. Publishing under two names has never been beneficial to an author's reputation. Kurt Tucholsky, by contrast, used up to five pen names. But this was a market-oriented tactic on the part of a rapid, facile writer: it may have also been a game of identity. Gertrud never tended to play these kinds of games. Whether in written or verbal form, I suspect that she didn't care if she was introduced as Kolmar or Chodziesner.

Later on, the Nazi regime no longer allowed Jews to use stage or pen names, so any potential choice was taken away from her. In the two decades prior to that point, however, it remained Chodziesner here, Kolmar there. And only a small, inner circle would have known that they pointed to a single person, whereas the word would hardly have gotten out to potential readers. So if someone saw a poem by Gertrud Chodziesner in print or heard one recited, wanted to read more of her poetry, and mentioned the name Chodziesner in a Jewish bookstore, he would scarcely be referred to Kolmar's new poetry volume.

| 65

That same year, "Die Jüdin" ["The Jewess"], another poem by the author who didn't want to make a name for herself, appeared in the September issue of the *Blätter der jüdischen Buchvereinigung* [*Pages of the Jewish Book Association*]. Here is a lyric sequence:

> I should like to set up a research trip
> In my own ancient land.
>
> I could perhaps discover Ur of the Chaldees
> Buried somewhere,
> The idol Dagon, the Tabernacle of the Hebrews,
> The trumpet of Jericho.
>
> That blew away those sneering walls,
> Blackening into depths, devastated, bent:
> And yet I once sucked the breath,
> That blew its tones.
>
> And in chests, buried in dust,
> Noble robes lie dead,
> The dying glow from a dove's wings
> And the stump of the Behemoth.
>
> I express my amazement. I am indeed short,
> And far from their days of magnificent might,
> But shimmering expanses gape about me
> Like protection, and I grow inside them.

| 66

At this time, Gertrud, who would have preferred a first name like Esther or Judith, would have approved of the following comments in the *Central Verein Zeitung*. They are an affirmation of Judaism as a commitment to the Hebrew language, which she may have already begun to study:

Hebrew is certainly the living language of Jewish Palestine, and anyone who goes there should be able to speak Hebrew, just as anyone who travels to Rio de Janeiro should understand Portuguese. But Hebrew is far more. If Judaism is everywhere that Jews unite as a holy congregation, then the Hebrew language is the basis for joining together in every place throughout the world. Palestine is small and would be of minor significance if it were measured by the number of those who are lucky enough to live there in the midst of the newly resurgent Jewish people. It would exceed all expectations if the Hebrew language were to attain international standing. "Not a day without a line of Hebrew," as Franz Rosenzweig says. And why does he say this? He says it because, without Hebrew, there would be no Jewish knowledge, and without Jewish knowledge, no Judaism.

But Hebrew was also a language that one could use to distance oneself from and to exclude the Nazi regime. Though not a language of resistance per se, it had a certain contrariness to it. Thus, the Gestapo office in Berlin saw itself forced to send out a circular, signed by Reinhard Heydrich, chief of the German Secret State Police and the German Security Police:

> I gather from various reports that at public Jewish political meetings, lectures and the like are frequently given in the Hebrew language. This renders proper surveillance of such meetings and the prohibition of subversive propaganda impossible.
>
> Therefore, pursuant to Sections 1 and 4 of the Decree of the Reich President for the Protection of the People and State, I request that, acting on your own responsibility, you forbid local Jewish political organizations to use the Hebrew language in public meetings and tell them to avail themselves of the German language exclusively. The only exception to this shall be closed meetings, evening practices and the like, at which members of the sponsoring Jewish organization gather for the purpose of practicing the use of Hebrew to facilitate their immigration to Palestine, as well as Jewish shul and religious community meetings.

| 67

No matter what was happening in the world, work in the garden continued for the time being, probably in concert with her father. She celebrated the little Garden of Eden in "Geflügelpark" ["Poultry Park"]:

> Behind hollyhocks black pines brood,
> Birch tops rocking, rattling gently.

Splintered piece of wood, pinecones, limestone and shale,
Where whirling feet of tines shuffle.

On grass-woven paths a mother lures
Her little ones to privet hedges,
Lets them dunk with pleasure, splashing, bathing
In the low, gray pool of sand.

Heavy Rhode Island Reds
Are taken for a stroll by a pretty rooster,
Proceeding deeply cautious, standing and thinking,
Showing him orache and chickweed,

Pecking at pennycress and pasqueflower,
Warning of the tiny colorful beetles,
In front of the ducklings on the muddy waves,
Brown as coffee and white as cream.

Retreating to mahonia thickets to teach
Wise bronze and golden wyandottes
Looking for seed, harvesting sweet berries,
Cleverly catch beetles and moths.

Dwarf knights, lie in the bushes,
Red combs quarrel over the spoils;
Their women, professional mourners,
Wear black wings they drag through the herbs.

Undulating dun-colored bridal veil grass,
Winding down from the hills face conceals:
Secrets: rare Easter eggs,
Fine and white, that little children will never find.

Rhode Island Reds, wyandottes, new words for me . . . I am curious, so I read and find out that wyandottes come from the United States . . . There are white and black wyandottes, often in dwarf form . . . Their color is silver laced with black . . . Rhode Island Reds also come from North America and are named after the state of Rhode Island. Internet offers describe them as "hardy," successful in "productivity and beauty," a "cross between red, Malay fighting cocks and other breeds of Asian origin." They are valued as "prolific egg layers over several years and good meat birds."

| 68

The 1936 Berlin-Leipzig Worldwide Poultry Congress was organized by the World's Poultry Science Association (WPSA). Double keywords!

First, I assume that Gertrud read reports about the conference or at least took note of it. I must point out with renewed emphasis that she wrote about small animal *breeding* and not about small animal *keeping*. Even if she took "breeding" to mean rearing, rather than interbreeding to form new breeds, she would have known a lot about poultry and would have had considerable interest in professional exhibitions. It wasn't simply a matter of little white rabbits or ducks waddling around the property and paddling about the little duck pond; nor was it only about scratching, cackling, egg-laying chickens that ended up in the soup as a welcome addition to a diet that, particularly for Jews, had deteriorated. Rather, it was about raising poultry according to a system with Gertrud as "poultry expert," wasn't it?

And could her sister also have taken part in the conference? In 1936, Margot was on the official, published list of members of the Berlin Ornithological Society. She had left Germany in the meantime and sought refuge in Bologna, Italy. She became secretary and translator-interpreter to Professor Alessandro Ghigi (born in 1875), a famous zoologist who was rector of the Royal University of Bologna at the time. Through her article in *Ornithology* (at the very least), "Dotoressa" Chodziesner had also proved herself in her host country. The collaboration could well have been so close that she, as Ghigi's right-hand assistant, could have been a member of the delegation from the friendly, Fascist country of Italy. It would not have been unlikely that, as a "German Jewess," she would have returned to the Reich.

So I had cherished the hope that Professor Ghigi, accompanied by his female colleague, took part in the Berlin-Leipzig Congress. As a member of the Italian delegation, she would have been under his personal protection and theirs, as well. And she would have been able to meet her sister in conjunction with the conference. They would have had plenty to talk about in Central Berlin or Finkenkrug.

But I must kiss my ideal scenario good-bye. Neither name shows up in the author index of the Main Reports and Announcements in companion volume 3 to the Sixth World Poultry Congress in Berlin-Leipzig. The Zoological Institute of the Royal University of Bologna was instead represented by Professor Anita Vecchi.

But right there, in one of the first reports, is a surprise entry! A report on preparatory work for an international dictionary of specialized, poultry-breeding terms reads: "The necessity for this type of dictionary arose from the fact that numerous poultry-breeding expressions cannot be found in standard books on the topic." The expert reported on the state of progress: "We have now come up with 745 terms as a basis for the dictionary, and Drs. Grzimek in Berlin, Wulff in Leipzig, and Miss Chodziesner in Bologna have offered me valuable support in compiling them."

So the collaboration of a Jewish woman was honorably highlighted at a congress that was organized by the Reich minister of nutrition and agriculture. Were they unaware or did they suppress the fact that the female colleague working on the dictionary was Jewish? Whatever the case may be, we learned something more about Gertrud's sister in Italy. Not only was she secretary to the rector of the university; she also did freelance work in a semantic field that was not unfamiliar to Gertrud. *Schlupffähighkeit,* "hatchability," is one example among hundreds of technical terms.

| 69

And family life went on! On June 1, 1936, Counselor Chodziesner took a request for motion of dismissal form and entered something personal on the empty page. In the matter of *Father v. Daughter,* he petitioned for: "All the best that a father can wish his beloved, youngest daughter for her trip southward . . ."

His good wishes accompanied Hilde on a trip to Italy. Sabina Wenzel later wrote: "My mother told me that, after it became increasingly difficult to sell good books, she was going to Italy to see if there were any prospects in that country." Letters to her were initially addressed to a hotel in Gardone Riviera.

It was a village on Lake Garda's "Lemon Riviera". . . The writer Gabriele D'Annunzio, also known as Il Comandante, resided there in the extravagant Il Vittoriale degli Italiani . . . Gardone Riviera was a spa with impressive hotel buildings but only around two thousand residents . . . A bookstore in this location would hardly have paid off. Did she, perhaps, figure on tourists and admirers of the famous, notorious Fascist D'Annunzio, who was a friend of Mussolini? Or did the village serve as Hilde's starting point for exploratory trips? Was Gardone the first stop? Sabina Wenzel suggested that her mother traveled on from there: "I no longer know if it was in Positano or Amalfi that she met a woman who loaned her house to Mother in her absence." Perhaps there were private reasons for making the trip. In any case, the keyword "bookstore" no longer came up. Hilde would flee to Switzerland two years later. So was the trip to Italy nothing more than an interlude?

At any rate, Hilde's little daughter Sabine stayed with her aunt and grandfather in Finkenkrug once again.

But it is a keyword in another excerpt from the biographical sketch that Sabina Wenzel sent me from Brazil:

I remember that I often sat in front of the bookstore with a picture book, sometimes in the company of an older girl, Steffi Goodman, who lived in the house and later immigrated with her parents to Philadelphia in the U.S. I don't have any other important memories of the bookstore, apart from the fact that we lived in the back rooms, which opened onto a dark courtyard with a tree. One person who has remained in my memory is our chauffeur, whom I called Uncle Bosy. He drove me to kindergarten in the mornings. He was a handsome young man, and I already liked good-looking young men in those days. I clung to him because he looked after me. I got the short end of the stick with my parents, of course, because they were very busy with the bookstore. My mother, in particular, chatted with customers until late at night, and my father woke me up in the mornings, dressed me, and gave me breakfast.

Gertrud wrote a letter to Italy in the middle of the month. The letter was a form of role playing in which she portrayed herself from the fictional perspective of little Sabine. For a long time, I considered whether I ought to introduce this sequence. The writing strikes me as terribly fussy. Yet the contrived scene shows how greatly people cut themselves off from ominous world affairs in Finken-krug, how they could very much confine themselves to family matters, at least temporarily. People adapted—and so they were no exception in that country at that time: "When I wake up in the morning and halloo, then 'Tjude' either has to get dressed, or she claims to be very tired and gets back into bed. In any case, something is thrown over me so that I don't catch cold. I sit at the window in Truden's room in front of a box called her 'desk' on a step I call a 'footstool,' study books and newspapers, or write up bills for 'one mark.'"

The role playing continues: "By the way, I have recently taken over the post of 'beautician': unfortunately, she has placed little value on skin care up to now. While she does her hair, I dab 'powder' on her cheeks from an empty crème jar into which I vigorously squeeze all five fingers. Today I also practised on her lips with lipstick in the form of a tiny, empty perfume bottle. It hurt her just a little, but that doesn't matter. Pride knows no pain, and our 'paths to virtue and beauty' are organized in such a way that I tread the path to virtue so that Trude can walk the path to beauty."

I'll make one comment about the box that supposedly served as a desk. This box was surely identical to the box in Gertrud's childhood room that was a storage container for newspaper clippings. Manuscripts and typescripts were deposited in this box, which was originally for shipping starch. It surely didn't double as a writing pad: for that, there was a mahogany writing desk that Aunt Gertrud had placed by the window with a view of three birches in front of the thick stand of trees at the back of the vast garden.

| 70

In July 1936, Ludwig Chodziesner's license to practice law was "revoked" after forty-five years in the profession.

Reichsrechtsführer Hans Frank, commander of law in the Third Reich, did the propagandistic groundwork, primarily in his speech at the Conference of the Reich Law Office of the Nazi Party on the occasion of the 1935 *Reichsparteitag*.* "The idea that a Jew should have anything to do with German legal life, either directly or indirectly, is absolutely intolerable to us National Socialists. And so it must be stated here as powerfully as possible that we can hardly wait for the moment when the last Jew has been eliminated from the German legal system."

Here is Dr. Frank again that same year at the congress on the "restructuring of German law": "National Socialist laws can never be properly used by a Jewish judge or a Jewish lawyer. That's why it shall remain our incontrovertible goal to permanently shut the Jew out of judicature in the course of time."

And so it was that Ludwig Chodziesner was "shut out." We don't know how he responded personally. We only know that he continued to behave properly in private correspondence. He left the title *Justizrat* on printed letterhead but crossed out *Rechsanwalt* [lawyer] and, subsequently, *Notar*.

The Berlin Bar Association also documented the disbarment of family members. The admission of the lawyer and *Notar* Chodziesner had already been revoked in 1933. Ludwig's daughter-in-law, Dorothea, was not allowed to be employed as a lawyer after June 1933. Even Fritz Chodziesner, who occasionally worked in his father Max's office, was already forbidden to practice law as of spring 1933.

On the other hand, Max (the second of the younger brothers, also a lawyer and *Notar*) wasn't prohibited from practicing his profession until 1938.

Factition: My Dear Hilde, as you know, it now happens that my professional life has not only been called into question but also, in fact, terminated. My admission to the legal profession has been definitively revoked by invoking a new law that I, as a jurist, cannot recognise. In this totalitarian system of perverted law, I am almost afraid to write a word like "jurist" or "lawyer," which we are prohibited from doing anyway. I was a lawyer and Notar for four and a half decades, though in recent years for a shrinking number of Jewish clients who all had the same problems: How do I get out of the country? How can I keep a portion of

---

* *Reichsparteitag* [Reich Party Day] was any of the massive Nazi Party rallies held as propaganda events from 1923 to 1938. In the 1930's, the *Reichsparteitag* took place at the Rally Grounds in Nuremberg and so were called the Nuremberg rallies.

my assets in the process, secure my savings and a small portion of my personal effects? I've reached saturation with regard to the accompanying stories of oppression and misery. And so I could, purely theoretically, be relieved about the fact that I will no longer be confronted with this collective misery and can close my "branch office."

But this is happening under such a cloud of shameful attendant ills! Whether or not this can be used in a family chronicle, I cannot help but report on all of the private adversity that has weighed on me, indeed shamed me, as though it were intended to insult me personally as an ex post facto devaluation of all that I have stood for throughout my life. I mean the Act to Amend the Penal Code, as well as the Act to Amend the Code of Criminal Procedure. Both of these interventions or, better put, encroachments were touted as a "tremendous upheaval" in the cowed trade press: and that's what it is, in fact, because it spells the end of the rule of law! The law has already been perverted, indeed usurped for a long time, but has now been officially abolished.

Section 2 of the Penal Code is at the heart of it. Until now, the principle of nulla poena sine lege* applied. They now brazenly refer to it as "outmoded irrationality and illegality" that has been superseded by (watch out!) "the German people's sense of justice." As has been sufficiently shown, that in turn has been driven by propaganda and acts of terror. To put it bluntly, despotism reigns officially and totally. And I must stand by and watch this, must still witness it at seventy-five years of age! As a colleague said in a confidential discussion, and discussions such as this must be held in the strictest confidence in this society infested with informers and stoolies: If an offence seems punishable to him and is not punishable at all under the law, any judge can simply borrow a paragraph that appears suitable to him and declare that, although according to the applicable provisions, the defendant is not punishable and must therefore be acquitted, I will penalise him anyway simply by arbitrarily applying another clause by analogy.

Here is an additional quotation taken from a professional journal that I still subscribe to: "Judges and public prosecutors have been exempted from all formal constraints, and been given greater freedom of movement and action." As a colleague jotted down and slipped to me, "anyone" can "be arrested at any time and held in detention for as long as suits the authorities, especially the party and the SS.† There is no longer any judicial review of arrest warrants, no examination at certain intervals of grounds for detention, no right of persons held in custody to hire a lawyer and to consult with him in person." In short, there are no longer any legal remedies!

---

* *Nulla poena sine lege* [no penalty without law] means that any punishment must be in accordance with the law.

† The SS [*Schutzstaffel*] was the special police force of the Nazi Party.

Where was the thousandfold outcry of German jurists? We non-Aryan lawyers could have at least raised our voices. On the other hand, what was and is wrong with our Aryan colleagues? Totally intimidated, totally incapacitated? I can only be thankful that, in this miserable situation, I am no longer a practising lawyer.

And what about Gertrud? With the closing of the law office, she's also been deprived of a job. She will no longer take phone calls and forward them if necessary, will no longer sort incoming mail, no longer type fair copies, and so on. In short, even she will abandon the language of jurisprudence. I must mention again, and you should emphasise in the chronicle, that Trude learned my professional jargon voluntarily. No one suggested that she take a course for legal assistants: she wanted it that way. I could have justifiably insisted on another assistant. And so many good employees have been fatally "freed" in the past three years! Financially speaking, it would not have been a problem to have an additional employee in the house during recently reduced office hours, but Trude would have protested most vehemently. She wanted to take over the secretarial work, and that must be recorded. Now it has been taken away from her.

Yes, my daughter, we suddenly have a lot more time. Fine! The house and garden make for plenty of work, but loads of time has now been freed up that, up to now, called for working together in the ground-floor office.

I've cleared my desk, no longer want to see law books and trade journals: the law has been disabled. I now write on an annoyingly empty wooden surface. Gertrud will also clear off her little desk in the other room, will surely also empty the drawers. Everything will go in boxes, and they will be stored in the cellar. What next?

| 71

Reality was still not monolithic in the fourth year of the Third Reich, so I am not permitted to portray it as though it had been.

In spring 1937, Willy Cohn traveled with his wife from Breslau to Frankfurt, then on to Palestine for the purpose of visiting their son in Paris and Jerusalem. Their son had recently emigrated, and they wanted to look at Eretz Israel* with an eye to potential future plans. They were no exception. Something akin to German-Jewish tourism to Palestine must have developed at that time, and it always had the same objectives: to visit family members and to get the lay of the land.

The question arises now arises as to whether the Chodziesners were under "house arrest" in Finkenkrug, so to speak. Or could Gertrud have taken a trip to

* Eretz Israel, in Hebrew, means the land of Israel.

Bologna, Paris, or London to keep her ears open and see for herself—so that she and her father could make a long overdue decision together after her return?

Even so, a fact-finding trip such as this required the completion of quite a few bureaucratic formalities. A Jewish adviser, also by the name of Cohn, wrote: The "prospective Jewish émigré must demonstrate to the responsible emigrant advice center on the basis of documentation that the proposed fact-finding trip is with emigration seriously in mind." Only then "would they issue a passport certificate for issuing a passport to an applicant. . . . Before a passport is issued, the applicant has to present certificates of good standing from the tax office and metropolitan tax authorities to the police department."

Such trips were not allowed to appear nonbinding; they were largely obligatory. The bureaucratic hurdles were high because one assumed "that Reich Jews put considerable Reich interests at risk by traveling abroad." These risks were mainly fiscal.

Despite the difficulties, Willy and Gertrud Cohn's trip should bring to mind what was still feasible in 1937. Unimpressed by the many warnings of unrest and attacks in the tense situation between Jews and Arabs, they wanted to look around—with round-trip tickets in hand for passage on a ship.

They booked with the Cohn Travel Agency, which took care of visas and foreign exchange permits: "Woe to you if any stamp is missing at any border." A visa for Palestine required a deposit, a considerable sum. People heard about unrest in Israel, but they didn't become unsettled by it: "I am glad that I may see my children and our country." Concerning the train trip via Berlin to Paris: "Every border control went smoothly!" Their son Wölfl picked up his parents at the train station. A few days in Paris, a trip to Marseille, and they boarded the *Mariette Pacha:* "Everything went smoothly in Marseille." They sailed in the direction of Alexandria: "One gets a little distance from things out here in the middle of the sea." There was a "German warship flying the swastika flag" in the Alexandria harbor. Port Said, Haifa, and they docked. They again reported that: "The passport check on the ship went smoothly. The commission worked very quickly—we were taken ashore." The information from initial conversations about chances of immigrating to Palestine was contradictory. They met their son Ernst, traveled to the Giwath Brenner Kibbutz, where they were lodged in tents. There was disillusioning news in conversations: Zionists were happy all the same. They heard disturbing things: "It is still not advisable to walk through an Arab village by oneself." Concerning Jerusalem: "A person must not get lost on a side street. These days, any Jew who does so can risk disappearing without a trace." But the kibbutz was booming: "I watched as they tilled and harrowed. All of it took place with the most modern machinery. I smelled the hay of our country. I am intoxicated by what Jewish people are doing here. Building is going on everywhere." And then: "I've talked over the problem of our future with Trudi, explained everything to her, how I would be tempted to stay here. It's a dream of a lifetime! If I could act on the basis of my feelings, then I know what I'd have chosen. But one must still consider many things."

Exploratory discussions, sightseeing, and tours. Back to the kibbutz. No luck in discussions with his wife: "I really don't think that Trudi will be able to decide in favour of moving to Giwath Brenner. And the climate certainly doesn't appeal to her. We have entirely different outlooks on things too. Trudi cannot understand my rather romantic view and sees things more plainly. If often pains me, but I see no possibility that this will change." He was disappointed that Jewish piety apparently played only a minor role. On a commemorative plaque, he "also found the mention of God, which one otherwise doesn't mention here. Nevertheless, I hope that a new devoutness will develop." He made several observations: "The cars all have bars, which is the best protection against rocks thrown at them ... Fortresslike Arab houses with embrasures. The solution to this entire set of problems seems extraordinarily difficult to me." Repeated debates with his wife, who absolutely refused to go to Giwath Brenner, "such that one of my dreams shall come to a close." He also expressed personal disappointment, particularly with his fellow countrymen: "The older German Jews are undoubtedly not welcome additions; they are looking entirely to the past and mourning dashed hopes. These middle-class people are not very adaptable. They hurt the building of Palestine more than they help it." Farewell, vain hope: "God grant that I may soon come back and take part in the development."

They traveled by ship and train: "There were extensive checks in Aachen. The customs officer came first; that went fairly smoothly. A civil servant then came to censor everything by the book. He was very proper, offered apologies to some extent."

Since everything went without a hitch at the border crossings, even at the German border, Cohn set off on a journey one year later, this time to Switzerland. His wife had to stay in Breslau, as she was expecting another child. So he was not attempting to flee, more likely checking things out. But he would give up hope: "Given my impaired health, there's no place else in the world where I see great opportunities to earn money. With God's help, the children will win through. In spite of my command of multiple languages, hardly any earnings will come from it. I believe that my life has arrived at a great turning point, has perhaps come to a complete halt."

An increasing number of emigrants returned in 1937. Their return again became a topic of discussion, for example, in the Reich Office for Emigration Affairs. A confidential circular said that "return to the territory of the German Reich by persons who are citizens of the Reich" could "not be prevented." How, then, were the authorities to handle emigrants who came back?

Answers to this question are not a priority here. We're more concerned with a trend that might have affected the behavior of father and daughter. Thus, a report from the security service of the *Reichsführer* SS* on the present position of Jews in Germany stated: "In recent months, a powerful 'emigration fatigue,' founded on the 'great pacification of the Jewish Question' in Germany, the comment of numerous Jews who were polled, has made itself felt, accompanied by the complete freedom for Jews to be profitably engaged in German economic life; the difficulty of immigrating—to Palestine, due to rioting in 1936; to other countries because of strict immigration regulations; the large loss of capital upon emigrating (Reich Flight Tax, exchange rate for blocked reichsmarks, Haavara payments† in case of immigration to Palestine, etc.)."

After that, they considered how "the expulsion of German Jews" could still go forward. Here are two additional paragraphs excerpted from the written statement, the first under the heading of "enlightenment" and the second under the heading of "intimidation":

Although attacks as mounted by hooligans seldom meet with understanding, because an enlightened people consider this type of fighting too primitive and nasty, propaganda that is geared more to "enlightenment and objectivity" would nevertheless achieve something useful.

The most effective means for removing the Jews' sense of security is the wrath of the people, which indulges in violent clashes. Even though this practice is illegal, it has a long-lasting effect, as the Kurfürstendamm Pogrom showed. Psychologically, this is even more understandable, for the Jew has learned a lot from the pogroms of recent centuries and fears nothing so greatly as a hostile atmosphere that can turn against him spontaneously at any time.

| 72

Moonlight in Vermont . . . In her edition of poetic works by Gertrud Kolmar, Regina Nörtemann has presented a chronological table in the appendix to the commentary volume. Her commentary points to "letters" that the poet sent to the actor Leni Steinberg during that period, letters that left the country for

---

* The *Reichsführer* SS was the top officer of the SS, at that time Heinrich Himmler.
† Haavara payments were payments made under the Haavara (Transfer) Agreement of 1933, in which the German government agreed to allow the Zionist government to transfer property from Germany to Palestine to encourage Jewish immigration to Palestine. It forced German Jews to give up most of their property before leaving.

North America. In her correspondence, Gertrud Kolmar asked "about possibilities for finding work in Vermont."

The epilogue also points to this correspondence, which indicates "that she was still contemplating emigration and was very concretely on the lookout for the possibility of working on a poultry farm in Vermont."

I wrote to Nörtemann and asked her to provide me with these previously unpublished writings. Much as she tried to help, it was not easy: the correspondence was purchased on the antiques market and is privately owned. The owner sets great store by privacy and wishes to remain anonymous. But Nörtemann passed on my letter, and I received a response. Still wishing to remain anonymous, the owner, an antiquarian bookseller in southern Germany, proved gratifyingly accessible and agreed to send me copies of the correspondence, which I received as promised. And so I worked my way with a magnifying glass through the very tiny, orderly Sütterlin script that was accentuated with numerous descenders and not always easy to read.

There are two postcards, a lengthy letter, as well as the draft of the addressee's response. The first postcard, dated May 22, 1937, is not of interest biographically. In contemporary terms, Leni Steinberg introduced herself as a "fan." The poet wrote to her and—what a strange oversight!—gave the wrong return address in the process. For this reason, the reply arrived at an uncle's house to begin with, and he forwarded it after a while.

A second, critical document, dated June 22, 1937, is a small, thickly inscribed postcard with a precise address: "Miss Leni Steinberg, c/o Paul A. Benjamin, Warm Brook Farm, Arlington (Vermont), U.S.A." The United States!

It goes back and forth about the previous address at first, but then gets exciting. The following sequence may well be appearing in print for the first time:

Along with this card, I am sending you eight poems as "printed matter." None of this has appeared in book form as of yet: it's hard to find a publisher for one's work.—And I live out here "in the country" (F. is a popular day trip destination for Berliners), and I gladly work a whole lot in the garden. Your language studies are of interest to me as well, since I am "by nature" a qualified language tutor and interpreter (of English as well). I hope, as you do, that an opportunity will arise for you to pursue your art, even if I would personally also gladly be working on a farm, breeding poultry in particular, about which I know a bit, as I do about horticulture . . . I've brushed up on my knowledge of geography just now and looked up Vermont in the atlas. I already knew that it was a northern state . . .

I'll be pleased if you like the poem "Gruss aus der Heimat" ["Greetings from Home"], and if I receive word from you again. Yours, Gertrud Chodziesner."

That's all there was to it! Her inquiry was apparently not all that specific. What stands out is that she didn't broach the subject by starting a new sentence but syntactically orchestrated a smooth transition: "I hope, as you do, that an opportunity will arise for you to pursue your art, even if I would personally also gladly be working on a farm, breeding poultry in particular, about which I know a bit, as with horticulture . . ." Thereupon, she closed the letter in an absolutely noncommittal way. There was no clear or urgent request to keep in touch, only the mention of the subsequent "printed matter" and the "poeticized greeting from home."

Should we conclude from this postcard sequence that she was not really serious in wishing to immigrate to Vermont? Or was she simply fishing for information in an entirely gentle manner? A bit of walking on eggshells in front of a chicken farm?

Here's how I read it: The sender presents herself indirectly as a woman who expects from the recipient, hopes, that she may pick up on what is being discreetly suggested—for example, that she is familiar with chickens and would gladly work on a farm in Vermont . . . She doesn't even mention in the course of this that she has agricultural training, merely points to her gardening experience . . . But don't make a fuss: just weave everything gently into the text of the postcard . . . This formally emphasizes the unassuming nature of the indirect inquiry, by the way. Theoretically, the inquiry would have certainly merited a separate letter . . . But she doesn't want to barge in through the front door in Vermont, merely knocks at a side door . . . What she really wants, and really doesn't want . . . In short, may the addressee be so kind as to understand the indirect appeal. Miss Steinberg certainly didn't flee Germany for no reason, and she did so without the prospect of a new job, though she dearly desired one . . . The sender double-checked as to the precise location of the state of Vermont . . . But, of course, it was primarily about the poems that would follow under separate cover . . .

Wasn't self-appeasement (also!) operative here? She could tell herself later on that she had absolutely tried to do something, had contacted a farm in Vermont, but they hadn't picked up on her subtle hint: no encouragement had been forthcoming, let alone an exhortation or even an invitation. The matter had unfortunately come to nothing . . .

From the incidentally passing remarks, those in Vermont could hardly infer urgency or, possibly, existential threat. It doesn't work to call so silently for help!

The noncommittal response of the addressee, who was apparently about to head for New York in the hope of finding work, is also significant: "It interested me greatly that I was able to learn a bit more about you, and I am glad that you can live in the country, which surely best suits your character."

This was admittedly a quotation from the draft of a letter, but Leni Steinberg could have transferred something similar to a fair copy. Apart from that, the four casually inscribed pages concerned the poems, which had arrived in the meantime, accompanied by her assessment and esteem, as well as mild, discerning objections and questions of interpretation.

Which poems did Gertrud Kolmar send to the United States to perhaps gain entrée there? She would have thought long and hard about what would generate the best response in Vermont.

While it would be going too far to insert the little collection here, I will present a single, exemplary verse from each poem that is frequently also my favorite verse. First, here is the magnificent opening verse of "Fischkönig" ["Fish King"] that I cited earlier:

> Where are the names that I knew?
> A scream tore them to pieces.
> One of them sails through my breast
> Along with my gray conscience,
> Wavers upon reaching my weighted mind,
> Increasing in its light:
> Go, king, go on,
> Let your crown lie!

The following poem, "Die Unerschlossene" ["The Undeveloped"], also came up in an earlier sequence of works in this book. But here is the magnificent opening verse again:

> I, too, am a part of the world.
> I have never reached mountains,
> have left bushland unpenetrated,
> Pond bays, river deltas, salt-licking coastal promontories,
> Caves, wherein huge dark green reptiles flash,
> Inland seas, flaunting orange jellyfish.

It remains a mystery to me how the reader and letter writer at Warm Brook Farm was able to draw parallels to Hans Carossa,* of all people. Moving right on to the next example, however, we come to the fourth verse of "Das Götzenbild" ["The Idol"]:

---

* Hans Carossa was a German poet and novelist known chiefly for his autobiographical novels.

My breast is smeared with milk;
Two white rivulets run to my hips.
The moon dog must not see, what she has given birth to,
So the pregnant one scatters herbal fragrances to me.

I would not like to separate the final two verses of the poem "Die Lumpen-sammlerin" ["The Rag-and-Bone Woman"]:

The key calls the mother locker,
Her brother's worn-out shoe,
And rags boast downwind
With red dances, poor so-and-so,
They're ugly, used-up long ago.

Gently the great shadow wallow
With bag and cart before my feet,
Growing thick and gray: and if I
Bristle, propping up the hot cudgel,
Throws me too into the trash bin. Me too.

A poem follows that was written on April 1, shortly before she sent them to Vermont: "Mose im Kästchen" ["Moses in the Basket"]. It's difficult to extract a handy quotation, so I shall stick to three lines:

It's just a poor weeping mother getting lost in the rushes,
Rocking a box of reeds, crying silently for help
From the terrible world, where the idols live.

This line reverberates: "Crying silently for help . . ." The poem "Dagon spricht zur Lade" ["Dagon Speaks to the Ark"] was written three days after this poem. Leni Steinberg copied the following verse from the poem "Die Gauklerin" ["The Clown"] in her draft:

Surely what I did while smiling,
Deserves a laugh;
There's certainly nothing so elfinlike,
Insignificant and done without so easily.
A cup, shy of violets
Carried the lesson I drank,
Taking delicate flight from its coarse wood,
And adventure from mere stone.

And as a quasi swan song, here is the closing verse of the six-verse poem "Der Schwan" ["The Swan"]:

> Silently,
> Gold turning gray,
> He sings a song,
> That ends in sadness.

By presenting this poem, Gertrud showed that she wanted people in Vermont to see her primarily as a poet and not as a gardener and chicken breeder. There's nothing more to be said about it.

Coming back to the draft from Warm Brook Farm in Arlington, dated August 27, 1937, I don't need to address specific questions relating to the understanding of several passages in the text. The only important thing is the reaction in Vermont to the extremely discreet inquiry.

Here are several excerpts from the letter: "At last no poetry that deals solely with one's own self or our present-day, Jewish fate . . . In nearly every poem, I found lines filled with power and individual character, whereby I exploded with delight . . . "The Untapped" reminded me a little of Alfred Mombert who, along with Hans Carossa, is one of my favourite poets. But this comparison should not in any way deprive you of your own uniqueness . . . I would sincerely ask you to shed light on my question . . ."

The poet would address her questions in a long letter, dated October 18, 1937, on two thickly inscribed pages, surely room enough to return to her inquiry about agricultural work, poultry breeding or Vermont . . . But the first lines nip such prospects in the bud:

> Last night there was a "poets' evening" at which my works were also
> discussed. I came home late. As is the case after "bar-hopping" of this kind,
> I was not exactly hung over, but a bit too sluggish to do much mental or
> physical work around the house. So I tackled your letter of late August in
> the early afternoon, and since I was reading it, I immediately got the urge to
> answer, to write to you . . .
>   First of all, I thank you most cordially for your kind words and the loving
> comprehension of my work to which these lines attest.

The entire letter will certainly appear sometime in an expanded edition of her letters. I will merely cite an additional remark about her work that is biographically interesting: "Once a work is finished, I make very few changes to it.

As a beginner, I often did this on the advice of well-meaning experts and merely spoiled my own creations."

No matter how closely I read this letter, I cannot find the slightest reference to the subject of emigration. Kolmar presents herself solely as a poet and not as a woman who has emigration in mind. She seems to have forgotten all about it. Poetry is the main topic, not poultry breeding. So the question arises once again: how serious had she ever been about plans to emigrate, or how seriously had she considered emigrating at any rate? It remained a discreet allusion that was counterproductive in this case, and she thereby squandered all her chances, as the response from Warm Brook Farm showed. The addressee did not spot the proper cue for inquiries or offers. And so I presume that earlier attempts, such as the idea of immigration to England, remained equally noncommittal.

Assuming that Leni Steinberg had loudly and clearly picked up on the hint, conveyed on the q.t., so to speak, how would she have reacted? About like so?

"Dear Miss Chodziesner, if you are as knowledgeable and active in gardening as you mentioned and know something about keeping poultry, then please do your utmost to come to Vermont. There is plenty of work here for women who can seize the opportunity." And she would have immediately turned to the landlord Paul A. Benjamin (related to the Benjamin cousins, perhaps?) and asked, "Is there an opportunity for a German poet who knows a fair amount about horticulture and poultry breeding to work here in Vermont, perhaps on your farm?"

Warm Brook Farm would, indeed, have been a wonderful location for the poet! It had all the makings for her employment in house, garden, and on the farm.

The sparsely populated state had no more than half a million residents back then. The mainly hilly, thickly forested landscape had numerous bodies of flowing water and lakes rich in fish. These beautiful landscapes are very popular with tourists nowadays but are not suitable for cultivating wide swaths of fields with farm machinery. The residents consequently set up poultry farms that didn't require much space. Keeping goats was also viable, as was pig breeding, and cattle grazing besides. Maple syrup production was and remains economically important for agriculture. During Indian summer, the trees finally produce the brilliantly glowing autumn leaves that are so highly celebrated and sung about, and I don't just mean "Moonlight in Vermont" that Frank Sinatra recorded for Evergreen. Indeed, Vermont could have been an almost ideal second homeland for Gertrud (and her father!), particularly because of its moderate summer climate.

Carl Zuckmayer described the new ambience of Vermont to Ina's sister, Annemarie Seidel:

Beginning in July, we'll be renting a very isolated, entirely basic farmhouse here in the Green Mountains. It's a blend of old backwoods settlement and Carinthian farmstead, and lies on a hill above the lake on the edge of endless forests that already sport fall colours such as I have never seen before. This comes from the many species of maples and red oaks, etc., that are found in our area. The undergrowth is also thicker and more compact, such that the wooded mountains and forest edges look like a single, flaming red mass of leaves with dark, violet-black shades. The nearest neighbour lives a half hour away; the silence is primeval. . . . A cowgirl on a pony in long blue pants brings milk, butter, and homemade bread. The meat-and-fruit car from the nearest general store comes by every few days, and we purchase provisions from them. It is wonderful to be getting acclimated to the soft light of kerosene lamps and flickering candles in the land of Edison.

Additional keywords for Gertrud's virtual second homeland have been snapped up from a report by the historian Gert Niers. They are based on the question, "What would the energetic poet's field of activity have been like?"

Just before Gertrud was born, Jewish emigrants founded poultry and egg farms in the United States . . . Of course, they also had to fight against the prejudicial view that Jews could only be successful as merchants in big cities. They couldn't succeed as farmers, however, because they had absolutely no work experience in this line of business! . . . Yet the number of chicken farms belonging to German-Jewish emigrants grew . . . The Jewish Agricultural Society supported new establishments with low-interest credit and loans through the Federal Land Bank . . . A professional journal, *Der Yiddische Farmer* [*The Yiddish Farmer*], appeared . . . Most poultry farms were isolated, so this created new contacts . . . Far-reaching isolation very nearly made assimilation unnecessary . . . To be profitable, new farmers each had to purchase or take on several thousand hens and chicks . . . This was hard work: ten to twelve hours per day, seven days a week . . . Feeding, cleaning stalls, rearing chicks, vaccinating, gathering eggs, weighing, packing . . . Laying out fences to protect against stray dogs, martens, raccoons; occasional use of firearms . . . Farmers had to search for and secure potential sales, primarily to restaurants and markets . . . The U.S. poultry and egg sectors would eventually be dominated by German-Jewish farmers to a large extent . . .

In *Im Labrynth der Paragraphen* [*Lost in a Labyrinth of Red Tape*], Armin and Renate Schmid confirmed the bureaucratic hurdles on the road to North America. So the question arises as to what could have impeded father and daughter on their way to Warm Brook Farm in Arlington, Vermont? What could possibly have hindered their departure, however late?

Prospective immigrants had to post bond, file an affidavit of support. An American sponsor, for example, Mr. Benjamin, had to furnish proof of income and assets, had to leave a security deposit at a bank, including an affidavit of support, savings account, life insurance, real estate, stocks and bonds . . . and send a confirmation of deposit. The affidavit might be rejected by an American authority with demand for a better guaranty. Deposit the affidavit of support with a lawyer. Sponsor makes advance payment for passage by ship at an American Express office. Written, certified proof that booking took place and proof the reservation was made. State Department registration at the consulate general in Berlin. Scheduled summons from the Consular Division for a medical examination and for delivery of the documents required to issue a visa. Registration of the quota number . . . handing over the passport . . . tax clearance certificate from the German tax office . . . copy of the receipt from capital levies paid . . . certificate of good character . . . payment of Reich Flight Tax . . . proof of amounts committed to Jewish cultural associations . . . registry office notice of departure from the police . . . request from Federal Tax Authority to open a limited-access security account at a foreign exchange bank . . . request to make a nonrecoverable payment to the Deutsche Gold- und Diskontbank in Berlin . . . obtaining permission to transfer household goods to be sealed by customs officials . . . drawing up a list of household goods . . . additional tax statement of household goods to be taken abroad that were bought after December 12, 1932. Deadline for immigration . . . possible Department of Justice notification that even two affidavits are not deemed sufficient . . . getting hold of a third affidavit. A new obstacle: A duplicate of the reservation for passage on American Export Lines no longer satisfies the requirements and regulations. Statute of limitations for submitting documentation runs out. Starting over?

| 73

Hilde, the bookseller: A conversation about the book trade may have occasionally taken place in Finkenkrug. Or did Gertrud go into the metropolis and visit the bookstore on occasion? What might she have heard there about the state of the book market?

First, here are three quotations from an article in the November 11, 1937, edition of the *C. V. Zeitung*: "In today's period of transition and regrouping," the Jewish book trade faces "the most difficult tasks. People used to say, 'Which book?' Today, they must say, 'Which Jewish book?'. . . Apart from financial considerations, everyone used to be able to satisfy his or her learning requirements and entertainment needs from the literary creations of the world. Despite every individual effort, the idea has not yet sunk in that today's new order of things has made it necessary—as a spiritual commitment to oneself—to turn one's attention in the main toward the Jewish sector. . . In the realm of books, a voluntary, radical spiritual upheaval in Judaism has only taken place among a small social stratum." And so booksellers and distributors still had to work hard to persuade people in those days.

Hilde Wenzel could have cited figures that shed light on the status of a Jewish poet like her sister in the Nazi state. Within the previous four and a half years, the total number of books published in the Jewish segment of the market was around five hundred: "The total number of all books published within this period of time was 892,000." This figure referenced the sum total of all editions. More than 80 percent were new publications; the remainder were reprints. A quarter of new works were books with religious or philosophical content. Literary works accounted for 20 percent, books on Jewish history around 10 percent, books in the Hebrew language around 7 percent, and literature on Palestine 5 percent. We now come to two surprising figures: 6 percent of new works were poetry volumes, and only 5 percent were biographies. Hilde could also have spoken about the "three thousand mark." The average number of copies usually only exceeded this mark in the case of reference books. Books in Hebrew sold around 4,700 copies on average, books on Palestine around 3,500, literary works in general a little over 3,000, and the average number of poetry volumes—not bad!—stood at 2,500. And this at a time when about 100,000 Jewish families were still living in Germany.

At the beginning of November 1937, the concert and lecture column of the *C. V. Zeitung* reported on an event sponsored by the Berliner Künstlerhilfe:* Erna Leonhard-Feld and her colleague Leo Merten recited poetry by Gertrud Chodziesner, Jacob Picard, and Martha Wertheimer, which they presented under the title of *Ungehörte Stimmen* [*Unheard Voices*].

The actor Erna Leonhard-Feld was a contemporary of Gertrud Kolmar. Erna's father furnished a "proposal for the comprehensive new rendering" of the Bible, published in 1934 and edited by the biblical scholar Harry Torczyner in Jerusalem. It was a four-volume edition with a large number of copies printed.

Erna Leonhard-Feld had recited poems by Gertrud Chodziesner half a dozen times in all. These events took place at various venues: a private home, the Private Instruction Community of Grunewald, the clubhouse of the Jewish Women's Federation, and the podium of the Jewish Cultural League. As was the custom back then, poetry was recited from memory, although this is hardly ever the case today. (An impressive exception was an evening with Joseph Brodsky, who brilliantly declaimed his own poetry.) Leonhard-Feld, who was Jewish,

---

* The Berliner Künstlerhilfe, officially the *Jüdische Künstlerhilfe* (Jewish Artists' Aid) of Berlin, was an organization that helped Jewish artists to emigrate from Germany.

recited poetry by Jewish poets, including Franz Werfel, Karl Wolfskehl, Nelly Sachs, and Else Lasker-Schüler. It seems that Kolmar's poems were specially highlighted and presented under the name Chodziesner again!

The reviewer, signed "H. L.," was surely Hugo Lachmanski:

> The voices of three poets have certainly no longer gone entirely "unheard." But as Erna Leonhard rightly noted in her opening remarks, the Jewish public has hardly given them a broader, more enthusiastic reception until now. I got the strange overall impression from the inaugural evening that Picard was actually more feminine in his poetic renderings, though he was the lone male in the group of three. His lyric poetry is lighthearted, emotional, based entirely on longing, dreams, pain, and reminiscence. On the other hand, Gertrud Chodziesner's poetic path proceeds from the personal realm of poetry in which the lyric *I* is realized as pure confession in a fantastically heightened reality of strange occurrences and creatures, and her difficult verses become intoxicating, as if they had been inspired by the colours and images of Arthur Rimbaud.

There are still no hints about the form these events took. Did they draw large crowds? Were the audiences small? Did the speaker comment between recitations? Did she communicate with the poet about the choice of poems beforehand? Or was the selection entirely up to Leonhard-Feld? Did the poet always attend? At any rate, the letter to Vermont attests to her presence at the event in 1937. Did they applaud her? And can we allow ourselves to imagine that she at least stood up briefly to accept the applause and was only partially dismissive?

| 74

"For the Jewish Book" was the headline on the front page of the November 11, 1937 edition of the *C. V. Zeitung*. A great plea, not only for Jewish books but also for reading "on behalf of Jewish culture" in general.

Along with twelve colleagues like Leo Hirsch and Gerson Stern, Jacob Picard also wrote a statement on the topic of the "creative moment." Had the author not taken the opportunity to mention his colleague, Chodziesner, Picard's contribution would hardly be worth mentioning for its pathos: "We read, yea, hear the mythical sounds such as those of Alfred Mombert or the great verses of Gertrud Chodziesner, our kind of poets, both of whom live among us poor, modern-day people."

A delighted Kolmar expressed her thanks almost immediately, acknowledging this remark in an accompanying letter:

When I picked up the *C. V. Zeitung* day before yesterday and read your essay on the "creative moment" with great interest, "not thinking anything nasty," then suddenly saw my own name after Mombert's and before Dostoyevsky's, do you know what I felt like? It's not easy to describe. But maybe Andersen's "ugly duckling" felt like this when it finally ended up among the swans, and the watery mirror showed him that he was a swan himself . . . I thank you sincerely for these printed words, and likewise thank you from my heart for the thoughts expressed in your letter. Now I don't wish to feign false modesty and say that I have not earned the praise that you gave to my verses . . . No, you see, I openly admit that I have not known the great artistic struggles of other poets: I have merely always struggled to become a strong, kind-hearted woman. And if I hear from the mouth of a real expert that my art has unexpectedly grown along with my pursuit of personal growth, then I am deeply glad. You will not think less of my writing because of this admission, will you? I was pleased when Frau Feld told me that your poetry and my own would be recited on the same evening, and I was even happier when you told me the feeling was mutual . . . For I don't care to shine as the brightest star in a canopy of minor constellations, and surely you don't either! Oh, how gladly I would have written to you, "Dear Herr Doktor, your words of recognition honour me. But there are many, more important Jewish poets than I here in Germany . . ." You know yourself that I cannot write this way, that my words would have been nothing more than a white lie, and I am sorry to think it . . .

So please allow me to thank you cordially once again for every good word that you wished to bring before the public about me and my work. And rest assured that I am already looking forward to expressing my gratitude again verbally in December. I send you many greetings and call myself by the name with which you honour me,

Your friend, Gertrud Chodziesner.

Here is a small postscript: Some two months later, Picard telephoned Finkenkrug to ask if there was a convenient time for him to come for a visit. She later wrote:

If I'd only known your number, I would have called you right back after I hung up the phone on Sunday. It occurred to me that declining your visit must have hurt you after all, and I should have asked you to come here in spite of the fact that family members were expected. But it's not customary to talk about my "poetic activities" among extended family in the first place—quite apart from the fact that the little children would have required attention and been bored by such conversation. And since I must be hostess and servant to my guests all at once, it would have been impossible for me to sit comfortably off to the side with the two of you.

These two statements typified her role as servant. Was this behavior only circumstantial? Surely she would have planned the family visit ahead of time. Hilde was certainly in on it, so Gertrud could have said to her or another woman in the group, "Please make sure that everyone has something to eat and drink; I'd like to sit in the upstairs room with my colleague."

Something like this was inconceivable to her. She kept the apron on, literally and figuratively, although a chat about the status of poets and literati would surely have been important to her. It would have nearly had novelty value, but no! The continuation of the regular family routine took precedence over a discussion of literature, over the decidedly changed working conditions and prospects of publication, and not just for Jews. What was going on in the academy? What did the publishing landscape look like? Who else had left the country by now? What would you prefer then, Herr Doctor, to stay or to leave?

Seven months later, she was still hoping "to see" the Picard couple "sitting here cosily at my place in the fall—of course, you will find me to be an entirely simple, 'unliterary' person."

But, finally, there were visits and discussions. Writing on vacation in Vermont, Picard would later reminisce: "I occasionally got together with her during my last two years in Germany, usually in the company of her elderly father, that wonderful man from the old days."

| 75

Required reading was connected with a shocking discovery: Karl Josef Keller continued to publish as a Nazi poet. This time, five of his poems were featured in the slim solo anthology *Wir glauben* [*We Believe*]: "Junge Dichtung der Gegenwart" ["Young Poetry of the Present"], softcover in the Deutsches Wesen [German Essence] series, first printing in 1937.

The foreword sets the tone, is mercifully short but over the top: "Poetry must always be a service, a service to the tremendous mission of the *Volk** . . . The poet of our day is a soldier first and foremost . . . Called up as custodian of the German

---

* The Nazi use of the term *Volk* [people] went far beyond the literal meaning of the word, adding a sense of German identity and superiority. Nazi propaganda often portrayed individuals as part of a great whole called the *"deutsches Volk"* and used the term in nationalistic political slogans such as *Ein Volk, ein Reich, ein Führer* [One people, one empire, one leader]. The Nazis also used the word in such compound words as *Herrenvolk* [master race], *Volksgemeinschaft* [people's community], and *Volksgenosse* [fellow countryman].

soul, to bear witness, to proclaim and reflect the dawning of the new Reich . . . That faithful loyalty to the *Volk* and their Führer became Word . . . We say yes to everything that prospers the eternity of the German people . . . We believe!"

I shall not introduce the rhymed contributions in detail, for this would honor them too greatly: extracts will suffice. I'll proceed in the order they appear. First, a "harvest song" by Keller. Offerings for harvest festival were held in high regard back then: "We harvest the grass . . . the waving crops . . . Death in brilliant colour . . . none in the country starves here . . . calloused hands . . . Praise be to all eternity . . . Land with life most radiant colour."

Consequently, his contribution to the Harvest Festival, which was played up propagandistically in those days, came after the "harvest song." Keller joined in the chorus: "Oh you glorious German soil . . . You offered yourself up and we sowed you beneath God's sun and wind . . . You, Oh Earth, are our great altar . . . We offer our lives and deaths in eternity."

Keller apparently did not versify any hymns of praise to Hitler, but other authors steered clear of this too. Nevertheless, they stayed in the mainstream of contemporary cultural politics and were not only tolerated but also promoted. Their situation in that era can be compared with that of painters, whose paintings were purchased for museums and art collections and to adorn office spaces. Artists were by no means expected to merely reproduce images of Hitler: they painted meadows, fields, forests, cows, horses, deer, water, mountains, and skies. Based on this division of labor, Keller dealt with grain and stars, bread and blood.

The same applied to the theme of Germany in general. Here are the first two lines of both verses from "Lied an Deutschland" ["Song to Germany"]: "Germany, you, the most-golden grape on the world's vine . . . Germany, you, the most glorious flower in the world's garden." And this line rhymes with it in German: "You receive our death eternally."* Must we now cite one of the many parallels that fit within the catchphrase "dying for Hitler's Germany"?

The next poem is "Anrufung" ["Invocation"]. The one who is being invoked remains nameless, so the associations are all the more numerous: "You here, you there, you in factories, on ships, you within vapour and streams, with the plough and the spade, you, you, you / Guide our senses, lead our hands, / so that our ways and efforts succeed / and do not burn out the fiery longing / for land that is free and a life well-mastered."

"Eiserne Landschaft" ["Iron Landscape"] is the fifth and final example. The poem equates steelworkers with farmers, cast steel with bread dough, molten steel with wine: "Blazing and hissing, aglow with flames, / their bread baked of

---

* The original German text is "Deutschland, du herrlichste Blume in dem Garten der Welt / Dich unsere Sterben ewig erhält."

native iron soil . . . They sow and reap bronze and stone / their fiery wine the essence of steel and molten iron."

With his five contributions, Keller was numerically among the top authors in this hundred-page volume. Kolmar must surely have noticed this! In any case, Keller later wrote that they had switched poems. If this had not been the case, then sister and brother-in-law would likely have displayed the new publication in the bookstore. And then what?

Retouching is not an option here. For a limited time, the Jewish poet who wrote poems against acts of SA terror had a close relationship with a poet of the "Blut und Boden" ["blood and soil"] school.

How might she have seen this in the quiet hours? The written record provides no clues. So until further notice—and judging from an outside viewpoint—it can only be stated: Here is an exemplary case of a relationship in which the connection between heart and head is lost at times, proving once again that understanding and feelings do not have to be identical.

| 76

Factition: Dear Father, consciously leaving aside fiscal questions (I have enough to do with accounting in the bookstore!), I shall come back to the topic of England. As I was obliged to learn in the meantime, I was much too naive in my previous letter on the subject. Wishful thinking was apparently part of the equation. My eyes were opened in various ways by two lengthy conversations with customers who became good friends. Both have contacts in England, one through a nephew, the other through a friend. I must share the results of these two long talks with you. As you can see, I still shrink from writing to Trude about it. As much as conversations with her matter to me otherwise, the entire subject seems something of a nuisance to her. The decision as to whether preparations will finally be made to flee the country depends entirely on your stance in the end!

First of all, as far as you're concerned, what might have affected you or what could possibly affect you, it would hardly be possible to publish sketches from everyday life in Nazi Germany in an organ like Senior's Watch. First, the British Interior Ministry would have imposed the strictest political restraint, particularly in terms of criticising Hitler and his followers. One does not wish to spoil things unnecessarily with this power broker and number one potentate: appeasement, please, in the finest British tradition. Add to that the second, fitting point that there is little or no interest in critical articles on the situation in Germany. Good old isolationism is still at work here: the English Channel also acts as a mental barrier, so events in Hitler's Germany are of very little interest.

This also comes out in the sales figures for the few books that deal with developments in Germany. The information Leopold Schwarzschild gathered about the Reichstag fire met with minimal interest, and his book, End to Illusion, lies like a deadweight in the retail book trade. I also heard from a relatively reliable source that not even two dozen copies of the paper Hitler Rearms are said to have been sold, although the fact that Hitler is massively rearming is contrary to the provisions of the Treaty of Versailles and should actually be of "vital interest" to England. Indeed, England even made concessions to the dictator by signing the Anglo-German Naval Treaty: build warships again by all means, but please don't overdo it . . .

So, you see, there's no real interest anywhere in information coming out of this country, including its apparently enviable strongman and his brutally energetic charisma. What emigrants say about him, sooner verbally than in writing, meets with apathy on the one hand and disbelief on the other. Isn't it true that these emigrants are simply exaggerating, just want to show off and act like big shots with their dubious stories of concentration camps? They simply have to dramatise so that we'll accept them as persons who in fleeing saved their own lives.

What makes matters worse is that a residency permit is linked to the requirement that the applicant accepts no employment. The worldwide economic crisis has also caused high unemployment in England. The remaining jobs should therefore be protected, and even unpaid work is prohibited. It's possible that an exemption permit could be obtained in your case, but that would depend on many factors over which you would have no control.

It would have been even more difficult for Trude. She would have had the greatest difficulty finding employment as an au pair, tutor, or teacher and, even then, the only subject would have been French. Add to that the overall age limit for single women. Female workers have the best chance of being accepted for housekeeping and child care, but only if they are between the ages of eighteen and forty-five. So the door would have gradually closed for Gertrud.

And as a translator? I must disappoint you there as well. The splendid isolation of the island inhabitants has direct repercussions here. There is absolutely no interest in reading literature in translation. Whatever is available in the English language is completely satisfactory to the predominantly conservative clientele. Thus, Gertrud would hardly have the opportunity to translate a French novel into English, for example. She wouldn't even have the chance to translate her own poetry or other work for potential publication. She would seem much too advanced for England, which would only reconfirm the fact that Germans overdo it. One must therefore put activity in the literary field out of one's mind from the get-go.

Unless . . . you had the name Stefan Zweig, resided in London, and enticed the English with a biography of Mary Stuart. You wouldn't have to worry at all about *this author, who is translated and enjoys worldwide success. On the other hand, how can authors who are barely known in Germany and completely unknown over there—and Trude is among them, so let's not kid ourselves—gain acceptance?*

Things would probably go about the same for her as they have for a poet whose name should not be mentioned here out of tact and discretion, except by the initials MHN:* an "Aryan," but one periodical called him a "crypto-Jew," a Silesian with very, very little knowledge of the English language. He's gotten nowhere in London, and he'll never live to see the day when they praise him to the skies there. He would have preferred to stay in Zurich, but the Swiss authorities didn't want to renew his residency permit, so he went to London. And there he signed a declaration that forbid him from taking any kind of work. The odds were extremely slim that the Foreign and Commonwealth Office would raise any objection to his resumption of work as a freelance writer. Incidentally, this wouldn't be taking work away from anyone, since you can't earn a thing from it anyway. So MHN continues to write poems without the slightest possibility of finding a publisher, certainly not in England. This remark made the rounds: "Pity that no sod will print this stuff." Maybe he'll succeed in placing one or two poems in emigrant periodicals later on, but they don't pay any fees as a rule or they'd forever be owing money—they're always teetering on the edge of bankruptcy as it is. MHN supposedly also wrote a novel, by the way. He didn't even look for a publisher, of course, be it in England or Holland. He resignedly stuck the typescript in a drawer, which is somewhat familiar to us in view of Gertrud's novel, isn't it? This is how resignation grows and grows, paired with social isolation. And no one knows how long the exile could last. "I incorrigibly continue to write verses." Such a remark is also familiar to us, isn't it?

What can we conclude from this rather pessimistic-sounding account? First of all, and this should be fine with you anyway, there's nothing more to do with regard to England, nothing to jump-start on that score. No need to drop the subject: it simply mustn't be brought up anymore, no matter how casually. Trude surely won't ask about it. Or do I misjudge her on this topic? On the one hand, she certainly doesn't seem to want to leave; on the other hand, Palestine has come up in conversation. If I were you, I would not necessarily introduce the subject. But if it were to come up again, then I would ask you to seize the opportunity posthaste. Speaking of which, it should again be made clear that London's restrictive immigration policy of allowing as few Jews as possible into Palestine also has an adverse effect in the British mandate. As Jews become a larger portion of the population, one fears that the potential for conflict with the Arabs will increase. Just how highly explosive the situation is there can be gleaned fairly often from the papers.

---

* MHN is Max Herrmann-Neisse, a German poet and writer who went into exile in London in 1933, where he lived until his death in 1941.

I must say in general that the idea of a Palestine in which as many Jews as possible ought to settle is turning out to be more and more illusory. The area is simply too small and too poor! The word "settle" further suggests that the freely available land can be cultivated. Large areas of land will not be allocated: land must always be purchased, that is, bought from Arab inhabitants.

A red-on-white map has been placed in the back inside cover of a book on Palestine that is on display in our store. The map makes it clear that Jewish settlements lie far apart in Palestine: areas in red hatching stand for Jewish lands, solid-red marks for KKL lands.* Points along the coastal plain are especially thickly settled, particularly near Tel Aviv. As you go inland, however, they get farther and farther apart, and are even scarce in the vicinity of Jerusalem.

After a short break from writing, I must therefore bring up the idea of France (!), which makes considerably more sense than Palestine and is closer than the British Isles. Does this come as a surprise? From all that we've been told, half of our emigrants must have taken refuge in France, certainly ten times the number of those taken in by England so far.

Now, please don't ask me why I'm only advancing this suggestion now. And I ask that you read this "written statement" with your usual care. The slogan now reads: "Forget England, Vive la France!"

I imagine that Trude's time in Dijon would be a good point of departure. She apparently enjoyed her time there seven or eight years ago and completed the French course with an outstanding result—something like this can only be favourable! There might still be one or two people in the university system to whom you could speak about it, but be careful how you ask. If you don't have any luck there, then Trude could try to gain a foothold in the publishing or bookselling world. To improve her chances, she could translate and present two or three of her poems (not the most difficult ones)—or a piece of prose—as a calling card of sorts. But maybe it would suffice if she approached them with her two little poetry volumes. If she still didn't find a position with a publisher or in a bookstore—even in France, we Juifs [Jews] aren't overly popular—then perhaps she could find work keeping house for a bookseller or publishing house employee. One can safely assume that she would be treated with a modicum of respect that, all modesty aside, she truly deserves. Unfortunately, one does hear that Jewish immigrants are treated with condescension, even mistreated, both in households and in smaller firms. By presenting a sample translation, however, she could set a tone that would prevent humiliation or at least make it less likely. A translation to signal that: "I am not a stranger to you, and you are not strangers to me. France was no random choice, no makeshift solution. Mon dieu [My God], this trip to France was

---

* Keren Kayemeth LeIsrael [KKL or Jewish National Fund] was founded by Zionists in 1901 to purchase land in Palestine for Jewish settlement.

"prearranged" ten years ago, which is to say I'd already gained a foothold in La douce France [gentle France] a decade ago, albeit in Dijon, a place I would have naturally bypassed to head straight for Paris, where the more interesting book- shops are and an intensely active, bookselling married couple (I know of a certain example in this case . . .) might be happy if relief were offered, at least in the form of in-home help.

Nor can a new position as governess and private tutor be entirely ruled out. In light of the tense political situation at present, one would hardly be interested in German lessons, but what about English? After all, it's the language of the nominal brotherhood-in-arms, the Allies.

In the course of typing this, I have everything clearly in my sights, and it strikes me as almost within reach. If you deliver the proposal with your usual authority, discuss it forcefully, then it would trigger a response no matter how much inner resistance you encountered. And the two of you would pull yourselves together while it's still possible. You would also be doing this for your own good, Father. After so many years in Finkenkrug, life could possibly gain new vigour in Paris. I don't want to lapse into daydreams, but this opens up good prospects: letters wouldn't be opened by the censors anymore, no one would be listening in on tele- phone calls, being arrested on the street would be gone, you wouldn't have to fear abduction, and Trude could breathe a sigh of relief.

So, stern father of mine, I implore you to take this suggestion. Persuade our hesitant, sometimes much too introverted Trude. Make her enthusiastic about France, the land of Rimbaud and Verlaine, and stay at her side. You don't have to leave straightaway with tons of baggage. With Helene's help, Peter and I could organise the transfer of books and furniture as soon as you get settled. Now you, too, should begin to get ready like our family all around us. The horizon is darken- ing, and you need only look up to see it.

When I hand you these pages, my written salutation will be accompanied by a personal embrace. A bientôt, See you soon, Hilde.

| 77

In the final quarter of 1937, Gertrud Kolmar wrote the cycle *Welten*. A miracle took place here: in a time of increasing pressures and restrictions, she freed herself through writing, gave up her corset of rhymes, and expressed herself in free verse.

After the Second World War, Peter Wenzel would compile his sister-in-law's typescripts and manuscripts. His own "depot" came along with that of his ex- wife, who continued to support him greatly. To begin with, he would initiate the publication of *Welten* in 1947.

A little paperback lies beside me, more like a cardboard notebook, blue-gray, name and title in red lettering from Suhrkamp Verlag, formerly S. Fischer Verlag, sixty-three pages, including an epilogue by Hermann Kasack.* On three pages are a biographical sketch, a longer passage from one of Kolmar's letters, and a quotation from a piece of lyric poetry:

> When I am dead, my name will hover
> For a little while above the world.
> When I am dead, may I still
> Be found somewhere along fences behind fields.
> Yet soon I will be lost,
> Like water flowing from a scarred pitcher,
> Like fairies' secretly forfeited bounty
> A little cloud of smoke from a speeding train.

This high point of linguistic flowering came in the fifth year of the Nazi dictatorship! And it took place in poems that she didn't include in the subsequent poetry volume that came out the following year. Did the tone seem too novel to her and, therefore, too risky in a country that fought against artistic innovation or crippled it at the very least? At a time when many colleagues became faint-hearted and fell silent, she reached an apex in several of the poems.

There are seventeen poems on fifty printed pages, which is already a good indication of their average length. Even in this narrative of her oeuvre, I will quote each in its entirety.

First, the poem with the editorial title "Zueignung" ["Dedication"]. She opens with a stylized self-portrait of a female artist for whom a modest manner is characteristic, but who finally celebrates herself in an apotheosis. The original title was "Kunst" ["Art"]:

> She took the silverpoint instrument
> And bade it go over the matte white satin surface:
> Her country. It drew
> Creating mountains.
> Bald mountains,
> The bare-edged stone foreheads of summits,
>   meditating on the desolation,
> Their bodies
> Dwindling, wrapped, vanished behind the pale cocoon
> Of a cloud.

---

* Hermann Kasack was a German poet, novelist, and writer of radio plays.

Thus the picture hung over the gloomy plot, and people
    looked at it.
And people said:
"Where's the fragrance?
Where's the sap, the filling luster?
Where are the greens, brimming with emergent power
And the brown, burnt red of the cliffs
    or their silent, gray gloom?
No falcon hovers on the lookout, no shepherd piping.
The mild blue evenings never shaded with beautifully curved
horns of wild goats.
This is colorless and insubstantial, without a voice; it does not speak
    to us.
Come farther."

But she stood and remained silent.
Small, unnoticed, she stood in a heap, listening in silence.
Only her shoulders flinched, her eyes slaked in tears.
And the cloud that wafted her drawing hand,
Sank down, enclosed, lifted and carried her up
To the bald mountain's crevasse.
Someone waiting,
With a crown snaked by two golden-green basilisks,
Stood in the twilight, glowed and bowed in greeting.

In the next poem, "Dienen" ["Waiting On"], autobiographical material again becomes highly stylized. The text is widely draped, evokes alchemical effects, and confronts us with the vastly modest actions of the lyric *I*, who is preparing a meal for someone she loves:

Whose substance you bind and release, cool and glow,
    weaken and affirm,
Who you irritate with acid, torment with ore, hide secret potions in capsules
    brewing in test tubes and crucibles,
Though the alkahest is neither the red nor white lion,
    what you,
Adept in alchemy, are simmering, I find strange and wonderful;
What you, lord of fire, restrain in a bronze cage, that now
    crawls and crouches ready to leap like a prowling predator,
Shooting up, shattering the bars, claws enraged
    tearing your limbs (oh, I tremble to think of it!):

I want to attract a different sort of flame, a milder, tamer blaze,
    which caresses me by the hearth, purring and playing
    like a domestic kitten;
For I want to prepare varied dishes, a small meal,
    designed to please you,
When tired yet smiling you into my darkening
    rooms come.
Why do you scold me?
Why do you mock me?
Is it because my world is plain, just a few square steps, hemmed in,
Full of inglorious, petty things, minor chores,
Filled with clattering cups, bubbling pots, ugly
    steaming splattering fat, overflowing milk?
Is it because I lift bulbous barrels of flour, open little spice boxes,
    grate nutmeg,
Weigh herbs, squeeze lemon juice into glass bowls,
    or whisk golden-yellow egg yolk in blue cups? . . .
Yes,
Do you know what the Turkish copper coffee grinder
    saw in Sarajevo
And my pitcher with brilliant white and red spots in Bohemia's Ohře
    like fly agaric in the forest?
Do you know,
That big ships, smoking black, navigate all the oceans for me,
    hauling freight to every coast,
So that when pale grains trickle through my fingers,
    the silent faces of the men of Rangoon look at me
Or the dark face of the Negro, singing, reaping rice
    in South Carolina's fields?
Or that an Indian woman climbs unseen from a wooden tea box
Adorned with silver, in woven ocher and terra-cotta
    flowing and waving?
The voices of Bulgarian farmers echo back to me
    sharp as onions.
And I ask the slowly pouring drops if the olive trees
    from my strange, lost homeland didn't make them.

Oh sunny meadow, into which my thin, anxious kitchen overflows,
With a belt made of viper's bugloss, yarrow, wall barley, Scabiosa,
With quietly grazing spotted cows, and the rhythmic beating
    of their tasseled tails,

Oh golden-brown streak, interwoven with poppy-red and
    cornflower-blue,
The silence of midday and the warm scent of coming bread breathing
    about us!—
Then I threw crumbs into hot, sizzling butter,
Still shaking from the blackened pan pounding
    with a thousand hammers in the veins of the earth,
Still hissing and crackling the tortured iron rises up,
Robbed by the mother, raped in the oven, was forced to take shape.
Then, my spoon, tasting the steaming soup,
    carved by expert hand,
A linden branch grew again above the low roof,
Blossoming, surrounded by choirs of singing bees.

Let my friend come and eat.
And see, all nature helped me, so that I may serve the One.
Today as yesterday love decks out the table.
Take then with love, what the bowl carries:
May it please your eyes, its aroma agreeable,
    and may whatever enters your mouth be a blessing to you.

Gertrud Kolmar wrote about her identity as a poet who emphatically distanced
herself from other people's approaches during the creative process:

Yes, I know that I am a poet, but I would never like to be an author.
Papa recently received one of Mary L's letters. It was sent to him by
an acquaintance who is also a friend of hers. In it, she talked about
completing her biography of Catherine the Great and said she wrote
the ending while the beginning was already being printed. Since I don't
know the work, I may not claim that a book written in this way would
not turn out well. But I am really alienated by what I would like to call a
lack of respect for one's own work. Imagine not having it in its entirety,
if only for a short time, so as to read the whole thing from beginning to
end before it goes to the publisher! I certainly don't demand that it be
set aside for weeks or months, as I consider proper for a manuscript and
also allow in the case of my own works. . . . I will not imitate the way
she creates or her working tempo. But something about it disconcerts
me, is very foreign to me . . . She creates for today, and I try to create for
eternity, probably without sufficient strength. She is successful, at any
rate, and I—well, success isn't important enough to me, the essential
lies elsewhere.

Here is the great narrative poem "Die Stadt" ["The City"]. A pair of lovers explores a wintry city in the north. Is it Hamburg, as Kolmar intimated in a letter? Associations with autobiographical events turn up of their own accord and need not be more closely cited. Beneath this poem like a watermark are the initials K. J.:

They walked
Through the cool, light mist of a winter morning, lovers, hand in hand.
The hard earth crumbled and tinkling frozen puddles spurted under
    their shoes.
Down by the riverside path
Someone in a brown velvet jacket sat before his easel
Painting a drooping, leafless willow.
Curious children crept closer,
And the adults ceased walking for a moment,
    blaming, praising.
Toward the bridge covered with slippery, green algae
Floated a deliciously dilapidated boat.
Three swans on the waves
Arched their slender necks, silently,
    unfolding their wings with a flourish.
The woman tore bread and threw it far out into the water.

Beneath rigid oaks,
Branches black and twisted, stretched like tortured limbs,
There they stepped onto frosted grass, and the ivy-covered pillars
    closing the gardens.
As they set foot onto the long stone bridge,
The sun tore the mist away like a robe,
And the city stood up, diagonally behind the broad basin of the river.
Shiny gray-black roofs intertwined and overlapped
    like the plumage of crows, the higher ones with a green patina;
    golden cupolas flashed.
Gulls screeched on the bridge railing, flapping hungry beggars.
They were now on the other side
And looked at the boys in front of the sullen everyday house,
    binding their yellow dog's sore, bleeding paw.
Women with net shopping bags, baskets with handles, hurriedly eyeing
    the unfamiliar idlers warily and mistrustfully,
Disappearing behind the doors of gloomy, small and puny shops.

The streets became louder and stronger, more prosperous, fuller.
Stately inns beckoned with bold letters;
Redbrick walls stood there, heavy and powerful
    as did old-fashioned aldermen with quilted doublets and berets
    and ostentatious coats.
Streetcars clamoring merrily, rapidly ringing, like a street urchin
    slipping away at a park gate.
Men in thick, warm coats smoking and discussing
    and fast-moving trade and commerce,
And soon enough the snack bar started up, its stand extolling
    the nourishing smells of roasting.
Shops all lined up,
Offering tender, juicy meats and venison, fish,
    smoked eel and herring,
Offering long and crispy brown bread, sweet, filled with currants,
    and tangy ones, dusted with flour
    or strewn with salt and caraway.
A tiny Chinese teahouse tucked between copper sheets
    made of lacquered cherry wood,
    its gilded roof curled.
Yet this archway, where, for quite a sum, potions and salves and powders
    are mixed and dispensed as medicine,
Showed an old man through the window, alive, stooped in his chair,
In a woolen coat, with flowing, snow-white beard;
He has closed his eyes.
Behind him grins a long, horrid skeleton with a skull,
    sneering eye sockets and teeth,
A glittering scythe in one hand and the other
    clawing the sinking shoulder.
A clock showed midnight.
Then the woman was frightened and grabbed the man—

But he just nodded and smiled;
Because he saw nothing but her dark hair
    and her pale, dark-eyed face.

Gertrud Kolmar hardly wrote any poems after this cycle. Was this due to the mounting pressures of the Nazi dictatorship? Or was it ultimately unrelated to external factors?

Whether we interpret it as the result of independent literary development or the outcome of external influences, the poems finally stopped—poems in her mother tongue, at any rate. But Kolmar would later try to make a fresh start in the tongue of the ancient Hebrews.

| 78

Hilde Wenzel immigrated to Switzerland in March 1938. Her husband was expelled from the German Reich Association of Booksellers. Compulsory membership in the RSK professional association was terminated because he was still married to a Jew.

The direct catalyst for her hasty emigration was that Hilde had been summoned to the police station "for the purpose of passport inspection," so she was afraid that her passport could be seized and wanted to forestall it: "I telephoned my father. 'I'll be back soon,' she said. My siblings showed up at the store that evening. They'd found out what I was planning. My brother was pale. 'You won't make it to the border,' they said. 'They have taken down the passport numbers, and it's not all right for you to still have your passport.' 'I'm going to try,' I said. . . . They still didn't understand what was in store for them."

Hilde traveled to Switzerland by herself. She went on to Italy from there, probably pursuant to a stipulation of the cantonal immigration authorities. Sabina Wenzel wrote: "But it was precisely the moment in which Hitler visited Mussolini in Rome, and all Germans were being interned on those particular days." Hilde returned to Switzerland. Of course, she only got a temporary residence permit "for the purpose of preparing to emigrate."

Additional information from her daughter: "At some point she arranged for me to be brought to Switzerland by a rather distant Aunt Paula, my father's cousin, who called herself 'countess.' She also crossed the border with ease, so you had to wonder what kinds of connections she had. I believe that she took me to foster parents in Montagnola first, a dentist and his family who owned a villa next door to Hermann Hesse* with a beautiful view." She remained there for a half year.

Factition: Revered Father-in-Law, I hereby go on record with what I've already let you know in short by phone: we had to close our bookstore, our antiquarian bookshop, and our little rental library. The Reich Culture Chamber has stricken my name from the list of bookseller members because I am "Jewish by kinship," that is, in spite of geographical separation, I am still married to Hilde. One of my

* Hermann Hesse was a famous German-Swiss poet, novelist, and painter whose best-known books include *Steppenwolf* and *Siddhartha*.

grandmothers has also been brought into the mix; she is apparently not entirely compliant in terms of racial ideology. In short, I defile the pure image of the German National Socialist book trade.

In the past few months since Hilde escaped to Switzerland, followed by the delayed "transfer" of little Sabine, I was alone in my rooms a great deal. And feelings caught up with me that previously had almost no room to unfold during periods of compulsory activity. But sometimes I feel ashamed when I stand in front of the shelves "reflecting" (one could have said this while glancing through the shop window), or at the table with new publications, "reflecting" more than ever. OK, new editions, reprints of classical texts were lying there. OK, contemporary American novels were lying there, amazingly enough still deliverable. But the professional association urged us not only to place new books by German authors on the shelves but to give them special consideration in designing window displays as well. And did we ever get deliveries! At times, I got the impression that the table bent and its legs buckled under the weight of lies. If mendacity didn't weight it down, dishonesty did. I did not, as tacitly assumed, spread out and fraudulently display them on the table in the middle of the store; for example, books by dignitaries who took part in the Lippoldsberg Poets' Meeting last year. Yet I was forced to keep them visibly on offer. However, I would have preferred to merely hand them over upon request—books like those by Beumelburg and Kolbenheyer* (or, as I allowed myself to jokingly say to our employee, Kurt, Beumelheyer and Kolbenburg). But I've mainly displayed books on animals and gardening on the main table (not only for your sake), and books by your favourite authors, Paul Eipper and Hermann Löns, one or two of whose titles I've already sent to you in Finkenkrug: Animals Look at You . . . Senta, the Yellow Mastiff . . . My Green Book . . . And germane to Löns, My Brown Book.

It is with a certain melancholy that I look at the little stack of order cards I have saved from the bankruptcy assets: Peter Wenzel Bookshop, Berlin-Charlottenburg 2, Grolmanstrasse 30/31. I close my eyes and see only a single name written on the reverse side in spooky script and only a single title, The Lyrical Work: linen binding, dust jacket, ca. 500 pages . . .

But this dream book presupposes, and here is our letter of intent, that we do everything in our power to collect and place Gertrud's poems in safekeeping. She fancies that her work is sufficiently protected in her "starch box." Even in these brutally barbaric, regressive times, she cannot imagine that what is commonplace in house-to-house searches could also happen to her.

The box with her memorabilia, writings, and typescripts could be overturned and everything trampled underfoot by men in boots. Yes, the box could possibly

---

* Werner Beumelburg of Germany and Erwin Guido Kolbenheyer of Austria were authors favored by the Nazis.

be dumped out the window, and she could be forced to "kindly burn the Jewish rubbish." Everything, everything, everything would then be gone in one fell swoop, and we'd never get over it. So that this nightmare does not come true, we should devote everything to taking the poems to safe places in time, just in time, indeed at the eleventh hour, insofar as they are still accessible.

I beg you to support me, even more so than previously. Encourage your daughter—as her former "senior clerk," you certainly have the authority to instruct her—to make copies of the typescripts, to place them outside of the house, and to give them primarily to Hilde in relatively secure Switzerland. Where this is no longer possible, as with older poems, I'd gladly type them out, also with carbon copies. They mustn't be stored in a single, allegedly secure place: it's advisable to distribute them over greater distances instead.

Even if this letter is delivered via our apprentice, Kurt, on one of his cycling excursions, we should discuss this matter as soon as possible in person. This letter should get you in the right mood for it, as it were. When this Nazi Walpurgis Night is finally over, and the poems and other texts no longer have to remain hidden, then I will collect everything again and see to fitting publication—even if I have to go from pillar to post. I tend toward pathos but sometimes see myself as a kind of Saint Christopher who carries little people on his shoulders through the sweeping, brown flood. She and her work must reach the other shore. And you must help me get there. Greetings, Peter.

In retrospect, Hilde, the émigré, would have been able to tell the family things from Switzerland that made it more difficult to harbor illusions. Combining the experiences of others into a classic case, here are a few pointers that might have spared Gertrud:

You move into a little hotel ... need support and find it, both privately and organizationally. The Jewish community pays hotel costs for the time being ... Numerous confrontations ensue with the Swiss immigration authorities ... Restrictions increase: The Swiss authorities don't wish to attract the displeasure of their expansionary, aggressive neighbor. There is constant fear that Switzerland could be annexed like Austria, so-called "Return" (to the Reich) ... You leave costly Zurich and take lodgings in Ascona, for example; look after yourself in the little hotel room, perhaps get a spirit stove ... Feelings of loneliness set in: there's no longer anyone who addresses you on a first-name basis ... The main problem of a residence permit remains, and growing numbers of Swiss immigration officials prove to be antagonistic ... You have to show up at the police station with your passport every month ... Residence permits remain strictly limited timewise ... As a matter of form you must leave the country, travel to Italy, and come back, until revoked ...

| 79

Gertrud Kolmar stayed. From mid-March to mid-June 1938, she wrote a second play, *Nacht* (*Night*): *Dramatic Legend in Four Acts*.

After the war, senior editor Hermann Kasack noted, "Better to omit from
the complete edition. Dramatic without vigor, but also linguistically without
exceptional realization—publication not opportune for the time being." It took
a long time before a theater was found for the premiere. It took place at the
end of February 2000 in the small theater of the Düsseldorf Schauspielhaus,
sixty-two years after it was written. It hasn't been presented in another theater
in this country, at least not so far. And yet a translation exists: *Notte. Leggenda
drammatica in quattro atti*. Was this edition also meant as a script for the Italian
premiere? It hasn't taken place so far.

What were Kolmar's expectations or intentions in writing this piece? Did she
ever have the slightest hope that it would be performed sometime? There was
just one theater in Berlin that could have performed the work, the Theater of
the Jewish Cultural League. Plays and operas were performed there under the
artistic direction of Kurt Singer, producing a wide range of dramas on the theatrical side. Gotthold Lessing's *Nathan der Weise* [*Nathan the Wise*], a natural
choice for the opening, was performed on October 1, 1933, with Kurt Kartsch
in the leading role. He would also eventually leave Germany and would be typecast by Hollywood in the role of the villainous SS officer. Shakespeare's *Othello*
was the second premiere. The role of an outsider followed Lessing's gospel of
tolerance: "The Jewish audience is often inclined to substitute the word 'Jew'
for 'Moor' . . ."

The spectrum broadened quickly, and Shaw, as well as Priestley, Goethe,
Carlo Goldoni, Molière, and Pirandello were performed. But there was an
increasing tendency to expand the percentage of Jewish plays in the repertoire.
Stefan Zweig's *Jeremias* [*Jeremiah*], written in 1921, was a triumph. Schnitzler,
Molnár, Wertheimer, Wolffsohn,* and others followed. Plays by Jewish authors
would eventually be the only ones approved by the Reich Culture Chamber. The
theater continued to operate with some interruptions until August 1941, so a
play by the Jewish author Kolmar might have theoretically had some chance of
being performed. Did she see performances at this highly professional theater?
Did she come into contact with the theater or, possibly, with the artistic director's office? Did discussions take place—or preliminary discussions at any rate?
The typed fair copy of the play indicates that the usual stage directions were

---

* The writers mentioned are the playwrights Arthur Schnitzler of Austria and Ferenc Molnár of
Hungary, and the German journalist Martha Wertheimer. Wolffsohn may be the German writer Julius
Wolffsohn.

provided, so it was adapted for the theater, at least according to how the author conceived it.

I suspect that she initially wrote the piece for herself, for the inner stage in her head. Was it a closet drama, as people would have called it back then? But who would have read it, who could have read it, when only one or two typescript copies were available? It's not as if Germany had a conspiratorial sub-culture like Samizdat* that produced handwritten or typewritten copies. So for whom did she write the piece, or whom did she have in mind?

As we've already seen, she was not a woman to produce a flurry of activity in the literary field, developing, cultivating, and expanding her connections. And so this piece was also forgotten.

The opening cue: "The action takes place on the Island of Rhodes in the year 2 A.D."

No summary in the style of a theater guide follows. I will simply highlight the main outline of the plot, which is the story of a young Jewish woman who sacrifices herself.

Tiberius Claudius Nero is the main character. He supersedes the historical person of the same name, of course: he has been lifted out of political context and could actually bear a fictitious name.

Moving directly on to the plot, an animal must be sacrificed so that a connection to the godhead ensues. A black goat is the offering. A slave pro-cures—which is to say, steals—it. The people robbed are an old man and a young woman, Ischta, both of whom live in a cave. They depend on the animal for their livelihood, so Ischta abducts the stolen goat. But when it becomes known that the goat was meant to serve a higher purpose, the perpetrator surrenders to the guest from Rome, "throws herself at his feet: Sire! Do not punish us! Have mercy! . . . The goat is ours . . . our only one! Thy servant took it . . . I brought it home . . . I set it free . . . Sire, we are poor, we shall perish!" She begs for mercy.

Tiberius orders the kneeling Ischta to rise. She obeys but soon wishes to kneel down before him again: he demurs. She reveals that she is Jewish and declares her willingness to atone through service: "Sire, take me into thy house above the cliffs! Take me into thy white house so that I, but a maiden, may be thy slave! I shall try hard . . . and not complain if thou punishest me! I want to learn everything, everything . . . to prepare the bath, to mix spices, and to anoint and braid hair . . . That I may serve thy wives . . . and adorn them, softly: so that each may be beautiful when thou callest them to thy chambers . . ." And so we see labors of love, indirectly, in the submissiveness of a slave.

---

* Samizdat was an informal system in the Union of Soviet Socialist Republics that secretly printed and distributed literature that had been censored by the government.

The motivation behind love and affection for the great man cannot be easily understood. We certainly cannot find the answer in the character of Caesar, who is merely a catalyst for intensification, so that enslavement proffered becomes an offer of self-sacrifice.

The indirect suggestion of erotic love does not fit into Tiberius's concept of self-discovery, however: "Be gone!"

But just as she is about to retreat to the cave: "She hesitates, turns around, rushes up to Tiberius and falls down before him. 'My lord . . . oh, my lord . . . I *cannot* run from thee . . . I *cannot!* . . . Cast me not from thy presence . . . I shall endure everything, everything . . . I simply *cannot* go!' "

That is the sore point! She, a sinner, offers herself as a sacrifice. So the question arises, "Oh, maiden, what are thy sins?"

Indeed, what sins could there be that Ischta regards as deserving of death? "I *cannot* name them, my lord . . ."

But after a short interval, she passes on keywords from two biblical stories that are meant to indirectly impel him to accept her self-sacrifice. First, she alludes to Abraham, who was willing to sacrifice his son, Isaac. She then obliquely becomes more direct: "And if thou commendest me to him" (God) "for the sake of thy victory, as Jephthah the Judge did his daughter . . . but he did not know it . . . fell silent."

This condensed, abbreviated version is puzzling. How should the Roman understand it? And what are we to make of it?

The reference is to the eleventh chapter of the book of Judges. Jephthah wages a military campaign against the Ammonites. He promises God a burnt offering if he is victorious. The first person that he meets upon returning home after the victory shall be the one offered up. The Lord God accepts Jephthah's offer and allows him to win. He returns home and "behold, his daughter came out to meet him with timbrels and with dances: and she was his only child; beside her he had neither son nor daughter. And it came to pass, when he saw her, that he rent his clothes, and said, 'Alas, my daughter! thou hast brought me very low, and thou art one of them that trouble me: for I have opened my mouth unto the LORD, and I cannot go back.' And she said unto him, 'My Father, if thou hast opened thy mouth unto the Lord, do to me according to that which hath proceeded out of thy mouth.' "

Without further inquiry, without discussion, she agrees to be sacrificed by her father. She only asks for a period of two months in which she withdraws to the mountains with her women friends to bewail their "virginity." She returns punctually from the mountains and stands before her father. No questions asked, not even any opposition, just a victim who cannot resist, who does not even want to resist. So it was pure coincidence that decided her fate:

this random choice, this random decision was included in Jephthah's plan, in his deal with God. Even when chance chose his only daughter, no questions were asked of the father: "He did with her, according to his vow." Martin Luther wrote in a marginal note: "One wishes / he had not sacrificed her / But the text stateth it clearly here."

Returning to Ischta's conversation with Tiberius, she identifies herself with Jephthah's daughter from the outset. And she passes on the offer to Tiberius with this suggestion: do as Jephthah and sacrifice me. Surprisingly, Tiberius understands this veiled offer and, after briefly contemplating it, accepts the offering, though it's immaterial to him who shall decide, the God of Israel or the goddess Ischtar: "I will sacrifice to the one who accepts it."

His retraction follows immediately: "Flee and live." But Ischta touches the ground with her forehead: "My lord, I am your slave."

Tiberius does not want to accept this: "Do you know who I am?"

She insists, "The one who sacrifices me . . ." This time it is intended to be a love offering. "My lord . . . I am burning . . ." she cries at the end of the third act. To which he responds laconically, "Come. He pulls her to him, wraps his garment around her, and leads her away into the darkness."

This young Jewish woman does not ask the questions that we ask ourselves. She goes into the trap with eyes open. She does not ask herself whether the sacrifice could possibly be meaningless, whether the goat should have, perhaps, been sacrificed in her place. Ischta is prepared to sacrifice herself without inquiring about other options. Even so, this is about her young life, which will be given up. She increases the value of meaninglessness and futility through intellectually erotic devotion, at least in her own eyes.

The sacrifice takes place in secret. The sign of the sacrifice will be reported on but not visible on stage: "His clothes are splattered with blood." Tiberius insisted on slaying Ischta himself. But as the drama unfolds, he must soon realize, "The sacrifice was made in vain."

Kolmar's imaginary figure symbolized the embodiment of total self-sacrifice to the point of self-destruction, be it surrender or be it death. She created the role of a woman who ignores herself to the extent possible, abandons herself, places herself last, meekly sacrifices herself, and allows herself to be sacrificed.

The central theme, sacrifice and victimhood, comes up repeatedly in Gertrud Kolmar's oeuvre. How might we understand this in each case?

To sacrifice oneself for *someone*, such as her father. This can be plausibly demonstrated within her inner circle.

To sacrifice oneself for *something*, such as an ideology. This can be understood within wider circles but still cannot always be comprehended by outsiders.

To *be sacrificed* without reluctance, resistance, even without a clearly definable reason? Explanations are hard to find in this case. Was she secretly hoping for remission of sins, rather than to compensate for minor offenses? Was the prevailing idea to achieve something good, something essential as Marcus Curtius* once did?

First Jephthah's daughter, then Ischta, the poet's counterparts: Did she envision these figures to understand herself? Or to justify herself to herself?

In any case, to be sacrificed without knowing why, without understanding what it means, and to agree all the same requires a means of explaining this victim syndrome that I do not have at my disposal. I see a type of role behavior here that one can hardly identify with today.

I look for clues in the secondary literature on Kolmar and see that I am not the only one having a hard time with this issue. Particularly in view of *Nacht*, Marion Brandt writes: "When I read this play, as well as particular poems by Gertrud Kolmar, I am taken aback or even repulsed by the fact that several female figures offer to sacrifice themselves." Marion Brandt also tries to understand but only suggests possibilities that might lead to solving the problem. Regina Nörtemann also sees it as a "research necessity."

So this isn't a chapter of a biography, but rather a topic for scientific research. First of all, the meaning of sacrifice and victimhood in Jewish religion and philosophy would have to be analyzed.

This thought pattern would have to be strictly differentiated from the concept of sacrifice propagandized by the National Socialists in those days. In this context, Christina von Braun points to a book by Lydia Gottschewski that was published in 1934, *Männerbund und Frauenfrage: Die Frau im neuen Staat* [*Male Society and Women's Rights: Women in the New State*]. In it, you can read about women in the Nazi system: "The decisive criterion for these women is their willingness to sacrifice." The same is true of their readiness to serve. "Service" is realized "most beautifully when I takes a back seat to you or we, where it abandons itself and dissolves into something greater: child, family, and *Volk*."

Tricky subject! Especially when it becomes linked to the usurpation of thought patterns in National Socialist writing. The publisher Langen Müller opened its Die Junge Reihe (Young People's Series) with the little volume, *Ich dien!* [*I Will Serve!*]. Characteristic concepts include: "And place yourselves in line to serve . . . *Ich dien* is the freely chosen dictum that drives us . . . Oh, they who serve it will freely harvest the seeds . . . Its spirit is service. And it will gladly serve."

* Marcus Curtius was a legendary hero of ancient Rome who sacrificed himself to save the city.

Indeed, willingness to serve and readiness to sacrifice were ceaselessly prop-agandized. All of this finally boiled down to active duty in the military.

The obvious thing is to develop and reproduce the following explanatory model: In the end, Gertrud Kolmar sacrificed her own life for her father. Absent the very strong bond with him, she might have gone with Hilde to Switzerland or followed Margot to Italy. Either by herself or with her father, she might have survived the Shoah [Holocaust].

Yet her basic attitude was not all that homogeneous. After all, there were early signs or at least overtures in preparation for immigrating to England. And what about the cautious, nearly hidden indications regarding Vermont?

And readiness to settle in another world was in the offing, after all. Thus, she wrote to her sister that same year: "When I began to learn languages, I did not sense, of course, that languages would one day become a 'trump card.' But when I now find myself in better psychological shape than many who are otherwise no worse off than I, that's certainly owed in part to the awareness that, 'wherever I wind up, I'll surely be able to communicate immediately or within a short time.'" But she didn't dare put it to the test.

Here is an interim analysis for possible reconsideration later on: Up to 1938, she did not determinedly pursue plans to emigrate. She admittedly went to some effort to leave Germany but did not explore every option. When she explained that she couldn't abandon her father and had to carry on with the "affairs" as head of household, this was always a convincing argument.

And what about her father? Would he have ever said to her, "Trude, we cannot stay here any longer. It's high time that we got out of here!"

| 80

Time to pause and take a deep breath. In a letter that "Father and Trude" sent to Switzerland, the senior partner wrote:

> The holidays are now over. The weather was absolutely paradisiacal on Good Friday. The sun shone on every path, on every creature, sweet, bright, warm sun. And I went through the green forest, through thousands of white and pink-coloured windflowers with my Little Bee and Flora. And your father shares in Goethe's tragedy—*si parva licet comparare magnis* [if one dares compare the small with the great]: a young feeling, youthful enthusiasm in decrepit body. . . . Trudchen hid a dozen Easter eggs and the little doll searched and found them all, and finally even saw the rabbit that slipped through our fence. . . . That same evening, Aunt Clara and Uncle Alex

came unannounced to say good-bye. They will be leaving us forever in just a few days.

It must have been a shock for Gertrud, because she particularly admired this uncle. Here's what Hilde had to say: "Yes, in her own sincere, reserved manner, my sister Gertrud was frankly partial to our uncle. She admired his vivid imagination. 'He is a poet,' she liked to say, 'even if he's never written a single line.' . . . 'What Uncle Alex told,' was proverbial with us, and it was a very bad sign when we couldn't get him to tell us the story about the silver leg or some other exciting tale."

| 81

The name of the poet Gertrud Chodziesner shows up in July 1938 in a very surprising context—namely, as a member of an action group.

In the archive of the Jüdisches Museum in Berlin, there are twenty-seven microfilms from the extensive Jacob Picard Collection of the Leo Baeck Institute. There are three letters that have not been published until now, and the writer Martha Wertheimer authored them.

She wrote the following to colleagues in Berlin:

> The suggestion has come to me from Artist Support and Reich Association of Jewish Cultural Leagues circles that Jewish authors, whose published and unpublished works have been recited at meetings of Jewish cultural leagues in Germany, at artist support groups, congregations, and other organizations, join forces in a community whose purpose is to get organizers (and not those reciting, who receive honoraria themselves) to compensate authors living in Germany with the help of the Reich Agency for Jews in Germany. What they have in mind is a union that is in no sense an association but simply a sort of emergency action group. I therefore ask you to inform me as soon as possible at the above-mentioned address whether you are prepared to send a letter concerning this matter to the Reich Agency and to sign your name to it. The draft of the letter is enclosed.

Just a week later, on July 19, Martha Wertheimer could report the following in a second newsletter: "Regarding my first letter, everyone to whom it was sent has responded positively and assured me of their signature on the letter to the Reich Agency."

Wertheimer sent the letter to "the Reich Agency for Jews in Germany" in Charlottenburg's Kantstrasse:

In countless presentations by Jewish culture leagues and cultural presenters (Jewish congregations, artist support groups, educational associations, women's leagues, etc.), performing artists recite from our published and, at times, yet-to-be-published works. Whereas it is considered a given that the organizers will pay an honorarium to the performing artists, the authors who play an essential, indispensable role in these events have come out of them empty-handed up to now.

For this reason, it is our suggestion that an emergency action committee of Jewish authors living in Germany, who should be incorporated into the Reich Agency for Jews in Germany, get all presenters to pay a small contribution to this emergency action committee, with plans as to the amount and distribution still to be worked out. . . . Jewish authors are of the opinion that the measures suggested here also represent support, both for the publicity of the Reich Agency for Jews in Germany and Jewish books, and so it may be expected that intensive publicity for the works presented at evening recitations will have a positive effect on book sales. . . . With the greatest respect and on behalf of:

Gertrud Chodziesner, Karl Escher, Herbert Friedenthal, Leo Hirsch, Georg Hirschfeld, Josefa Metz, Arno Nadel, Jacob Picard, Arthur Silbergleit, Manuel Schnitzer, Manfred Sturmann.

Dr. Martha Wertheimer

The poet, who liked to portray herself as a loner and was largely seen as one, shows up here as a member of an action group!

Here is something new that indicates the existence of a circle of literati who knew one another. Karl Escher, for example, either got to know Kolmar at the Stomps publishing office or saw her there again and wrote down impressions of her that have been previously cited in this book. She would have met Martha Wertheimer at Leonhard-Feld's recitation evenings. And Picard's name has already come up repeatedly.

Furthermore, one of Kolmar's anecdotes shows that, even when her work was not being presented, she attended recitation events and came into contact with other colleagues there:

At an "Unheard Voices" evening where, by the way, my verses were not recited, the writer Josefa Metz introduced herself to me at an informal gathering that followed the performance. She sat down next to me and asked, among other things, whether creating was difficult or easy for me. "Difficult," I responded. She found it very easy, she said. One or another Viennese newspaper had praised her, and she even won first prize from the Berlin Gasworks at that time. An advertising poem of hers received the award. "Just imagine, first prize from the Berlin Gasworks," she repeated and seemed completely unable to let go of this happy memory. That struck me as such a . . .

However, I will not be introducing Josefa Metz or any of the other cosignatories of the petition in brief portraits, as they are listed sufficiently in the *Zentrales Verzeichnis Antiquarischer Bücher* [*Central Directory of Antiquarian Booksellers*]. What's more important here is the question of communication between colleagues. Did Kolmar shut herself off from or open up to conversing and communicating? The contours of the largely isolated poet who isolated herself become softer. In a three-page printed letter to Hilde, she reported on a newly established connection:

> The young poet—that is, she is around fifteen years younger than I—sent me a letter after the event at which poems by both of us were recited. She had my book but would gladly like to know more of my poetry, and would I like to send her some to copy? I did so, and we've been in contact with each other ever since. This doesn't make me especially happy, however. She is undoubtedly very talented, still hopeful, and already in part accomplished, but her nature is apparently completely different from my own, which also doesn't bother me. What rubs me the wrong way is that she insists on addressing me as "fabulous creature," "person to be respected," and "master." First, I am not a suitable object for such things, and second, it doesn't fit her fresh and self-assertive manner in which she doesn't mince words (at least, that's how I experience it, but I could be wrong, of course . . .). Now we are just at the beginning of our acquaintance—albeit I already have five letters from her—so perhaps this newly planted tree will bear fruit someday . . .

The appeal came again, but did it have any effect? Two months later, Picard wrote a critical article in the *C. V. Zeitung*: "The Cultural Leagues as an Author Envisions Them."

It arose from the fact that authors still didn't receive any honoraria for texts that were read aloud in public. Did the negotiations drag on? Was the petition rejected? I cannot go into the question further but can only state that Jewish authors were marginalized by the Reich Literature Chamber and the Reich Agency for Jews, and not only in Berlin.

Jewish Cultural Leagues mainly stressed theatrical and opera performances, symphony concerts, and presentations of light entertainment. "Authors of literary works," on the other hand, found almost no possibility of being performed:

> Weren't there lecture halls where people like us could read their work aloud? No, that's precisely what the cultural leagues only allow in few cases,

and almost not at all during these years. But, one would counter, haven't interpretive performing artists recited your works occasionally? True, true! But therein lies the point with which we were only partially in agreement. While they could actually have been missionaries for our literature, had they properly assessed their role, the directors of the big cultural associations, caring only for those artists who reproduce someone else's work, have set an example for others. Neither have they put in a good word for us, nor, more importantly, have they allowed us to have our say, as would have been appropriate in this matter. They repeatedly justified it by saying that authors did not do well at reciting their own work. That may be so, although it does not apply universally.

But it was not simply a matter of "experiencing mnemonic wonders, but more about being in direct contact with the creator. These are facts that have always been recognized in every country outside of Germany and are being recognized more than ever today: how bitter to have to state it here."

| 82

Martha, their deceased mother's sister and a potential aid to Gertrud later on, immigrated to Palestine with her husband and son in July 1938.

Papa Ludwig wrote to Hilde in Switzerland: "They left me forty volumes of Johann Gottfried von Herder in the 1853 Cotta'sche Verlagsbuchhandlung [Cotta publishing house] edition as a keepsake. I leaf through it a lot. I especially liked the aphorism I wrote to you about, and it is always on my lips nowadays, like a cigarette in a smoker's mouth, just as calming, yet much less harmful than nicotine." And what, to him, was the ultimately harmful double dictum reads: "Whatever providence sends, endure; / Whoever perseveres will be crowned."

His gaze had fallen on the first lines of a long, devoutly balladlike poem, "Die wiedergefundenen Söhne" ["The Recovered Sons"]. Here is the first verse:

Whatever providence sends, endure;
Whoever perseveres will be crowned.
It knows how to repay in plenty,
Rewarding a peaceful mind with glory.
Brave is the lion tamer,
Brave, the world conqueror,
Brave, whoever masters himself.

Chodziesner made the two opening lines his own. They were tailor-made for his "peace of mind," and he abided by them.

Chodziesner liked to quote classical authors and traditions anyway. So he implored fate to grant his grandchild every imaginable good and added, "The ancient Greeks called the Fates that determined human destiny 'Moirae,' and the Romans called them 'Parcae.'"

This illustrates the jurist's fatalism, too. As a man with a classical education, he could point to traditional thought patterns that he had developed, thought patterns that would influence his behavior. Persevere, for no one can escape what fate has predestined. So he fortified himself with cultural material that deterred him from making necessary decisions.

Factition: My Dear Hilde, confirming receipt of your latest attempt at writing, I would like to, no, must ask you categorically not to incessantly prompt me as to what to tell Gertrud with regard to what we, possibly together, should set in motion. At seventy-seven years of age, I am experienced enough to be able to assess this properly myself. I cannot fathom or even concur with your repeated outbreaks of emigration hysteria. My brothers and sister badgered me sufficiently before departing for South America. And your sister Margot did not spare me from dark omens to convince me that I should also seek my salvation by means of flight.

My dear, I am slowly approaching my eightieth year. Perhaps you will very gradually factor that into your considerations. I won't be able to put down any more roots on foreign soil. People would have no more use for me abroad in any case. I would merely be a burden to various people and institutions. And I would primarily be a burden to the eldest of you. I cannot exploit Gertrud's attachment to her father, certainly not unscrupulously. In a foreign country, she would be all the more absorbed in caring for her elderly father, who would be increasingly afflicted with rheumatic aches and pains and would therefore need more help if, in the worst case, impending immobility occurred. I therefore support her efforts to go abroad, to flee, which flare up on occasion. She should not be saddled with her elderly father like Anchises carrying old man Aeneas on his back from the burning city of Rome. Such a burden would bring this small person to her knees, tough as she is. She should be on the lookout without being burdened by her father. You should leave me here in peace. Emigration is only appropriate for the younger generation. As far as my siblings are concerned, well, all right, there must also be exceptions. I do not stay behind gladly, however, but of necessity. When the "Chodziesner" ship goes down then, as captain, I want to remain steadfast on the bridge up to the final minute.

As I have already written to you, sister-in-law Martha has left me the complete Herder, forty volumes in the Cotta edition. If I may, I see something like this as a sign of fate. Almost without thinking, led by superficial curiosity to begin with, I have leafed through several of the volumes and stumbled on the double dictum in the process, the one I've already shared with you. And I will repeat it regardless, because it has become a guiding principle for me, a motto, indeed a slogan: "Whatever providence sends, endure; / Whoever perseveres will be crowned." The poet and preacher Herder formulated it from sufficient experience of life, so I can safely appropriate it for myself.

And the forty volumes that I've lined up on the cleared-off writing desk, flanked by marble and bronze bookends, indicate something else, too: The volumes provoke me to go into them more deeply. That would no longer be possible in exile because a person is eaten up, as it were, by demands that come at him from all sides, or so I hear. "Take up and read!" the volumes seem to call to me, as freely adapted from Saint Augustine. Take us in your hands and read us! In fact, take every one of us and read us all, beginning with his Letters for the Advancement of Humanity, which proves to be strongly desirable at this time. In these generally unsettling times, made even more disturbing within the family on account of you, I have not yet found the inner peace to let myself read this great humanist. But, as already indicated, I've leafed through him plenty. As if led by a helping hand, I stumbled upon two places right away that will most certainly spur me on to future reading.

In case you want to look this up, since you have enviably free access to everything that's available in print and bound, I refer here to Third Conviction. By this, does he mean reflexion? Anyhow, this is what the first, exceedingly momentous sentence says: "Increasingly, what must show its true colours is false statesmanship that places the fame of its ruler and the good fortunes of his reign in expanding the borders, pouncing on and capturing foreign provinces, increased revenues, clever negotiations, and in despotic power, cunning, and deceit." Isn't this a brilliant statement?

Now the second example, First Conviction, which I also caught by chance. But I would rather say and write, "apparently caught by chance," since I take it as a sign from on high. "The Abhorrence of War" appears as a crosshead. We are confronted with this topic nearly every day. By means of ceaseless repetition, they get us in the frame of mind to accept the ultimately, indeed probably soon-to-be-engineered, war as a fact. Here's another opening statement of the utmost, specific importance: "When a nation is not compelled to self-defence but horribly attacks a peaceful, neighbouring nation, then war is an inhuman, worse than beastly effort, in that it not only threatens the nation being attacked with devastation and the death of innocents, but likewise undeservedly and heinously sacrifices the nation that wages it."

No, I cannot leave it at this, for all good principles come in threes: "And what follows in its wake, more terrible than war itself, is disease, military hospitals, hunger, plague, looting, acts of violence, barren land, brutalisation of the spirit, destruction of families, and corruption of ethics that lasts for generations."

Are those not statements that take your breath away at a time like this, when propagandistic bellowing (above all, with the use of keywords or, better still, slogans like Sudetenland and Poland) is meant to get us in the mood for war? War that spreads like wildfire and could even drive emigrants like you from their places of refuge? Assuming that you do not face an immediate threat, you may almost certainly be interned. In that case, as long as I am not denied access to the garden, I'll let myself be forced to live under house arrest here in Finkenkrug.

Yes, I will hold fast to all forty volumes of Johann Gottfried von Herder. They will support me, give me inner stability, and put things in perspective. Only those who see things in perspective will survive. Then, perhaps, I will be rewarded for my resolute hope, and this horrific episode will draw to a close by the time I've read the fortieth volume. Then I would pile the volumes atop one another to form a triumphal column on the desktop.

And so I greet you, dear daughter. And give my love to my little granddaughter, Sabine, Your Father.

| 83

In August 1938, Gertrud Kolmar's third poetry volume, *Die Frau und die Tiere* [*The Woman and the Animals*] was published by the Jüdischen Buchverlag Berlin [Berlin Jewish Book Publishing House]. It contained sixty-four poems, mainly from an earlier period, on eighty-six pages.

She had already given up her pen name, and the volume was published under her surname. This was now according to regulation. *Reichskulturwalter* [Reich culture manager] Hans Hinkel wrote to the Reich Association of Jewish Cultural Leagues: "I find myself bound to point out once again that members of the Jewish Cultural League are forbidden from using noms de plume (pseudonyms). I beseech you to announce this directive to your members again and point out at the same time that contravention of this directive would entail an immediate ban from the profession and expulsion from the Reich Association."

The Jüdischer Buchverlag was not the same as the Jüdischer Verlag that specialized in scientific works and Zionist writings. The publisher Erwin Loewe incorporated the Jüdische Buchvereinigung, a book association that would soon have six thousand members, into his Buchverlag. Members paid one reichsmark per month (about ten euros in terms of present-day purchasing power) and received four new books per year.

Jacob Picard was one of the authors from the previous year. The title of his novella volume was *Der Gezeichnete* [*The Marked One*]. This was one of a number of texts on Jewish country life in the Lake Constance region. Here's a sample: "He greeted her in passing, but seldom spoke to her. But one time he said, 'Gelele, you look like a little canary.' Then the girl sensed what had come over him and began to run after him calling out: 'Are you meshuga?' "

This fourth-quarter volume* from the book club was very successful. Seven thousand copies were printed, most of which went to subscribers, although a small portion was sold in the ghettoized Jewish book trade.

Picard was also the one who staunchly supported the publication of Kolmar's poetry volume:

> From 1935 until the end of 1938, I lived in or near my hometown on Lake Constance. During that time, my volume of Jewish stories, *Der Gezeichnete*, was published by the Jüdische Buchvereinigung in Berlin. One day, the publisher sent me the manuscript of a poetry notebook by Gertrud Chodziesner, a poet with whom I was not familiar, asking me what I thought of it. I didn't even have it for two days before I wrote to him that he should publish it immediately. We all had the feeling it wouldn't be possible for us to do so much longer.

The poet ran into a precarious set of circumstances: The incorporation of the Jüdische Buchvereinigung into the Buchverlag unleashed protests within the Jewish retail book trade. New books were delivered to subscribers while excluding the book trade, and this at a time when the Jewish book trade was in an extremely critical position: customers were emigrating, repressive measures were on the rise, and money was tight.

Kolmar thus became an author at a company that was unpopular in the Jewish book trade, and this might have had repercussions for distribution and sales outside the book club.

Papa Ludwig was proud of his Gertrud, however, and his passionate letter to Hilde attests to this fact.

In the addendum to this letter, daughter Gertrud makes herself commendably inconspicuous. She reports on an afternoon invitation to "wine, ice cream, and coffee" at which her father "had to keep the *Damentoast*† warm, which I only found out about yesterday, by the way. This time, you'll find everything else I have to say in the little book. Kiss the little monster, whom I often long to see. Warmest greetings, Trude." Now the mention of the new book really couldn't have been more casual, embedded in family matters as it was. She really couldn't have downplayed it any further.

* * *

---

* The volume was Gertrud Kolmar's *Die Frau und die Tiere.*
† *Damentoast* is pork cutlet on toast.

On September 22, 1938, the little book was reviewed in the *C. V. Zeitung*. Hugo Lachmanski wrote, "Gertrud Chodziesner, one of the greatest, most unique talents among contemporary Jewish poets, has been mentioned several times in this publication."

The critic characterized the work of the poet "who takes her own, solitary path" as follows: Her "poetry is not the reflexion of a contemporary state of mind in the particular form of expression of the lyric *I;* rather, the lyrical concept springs mainly from reflexions that other figures cast onto the lyric *I.* . . . And yet, whether the poet only puts on a mask in the *I* form of her poems that she borrows from poor or spiritually joyless stepchildren—whether rag-and-bone woman or abductee, untapped or clown, sinner or old maid—even in costume, she becomes a confessor."

But her "own, painful lament" is also discernible in the poems, such as "Die Erzieherin" ["The Governess"]:

> I fill their outstretched hands, as I like.
> It's not their own . . . The day, standing without a head, tepid and flat
> Is like laundry and homework
> During the everyday stroll to the canal.

Or the lamenting in the previously quoted poem, "Die Verlassene" ["The Abandoned"]:

> I loved you. So much.
> I've cried so . . . in fervent supplication . . .
> And loved you even more, because for I suffered for you,
> When your pen refused to write any more letters to me.

The emphasis on "a lavish abundance" of images brings to mind the keyword "baroque." And Lachmanski continued: "The poet luxuriates in colours such as only the French symbolist Arthur Rimbaud, among modern-day poets, has on his palette. Whatever may have awakened this sense of colour in the poet—this suntan and rose, this peacock blue and orange, this greenish black and silver coloured, this orangey yellow and emerald, this copper and bluish grey—present themselves as the profuse, ornamental accessory to a language of verse, over which arch the most daring, most remote metaphors like heavy, dark cupolas. . . . This poetry collection is a luxurious symphony of colours."

Finally, Gertrud wrote in greater depth to Hilde in Switzerland:

> Reviews are now appearing everywhere—frequently "really great"—that
> most unreservedly admire and praise the author of *Die Frau und die Tiere,*

like the reporter from the *C. V.* just did. The contents of their articles are now being discussed on a wide scale with the conspicuous mention of our name, and I must think of Byron's remark now and then, "I awoke one morning and found myself famous." (But in my case it's still not all that bad!) Even if I've been declared "the most important Jewish lyric poet since Else Lasker-Schüler," it still gives Father more joy than me. It doesn't excite me very much. There was a time when external praise could please and encourage me (but I seldom asked for it back then, and mostly didn't get it for that reason). Even without the critics, I now know my worth as a poet, what I am capable of and what I cannot do.

She resumed her account in a letter from March 1939: "I was visiting the poet Jacob Picard yesterday afternoon, and he gave me an article that Bertha Badt-Strauss wrote about me in the *Morgen* [*Morning*] that she posted for him to give to me. The proof sheets were already done when the *Morgen* had to stop publishing, so that the report was already printed but not circulated. I already thanked the author by phone, and she wanted to meet me."

Here are two sentences from the review: "No book has been able to enchant me in a long time, particularly in these troubled times. But this one cast a spell, such that one could live in another world for a day and a night, a new, magical world full of hard, glistening crystals." The second sentence read, "This book seems to be shrouded in unbounded loneliness."

The poet again wrote to her sister in Switzerland:

In the end, it may strike you as strange for me to admit to the fact that, as gratifying as it is to me that my work gives something to others, it doesn't give me as much pleasure as the work itself. It's the same for me with my little works as it is for a mother with a newborn child: she is naturally happy about the father's and grandparents' enthusiasm, and the good wishes from relatives. Nevertheless, what makes her happiest of all is the fact that she brought it into the world. So my favourite poems are the two last (and best) ones, which have still not met with any kind of response because they have not yet been published. I mention them because I have a favour to ask of you: I'd like to send you a copy of each of these two works (a poetry cycle and a play). You should place them in "storage," so to speak, take charge of them, since I don't know what fate has in store for me, where I will end up.

In her volume, Kolmar presented an assortment of earlier poems from the cycles *Weibliches Bildnis* [*Female Portrait*] and *Tierträume* [*Animal Dreams*]. Thus, this narrative of her work has been inserted in her biography in chronological order. But at this point we shall also take a look back at poems written before 1936.

The volume starts off with a programmatic poem that makes, or rather suggests, a connection between life and work, between person and text. "Die Dichterin" ["The Poetess"] addresses the reader through the medium of a book:

> You hold me entirely in your hands.
>
> My heart beats like a small bird
> Inside your fist. If you are reading this, watch out;
> You see, you're turning the pages of a human being.
> Even if only made for you of cardboard,
>
> Of paper and glue, it thus remains silent
> Not meeting you with its powerful look,
> Looking out searchingly from the black characters,
> It is a thing, with a thing's fate.
>
> Yet it was veiled like a bride,
> And decorated, that you might love it,
> Shyly asking that you
> Drive equanimity and habituation from your mind,
>
> Shaking, knowing and whispering to itself:
> "This shall not be." Then nods to you smiling.
> Who should be hopeful, if not a woman?
> Her entire efforts are just one thing: "You . . ."
>
> With black flowers, and painted eyebrows,
> With silver chains, silk, and star-studded blue.
> As a child she knew many beautiful things
> And has forgotten those other, more beautiful words.
>
> A man is so much smarter than we are.
> In talking he converses with
> Death and spring, ironworks and time,
> I say: "You . . ." and always: "You and I."
>
> This book is a girl's dress,
> That may well be opulent and red yet pitifully wan,
> And can only, with loving care
> Tolerate crumpling, soiling, marks.

And so I stand, pointing at what happened to me,
For though caustic soda has indeed bleached it,
Nothing has rinsed it completely clean.
Thus, I call for you. My call is thin and light.

You hear someone speaking. Do you also hear someone feeling?

Gertrud Kolmar remains a difficult case in terms of the connection between her life and work. In this case, she facilitates, indeed provokes us to draw biographical conclusions; she cautiously lets us take her at her word, but with due reservations. As I have already stressed, her poems do not generally lend themselves to being used as biographical statements. But some of them can be incorporated into the biographical context in the form of reflections and refractions.

In most of the poems, however, the lines that connect her work and life are limited. If there is any point at all in asking how life and work are related, then it would only be with respect to the facts and what was made of them in the end. How were they stylized, transformed, or both?

| 84

In the same month that the poetry volume appeared, the Act on the Regulation of Jewish First Names was also adopted. Jews had to assume additional names: "to wit, male persons" had to take "the given name of Israel, and female persons the given name of Sara." By the end of 1939, these additional names had to be registered at the respective bureaus of vital statistics and delivered in writing to the responsible local police authorities.

Marie Simon, a contemporary of Kolmar, wrote: "This measure, vile as it was, evoked laughter from those affected. Jewish women had been ennobled, because Sara means princess." And to console the men, people quoted from Genesis: "Thy name shall no longer be called Jacob, but Yisrael: for as a prince thou hast power with God and with men, and hast prevailed."

Whether the poet may have seen this as a good or bad omen, she still had to call herself "Gertrud Sara Chodziesner" after passage of the Second Decree on the Execution of the Law Regarding the Changing of Surnames and Forenames.

If someone intentionally or inadvertently left out the additional name (e.g., in a letter to the authorities), then this would have met with an order of "summary punishment."

Her isolation intensified once again. To what extent was it still possible for the poet to communicate with colleagues?

Kurt Pinthus suggested that the poet occupied the position of outsider without pointing to her lifestyle. This narrows down how to ask the question: with whom would she have still been able to exchange views? Only three names occur to me.

She seems to have trusted Jacob Picard. The geographical distance alone between East Havelland and the Lake Constance region to which he first retreated was enormous. The relationship remained a distant one anyway. The poet insisted on addressing him as "Dear Doctor" and signed with "Very devotedly, Gertrud Chodziesner." But mutual, respectful recognition would hardly be characterized as a friendship between authors. The geographical remove would increase significantly when Picard emigrated, and written communication would break off.

And what about Karl Josef Keller? He had proved inclined to express himself in a literary form that was agreeable to those in power. Would this have stimulated discourse?

Or Ina Seidel at least? Even she came closer to the canon that the power brokers advanced. Jan-Pieter Barbian described her involvement in an article titled "Innenansichten aus dem Dritten Reich" ["Inside Views of the Third Reich"]. Ina Seidel "stood up for Adolf Hitler and his Nationalist politics at several public rallies, i.e., when Germany withdrew from the League of Nations in October 1933, when Germany occupied the demilitarized Rhineland and introduced compulsory military service in March 1936, and on the occasion of Germany's annexation of Austria in March 1938. The two eulogies that Ina Seidel formulated on the occasion of Hitler's fiftieth birthday are particularly embarrassing."

A synthesis of bombast and pathos shows up in these eulogies that was widely characteristic of that era. Thus, Seidel wrote, "that from among thousands there was one upon whose head the cosmic streams of German fate clustered, mysteriously accumulating so as to begin circulating an inexorably powerful order." A cosmic display of splendor, not of the earth, yet of this world. Thus overcome, the author of this profession of loyalty would like "to be thankfully and humbly engrossed in the work of the Chosen One of a Generation, in the work of Adolf Hitler."

Here, too, there was no longer any basis for literary discourse. At this point, Gertrud Kolmar became more of a versifying monad, the lexical definition of which is: "An image of consciousness in which the 'I' point comprises the entire universe." And it is also a "description of the private nature of perception." While the monad is a self-contained element, Edmund Husserl stressed that "even so, monads have windows." And it was becoming increasingly dark and gloomy outside these windows, so she had to generate light and color from within.

| 85

A glimmer of light shone through the monadic window. In August 1938, Leonhard-Feld and her son, Leonor, visited the poet in Finkenkrug, and she stayed "out here for the entire day." This was not the first time they saw each other in private: mother and son had already been in Finkenkrug "around two years" earlier.

The basis for her relationship with Leonhard-Feld was a positive one. Gertrud told her sister Hilde about it in October: "I've made up my mind to learn to cook again. Since last Monday, I've been taking lessons with 'my' reciter, who is a very good, experienced cook and has practised her art on a large scale up to now, in that she has cooked for the children at a school. She lives in Eichkamp, which is very convenient for me, and we currently have a guest at our table, a grass widower who has to eat whatever we cook."

I must immediately add that Gertrud did not tell Helene Köpp about this private cooking course for the time being: "She surely assumes that I am engaged in writing elsewhere." But perhaps this, or something like it, was the subject that led to resentment: "Helene, who certainly cries very easily, has often said to me, 'You are very hard-hearted . . .' But I am no such thing . . ."

Anyway, she made plans to sometimes cook for Papa herself. She didn't want to get in the way of the cook and housekeeper in the process, so she limited herself to desserts. Lemon blancmange was in her repertoire. As one housekeeping book that I will present later shows, lemons were occasionally still available in the stores.

A brief glance over the poet's shoulder in the kitchen: Does she look sideways at a cookbook? Stir cornstarch with egg yolk and a bit of milk until smooth . . . Place the remaining milk with sugar, salt, and grated lemon rind in a pot and bring to a boil . . . Add the blended cornstarch and bring to a boil again while stirring constantly . . . Beat egg whites until stiff and fold into the cream . . . Let come to a boil once more and remove from stove . . . Stir in the lemon juice, place the mixture in little molds and let cool . . . Remove the lemon blancmange, then garnish with a bit of lemon peel, and voilà!

| 86

Fifth Decree of the Reich Citizenship Act (September 27, 1938): "The Elimination of Jews from the Legal Profession. Section 1: Jews are barred from the legal profession. Insofar as Jews are still lawyers, they are eliminated in accordance with the following regulations."

This meant the end of professional employment for the last jurist in the family, Ludwig Chodziesner's brother, Max Chodziesner, who also received a letter with a "certificate of delivery" that read: "Your admission to the legal profession at the local and regional courts in Berlin has been revoked by the Reich Minister of Justice by means of the decree of 10.17.1938 on the basis of Section 1 of the Fifth Decree of the Reich Citizenship Act with termination on 30.11.1938, provided that you have not already left the legal profession prior to this date."

A National Socialist lawyer wrote a commentary for the *Juristische Wochenschrift* (*Jurists' Weekly*). By means of the *VO. zum RBürgerG* (Fifth Decree of the Reich Citizenship Act), the dejudification of the German legal profession had been brought to a close: "Our thanks to the führer, whose ideas established the conditions for the act that has freed us from Jewish pests, and thanks to our Reich commander of law, who never stopped his fervently fanatical call for the removal of the last Jew from German legal life."

This news was not at all surprising, but once again depressing, and certainly so for father and daughter in Finkenkrug.

| 87

Storia e futuro: Incontro con la memoria de Alessandro Ghigi, rettore dell'Università di Bologna negli anni Trenta. [History and the future: encounter with the memoirs of Allesandro Ghighi, rector of the University of Bologna in the thirties.]

In October 1938, Ghigi, director of the Istituto di zoologica [Zoological Institute] and former president of the World's Poultry Science Association, wrote to his professor colleague Giuseppe Prezzolini, the president of Columbia University's *casa italiana* [Italian school], who was responsible for preparing the Seventh World's Poultry Congress that was to take place in the United States. In his letter, Ghigi requested help for "*la dottoressa* Margot Chodziesner, a German Jewess, his secretary and interpreter for some years."

Meanwhile, Hitler had persuaded, nearly compelled, his "Axis partner" Mussolini to introduce so-called racial legislation (i.e., the Nuremberg Laws) in Italy. Thus, Ghigi's colleague not only faced dismissal: "As a result of measures taken by our government to protect the Italian race, she must leave Italy by March 1, 1939." And Ghigi asked his colleague to find a suitable position for the *dottoressa*. She would also need a place to stay, so he was called on to provide hospitality, at least initially, since Margot was "not permitted to take along a proper amount of money, and she was also not allowed to accept a gift of money from her father, who lives in Germany."

In December 1938, Papa Chodziesner wrote to "dear, sweet Hillechen" stating, "Yesterday I received an airmail letter from Margotchen in Rome that pleased me greatly and set me fairly straight. Through the efforts of her boss, she got a visa to the United States without registering or other formalities and, in fact, on the basis of her earlier accomplishments as a 'skilled agricultural labourer.' Maybe you will now also succeed, my dear, sweet little champion, in going to the country of your dreams to find peace, tranquillity, livelihood, light, and warmth. And then I, too, will be happy."

But neither Margot nor Hilde succeeded in escaping to the United States. Hilde had already tried to secure the necessary guarantee several months prior, but she received a letter in October, the wording of which may have been typical of numerous rejections in those days: "I would like to help you, but it will be impossible for me to sign an affidavit for $5,000 as required by American law." She therefore remained in Switzerland, where she was gradually tolerated by the immigration authorities. And Margot emigrated to Australia.

Here's what the *Philo Atlas* has to say about Australia: "Emigration only on the basis of a special emigration permit." One of the prerequisites was, "Named [persons] may only practice professions that do not harm the interests of workers and benefit the economy." For a zoologist, an ornithologist, there were no opportunities to work in independent basic research, so Margot had to put her scientific knowledge to use. The work she published ten years earlier in the *Journal of Ornithology* ought to have been something of a passe-partout. Here's the title once again: *Scientific Results of Applied Poultry Breeding*. And so she was expected to contribute to the improvement of the food situation on the fifth continent.

| 88

Continuing with the keyword "emigration": V. O. Stomps, publisher of the *Wappenbüchlein* [*Little Coat of Arms Book*], apparently wanted to speak with his new author about political developments but had to note "that Gertrud Kolmar, who last visited me in 1938, actually declined to have any opinion about these events. She countered my suggestion that she still try to emigrate with the reply that she was born in Germany and wanted to stay here. The subject of her own situation simply didn't exist for her. One got the impression that she was not willing to pay it any heed, that she was only interested in her work."

Gertrud's refusal was also the subject of letters between Peter Wenzel in Berlin and his wife, Hilde, who continued to try to bring her father and sister to Switzerland: "Your irritation at Trude's fickleness is completely justified. The children and I were very touched by the energy that you've expended on their affairs. In my opinion, Trude will be free to pursue other things as soon as Papa is lodged somewhere. And I think the same will be true for him. Papa has fought retirement up to now, but maybe this will change sometime. I am going out there on Sunday. You are definitely dealing with Trude's affairs in the right way."

The father's fickleness matched his daughter's, or the other way around: Gertrud's fickleness corresponded to her father's.

It was very likely that they also consulted the *Philo Atlas,* a "guide to Jewish emigration," in Finkenkrug, so here are a few quotations:

> As a rule, emigration means a complete and total change in familiar circumstances: Even if emigration occurs within Europe, climate, diet, language, customs, professional opportunities, and political conditions in the country to which a person immigrates deviate almost entirely from the familiar. Therefore, emigration places a tremendous demand on physical, mental, and emotional adaptability; usually only young people are up to the task.

It listed all of the countries that could possibly come up in terms of immigration, countries that German Jews mentioned again and again. But the lexicon offered only a depressing litany of warnings: "Latest developments unfavourable . . . naming of a guarantor to bear the cost of return trip if need be . . . hardly qualifies as an immigration destination for Jews . . . immigration only on the basis of special immigration permit . . . no possibilities . . . only opportune for settlers who can handle the tropics . . . up to the discretion of the authorities to grant . . . very few possibilities . . . limited possibilities."

As early as 1933, Annemarie Seidel, who later married the publisher Suhrkamp, wrote to her sister Ina: "All of my friends are scattered throughout the world."

A number can be placed on the cultural exodus: By this point, more than fifty-five hundred cultural and scientific figures had already been driven out, and the exodus continued. Even that most cynical of rabble-rousers, Goebbels himself, became sarcastic about it. He recorded the following in his diary: "Some senior know-it-all has discovered that Johann Strauss was one-eighth Jewish. I've forbidden this to be made public. First, it has not yet been proved; second, I do not care to allow the entire body of German culture to be gradually pushed aside. In the end, all that would be left of our history would be Widukind, Henry the Lion, and Rosenberg.* And that's a mite too few."

---

* Widukind was the leader of the Saxons against the Frankish king Charlemagne in the 700s. Henry the Lion was duke of Saxony and Bavaria in the 1100s. Alfred Rosenberg was the propagandist who drafted many key Nazi ideologies.

But this tiny, insightful phase was immediately covered up and drowned out. Just one day later, on June 11, 1938, he noted: "Spoke about the Jewish question before 300 police officers in Berlin. I really stirred them up. Flies in the face of sentimentality. Harassment, not law, is the watchword. The Jews must get out of Berlin."

The Gestapo forced people to emigrate and made it more difficult at the same time. In quite a few countries, antisemitism also constituted an almost total barrier to immigration. And the ongoing global economic crisis also reduced opportunities for émigrés. Prices of raw materials fell, industrial production declined, and unemployment figures rose, so many governments wanted to keep the number of immigrants as low as possible. Leaflets from emigrant counseling centers contained information on the topic.

Regarding one of the leaflets from 1938, Walter Laqueur wrote:

I want to cite several excerpts from it, for they are beyond human imagination. Luxembourg: the border is completely closed to immigrants and hikers. Amsterdam Ministry of Justice: in future, refugees are to be considered undesirable aliens. The Consulate General of the United States in Berlin advises that, due to the extremely large numbers of immigration applications, quotas have been exhausted for the immediate future. The Fiji Islands are looking for a Jewish pastry cook and a watchmaker, single, who is not younger than twenty-five but not older than thirty. Paraguay seeks an independent expert candymaker. British Bechuanaland wants an expert furrier. Central Africa seeks an unmarried Jewish butcher (specializing in the production of cervelat). San Salvador is looking for an unmarried Jewish engineer to build electrical machines. Manchukuo still offers the best opportunities.

And he stated:

No country in the world needed Jews. But the words that were on everyone's lips and, in my mind, characterized the whole era were: "restructuring," "existence," (plus "create a life" and "secure existence"), character reference, *shnat hachshara* (year of preparing for Palestine), health certificate, certificate of good conduct, travel cash, certificate (entry permit to Palestine), affidavit (a precondition for American visas), *chamada* (Brazilian visa), and much more. Added to these were many new acronyms such as ICA, HIAS, HICEM, Altreu, Paltreu* and the like, which suddenly became

* All were organizations that helped European Jews emigrate. ICA was the Jewish Colonization Association, HIAS the Hebrew Immigrant Aid Society, and HICEM the organization formed by the merger of ICA, HIAS, and Emigdirect. Altreu was a Jewish bank that financed emigration; Paltreu was the Palestine Trust Office for Advice to German Jews.

crucially important. All of this seemed strange and a little weird, but it would soon become clear that these certificates, affidavits, and *chamadas* were matters of life and death.

The word "emigration" sounds far too neutral. What actually took place was *expulsion,* combined with systematic humiliation and robbery. Above all, the plundering of emigrants by means of the Reich Flight Tax and other fees was systematic. A circular from the Foreign Office to all international offices said, "We expressly point out that it is in Germany's interest to hunt Jews across borders as mendicants because the poorer the immigrants, the greater the burden to the host country." Émigrés were thereby supposed to stir up antisemitism abroad and, in turn, reinforce the actions of the thieving, murderous government indirectly.

Here's another set of figures: In the six years since the *Machtantritt,* 236,000 Jews, or approximately half the Jewish population, had fled Germany. The largest number, 57,000, immigrated to Palestine.

A woman like Gertrud would have been welcome in Palestine. Her combined skills in home economics and poultry keeping were particularly desirable. Due to her apprenticeship at the women's school in Arvedshof, she was extremely well prepared, to which must be added her long-standing experience in raising small domestic animals.

"Palestine is primarily an agricultural region. To consolidate and take root in the first place, the Jewish community also requires an agrarian population. Craftsmen and industrialists are second in line, while merchants and members of the liberal professions (teachers, doctors, etc.) are last in terms of need. . . . With the small number of European Jews employed in agriculture, it is to be expected that this stratum will not provide enough immigrants to Palestine." Arthur Ruppin, a senior official of the Zionist Federation, stated this way back in 1919.

Under the title *Die Auslese des Menschenmaterials* [*The Selection of Human Material*], he certainly anticipated vocabulary that the Nazis would pick up on and that became politically charged. Ruppin not only called for "healthy selection," such that "the mentally ill, the incapacitated, and epileptics" were "a burden to the community in Palestine, for example; to work towards the purity of the Jewish race in Palestine" was also important. It would be desirable if only "*Rassejuden* [racial Jews]" came to Palestine. Once again, "morally inferior human beings" were not desirable, and "the eradication of antisocial elements" was essential.

In the event that word got out about this in the 1930s, it may well have deterred Jews who wanted to immigrate to Palestine, as there were Nazis there, too!

Swabians who had already immigrated and founded settlements in areas purchased in the previous century were mainly Pietists or former Pietists. They often developed rightist leanings and, after a long period of inactivity, they now began to organize quickly. They established a local branch of the Nazi Party in Jerusalem and a regional branch of the Nazi Party in the Mandated Territory of Palestine.

The overall number of Nazi Party members in Palestine was said to be small. Yet even in Jaffa and Haifa, cells formed and were headed up by *Stützpunktleiter* [base action leaders]. National Socialist propaganda resonated greatly with German-Palestinian youth. Teachers were the primary intermediaries who "ensured order," taught children "decency" and the Horst Wessel Song. These German settlers had lived on the sidelines for a long time and felt forgotten by their homeland. But this changed in a flash after the *Machtergreifung*. Nazi propaganda was mostly broadcast over the Reichsrundfunk [Reich Broadcasting Company] via short wave. But long wave also made it possible to receive the programs in Palestine, including broadcasts of Hitler's speeches at public events. And propaganda material was shipped to Palestine as well.

Wherever possible, the material was confiscated by customs officials at ports or made to disappear by Jewish workers. Pietistic Nazis were generally viewed with suspicion by Brits, Jews, and Arabs, and were often treated as enemies. This forced the little throng of Hitler Youth that sprang up overnight in Palestine to behave more conspiratorially, making it all the more exciting for the boys. Thus, a "South Beach Company" was formed with military training as a major component of the program.

These Nazis viewed Palestine as a homeland on whose soil German blood had flowed in shoot-outs with Arabs. The fear could thus have arisen among potential Jewish immigrants that, even under the British mandate administration, the generally heated, highly explosive climate in the interior could lead to attacks by Palestinian Nazis.

| 89

The November pogrom of 1938 is appropriately emphasized in numerous works about the history of Jews in the Third Reich, as in the documentary report *Juden in Berlin 1938–1945* [*Jews in Berlin 1938–1945*], edited by Beate Meyer and Hermann Simon.

This pogrom had an extensive prologue, however. Contemporary witnesses would later report, "From the beginning of 1938 onward, people sensed that disaster hung in the air. We had no more time to slowly plan and prepare for emigration." The situation became critical in May and culminated in the "June

Action." Word about what happened must have reached Finkenkrug at the time and would have shocked father and daughter anew.

In Berlin, numerous signs and shop windows of Jewish businesses were defaced, some with crude caricatures depicting "decapitated, mutilated, and hanged Jews." Windows were bashed in and shops demolished. An eyewitness report said:

> We were just entering a small jewellery store when a gang of ten teenagers in Hitler Youth uniforms struck the shop window and stormed into the store. They brandished butcher knives and shouted, "To hell with you pack of Jews! Make room for Germans from the Sudetenland!" The smallest boy in the gang climbed in the window and began destroying everything by throwing whatever he could grab into the street. Inside, the other boys smashed glass shelves and counters. They threw alarm clocks, cheap silverware, and miscellaneous small items to their accomplices, who were standing outside. One little lad squatted in a corner of the window, put dozens of rings on his fingers, and stuffed his pockets full of wristwatches and bracelets, so that his uniform bulged with the loot. Then he turned around, spat right in the manager's face, and raced off.

There were many arrests in those first weeks of summer. Jews were hauled off to police stations, where they were humiliated and beaten. Jews were taken to SA buildings and SA barracks, where they were mistreated and tortured:

> All summer long there were raids on Jewish cafés and eating establishments. It so happened that the infamous police captain would suddenly appear with a squad of police cars, and the *Schutz- und Kriminalpolizei* [constabulary and criminal investigation division] would cordon off the restaurants. The captain had the innocent customers show their ID cards, knocked the cigarettes out of the mouths of old people, handcuffed those who objected, and drove his quarry of thirty, fifty, or sixty people to Alexanderplatz. They held them there for days, even weeks, for there was now a "legal" solution to the Jewish question. No Jewish boardinghouse, not even the most secluded restaurant was safe from these lightning raids.

And that is how Goebbels's inflammatory speeches to police officers in Berlin and his calls for harassment by the constabulary, who were supposed to "protect," were transformed into atrocities.

The report continues: "Ever since those days in June, there has been no more peace for German Jews. We lost our feeling of normalcy that summer. We no longer see that the sun shines: it no longer warms us. We take no pleasure in summer, and the harmony of nature offends us. We are wounded. But people don't see our wounds, and we bleed to death internally."

The so-called *Reichskristallnacht* [Night of Broken Glass] took place a quarter of a year after the appearance of Gertrud Kolmar's new poetry volume, and far more than glass was broken that night. The assassination attempt on a secretary at the German Embassy in Paris by a young Jew, Herschel Grynszpan, served as pretext for what were now collective actions. Along with thousands of others, his parents had been driven out of Germany to the Polish border in the course of the "Polish action." Fellow sufferers "stated that they were chased by the SS into the no-man's-land along the border, and shots were fired at them from behind. The Poles did not let them in for a long time, such that they had to camp out in the open in the cold and rain."

The pogrom developed its own dangerous, often deadly momentum. The Nazi Party leadership actually wanted to prevent such developments, but things got out of hand.

On the eve of "demonstrations against the Jews," directives were issued in a telex signed by Reinhard Heydrich from the Geheime Staatspolizeiamt* to all Gestapo district headquarters and Gestapo regional offices with the comment, "Flash, urgent, for immediate release."

I'd like to stress point 5, which reads: "Once the events of this night have reached a point that allows for the use of deployed officers, as many Jews—wealthy ones in particular—are to be arrested in all districts as can be accommodated in the available prison cells. Initially, only healthy, male Jews who are not too elderly are to be arrested. After carrying out the arrests, the relevant concentration camps are to be contacted at once in the interest of housing the Jews in the camps as quickly as possible. It is particularly important to take care that there is no abuse of Jews arrested on the basis of this directive."

However, the course of events was more chaotic than organized. Several different authorities issued instructions and commands, and the SA was mainly responsible for carrying them out. But members of the SS, the NSKK,† and sometimes even tax officers and customs officials took part. In retrospect, even Prussian Minister of the Interior Göring found it difficult to reconstruct the chain of command.

This was a poorly organized action with a great momentum of its own. Papa Chodziesner would, it was hoped, be spared from the many side effects

* Reinhard Heydrich, a high-ranking Nazi official, was one of the chief planners of the Holocaust. The Geheime Staatspolizeiamt was the main office of the Gestapo.

† The NSKK [Nationalsozialistisches Kraftfahrkorps, or National Socialist Motor Corps] was a para-military organization of the Nazi Party that trained its members to operate and maintain cars and motorcycles.

associated with it: the usual beatings, even of old people, rapes in apartments and homes, stealing and plundering that largely took place under the euphemism of "safekeeping." Contrary to all instructions, the norm was that, after breaking into an apartment or business, items were swiped under the pretext that they needed to be placed in safekeeping. They were then handed over to party organizations and often "forgotten" in the process. People were also blackmailed into making check payments.

Two people reported on their experiences. A legal trainee, who was no longer allowed to take the second state examination after 1933 and worked in the administration of the Leipzig Jewish community, made the following contribution to oral history:

On the ninth of November, the phone rang at one in the morning, and ever since that time, I cannot stand it when the phone rings: "The synagogue is burning, what should we do?" I called the police: "Oh, so you're a Jew?" Bang, hung up. And then they knocked at our doors all night long. We did not open, so a locksmith broke the lock in the early morning, and there were two SA men standing there: "Why didn't you open your door?" I said: "I didn't know that you were officials. I was not expecting officials in the middle of the night. And I didn't expect them to make so much noise." From there to prison, and from there to a concentration camp. And my wife still had to pay the locksmith for his trouble. I was released five weeks later, and my wife had already prepared everything for emigration.

Another émigré wrote a report to her family from New York:

At around two-thirty in the morning, there was a persistent ringing and bellowing at the front door. They were trying to get in, and the door shook as they opened it. One, two dozen men, mainly SA brownshirts, forced their way in. They spread out inside the house, tore open or kicked in all the doors, and ran around the rooms, yelling. Everyone in the house had to assemble in the bedroom, a tightly gathered little group in nightgowns and pyjamas. A man in civilian clothing spat out, yelled, "No one leaves the room! Nothing will happen to you: we are human."

We looked at each other, speechless, and then—all hell broke loose!!! They smashed everything with axes, hammers, hatchets. All of the chandeliers, windowpanes, furniture, smashed to pieces. Sofas, etc., were shredded. They tore out the contents of cupboards, the desk, etc., and rendered them useless. In the little parlour, the desk, Grandmother's bookcase, red couch, portraits—everything just a pile of rubble. In the smoking room, they pulled the large built-in bookcase out of the wall, smashed it, and chopped the desk into firewood. We could no longer find the contents (around 1,100 reichsmarks). Marble fireplace in ruins. In the dining room, they destroyed the corner cabinets with the precious antique porcelain; well, all the contents. Table overturned, chopped up with axes. All of the chairs unusable. In the dressing room, the vanity and mirror smashed beyond recognition, the WC [toilet] ripped out of the floor. They ripped the water tanks from the wall, and our coats, hats, furs, etc., were floating in the water.

The man in civilian clothes came back into the bedroom:

"Well, ladies, how are you feeling now? . . . Ladies, alas, you're not doing well yet. Then—let's get going!" And so he "took a chair and began to smash everything in the bedroom. . . . The contents of my clothes and linen cabinet flew over the railing onto the flowerbed. A giant of a storm trooper threw matches to me and cried, 'Burn your rubbish, you Jewish sow!'"

Ludwig Chodziesner was one of twelve thousand Jewish citizens of Berlin and twenty-six thousand persons in the Reich to be arrested that night. In this case, however, "arrested" is the wrong word, for they did not present an arrest warrant at the front door; a detachment simply forced its way in and abducted him.

The excessive number of experiences that the daughter was burdened with must at least be brought up to some extent and not merely mentioned in passing. During that night of arson and demolition, hundreds of Jews were maltreated and injured. Nearly a hundred were killed, and in most cases that meant beaten to death. There was also a fatality in Falkensee.

It's likely that a vehicle, perhaps a truck, drove into Manteuffelstrasse with an SA detachment that had just stormed through Falkensee and the surrounding hamlets. Now it was Finkenkrug's turn. They would arrive, hollering and bellowing out songs, singing the verses at least, the choruses at any rate, and they would repeat them incessantly in those days, though I won't quote any here. As usual, the squad would have beaten and kicked at the door. Gertrud would have probably opened up. They would surely have pushed her aside. The SA men, often slightly drunk or even plastered, would have tramped through the ground floor, yelling. Some of the men would have stomped up the stairs, pushed the doors open, dragged the father out of bed, possibly beaten him, and snarled at him to get dressed right away, to get a move on! In the meantime, they would have ripped drawers out of cupboards as usual, swept shelves clean and overturned pieces of furniture, while other SA men on the ground floor would have continued raging, throwing leftover food at the kitchen walls, smashing crockery, and turning on all the faucets. During the pogroms, such procedures were the norm nationwide. Even if she didn't protest or beg for mercy, the daughter would certainly have been threatened and showered with abuses: "You're next, but we'll take care of the old man first . . ." And like hundreds of other victims, he would have been grabbed, pushed, or dragged to the vehicle. And while they continued shouting and jeering, he would have been struck and kicked until forced to crawl onto the truck bed. And then the vehicle would have driven off amid shouting and jeering.

At first, it was entirely uncertain what had happened to her father, how long he would be gone, in what condition he would return, or whether he would come back at all. Had they taken him into "protective custody," put him in a bigger prison, or sent him to a camp? People had already heard the worst about it in a roundabout way, primarily in the form of rumors. There was usually something to the rumors, yet they were frequently surpassed by the facts. The terrorist regime was also a torture regime.

Indeed, it would have been nothing short of a miracle if Ludwig Chodziesner had not been brutally mistreated during his abduction. The brutality scenario had a very high degree of probability. Gertrud said nothing about that night in her letters, of course, for it would have been too risky. As someone who had formerly censored letters, she knew how easy it was to look through and examine pieces of mail, so she was careful, especially in the case of letters to Switzerland.

In accordance with Heydrich's directive, Ludwig Chodziesner was incarcerated in one of the "available prison cells," which seems to have been at the local prison in Falkensee. They released him after four days in detention. Thus, he was spared deportation to the Sachsenhausen concentration camp.

Had he also been abused? Hilde Wenzel wrote from Switzerland:

> The news I have from home is gloomy enough. One hears nothing directly, because nobody dares write anything.
>
> One must therefore rely on personal accounts, according to which things are supposedly far worse than what has already been reported rather openly in newspaper reports. My father, who is seventy-seven years old, was in jail for four days. He is still not capable of writing to me, and I'm quite worried about him. . . . They wanted to arrest my brother, so he went to stay with relatives that same day.

| 90

Shortly after the pogrom, Ludwig Chodziesner faced a fiscal measure that would further rob and deprive Jews of their rights in Germany.

I must at least outline it briefly here because Gertrud's livelihood was also under attack. She lived not only for her father but also from his wealth and savings, and the Reich Tax Authority was out to get both.

As early as April 1938, Jewish citizens who owned more than five thousand reichsmarks (approximately fifty thousand euros in terms of today's purchasing power) had to register their assets. Whoever did not file the documents on time was threatened with up to ten years in prison, as well as "seizure of assets." This threat ensured that the tax authorities received all information on time. The measure was supposed to facilitate the later "grab" that followed shortly thereafter.

In the wake of the pogrom, the Nazis discussed and agreed upon further measures, as they did at the so-called Göring Conference of November 12. It took place in the Reich Ministry of Aviation, the building that houses the present-day Ministry of Finance. In attendance, with Prussian Interior Minister Göring presiding, were Propaganda Minister Goebbels, Reinhard Heydrich (head of the Gestapo and Sicherheitsdienst),* the Reich minister of finance, the Reich minister of economic affairs, an executive board member of Allianz AG, who was also the head of the Reichsgruppe Versicherungen [Reich Insurance Group], and other dignitaries.

According to the stenographic transcript, Goebbels proposed that all of the burned-down synagogues should "be razed by the Jews. And the Jews must pay for it. Here in Berlin, the Jews are prepared to do so. The Jews themselves will level the synagogues that have burned down in Berlin. We can turn some of them into parking lots and erect new buildings in other places. And this, I think, will impart a guiding principle to the entire country."

They then debated the question of how the insurance companies should handle this aftermath of the pogrom. Göring was opposed to paying claims to Jews whose homes or businesses had been destroyed. They summoned the representative of the Reich Insurance Group, who saw it differently: "If today we were to refuse to fulfil a contractual obligation that is clearly and legally incumbent upon us, this would be like a black stain on the honourable name of German insurance companies." To which Göring replied, "Just a moment! You're going to have to shell out in any event. But you will be legally prohibited from making direct payments to Jews. And you must pay the damages that you would have paid to the Jews—not to the Jews, however, but to the finance minister instead." The head of the Reich Insurance Group answered, "I see." Göring argued for "giving the Jews one blow after another to the head this week, lickety-split." He then asked the main question: "What would you think if I were to announce today that we're compelling Jews to contribute one billion as punishment?" And he provided further details: "I'm going to word it so that German Jews will

* The Sicherheitsdienst [Security Service] was the intelligence agency of the SS and the Nazi Party.

collectively have to make a contribution of one billion as punishment for their abominable crimes, etc., etc. That will work: the pigs won't make another killing quite so fast. Incidentally, I must point out once again that I wouldn't like to be a Jew in Germany." One billion reichsmarks was a tremendous burden on the Jewish minority that, by this time, numbered just a few hundred thousand citizens! By today's standards, this would amount to approximately ten billion euros!

As early as November 26, the *Deutsche Steuerzeitung* ran an editorial with the headline, "The Jewish Billion." It began by stating, "As defence and atonement for cowardly attacks by the Jews, General Field Marshal Göring, the authorized representative of the Four Year Plan by means of the decree of November 12, 1938, has imposed on Jews the payment of a contribution of one billion reichsmarks to the German Reich." In concrete terms, this meant that Ludwig Chodziesner also received the printed form *Bescheid über die Judenvermögensabgabe* [Notification of the Jewish Capital Levy]. Here is a condensed version of the text: "By virtue of the regulation for the implementation of the Jewish atonement tax . . . the amount of the levy to be paid by you shall be assessed at ___ reichsmarks. The levy amounts to 20 percent of your registered assets. The tax is to be paid in four instalments of ___ reichsmarks each and designated as Jewish Capital Levy, specifying the aforementioned street number." Reference was then made to coercive measures that would be taken in the event that payments were not made on time. I do not know how big Papa Ludwig's fortune was, but one-fifth of it was taken from him. This was just one of many pseudolegal plundering and pillaging measures.

In addition to the so-called atonement tax, Chodziesner was also required to pay a "voluntary penance" to the "Berlin Broken Glass Fund." The party leadership cooked up and quickly adopted the Ordinance for the Restoration of Streetscapes so that, in addition to the contribution, Jews would have to pay compensation for the damages inflicted on their own people. Above and beyond the contribution, the Jewish community had to wire a sum of five million reichsmarks to Deutsche Bank! The main purpose of this "reparation" was supposedly to reimburse all expenses "for deployment of forces to protect Jewish property": fire department, police, and garbage collection. Immediately converted to euros, the fire department and street cleaning got the equivalent of 1.7 million, the SA and SS got 700,000, and 2 million went to the Nazi Party "for operations that lasted for days." Göring pocketed thirty million for his ministry. Thus, the Jews had to pay drastically inflated amounts for the pogrom itself and the consequences thereof.

And they carried their criminal lunacy to extremes by declaring that even Jews who had long since emigrated were "taxable." Anyone in exile who believed himself protected from these financial demands was told "that foreign residency alone was not grounds for granting leniency." However long the paths to enforcement may have been, most German expatriates of Jewish origin did not simply file the letters away because they were law-abiding and also feared reprisals against their remaining family members and possessions in Germany.

Here's another example of criminal insanity: a small portion of the total served to compensate "Aryans" for damages suffered during the "Jewish action." (The latest insurance jargon included a new term, "tumult damages.") In practice, it looked like this: A party member named Fährmann received compensation of 150 reichsmarks for a tear in his trousers that occurred during demolition of the synagogue on Fasanenstrasse. Party member Rudat pocketed no less than 1,000 reichsmarks for his coat, which was no longer good enough for a Sunday stroll after participation in the destruction of the synagogue.

Enormous compensation for items of little value! The purchase price of a coat was about 70 reichsmarks in those days. By way of comparison, here are some additional figures: A female stenographer in a law firm earned about 70 reichsmarks per month. The hourly wage rate for a mason was 75 pfennigs, which came to 124 reichsmarks per month, and at a higher pay scale, he took home about 200 reichsmarks a month. In this period, the salary of a white-collar worker was between 200 and 230 reichsmarks. What the party member got for the hole in his jacket amounted to approximately fourteen coats in mint condition or a bricklayer's earnings over a five-month period.

There was no relief for Jews in Berlin or in the Third Reich. After the pogrom, they were plagued with additional regulations, ordinances, and prohibitions. Goebbels wrote in his diary: "I issued a directive that forbids Jews to go to cinemas and theatres. This was necessary and appropriate."

A list of other prohibitions accompanied this. The *Jüdisches Nachrichtenblatt* [*Jewish Newspaper*] published each of them in "Aus den Verordnungen" ["From the Ordinances"]. From then on, Jews were not allowed in museums, were no longer allowed to attend concerts or to use public libraries, and could no longer go to bathhouses, the zoo, or parks. Promenades in city centers were likewise restricted by signs reading, DISTRICT BANNED TO JEWS. Jews were forbidden from entering Wilhelmstrasse, for example. And Jews were also forbidden from entering Unter den Linden.

Over the next four years, the number of "districts banned to Jews" would grow in Berlin, although they had to refrain from giving "written notice," especially in the press. People in foreign countries could have made critical mention of it. Thus, the Gestapo ordered the Jewish community to announce the streets that were no longer accessible "in an appropriate manner by word of mouth among the Jews of Berlin."

| 91

And what happened to books put out by Jewish publishers after the pogrom?

"Orders to close down" were sent to all Jewish publishers in mid-December 1938: "I herewith order that your business, up to now licensed by me within the framework of the Jewish book trade under company N.N. and revocable, is to be dissolved by December 31, 1938."

Following these liquidations, a central publishing house called the Jewish Cultural Association Press was founded. Jewish bookstores had to close as well. Only a few outlets of the central publishing house or, more precisely, the publishing department of the Jüdischer Kulturbund in Deutschland e.V. [Jewish Cultural League in Germany, Inc.] were allowed. The book inventories of twenty-five former publishers were transferred to a central depot. Books from these collections could only be purchased through the Cultural League.

Picard was the source of the report that Kolmar's poetry volume had been pulped. This was probably one of many rumors circulating in those days. Although it is not very likely, we cannot rule out the possibility that her poetry volume actually was pulped. That's because the liquidation of Jewish publishing houses and bookstores involved strict regulations for further utilization of existing stocks.

Hinkel's office was in charge of writing these measures. It established guidelines and issued directives. Hans Hinkel, a party member with a very low membership number, was considered an expert on the *Entjudung* [dejudification] of German cultural life. His official "prelims" read: "Special Section Reich Administrator of Culture Hinkel concerning the supervision of intellectually and culturally active Jews within the territory of the German Reich." He served as "special representative to Reich Minister Dr. Goebbels." Within the scope of this special assignment, Hinkel ordered the liquidation of Jewish publishers and the Jewish retail book trade. The "economic values of the German *Volk*" were to be preserved in the process. Thus, all book collections had to be handed over "by way of a proper business transaction to the newly founded publishing house of the Jewish Cultural League." In individual cases, permission to pulp had to be obtained from Division IIa of the Ministry of Propaganda. In Kolmar's case, the "Erwin Loewe i. L." (i.e., in liquidation) Verlag would hardly have made such a request, and Loewe would have obeyed the order to hand over inventories en masse. The retail price was rescinded, and the books were mainly sold off for a pittance. Even Gertrud Chodziesner's volume of poetry was offered on a list in the *Jüdisches Nachrichtenblatt* at the reduced price of one mark sixty pfennigs.

The sale of Jewish publishers' inventories to exclusively Jewish clientele continued, albeit on a limited basis. Not until January 1943 was the last outlet for books from the twenty-five Jewish publishing houses "in liquidation" shut down.

The final phase of liquidation may have taken a macabre turn. By order of the SS, leftover books from the central warehouse were transported on Elba barges and by rail to the Ghetto Central Library at the Theresienstadt concentration camp, which ultimately boasted 180,000 volumes. Thus, we cannot rule out the possibility that Kolmar's last volume of poems was on the shelf in the library of the very concentration camp to which her father would be deported in 1942.

| 92

On November 24, 1938, Gertrud wrote to her sister in Switzerland, "*Yesterday we sold our house,* probably must be out in 4 to 8 weeks." Knowing that the letter would be censored, she did not write that they had been forced into selling the house.

Another instance of dejudification, this time of real estate holdings. The authorities used the euphemism "redistribution." The official form letter from the office in charge read as follows, most likely in the Chodziesners' case as well:

> You must offer to sell your property in the town of Falkensee, including the residential house, to N.N. N.N. has been advised of this directive. Within a period of six (6) weeks after delivery of this directive, the finalized sales contract must be submitted here for approval by way of the district administrator of Nauen, pursuant to Section 8 of the aforementioned regulation.
>
> Failure to comply with above directive will be punished. Moreover, a trustee will be appointed in the event of refusal to effect the sale.
>
> You must also immediately notify the mayor of your place of residence if you own any other real property. If applicable, you must also specify the location, size, assessed value (according to the most recent notification), and encumbrances (by giving a precise description of the creditors). In addition, you must state whether and, if applicable, what buildings are on the property.

The house supposedly became a branch office or department of the Reich Ministry of Aviation. Another version of the story is that an officer moved in, and he may well have served at the nearby Gatow Military Airport.

Thus, the house was not privately Aryanized but taken over as an official residence. It was in the hands of the state and has remained so. This government ownership has had long-term consequences: After the war, it became a meeting place for Young Pioneers and then an extension of the neighboring Lessing Oberschule. The property was completely deforested as a result.

What a *Wendezeit* [fall of the Berlin Wall in 1989] photo reveals, however, is relatively harmless as compared with the encroachments that came shortly before the turn of the millennium, when extensive clear-cutting transformed the sprawling gardens into a sports complex. The back semicircle of the porch had long since been removed from the house itself, which had been newly reconstructed, modern windows installed. Apart from the commemorative plaque, all traces of the former owners had been removed.

Not even during my second stroll around Neufinkenkrug did I see another property that had undergone such brutal clear-cutting. Conversion first took place under the Nazis, then under the GDR administration, and finally by way of the German federal authorities. This house in the midst of a sports arena is no longer suitable as a destination for pilgrims or friends of literature. The genius loci, the spirit of the place, has been driven out and extinguished.

Several years later, I was told that another huge gymnasium had been erected on the property. Hardly anything worse could happen to it now.

| 93

The forced sale of the house was again linked to the idea of emigration. Gertrud told her sister in Switzerland that: "Helene wants to withdraw from active life, and since plans that Papa made in case I go to England as a governess have had to be shelved for now, I will remain here for the time being. I neither want to, nor can I leave Papa alone now, given his situation and advanced age. You understand this and aren't angry with me, are you?"

On the day before Christmas Eve, she wrote:

> I have already telephoned about this matter but will only be able to pursue it properly when we are living in Berlin. That's because tackling it requires all sorts of running around, which in itself takes time, and I have absolutely no time at the moment. We have to be out of here sometime between January 15 and 31, and we want to seriously scale down. You can imagine—no, you can't imagine—what all has accumulated in our household since 1923 and as far back as 1894, and must now be unpacked, collected, sorted, and largely given away (insofar as there is anyone who wants it). I started working on it right after the house was sold. Although I usually rummage through it from morning to night, I sometimes despair of getting through it by the middle of January.

The subject of England came up again two months later:

I'd like to talk with you about the matter of England. Whenever I think about it, I feel badly that, given the pile of work on your plate, you went to so much expense and effort on my account. We planned it like so: I was supposed to make sure that I got to England and then somehow try to get Papa to join me there. He wanted to give up the apartment when I left, wanted to sell some things, put some of them in storage, and move into a boardinghouse, a retirement home. But the plans he made for himself are no longer practicable—partly due to external considerations, partly for personal reasons. And so just one arrangement is possible for my immediate future, and he is included in it. We are about to do something but cannot talk about it yet.

Gertrud gradually began to send typescripts to her sister in Switzerland: "My 'collected works' are still packed from the move. Over the course of the coming week, I'll probably get around to picking out what I want to send you. I am thinking of three things: two cycles of poetry and a play. This winter-and-spring move has evidently not done my Pegasus any good, but he will get back on his feet again . . . and carry me on his back to a more beautiful shore . . ."

Even at a time like this, her little niece was still included in her correspondence: "I really missed the little *Binelein** during the move. Of course, she would have been in the way the whole time. But I can just imagine her joyfully taking part in all the very interesting goings-on—'helping Grandpa, watching the men,' the packers, the transport operators, collecting, packing, and carrying everything away, emptying out the entire house. She would surely have been most keen to take part in all of it."

| 94

At the end of January 1939, father and daughter left their village and moved back to the city. Their new digs: Speyerer Strasse, Bavarian Quarter, the Schöneberg District of Berlin. Did this quarter fit into the new tenants' self-image? Or were they in danger of becoming downwardly mobile? In the Kolmar literature, the premature introduction of terms like "Jewish apartment" and "Jewish home" often suggest this to be the case because we immediately associate these terms

---

* *Binelein* is an endearing diminutive that is also a wordplay on her name, Sabine—*Binelein* means "little bee."

with painfully cramped conditions. But, fortunately, the facts were different in the initial period after the move.

Upon inspecting the district, beginning at Bayerischer Platz, I found the atmosphere disappointing. The central square at the underground station has a large area with grass, bushes, trees, and a few benches. The streets emanating from the square or feeding into it are mostly broad in scope, many of them avenues. Postwar buildings predominate, as three-quarters of the district was bombed out! The reconstruction was largely marked by the kind of demolition that is typical of urban planning. Only a shadow of the former Speyerer Strasse remains, and only one side of the street has been developed.

But the moment you look at photos from the early decades of the twentieth century, you get a very different image: Bayerischer Platz was a sprawling complex with a large fountain jetting watery accents high into the air. All around it were grassy areas, flower beds, white painted benches, hedges, and trees. Pictured are ladies and gentlemen in elegant clothing and kids from obviously good homes.

The area around Bayerischer Platz was what we would now call prime real estate. The district was laid out in the course of the urban expansion that took place at the beginning of the twentieth century. The facades of the houses were uniformly representative. Those who lived here were mainly Jews who had "made it," which is to say, about sixteen thousand of the nearly eighteen thousand Jewish residents of Schöneberg. The district was also referred to as "Jewish Switzerland." Leading Jewish figures lived there, each of them for a time: the reporter Egon Erwin Kisch, the writer Kurt Tucholsky, the physicist Albert Einstein, and the chanteuse Claire Waldoff. Though the Bayerisches Viertel [Bavarian Quarter] did not possess the charm of Charlottenburg, it was still seen as a "first-class address for dignified living."

And Speyerer Strasse was one of these first-class addresses. It was a broadly laid out, tree-lined avenue, consisting entirely of four-story houses with variably sectioned facades. The Chodziesners rented an apartment with four-and-one-half rooms on the second floor of number 10, a house "with all the comforts of home." Gertrud was apparently enthusiastic: "We have our own warm and beautiful apartment!" And it's big! "I don't know if you were aware that, despite all the 'unloading,' we still couldn't fit everything in three rooms, as envisaged (we wanted to rent out the two front rooms unfurnished), so we had to furnish all five rooms."

From the window of her room, however, she looked out onto a courtyard. (Was it enclosed?) As if to compensate, she would instantly beautify the balcony with "rose florets of sedum in a flower box."

So how did they settle in? First of all, Papa Ludwig's behavior was very surprising. The man who seemed to need peace and quiet, garden and forest, seemed satisfied with the company of dogs, chickens, and ducks, settled in: he developed initiative, he approached and got in touch with people.

In February, he sent a letter to his "Dear, good Hillechen!" For starters, he declared:

> Things used to be very different. For the pure pleasure of writing, I used to compose letters ahead of time to you, Margotchen, friends, acquaintances, and relatives, and keep them in stock, as it were.
>
> Today it's just the opposite, and the thoughts plague me: "You've got to write to Hillechen, whom you think about so often, every day and every hour, and to your sweet, golden Binelein, whom you so long to see. And you've got to thank Peter for his card in your best Swiss German." And yet, and yet! I've got to pull myself together. My pen used to fly so lightly over the paper, and my thoughts flowed faster than I could write them down. Now everything has become slower and more cumbersome. I long for you, am worried about you. Write to me soon! I was at the Pakschers at Witzlebenplatz No. 6 last Tuesday, which was the seventh of May. They were both very cordial to me. I was enjoying the beautiful view over the entire length of the Lietzensee from their pretty, very tastefully furnished apartment. We were talking about you, about our little Binchen, and the time passed much too quickly. I've been in need of conversations such as this with like-minded people for a very long time. When he took me to the underground station at Sophie Charlottenplatz, I said to him, "Please tell your wife that I could have fallen in love with her." Yesterday we had Mila Pieck (Rosenberg) and her husband over for coffee, and the day before I went for a stroll in the park with my old friend, Counsellor Harry Priest, who lives quite close to us on Bayerischer Platz. You see, I seek compensation for what I lost, human replacements for what the forest and its residents offered me. Is that even possible for me at age seventy-seven? One has to try, to persevere despite all odds.

"To persevere despite all odds" was one of the phrases with which he armed himself, a phrase from a font of quotations belonging to a social phenomenon that has faded entirely in our time. I speak here of the educated class, the status of whose members was signaled by quotations, mainly from classic literature. For a short time, this saying provided something akin to support at a time when civilization and culture were being liquidated on all sides. This was a phrase to live by, to hold onto.

The second surprise came in March of that year. For the first time in decades, Ludwig Chodziesner entered a nearby synagogue on Münchener Strasse. This synagogue was part of the residential building at number 37. The damaged building was torn down after the war.

Chodziesner told his daughter Hilde in Switzerland about it:

> After my coffee, I take a short walk along a few streets, weather permitting. I was walking along Münchener Strasse last Friday when I encountered a large flock of fellow believers, all heading for a particular spot. I joined the group, which grew and grew, and thus reached the synagogue, which was completely full. I was able to get a seat. The service had already begun. After about sixty years, I was in a synagogue on a Friday evening once again and heard them singing Lecho Daudi. My childhood, my youth came back to me, and I was deeply moved. The cantor's melodious voice still rings in my ears, and I hear the dear old strains that I used to sing every Friday evening.

The idea of an assimilated Jew going to synagogue both astonished and disconcerted his daughter Gertrud, who had almost no ties to religion and was not affiliated with any denomination. She would later state emphatically that "I'm not keen on piety in old age." For her father, however, the following also came into play: before and after the service, there were lively exchanges of gossip, information, and messages, as well as lengthy talks, and he was always in on them.

On the other hand, his daughter found it more difficult to settle in. She retreated and kept to herself in their new surroundings. She tried a novel for companionship, the French novelist Jean Giono's *The Dreamer,* which Hilde had sent her.

The book arrived while she was still in Finkenkrug. She thanked her sister in a letter: "I've heard *about* Jean Giono on occasion but still haven't read anything *by* him. Now and again, the thought occurs to me that I ought to do it sometime. But even if they happen to be good, it's somehow become hard for me to read novels lately. Perhaps it's due to the fact that we are now experiencing things that are incomparable to what has been written . . ." A few years later, she would again emphasize "that this experience of history is like a river that has inundated and washed away everything I once read."

After the turmoil of the move, however, she decided to read the novel: "Since I have the afternoon off today (hardly ever happens with me), and the weather is really beautiful after a long, cool, and rainy period, I've had the 'good idea' (as Binelein would say) to sit on the balcony and—finally!—begin reading the 'Dreamer' you sent me. No use. Despite being two storeys up, the street noise made me feel as if I were in the thick of things, and I have apparently still not gotten used to various types of auto fumes in place of fresh spring air. So I decided to retire to my 'quiet retreat' instead."

Concerning the atmosphere of the city:

Incidentally, I've tried to take an interest in the local "scenery," or rather, "nonscenery," but I haven't succeeded. Day before yesterday, I went along Martin Luther Strasse, then Neue Winterfeld Strasse, which are streets I still don't know well. Somewhat nonplussed and contrary to my usual practice, I suddenly noticed that I was not actually seeing the houses, the shops, or the people at all. "You must pay attention, pay heed," I told myself. Very well. Not five minutes later, I'd stopped seeing again. My view was turned inward, so to speak, like an inattentive student daydreaming in the classroom. We will soon have lived here for six months, and I simply haven't managed to come to bearable or unbearable terms with the neighbourhood. I am as much of a stranger here as on the first day. Perhaps it comes down to the impersonal quality, the emptiness of the area. If we were living in another part of Berlin, things would have turned out differently. But perhaps I can no longer adapt to life in a large metropolitan area, so far removed from nature . . . Even though I was born in one. You can't transplant old trees . . .

As an aside, I'd like to comment that there's a big difference between the impression one gets from reading such letters and Gertrud's image of herself as a letter writer:

I'm glad you like to read my letters. Your message emboldens me somewhat to write. In general, I'm really not a great correspondent, and it's also true that I'm not very suited to so-called normal letters that describe concrete things, such as the course of daily life. Margot does this sort of thing really well, for example. I can only do it when I experience something really new, when I find myself travelling in a strange environment. Otherwise, I have to use great force if I am to write "informally." That's because it's simply not my style to write the way I speak.

Accustomed as they were to exercise, the Chodziesners would likely have gravitated toward Schöneberg's municipal park in the southern part of the Bavarian Quarter. You can reach the park from Speyerer Strasse in ten minutes. The tower of the adjacent Schöneberg Rathaus [Town Hall] is already visible from the central square, leastwise via the sight line of Salzburger Strasse. The free-standing building, including the massive tower that accents the structure . . . The geometrically shaped portion of the park . . . The "Stag Fountain" with the bronze stag on a high column, Schöneberg's famous landmark: did it have a golden shine in those days? . . . The subway station forms a crossbeam in a slight depression on the park grounds, serving as both a bridge over the garden and a way across the park hollow . . . Glass between pillars: from the outside, you see the tracks going in, coming out . . . The narrow, elongated area of the actual park, laid out in the style of English gardens, is on the other side of this facade.

But since the ban had gone into effect the previous year, father and daughter were actually prohibited from entering the park grounds. But Gertrud and Ludwig Chodziesner seemed not to have worried about it, and Papa Ludwig noted, "Took my walk in the town park." Although the Star of David patch hadn't been introduced yet, party members could have recognized and reported them. Would it have been less dangerous if they'd gone to the park in bad weather or at very early or late times of day?

Their longing for green space could have been assuaged a bit here. At the same time, their yearning for Finkenkrug's forests may have intensified. But at least father and daughter had a park within walking distance, as well as a street and a district with tree-lined avenues.

| 95

Abgabepflicht [tax liability] was a major theme for father and daughter at this time. After the forced sale of their home at what was surely "just" a slightly inflated assessed value, they were subject to further plundering: "In 1939, Jewish-German citizens and stateless Jews in Germany had to hand over all gold, platinum, and silver valuables in their possession, as well as precious stones and pearls. Even certain artifacts like paintings, rugs, etc., fell under the *Abgabepflicht*. On January 20, 1939, the Reich government designated municipal pawnshops as purchasing centres." A senior clerk for the city recorded this in a statement of account and remarked, "Jews could not raise objections to the amount of the purchase price. They had to be content with what they got from us."

Martin Friedenberger wrote: "There is a general obligation to hand over items of gold, platinum or silver, as well as precious stones and pearls. Only personal items of value, such as rings, watches, silverware, or dentures for personal use," were exempted. "In Berlin, well over fifty thousand Jewish citizens responded to the official order and handed over their jewellery at the two municipal pawnshops."

All that people received upon delivery were purchase receipts, and they only took the weighted value of the materials into account. "As a rule," the correspondingly low sums "would then flow into a security account at a foreign exchange bank to which people had very restricted access."

Friedenberger listed what one Berlin Jew had to hand over: one chest of silver flatware with eight tablespoons, eight dinner forks, eight teaspoons, and twelve dessert forks; two additional pieces of silver flatware; one silver Hanukiyah,*

---

* A Hanukiyah is a nine-branched candleholder or menorah lit during the eight-day holiday of Hanukkah.

one silver sugar spoon, one pin brooch with an emerald and two diamonds; one ring, platinum; one gold bracelet; one gold wedding ring; one gold brooch with cameo; one gold men's watch chain; one pair of golden cuff links; one gold watch case.

There is no record of what Ludwig Chodziesner had to hand over in the way of family possessions, but it must have been a substantial list.

Another central theme for father and daughter at this time was blackout. The first blackout drill was scheduled back in January 1933 and surely included Finkenkrug. People would certainly have kept a close eye on the home of the only Jews in town to ensure that they complied with the regulations.

"Who must black out? Everyone is obliged to properly black out his dwelling, business, workshops, and so on, as well as vehicles. And how do you black out? The interior lighting of the buildings is to be dimmed in such a way that no light penetrates to the outside, but the volume and intensity of the light remain sufficient for normal private and business life to carry on."

One week later, they were still saying: "We are going to conduct air-raid blackout drills. All streets, squares, and courtyards must lie in complete darkness. The most important crossings may be dimly lit. Entrances to restaurants, theatres, and cinemas may no longer be lit—likewise shop windows. Car headlights must be dimmed." Father and daughter lived in darkened surroundings at night.

In June 1939, the measures became more specific: "For every air defence community, which effectively means every house, twelve devices are required for self-defence: a fire extinguisher, fire pike, rope, ladder, medicine cabinet, two pails per stairwell, water tanks, *Feuerpatsche* [fire beater], sandbox, shovel or spade, axe or hatchet." These were words the poet had to take note of, words that even she had to follow.

And in July 1939: "Air-raid protection in the pantry. In the event of war, vital food items must be just as protected from gas attacks as human life itself. Airtight containers such as pickling jars, stoneware jars with lids, and the like offer the most effective protection. Canned foods are safe from chemical weapons. We recommend stovepipes or ovens to anyone who cannot store their food in the aforementioned containers. Ventilation flaps and the front openings must be sealed with insulating tape."

An anonymous diary entry from August 1939 gave this account:

If one does not complete the blackout measures properly, he will be taken to task or even asked to pay up. In addition, men are out and about with paint and brushes. They are painting clearly visible arrows on basement walls and exterior walls that face the street. In the event of an attack, this will give people who are out and about, in trouble, or coming home from work the chance to find an air-raid shelter in an unfamiliar location. House doors must open easily. People aren't very afraid of looters, because they would be convicted by a court of summary jurisdiction. As to where they would end up, people talk under their breath about labour camps. People are afraid of these camps, of course, for a lot gets passed on by word of mouth.

| 96

And we now turn to Georg. The last sentence of the certificate of employment from the Gesellschaft für Telephon- und Telegraphenbeteiligungen [Telephone and Telegraph Investment Company] issued on December 6, 1938, read, "Mr. Chodziesner will leave our company on December 31, 1938."

The bogus laws that were applied to officials, doctors, and lawyers did not count in the business world, and the company valued the assistance of a reliable expert like Georg. He'd worked in the central patent department on Alexandrinen Strasse for half a decade. After the pogrom, however, he could not continue working through the end of his contract, which was due to expire momentarily, so he went into hiding for the time being. When the immediate danger was over, he prepared to immigrate with his family to Chile by way of England. In June 1939, he wrote to his émigré sister in Switzerland:

The way things stand for me now is that I received notification yesterday that the permit from England should arrive in about ten days. During this time, I hope to also get all my papers in order. If things with Chile go quickly, then I won't have to go to England first, particularly as I do not know who would pay for my crossing from there.

On the other hand, I don't want to close the door on England, should I have to wait a bit longer to go to Chile on account of passage, for example. If the Chilean Consulate gets back to me soon, I intend to do my utmost to get my visa as quickly as possible and to, perhaps, scrape together money for my own passage. And since my papers would be ready, I could travel on ahead. But, as I said, one cannot reach a decision on all of these matters right now.

Meanwhile, the addressee in Switzerland was forced to repeat her request for an extension of her residence permit: "On June 6, 1939, the Cantonal Immigration Authorities in Zurich decided to grant me permission to stay until June 30 for the purpose of preparing for emigration. I will now present the respectful request for an extension of the deadline and cite the following grounds for my request."

| 97

I make a surprising discovery in the Marbach Literaturarchiv [Marbach Litera-ture Archive]: a brown envelope in DIN A 5 format once contained a registered letter from Gertrud Chodziesner to "Mr. Fritz Baumeister Crzellitzer, Tel-Aviv, Hagilboastr. 12, Palestine." The envelope is postmarked July 19, 1939, Schöneberg 5, Berlin, and has a sticker on it with the word "Registered."

The envelope is empty but nevertheless contains a message. Gertrud must have asked her uncle to help her immigrate to Palestine. To fill in the blank, the architect Fritz Crzellitzer was married to one of her mother's sisters, Magda. He had immigrated with his wife and children to Palestine in a timely fashion.

But the fact that she sent her uncle a comprehensive letter by registered mail surely indicates that she was serious this time, particularly as compared with the subtle hints woven into her postcard text to the farm near Arlington, Vermont.

In one of her letters to Hilde from early August 1938, Gertrud mentioned the keyword "Palestine": "What can I tell you that's new and interesting around here? I'm stuck in the middle of currant picking, which is going on in the blaz-ing heat, and so am training for Palestine." This was surely meant as a joke.

Now on to the envelope and what it might have held . . . There is a type-written résumé in which she points to her training in "agriculture and home economics at the Arvedshof School for Women near Leipzig." She also refers to her employment at a kindergarten, the "language teacher exams," "military interpreters' exam," her work as a governess in private homes, the transla-tion exam for the Foreign Office, the summer course in Dijon, caring for her mother at home, participating in a course for civil law notaries, her work in the Finkenkrug home and garden, "raising small animals," and her knowledge of the Hebrew language as well as Czech, Spanish, and Flemish.

"I also enclose . . ." A list of nine positions follows. She then gives special emphasis to her work as a governess in various households. One of the three pages contains Hebrew writing samples and the translation of a Hebrew poem.

The keyword "Hebrew" doesn't turn up in Gertrud's letters until 1940—but then appears in a context which indicates that she was already an advanced language student, that she took part in a conversation course and had written poems in Hebrew. The year before, she had already learned so much Hebrew that she could submit writing samples and translate a poem by Hayyim Nah-man Bialik. Did she take lessons, or did she acquire the knowledge on her own? There was certainly plenty of motivation to learn Hebrew in those days.

Records indicate that Gertrud's teacher was enthusiastic about Bialik, so the impulse probably came from her. But this was not exactly a hot tip! Even then,

Bialik was considered a major force among poets writing in Hebrew, and people referred to him as "the greatest poet of the modern Hebrew language." He made the resurrected language of the Bible suitable for literary use. He sought to do the same with Yiddish.

Even though she completed only four of the eight stanzas, the fact that Gertrud Kolmar translated at least one of Bialik's poems was also an affirmation. Her relatively free paraphrasing has that unmistakable Kolmar ring. Here is the first stanza:

> Stormy night. Wind whooshing
> With clouds tearing the town savagely;
> The whole little town sunken and submerged,
> Sleeping in the muddy darkness.

In the case of a translation like this, it's easy to forget a famous Bialik phrase that must have long since been a dictum: "A translation is like a kiss through a handkerchief."

Learning Hebrew was officially welcomed in those days, at least among Jews, who were newly motivated.

The extended documentary CD-ROM by historians Eberhard Jäckel and Otto Dov Kulka informs us that: "In Nazi Germany, as in modern times on the whole, the Hebrew language has played a role in two areas: (1) as a sacred language, the language of prayer in the synagogues and in religious education, both at traditional institutions (Torah study) and in religious instruction at secular schools; (2) as a modern colloquial and literary language used in the educational work of the Zionist movement with a focus on aliyah. Teaching modern Hebrew was explicitly promoted by the Nazi regime because it furthered emigration."

Early on, the *Jüdische Rundschau* started a series called "Hebrew for Everyone." The sequential lessons were summarized in a booklet with a red envelope. Later on, lessons for advanced students came in a book with a blue envelope. The sequels in the *Rundschau* were extremely well received. The books enjoyed wide distribution, but learning remained marginally successful. In Palestine, people would soon say, "Never before has a group of immigrants learned Hebrew so zealously, yet with so little success."

It was also a language that people in Central Europe hardly ever had occasion to hear in those days. Handed down almost exclusively by scholars, this language of the Bible and the Mishnah had hibernated for nearly fifteen hundred years. The language was now being revived in an experiment fostered primarily by Zionists. And Hebrew became the language of Jewish settlers in Palestine.

* * *

The quota of immigrants to Palestine was admittedly kept low by the British mandate administration. Only someone with training in a skilled trade or agriculture could receive the certificate that made immigration possible. These certificates were limited to one thousand per month, and the Jewish Agency acted as facilitator. They wanted Zionists in particular. One of the oft-quoted, standard questions asked by the immigration authorities was, "Are you coming out of Germany or out of conviction?"

Supposing Gertrud Chodziesner (though not a Zionist) had received a certificate, ignored all warnings, and disregarded all concerns—then how could a woman in her mid-forties have survived in Palestine? It's conceivable that she could have worked in a kibbutz. If she'd been too old for agricultural work, she could certainly have worked in a nursery. And with this in mind, she probably emphasized her experience in dealing with children on her application.

But people had received frequent warnings about Palestine, and the warnings continued. For years, the *C. V. Zeitung* had provided a special page called "Palästina-Umschau" ["News of Palestine"], and veritable litanies of horror were published there.

Here is a short retrospective from August 4, 1938: "Another week of terror." A fifty-year-old man and his fourteen-year-old son were "killed by Arabs as they were carrying water from the Jordan to their settlement." In Jerusalem, a Jew "at the Damascus Gate was seriously injured when stones were thrown at him and he was stabbed with a knife. Police discovered a highly explosive land mine weighing over sixty pounds at the vegetable market in the Old City." A Jewish special constable "was severely wounded by an Arab with a knife" as he "accompanied workers on their way home from the orange groves." A shepherd was guarding his sheep near a kibbutz when he "was shot by two Arabs. Despite his wounds, he drove the attackers away by firing his shotgun at them."

A bomb exploded between Jaffa and Tel Aviv, injuring a six-year-old Jewish girl and an eight-year-old Jewish boy. "Bandits" built a stone barricade on a country road "to possibly hold back reinforcements and began to bombard the settlement from all sides." These are just six reports from a total of about two dozen within a single week. Each report provided in-depth coverage and the names of those involved.

The "News of Palestine" headline from August 25 was "Victims Without End." The first sentence read: "The overall situation has hardly changed at all." A seventy-year-old Jew was stoned to death. One passenger was seriously injured in an attack on a Jewish bus and five others, including one of Martin Buber's sons, had minor injuries. And so on and so forth. The final sentence read: "With the exception of enclosed urban or rural settlements, a state of emergency has been declared on all main roads in Palestine from six in the evening until four in the morning."

This succession of reports was truly not inviting or encouraging! Additional reports of this kind apparently made enough of an impression on Gertrud Kolmar that she left it at a single attempt and no longer asked her uncle to pass on her application papers.

| 98

Gertrud kept Hilde up-to-date about their domestic life as well:

> After dinner and after washing up, I was so lazy that I put off this little remaining portion of the letter until today. Admittedly, I now sleep an hour or more after lunch every day, but I also get up much earlier than in Finkenkrug, around 6 A.M. or soon thereafter. That's because I always want to be at Bolle's shortly after it opens at 7. And if I get there at 7:30, the best rolls are already sold out, and then I have to go to the baker as well. He also lives right nearby, to be sure. But it's so nice to get our entire breakfast of milk and baked goods in one place, and at the house next door, no less.

She shopped, made breakfast and supper, did the washing up, and so on. There was hardly a day "when I am not 'running and shopping,' and if I'm not 'running and shopping,' I'm in a hurry to get my room all straightened up." At least she had nominal domestic help.

The Chodziesners rented one room of their much-too-large apartment to

> a lady who pays nothing for the room, but helps me with the housework in the morning. She is friendly and willing but a complete novice in manual labour of all kinds (which, in her case, includes grinding the coffee). And her inexhaustible chatter, as well as her inability to be alone, plus her tendency to come to me every quarter hour with some piece of news, a new request, some nonsense or other—all of this makes dealing with her much harder for me than any housework. I would send her away and try to do it myself, despite being overly burdened. But since she's 52 years old, unemployed, and homeless, I feel sorry for her and want to try to steel myself against her incessant jabbering by means of friendly but stubborn silence. I've already done that today and am actually not as beaten down and tired as usual.

Five weeks later, at the end of March, she wrote:

Well, the difficulties with our lodger haven't lessened for me. But I've now reached the point (especially since it's not a permanent state of affairs, or so I hope) where I see the humourous side of people and things. She comes from Landsberg on the Warta River, and a nephew addressed her in a letter as, "Lotte, you old, fat, sentimental river flounder," which describes her to a tee. She's wallowing in tears today because good friends of hers are off to Kenya, and that is understandable, given her nature. I'm sorry for her, but the announcement that she's decided to die of a broken heart has more of an effect on my funny bone than on my heart. A 52-year-old teenager . . .

Gertrud Kolmar transformed her ongoing experiences with her garrulous sub-tenant—who demanded attention but provided little help—into a dramatic monologue: *Möblierte Dame (mit Küchenbenutzung) gegen Haushaltshilfe* [*Furnished Lady (with Kitchen Privileges) in Exchange for Household Help*]. The furnished lady's torrent of words practically amounted to an aggressive act against the lady of the house, who took her in without asking for rent and, in a role reversal, demoted herself to the status of domestic help.

By writing this monologue, the author of two momentous, overstylized theatrical consecration plays freed herself. And she did so under social and political circumstances in which most other people would probably have quit writing. Though it didn't tilt the world's axis, this was nevertheless a Kolmarian turning point! With wit and brilliance, the thoroughly refined poet articulated the maniacal chatter of a woman hungry to communicate, yet so self-centered that, in a time of dreadful events, she was mainly interested in cooking a special pudding (while taking advantage of the landlady).

Although the text was seemingly lightweight, it nevertheless mattered to Kolmar. This is evidenced by the fact that she made a clean, typewritten copy and thus considered it a final version. She may have written the play in the late summer of 1939 but, in any case, it was definitely before the Wehrmacht invaded Poland.

There are two possible reasons why this dramatic soliloquy has never been performed to date. The first is the format itself: the piece is shorter than present-day one-act plays. The monologue would have to be paired with something else to make an evening of theater. This also holds true for radio performances, and that is why my attempts to motivate a broadcaster to produce it have failed.

The second thing that may have prevented it from receiving a premiere is that the text lacks a current frame of reference. In Kolmar's day, people would have immediately understood the innuendos. If she had read the text to her father or given it to him to read, for example, he would have gotten it right away. The blanks that he would have filled in by association would have to be reworked, added to, and reintroduced today.

The furnished lady unerringly follows the motto, "I talk, talk, talk, therefore I am." She talks everything to bits and pieces, even the highly topical theme of the Aryanization of homes previously owned by Jews. With her, the gravity of the measure is reduced to the mere loss of comfort, to heating with stoves in lieu of central heating. And she just blathers around problems. This mindless chatter points to a mentality that doesn't see the handwriting on the wall, refuses to accept it, and thus prevents necessary decisions from being taken.

Even her nephew, clearly an immigrant to Peru, was a nonissue. And she wasn't concerned that letters to him might be "examined" or that potentially incriminating wording might be discovered. Only the postage stamps seemed to matter, and you didn't want to spend too much time getting hold of them . . . These were attempts to create and preserve normalcy in catastrophic times.

I will insert the text here, as it seems to convey a lot about the atmosphere in the Chodziesner home. Three cuts were needed to maintain the balance with other citations in this book, but they do not concern the essentials:

> GOOD MORNING!—Where did you buy your rolls today? They were simply too delicious! Even if you've eaten only three, you're ready for a fourth right away. I always say, "Have a good breakfast, and half the day's work is already done." Don't you agree?—Oh, by the way, I have a request: Could you tell your brother Georg that he's to hammer a hook into the wall behind my bed for me?
>
> It's for my dressing gown. I don't like to lay it over the chair, as it's so disorderly. It now hangs on the latch next to the door, but I find it so annoying to have to run across the entire room to the door after just getting up. You can catch cold so easily if you run around naked, after all—don't you think? Especially now, with no more heat . . . I think I've already caught something . . . Did you sleep well?
>
> Unfortunately, I did not. I couldn't find peace of mind at all. . . .
>
> No, I won't get to your father's room until Monday. Today, I will start on my room and the rear hallway. Oh, you know, my room! It will be the death of me. I'd rather dust all three front rooms than scrub mine in back. I'm sick all the time . . . Couldn't we set up things differently? You really must advise me . . .
>
> Say—just a quick question—may I make my pudding first before I start tidying up? Otherwise it won't be cold by noon. Since . . . you see, I bought

a pound of veal neck yesterday, but it cooked down so much, and what was left over—I won't get enough to eat with that little piece of meat, don't you agree? What do you think, should I use semolina or cornstarch? I think cornstarch is better for me. Since, you know, something really strange happened to the semolina pudding I made recently—I'd rather not tell you about it. I'd eaten the usual things, a little plate of soup, some vegetables, meat and potatoes, a few noodles that were left over from the previous day, and then half of my semolina pudding. And then suddenly—for an instant—my heart stood still. Yes, really. And I was breathing so heavily—I couldn't get any air and had to set my spoon down . . . I simply could not go on eating and actually had to leave the remaining pudding for the next day. And I wasn't even sated, but what did that matter? I went to the doctor immediately afterwards . . .

The doctor? I can't really recommend him. I don't trust him anymore . . . I was supposed to go hungry! I was to eat no meat, no puddings, rice, noodles, cakes . . .

So what else was I supposed to eat? He didn't tell me. I didn't even let him finish talking.

I don't need that sort of prescription.

I know myself well enough to realise that I have to take care of myself. Yesterday I went to someone else. But I had bad luck. I got to his office at four, but he was out, allegedly called away to deliver a baby. Of course, that was just a pretext . . .

Why? Have you ever heard of babies coming in the early afternoon? Children arrive in the evening or at night. At least that's been my experience. My experience in terms of other people, that is, for fate has luckily spared me from childbirth. Would you want to experience something like that? Not I. That's the only thing, however, that I have not endured. Otherwise, I wouldn't want them to write on my gravestone that, "Nothing was spared her."

Nay, I know it, believe you me . . . they'll be taking me to Weissensee [the Jewish cemetery] soon enough. I've lived through too much hardship . . . suffered too much . . . I always get myself upset, and I'm not supposed to, not with my heart . . . you know, I'm a very sensitive person. Everything takes so much out of me . . . And now, my friends from Leipzig have left—I already told you that they've gone to England . . . It's been fourteen days, and I'm still not over it . . .

Alas! There just aren't good people like that anymore! You know, when I used to arrive in Leipzig—I came mostly on the morning train—breakfast was already on the table, and what a breakfast! Cold chicken and even

lobster, plus Malaga or Rhine wine, plus strawberries and cream if they
were in season! In huge quantities. I mustn't think about it now. Oh, how
emotional the loss of these people has been for me. No one can replace them
. . . While we were saying good-bye, were still at the railway station, they
gave me a two-pound can of pineapples. I was more delighted by it than I
would be if you gave me a hundred reichsmarks right now . . . Should I open
the can?—Would you be so good as to open it for me—and I'll eat a few
chunks with my pudding? But I don't think they go together . . . what do you
think?

Yes, I already have news from England. But as I've already told you
. . . my girlfriend wanted to immediately look around for a housekeeping
position for me over there. But she now writes me that it will be very
difficult, as too many unsuitable elements have pressed for such positions.
People who spoil the market for the likes of us . . . too bad! But it can't
be helped now. She wants to try anyway. In any event, I informed her of
my modest wishes promptly, for it's best to be clear from the outset . . .
but surely you agree? I'm not making any special demands, but if it were
possible to find something suitable for me in a larger city, perhaps London
. . . one prefers not to go to such a small town . . . And with my heart, very
hard or strenuous work is naturally out of the question . . . Making English
beds, for example, is supposed to be terribly exhausting . . . because of the
width of the beds . . . It wrecks your limbs . . . Such things are not for me.
Or crawling around on my knees to polish the hallway . . . I would like to do
that kind of housework in more of a sitting position . . .

No, I can't use a sewing machine. But if you're helping in the kitchen,
for instance, cleaning vegetables or peeling potatoes, you can surely do it
sitting! . . .

No. I can't. When am I supposed to learn English? I have no time. I help
you in the morning. Then I have to cook my own food, and I absolutely
need my two-hour afternoon nap. I go shopping afterwards, and in the
evening I must go to visit relatives . . .

Ah, you see . . . I have a couple of old boiled potatoes from the day before
yesterday. Could you perhaps use them? Otherwise I'll just dump them.

Do I? No. Never in my life have I heard of people eating two-day-old
boiled potatoes. I think they've already gone bad. So I've got to toss them
out. Look how full the garbage pails are again! Do we have to take them
out today? Couldn't it wait until tomorrow—oh no, tomorrow won't work,
it's Shabbat, and the day after is Sunday—well, perhaps it can wait until
Monday? This back staircase is dreadful . . . Oh God, if my aunt from
Hamburg were to see such a thing—I've never used a back staircase in

my life before . . . and now with the garbage pail . . . Really, one feels like a servant . . . I can no longer imagine that I was once an accountant, an office manager at a large company, the boss's right hand—a position of trust! . . . You must know that all I ever had were positions of trust . . . I've even written out cheques, once for over forty-six thousand reichsmarks, just think of it! And now . . .

Say, do you need your big glass bowl today?—Yes? Oh, sorry, I just wanted to use it for my pudding. But never mind . . . just keep it . . . I'm not that kind of person . . . I'll just use one of your other dishes.

Look how it's pouring outside! . . . If it's raining like this on Sunday, I will not go to Westend.

What am I supposed to do there? You only go out there to enjoy a bit of fresh air. Earlier, when my relatives still had their beautiful villa, it was even cosy in bad weather. But now that they've sold their house, and sitting around in that cramped room . . . with dogs and children all around . . . that's not for me. Although I am very fond of children . . . And what an apartment, so uncomfortable—oven heating, just imagine! I'm not used to it. Personally, I've always rented rooms in luxury flats. . . .

By the way . . . you know . . . this relative is my aunt's stepdaughter—I've told you this before—my aunt will celebrate her seventieth birthday on Wednesday. I am also invited, of course. If only I knew what to get her . . .

The can of pineapples? Yes, I have already thought of that. But I do not think it's the right thing . . . First, it would be ungrateful, because my Leipzig friends bought the tin for me and not to give away as a gift—even if they would never find out, I don't like to do such things behind people's backs. And I also know that my aunt doesn't like canned fruit compote: she prefers to eat fresh fruit. I recall that she once told me so . . . and don't you agree that it would look far too ostentatious if I, an unemployed bookkeeper, suddenly arrived with pineapple? One might think I had a rich boyfriend . . .

I beg your pardon! Don't you think my age ought to shield me from suspicion? Well, you know, I'm still not as old as all that. Recently, on Nollendorfplatz, a Jewish gentleman passed me and gave me a look . . . well! . . . I just looked at him condescendingly so that he didn't even dare to open his mouth and moved on sheepishly . . . I had on my little spring hat with the bright blue feather—bright blue always makes you look so youthful—it was crimped, too . . . I must go to the hairdresser again on Wednesday. Should I wear my black silk dress? Or the one with the lace insert? Which do you think is more appropriate? And, you know, I'll buy a box with darning thread for my aunt and have the florist shop tie on a few flowers, primroses or forget-me-nots—I still have a nice colourful ribbon from a box of chocolates—she'll like that for sure.

And that's that. Would you like to try my pudding? You'll notice at once that there's an egg in it. You don't find it too sweet?—If I may give you some advice, I'd put the roast on now if I were you, otherwise it won't be tender. And put a few whole spices on it . . .

You're odd. Whenever I give you a bit of advice, you say you were already planning to do it anyway. But that's the way it goes . . . I'm such a compassionate person and give everyone good suggestions, yet they aren't grateful for them . . .

Yes, I'll just go and fetch the vacuum cleaner. Only . . . before I start, couldn't I just run down to the mailbox? I wrote to my nephew in Peru last night, but I didn't have a postage stamp, and I didn't want to bother you. Would you be so kind as to give me a stamp? It's so annoying and time-consuming if I always have to get in line at the post office for just a couple of stamps.

Thank you. Afterwards, I'll immediately bring you the twenty-five pfennigs from in back. Can I get you something from the baker, perhaps? I'll just pop across the street for a little something to go with my coffee, a cinnamon roll or butter cake . . . It won't take any time at all . . . And if someone should ring me, I'll be back in a few minutes.

Thank you. See you later!

In the late summer of 1939, the enterprising, though not exactly industrious "furnished lady" was able to move around freely in Berlin—aside from the gradually expanding number of districts off-limits to Jews.

Yet what could or would a Jewish woman have seen during outings in the city? Elisabeth Freund, a contemporary witness, had this to say:

> All the way down the Kurfürstendamm, nearly every shop has a sign in it that reads, JEWS ARE PROHIBITED FROM ENTERING or WE DO NOT SELL TO JEWS. When you walk along the streets, you see "Jew, Jew, Jew, Jew" on every house, on every windowpane, in every shop. It's hard to explain how the Nazis, those rabid antisemites, have plastered the word all over their city when there are so few Jews still living in Germany. You can no longer look anywhere without coming across the word "Jew." And it's not just luxury shops or cigar stores, for example, which are off-limits to Jews citywide. These signs are now going up in bakeries as well as butcher and vegetable shops.

If a woman who looked "Jewish" was strolling through town, would she have been accosted, jostled, or shoved off the sidewalk? Did she ever have to show her identity card because she supposedly looked "suspicious"? And did people shout at her repeatedly in this country where bellowing was practically a constant? The voices were hoarse, barking, cracking, even on the radio, and just a few songs were repeated incessantly, particularly the Horst Wessel Song, which became a second national anthem: "SA *marschiert* [storm troopers marching] . . . SA *marschiert* . . . SA *marschiert* . . ."

After a long journey and additional travel on foot, the "furnished lady" was finally able to reach her relatives in one of the "Jewish houses." A family member who read the newspaper could bring the conversation around to the more-than-threatening situation. Yet, would he have expressed himself openly if the family circle had been widened by the presence of a close acquaintance, a female visitor, or a neighbor?

You could never be completely sure that someone in the group was not an informer working for the Gestapo or a voluntary informant. Even if you were among friends, you had to take precautions . . .

The telephone, assuming there was one, could have been set up* during a postal inspection to eavesdrop on the room, even if the receiver was on the hook. And if you made a call, how often did a thoughtless comment lead to an arrest, all the more so if you passed on a political joke that was going around? An acquaintance repeated a sharply barbed joke about the two new religious holidays introduced by Hitler: Maria Denunziata and Mariae House Search . . . This immediately led to a house search in which they rummaged through the linen closet once again, tore books from the shelves and cabinets, and turned everything upside down for hours on end. You were summoned to the Gestapo office, put through the wringer, went missing for ten to twenty days, and came back a silenced person. Or you were arrested because of a remark in a letter written six years ago! You didn't dare write down a single line spontaneously, as every letter could be opened and read. One wrong move and you found yourself in a concentration camp again. There were good reasons for hundred-meter-long waiting lines in front of travel agencies, especially Palestine and Orient Lloyd!

Gertrud Kolmar was also constantly confronted with hateful images of Jews, chiefly in the numerous display cases of the Jew-baiting, Jew-hating newspaper *Der Stürmer* [*The Attacker*]. Julius Streicher was Gauleiter of Franconia and leader of the Zentralkomitee zur Abwehr der jüdischen Greuel- und Boykotthetze [Central Committee to Repulse Jewish Atrocity and Boycott Agitation]. Not only was Streicher the publisher and editor-in-chief, he also owned the paper! He referred to himself as "No. 1 Antisemite" and thereby attempted to challenge Goebbels for the top spot.

* "Set up" probably means that wiretapping equipment would have been installed.

As early as April 1925, Streicher gave a speech in which he called on people to "make a start today, so that we can annihilate the Jews!" Drawings in *Der Stürmer* brought to mind stereotypical caricatures of hook-nosed, thick-lipped Jews. Jewish *Ritualmord* [blood libel] was repeatedly pictured with dark figures of Jews allowing the *Lichtgestalt* [creature of light] in the form of a naked German maiden to bleed to death over a tin pail . . .

Gertrud continued to communicate closely with family. In October 1939, she reported on the health of her sister-in-law, Thea, who had a serious "stomach ailment," possibly a stomach ulcer.

After an initially false diagnosis, followed by the right medication, Gertrud was able to report:

> Since she has been pain-free for a week, and the tablets could hardly have calmed down a stomach ulcer, the doctor said (which is what I thought from the beginning, by the way) the illness was mainly due to nervous tension. It's the result of outer circumstances and could improve right away if things were to change for the better. Maybe a ticket to Chile would be the best remedy. Unfortunately, it is only natural that Thea's subjective state is worse than her objective situation. She can easily become disheartened, deeply depressed, so that even her judgement of people and things is clouded, and many things look dismal to her that are much less darkly hued to an impartial eye. We only hope that we can manage to send her and the little boy on their way as soon as possible, because then everything else will quickly straighten out as well.

What a remarkably played-down assessment! She left out one weighty factor altogether: Gertrud's brother, Georg, could not travel to Chile with his wife and child because he was interned somewhere in the Commonwealth. In terms of the postal system alone, it probably took quite a while for his wife to receive word about where he was staying. It's certainly understandable that this long period of uncertainty caused Dorothea's severe stomach pain. These problems would hardly have been solved by booking passage for mother and son, Wolfgang (Ben).

Gertrud took care of three-year-old Wolfgang in her apartment for a "few days" to reduce the strain on her sister-in-law: "He's all boy, a lovable, animated little guy with a good eye and sharp ear for everyday things, for real life, and a profusion of apt remarks (like when he looked at my picture and suddenly said that Goethe could still ride a motorcycle. He deduced that Goethe was still young enough because, despite his strongly thinning hair, he wore no hat and could still read a letter without glasses)."

| 99

On top of all the troubles, there was the growing angst of impending war. People had spoken about it for years. Rumors had been circulating since the *Machter-greifung*, and the portents were now building.

In April 1939, a gigantic military parade in honor of the führer's birthday took place in Berlin before international guests and the Nazi "team." Goebbels wrote: "It lasted almost five hours. A dazzling image of German power and strength. Our heavy artillery was on display for the first time. Everyone was amazed and astounded beyond all bounds."

A day later, he noted, "The celebrations in Berlin, especially the führer's parade, have made an enormous impression everywhere outside of Germany. We have rightly bailed ourselves out again. However, a confidential report from Paris is very pessimistic. Everyone over there expects war."

This was true in Germany as well. Why else were working men being drafted and replaced by women? The mere fact of women conductors on the streetcars … And food, especially meat, was apparently being hoarded for the Wehrmacht. Only two decades since the end of First World War, and now another war? The chief cynic Goebbels wrote in his diary: "History is not there for people to learn from."

In a speech to the Reichstag that was broadcast over radio, Hitler shouted so loudly that people could hear it in Schöneberg: "If international Jewish financiers within and outside of Europe should succeed in plunging the *Völker* [nations, peoples] into a world war once again, the result will not be the Bolshevization of the earth and a victory for the Jews in the bargain but the annihilation of the Jewish race in Europe."

For Jews, the soon-to-be dominant theme of war was therefore doubly anxiety provoking.

Even if there was no response to the topic of war in Kolmar's surviving archived poems and letters, we must not exclude it. Though she left no written clues, it was still the reality she faced. What effect did it have on the poet?

There were widespread fears that any number of Hitler's hazardous ventures could have triggered a war: the occupation of the Rhineland, the occupation of the Sudetenland and Czechoslovakia, the occupation of Austria …

And now came the increasingly intensified propaganda campaign against Poland: "Incidents in Danzig [Gdańsk], mobilization of Polish soldiers, mistreatment of ethnic Germans, cases of sadistic brutality, and a harvest festival with naked knives …"

As a man with a Polish-sounding surname, how must Ludwig Chodziesner have reacted to the escalating agitation against Poland? As a man raised in a province where many Poles lived, where Polish was spoken all over, and where, over the course of many years, living together had not been superseded by confrontation, how must he have felt? Chodziesner had also contributed in his day by calling for justice and equal opportunity for Polish citizens. And now this aggravation?

In his diary of August 24, 1939, published in New York in 1941, William L. Shirer, an American foreign correspondent in Berlin, reported on visible preparations for war: "It looks like war tonight. Across the street from my room they're installing an anti-aircraft gun on the roof of I. G. Farben. I suppose it's the same one I saw there last September. German bombers have been flying over the city all day. It may well be that Hitler will go into Poland tonight. Many think so" [*Berlin Diary: The Journal of a Foreign Correspondent 1934–1941.* (New York: Knopf, 1941), 181].

August 26: "Our Embassy today issued a formal circular to all Americans here asking those whose presence was not absolutely necessary to leave. Most of the correspondents and businessmen have already sent out their wives and children." Then came the news that "rationing will be instituted beginning Monday. There will be ration cards for food, soap, shoes, textiles, and coal. This will wake up the German people to their situation!" [*Berlin Diary,* 184–85].

August 27: "Food rations were fixed today and I heard many Germans grumbling at their size. Some: meat, 700 grams per week; sugar, 280 grams; marmalade, 110 grams; coffee or substitute, one eighth of a pound per week. As to soap, 125 grams are allotted to each person for the next four weeks. News of rationing has come as a heavy blow to the people" [*Berlin Diary,* 187].

September 1: "At dawn this morning Hitler moved against Poland. It's a flagrant, inexcusable, unprovoked act of aggression. But Hitler and the High Command call it a 'counter-attack'. A grey morning with overhanging clouds. The people in the street were apathetic. . . ." [*Berlin Diary,* 197].

A blackout, and not only a meteorological one: "The city is completely darkened. It takes a little getting used to. You grope around the pitch-black streets and pretty soon your eyes get used to it. You can make out the white-washed curbstones. We had our first air-raid alarm at seven P.M. The lights went out, and all the German employees grabbed their gas-masks and, not a little frightened, rushed for the shelter. . . . No planes came over. But with the English and French in, it may be different tomorrow. I shall then be in the by no means pleasant predicament of hoping they bomb the hell out of his town without getting me. The ugly shrill of the sirens, the rushing to a cellar with your gas-mask (if you have one), the utter darkness of the night—how will human nerves stand that for long?" [*Berlin Diary,* 198–99].

Even more ordinances and prohibitions against Jews were introduced that September! The first of these was a curfew that started at 9 P.M. in summer and 8 P.M. in winter. Telephone lines were cut, and Jews were no longer permitted to use public phones. Radio sets were confiscated. Merchants were instructed to keep lists of buyers' names so that Jews didn't buy any new pieces of equipment.

There would certainly also have been a radio in the Chodziesner apartment. For added harassment, the authorities appointed the Jewish High Holiday of Yom Kippur as the day on which to turn them in. Did father and daughter borrow a little handcart and bring the radio to the collection site?

A contemporary witness, Leopold Marx, wrote: "Items were not allowed to be handed in by officials, for instance. Rather, all concerned parties had to appear in person, and people risked severe punishment for noncompliance with the order. For devout Jews, this decree meant a serious violation of the law against doing any kind of work on this special day. Non-Jewish help who could have assisted by taking or pulling the little carts was very rarely available. . . . It was an eerie situation, but the very vileness of this order strengthened people's inner resistance. It was just another link in a long chain that began with humiliation and, for so many, ended in the gas chamber. Anyone who lived through this day will never forget it."

Ten days after the start of the campaign in Poland, Gertrud wrote another letter to her sister in Switzerland:

> Summer is now over. We've had nice, warm days up to now, but I've gotten nothing whatsoever out of them. Going for walks on the streets of this city is not for me . . . If things should go on like this for years . . . But the future is dark. And even if it were possible for me to get away from here soon (which is not entirely out of the question), I still may not put the opportunity to good use, for I cannot and will not leave Papa alone right now. He doesn't want to stay by himself, since the boy is now gone, as well . . . and since only paid staff, which might actually be hard to find, would care for him . . .

With the outbreak of war, it became increasingly difficult to leave Germany. Here's a note about Peter Wenzel, who didn't want to and could not follow Hilde and his daughter to Switzerland: In the meantime, he was working for a fledgling company, Deulakraft, the German School for Agricultural Machine Operators, whose curriculum included general tractor instruction and training courses for motorized plow operators. Did Wenzel work in the office? Anyway, he wrote to the Brazilian consulate in Berlin on September 12 using Deulakraft letterhead: "On August 6, 1939, the Foreign Ministry in Rio de Janeiro sent telegram 64–21730, authorizing you to grant me a Brazilian visa. As a result of the current war, I'm not available at the moment. But I hope very much that, after a speedy end to the war, I can take additional steps in this direction and ask you to let the matter rest until then."

| 100

Want and need set in early on, at an incredibly early stage. By the end of the first month of war, there were reductions in food rations. A person (even if he were Jewish?) got "a pound of meat, five pounds of bread, three quarters of a pound of fat, three quarters of a pound of sugar, and a pound of coffee substitute made from roasted barley" per week. Our contemporary witness, William L. Shirer, who worked mainly as a Jewish correspondent for American radio, had this to say: "The papers inform us we can no longer get our shoes half-soled. No more leather. We must wait for a new substitute material not yet out." And then: "A decree says you can have only one piece of shaving soap or one tube of shaving cream during the next four months" [*Berlin Diary*, 224].

Would Chodziesner also, like Shirer, have considered whether he should grow a beard? A Wilhelmine-style beard for protection and defense?

| 101

Three days after the surrender of Poland, Gertrud wrote a detailed letter to Hilde with her own personal observations:

> Every day was jam-packed with events . . . with world affairs . . . But it's not as though the tide of world affairs touches me greatly or carries me along, as was previously the case. It seems to me that things are changing face and shape at breakneck speed today. Everything is morphing, in fact whirling, and nothing is standing still. What used to take years, even decades, to change takes only a few days. And so I have retreated deeper and deeper into the abiding, into what has being, into eternal events (eternal events not only involve "religion" but also can mean "nature" or "love"). From that perspective, current events look almost like kaleidoscopic images to me: no sooner does a shape emerge than a shake or rotation causes the colourful pieces of glass to join together in a new configuration, and it's almost impossible, pointless really, to call to mind the variously shaped coloured beams and crystals. On occasion, I do participate in something like I used to, talk about it, warm to it. But afterwards I always wonder about myself a bit, ask myself why I spoke of things so heatedly, things which hardly touch my innermost being. I've

written to you already about my sense of unreality regarding our life in Berlin. This may also add to my "detached" attitude. In the meantime, it has become even more intense, more spellbinding, especially outside the house, and on the street I often have the feeling of being in a daze, a stupor, and long—in vain—to awaken from it. Since I had somewhat less to do last Monday, Papa took me to a less familiar, remote part of the city park to "bring me out" for a bit. I didn't let on, but the walk made me feel hopelessly sad. And I felt so old when I returned home. I also know that, when I speak of Finkenkrug, I often say "at our place" . . . "At our place, we did it this way or that" . . . as if the Speyerer Strasse apartment were not "our place" but "someone else's." As long as we lived in F., I never realised how attached I was to not "being scared" at all of moving to Berlin. Maybe it's not even F. that I am missing but rather those abiding things, the animals and plants, the eternally recurring cycle, the constancy of passing away and becoming. There are several borzois in the vicinity. I can't look at them without being painfully reminded of Flora. And yet, for her sake, I'm happy that she didn't come with us. I stop in front of every newly discovered stationery store in the area, eyeing the usual abundance of dog postcards to see if there might be a "Flora" among them that I could send to Binelein. But my search has been fruitless up to now. I thought about Sabine again yesterday evening . . . how she was out at our place last winter—it had snowed—and how happy she was to go sledding (she said, "go ice-skating") with me in her thick, warm, woollen suit. Well, she's got something similar in Switzerland, only more so, but without her Aunt Trude, of course, which understandably hits Aunt Trude harder that it does the child.

Sabine, the child she was not allowed to have, the child that was denied her, was brought into the world by her sister as a surrogate, so to speak. And from the beginning, Gertrud, now Aunt Gertrud, lavished the child with motherly affection. She took part in each phase of her development, especially when it came to language, and noticed the specific stages of phonetic development. Over a period of weeks, even months, the little girl lived in Finkenkrug, and "helped" Gertrud with gathering and raking leaves. And Sabine was surrounded by animals, borzois, parrots, chickens, ducks, and rabbits, to which children develop strong, quasi-human attachments. A little Noah's ark, rising from the sand that was also abundant in East Havelland.

The fact that Hilde had left Germany was doubly painful for Gertrud: it meant the loss of a sister with whom she got along extremely well and the loss of the child who was out of reach from that point on. But the love and affection remained. This showed up mainly in birthday letters to her niece. Since she was not able to give the child any gifts, she at least wanted to write to her. I shall present three of these letters, for they allow us to see other facets of her character.

It was a month after the end of the Blitzkrieg in Poland and, in anticipation of continuing war in the west, Gertrud Kolmar outlined a fantasy flight from Berlin to Zurich, a game of make-believe based on a fairy-tale motif by Hans Christian Andersen. The flight took them away from their increasingly harried lives in Schöneberg to family life in Switzerland. She tells us the story of the flight to Switzerland. Berlin, October 31, 1939:

My dear little monster, do you know what I'd like right now? I'd like to be Doctor Golden Hair. ("Doctor Golden Hair" is a beautiful fairy tale that I'd love to tell you, if only you were here.) But why would I like to be Doctor Golden Hair? I will tell you. Here's why: A little old man comes up to Doctor Golden Hair. He takes a piece of soap from his pocket, pours water over it, gets it all sudsy, and dips a pipe into the foam. He blows into the pipe and makes a soap bubble, which gets larger and larger and finally gets so large that Little Golden Hair, who is a handsome little boy, and the old man can climb into it. Then the bubble rises slowly into the air with them inside, and they fly far, far away to a distant land.

I'd also like to have an experience similar to Golden Hair's. But instead of the old man, I would bring my big beautiful doll, Elisabeth, with me on the trip. I used to play with her as a child, and she has brown hair, blue eyes, and a pink silk dress. And who do you think I'd bring her to? Well then, I would sit down in the soap bubble, which is like being inside a giant glass ball, and soar over mountains, valleys, rivers, cities, and villages. They would all lie far, far below me and look as teeny-tiny as colourful wooden houses from a building block set. And I would fly on and on over fields and woods, until really high mountains came along, so that my soap bubble would have to go up in order to keep from bumping into them and breaking in two. And what are these high mountains? I think they are the Alps, and this is Switzerland. And suddenly I see a big city below me in the middle of the mountains. Do you know what it's called? And when I press lightly on the bottom of the ball, it descends, lower and lower, until it glides down past the rooftops of the houses into a street and gently hits the earth. And as I was floating down, I just glimpsed a sign with LANDOLTSTRASSE on it. But a second later there was a little popping sound—the soap bubble has burst and it's entirely gone. There aren't even shards, just a bit of wet, glistening soapsuds lying on the pavement. I don't look around at all but go up to the house that I just arrived at, doll in hand, and ring the bell. But I wouldn't have needed to ring at all because a rather tall young lady (well, she's not all that tall) just happens to open the door. "Oh," I ask, "Do Mrs. Hilde Wenzel and Sabine Wenzel live here?" "I am Sabine Wenzel," she says. I am amazed. "That can't be," I explain. "I know Sabine Wenzel of Grolmanstrasse very well: she is still a small child and not such a big girl."—"But I am she!"—"Impossible! Two years ago, Sabine Wenzel was a little bug, and you're almost a schoolgirl . . . I am Sabine's aunt, you see, but I never called her Sabine, just monster or Püppi—"What!" the big girl cries out, "then you're Aunt Trude!"

And her mother looks out the door, and she is happy. And the little "monster" gets birthday greetings and is presented with the big doll, and then there's coffee and cake—and that's it for the dream. Alas, I can't fly over to you, because I really don't have a magic soap bubble.

Repeated expressions of grief:

I know full well that I should not allow myself to be overcome by the darkness all around me, that I should kindle an "inner light." Yet this knowledge helps me little—which is to say, if I am unable to find the light to kindle. In summer, there was still the splendour of some beautiful tree along the way—a laburnum, a lilac bush in the front yard of a house—that lasted for a short time. But such splendour made me see Finkenkrug as a lost paradise . . . with many birches, beeches, the forest . . . And Flora . . . I've written to you already that when we came here, I didn't know that I was so attached to all of this . . . Maybe I wouldn't have missed it so much in another part of Berlin. But the Bayrisches Viertel is terrible in winter, even if it's not worse than, say, Tauentzienstrasse or Nollendorfplatz. Yes, I've sometimes been glad to go to the dentist in Wedding: it's green there, though still less so than Finkenkrug. But at least that neighbourhood has a face! And yet, would I want to live there? . . . Oh, I would occasionally like to put on my coat and hat, and walk away, far, far away. These days, I oftentimes think that I could go out to Finkenkrug when the first snow falls and stomp around the woods in the moonlight, just like I used to. But I also know that I probably won't follow through with this plan.

| 102

As Hilde wrote, Gertrud's brother evaded abduction by fleeing on the night of the pogrom. And so we have another chapter in the "chronicle of a Jewish family."

After the war, Johanna Woltmann tracked down Georg Chodziesner's address, and she encouraged him to write down his recollections of the emigration period. They turned out to be rather laconic:

After the Gestapo came looking for me in Nov. 1938 and I spent fourteen days in hiding, our local police urged me to disappear as soon as possible. . . .

Although I had affidavits for immigration to the USA, I would have had to wait two years for a visa because of the American quota system. Meanwhile, we learned from an uncle in South America that a Chilean visa was on its way to Berlin for us. The Chilean Consulate in Berlin promised to forward my visa to the consulate in London. But since the visa didn't arrive until war broke out in Berlin, this was not possible.

He managed to leave for England in the nick of time, right before the start of the Polish campaign. The report presents such an abridged version of what happened there that it hardly has any validity and could even lead to wrong conclusions. His emigration story must, therefore, be reconstructed on the basis of his own keywords and with the help of additional information.

He was taken from Dover to a transit camp in County Kent in southeastern England. Shortly after the *Machtergreifung* and the first wave of emigration from Germany, the Council for German Jewry in Great Britain took over a military camp from the period of the First World War. About thirty-five hundred people could be housed there, and it was known widely among emigrants as Kitchener Camp. I must stress that this was a transit camp and not a detention camp, so it was not surrounded by barbed wire and there were no armed guards.

The status of refugees changed rapidly after the Wehrmacht's violent invasions of Poland, Belgium, Luxembourg, the Netherlands, and France. England felt directly threatened by the apparently invincible Wehrmacht, and panic broke out. Those who fled the Nazi regime were promptly declared "enemy aliens." Three categories were devised or, better put, improvised: (A) intern immediately, (B) sequester and observe, (C) temporarily at liberty. The distinction between A and B swiftly blurred, however, and Churchill ordered, "All of them in the slammer!" The British government saw the victims and enemies of the Nazi regime as potential spies and feared that a fifth column could form on the home front. Interned along with them were the first prisoners of war, particularly members of the German navy, as well as persons who were in England for professional or business reasons. However, these Nazis (or persons labeled as "Nazis") constituted only a small fraction of the total number of people interned.

What happened in and to England at that time has still not been adequately researched, and documents have been kept under lock and key. One gets the impression that real hysteria must have broken out. After Poland was overrun in four weeks and France in six, people thought the Wehrmacht was capable of anything and expected a subsequent invasion of the British Isles. Trenches were being dug in Hyde Park. It is not possible to understand how or why people who fled the Nazi system were seen as sympathizers or even as members of that system and treated accordingly.

In any event, these "aliens" were classified as dangerous enemies whose internment in the British Isles could not be sufficiently secure, so Kitchener Camp was disbanded, and all male refugees between the ages of sixteen and seventy were shipped to the Isle of Man. And they also had to be fenced in and guarded on this island in the Irish Sea, at least twenty nautical miles from the nearest coastal point in England and just as far from the nearest point in Ireland. Even the writer Robert Neumann, known for his collection of literary parodies, *Mit fremden Federn* [*Dressed in Borrowed Plumes*], was arrested. Neumann kept a diary, *KZ auf Englisch* [*Concentration Camp in English*], on the island and, though it has not yet been published, the author Richard Dove was able to take a look at it.

Dove reports: "The internees were brought on land within sight of a silent and hostile local population and then had to endure a long march to Camp Mooragh near Ramsay. There, the government had seized groups of hotels and pensions along the coast and surrounded them with barbed wire. In his diary, Neumann wrote, 'Dilapidated house: ancient, dirty mattresses in barren, dirty rooms—but there's a view of the sea and just one other fellow in the room!'"

And here's another excerpt:

The internees were cut off from the outside world for all those weeks. Newspapers and even radios were banned, and the whole camp turned into a rumour mill. One of Neumann's journal entries reads: "Very exciting days. Collapse of France. Newspapers banned and a rumour inferno" (June 20). Although the threat of invasion gradually decreased, it still dominated the internees' thoughts. On August 7, Neumann wrote, "For no demonstrable reason, several people dreamed last night that the Nazis occupied the island." Often, there were rumours about German peace offers to Great Britain. This increased the internees' fear that they could simply be handed over to the Nazis.

When the wave of internment reached its highest point, there were about twelve hundred prisoners living at Camp Mooragh. They represented a cross-section of German-speaking emigrants: Austrian monarchists, German Jews, Social Democrats of every stripe, and Communists.

Even isolation in the Irish Sea did not seem to provide enough security. Only one ocean in the world seemed to fit the bill as a cordon sanitaire [buffer zone], so they chose Canada, which still belonged to the Commonwealth, as the central location for Germany's victims and enemies who were classified as dangerous. And those camps were also surrounded by barbed wire. But people in Canada were not prepared for such a large batch, and around twenty-five hundred internees remained on the Isle of Man in the interim. Georg Chodziesner was among them.

These internees boarded an old troop transport ship, the *Dunera*, in Liverpool. Its official name was HMT *Dunera*, or Hired Military Transport *Dunera*. These involuntary passengers were tricked into thinking it was also going to Canada, but the *Dunera* set course for South Africa. Thus began the "*Dunera* Saga," the "*Dunera* Affair," the "*Dunera* Scandal," about which at least three books have been written.

And there are Georg Chodziesner's notes! His son, Ben, mentioned a "diary" in an email. So I pricked up my ears, pumped him for information, and he told me the particulars. Georg jotted down notes on toilet paper during the voyage, then worked out the details and typed them up at a later time. I received a photocopy of the typescript via air mail—lines jammed together with hardly any margins, as paper was scarce after the war. Ben gave me permission to quote freely from these previously unpublished notes. And so, after Hilde and Margot, the poet's brother will finally also have his say.

Liverpool:

Everyone had to line up in four rows, luggage in hand, between a line of sentries in front of the staircase that led to the *Dunera*'s gangway. Getting on board went quickly after that. When we arrived at the top of the stairs, we saw soldiers across from us, outfitted with steel helmets and fixed bayonets, who greeted us with calls of "Hurry up." Nevertheless, there was enough time to see the piles of scattered objects and pried-open suitcases lying around at the head of the gangway that were being ransacked by soldiers under the watchful eye of the Liverpool military police. A new surprise awaited us on deck. All pieces of luggage, such as suitcases, bags, backpacks, and other accessories (violins, typewriters, etc.), were snatched by one of the wild, marauding soldiers and, regardless of content, went flying in a high arc onto a great pile. Those wearing gas masks even had them torn off their heads, and if things didn't go fast enough, kicks and jabs with a rifle butt helped them along.

Everyone walked in a complete daze through the cordon and down to the individual decks. Some sat on benches that ran along the long tables. Those who couldn't find a seat remained standing, and everyone waited anxiously for what was coming next. We didn't have to wait long, for the order came down to lay all cigarettes, matches, lighters, razors, and knives on the table, and they demanded to see our papers, etc. Then, soldiers appeared with buckets and began to collect everything that was lying on the table. As if that were not enough, they carried out another body search, during which they took away and tore up the most important papers. It was pointless to object in any way.

The internees were spread out over six decks in all. Cordons, masses of barbed wire. The ship departed, accompanied by a transport ship and a destroyer. There were more searches, frisking, ransacking. Anyone who didn't comply was threatened with, "You'll never get to see the other side." Everyone was still convinced that the ship was going to Canada, and that's exactly how it was announced:

> The decks' occupants consist of internees from a whole variety of English internment camps, such as the Isle of Man, Huyton, Lingfield, etc. All are refugees, the majority of them Jews, as well as political refugees, particularly those being looked after by the Czech Refugee Trust Fund. Since the initial impression prevails that the military does not know what sort of internees it has, a deck father who is supposed to represent the internees' interests to the officers has been chosen for each deck. But these deck fathers have not been admitted and been told that the ship would first have be out of the danger zone (two to four days) before there would be time to meet.
>
> The situation at the stern is even more complicated, because National Socialist internees, mostly sailors, are housed alongside Italian and German refugees. These detainees were supposed to be sent overseas already, but their ship, the *Arandorra Star,* was torpedoed on the second day of their voyage, and only a small percentage of them were rescued, and they've been shipped off a second time, despite an express promise to the contrary. You can easily imagine the mood, and reports of their first voyage do not exactly foster confidence. . . .
>
> Much of the conversation centres around the trip in the danger zone. You can see that there are no life jackets whatsoever on deck at the bow. If anyone observes the iron doors that close off the decks and the placement of guard troops, then he can imagine the ramifications. People are generally down in the dumps. They sit around idly and talk with acquaintances whom they've met again here after being interned in different places. . . .
>
> The wind picked up during the night, and the first signs of seasickness became apparent, especially given our frame of mind. The following morning, the entire premises were a miserable sight: seasick people lay everywhere, not only on the decks, but also in the corridors. All the sinks and floors were dirty.

At about nine o'clock in the morning, we suddenly felt a powerful strike against the ship. Everyone was awake at that moment, for we all suspected that the ship had been hit. Even so, things remained calm, and when we noticed that the ship's propellers were still running, we settled down again. But things looked different on the afterdeck. Since those who were shipwrecked on the *Arandorra Star* had reported the day before on all the lurid details of their torpedoing in the morning of their second day at sea, instructions had been issued on Thursday afternoon to prevent potential panic in case of emergency. Early Friday morning, an extraordinarily violent blow against the ship's hull caused everyone to forget their seasickness, to grab a life jacket on the afterdeck, and to rush toward the only staircase that goes to the upper deck and is supposed to lead eight hundred people into the open air. The staircase was completely blocked at the moment that we felt a second, even more powerful blow against the ship. Everyone thought it spelled the end of the ship. It was no longer possible to take even one step forward. On the Italian deck, everyone fell on their knees in despair and began to pray. After about five very long minutes, the call of "all clear" came from above, and we could hear the motor running again. But it took a long time before things settled down again. We later learned that a torpedo had grazed the ship's keel. . . .

The first stroll on deck took place on day three of the voyage, Saturday, July 13, 1940. You got to the deck through the barbed wire door, where sentries with fixed bayonets formed a tight cordon. The ship has apparently left the convoy. The sight of our baggage was depressing. Open, destroyed suitcases lay everywhere, their contents scattered on the deck. Toiletries, shoes, clothing, etc., lay in total disarray, and soldiers rummaged through them, sticking this or that in their pockets. . . . While going back down, every single person was subjected to another body search in which even his eyeglasses were removed. We still don't have any toiletries or towels. After the walk, they took some comrades on deck to clean up. The items lying around were randomly packed into suitcases or large sacks, and food, etc., went flying overboard or was pocketed by soldiers, and nothing could be done about it. Everything took place under the officers' supervision.

It's necessary to add here that twenty-five hundred prisoners were crammed aboard a ship that was meant for about fifteen hundred. Three hundred men were appointed guards, among them convicts who had been released on parole for this special mission. The captain, Lieutenant Scott, hated Jews and let the gang do as it liked. There were constant attacks by armed convicts and soldiers, who referred to refugees as "Jewish swine" and mistreated them. There were tensions on board between Nazis and Jews. Uncertainty about their destination was also a strain. Were they really going to Canada?

On the seventh day of the trip, the deck fathers were called to the liaison officer. When they returned, they only said that there would be an announcement after lunch. Everyone realised that it concerned the disclosure of our destination. People were incredibly tense as they waited for the announcement. And it was very warm that day to begin with. Soldiers turned up in tropical uniforms for the first time. The announcement was made simultaneously on all decks: Australia was our destination. This also explained the rise in temperature, as the ship had already reached the latitude of Tenerife. The uproar on the decks was hard to imagine. Many had voluntarily joined the transport after being assured they would be taken to Canada. In other cases, fathers or sons had already left for Canada on earlier transports. It was terrible to think of spending many more weeks on this ship under the previously described conditions. Some still had wives in England and had been assured that they would sail for Canada, etc., and these people formed groups. We compiled lists and even came up with the idea of asking the commander to discharge "travellers to Canada" at the next port. But any reasonable person realised that such attempts were completely useless and had to accept his plight.

The next day brought a new surprise: the water was shut off and only distributed in limited amounts. Nothing but salt water was available for washing. And it was so hot that everyone walked around barefoot with nothing but trousers on. The liaison officer did not keep his promise to get us soap and hand towels. Our handkerchiefs had to go on serving as hand towels. And soap isn't useful with seawater anyway. The lack of razors is clearly apparent in the seedy appearance of the internees. There's not even any pleasure in daily exercise. They're constantly rushing us as we walk around the deck, and anyone who doesn't go fast enough gets a blow from a rifle butt. . . . Lately, everyone has to come barefoot when walking on deck. They say it's to protect the deck. As we were walking one day, a sergeant threw a bottle on the deck, and the internees had to walk barefoot through the broken glass which, needless to say, resulted in a number of injuries.

At 11:45 A.M. on July 27, we reached Accra on the Gold Coast, and the ship moored at the quay. This time, they closed up all the hatches in the washrooms. The only way to catch a glimpse of the outside world was to look out through a hatch in the latrine, and since there was a great rush, a security force was set up straightaway. While one toilet was available for normal use, people stood in line by the other and, after climbing over the toilet to the hatch, each person was allowed to take a quick look through it. . . .

We reached Cape Town at 8:40 A.M. on the eighth [of August]. Morning exercise was still going on, so we could partially watch from the deck as we entered the harbour. Unfortunately, the upper portion of the famous Table Mountain was shrouded in clouds. Through the hatches I already mentioned, we could marvel at the bright lights of Cape Town at night and finally see a city without blackouts again. The voyage was set to continue the next afternoon. From the latrine, we saw Cape Town bathed in bright sunshine. . . .

We travelled on and on through the Indian Ocean in rough seas on our way to Australia. A strong wave hit the ship at around 3:20 in the morning of the forty-second day. The crockery flew all over the place with a loud crash, and some of it broke into pieces. Comrades who were sleeping on the tables got thrown to and fro or rolled onto the floor. A few days later, a breaker smashed in the wooden siding by the kitchen anteroom, and a torrent of water poured into the ship so that those sleeping on the floor had to make a quick escape. But we got used to the rough seas over time. The only real difficulty came at mealtimes, when you had to balance your soup plate in your hand and the teapots slid across the entire table. Washing dishes also had its exciting moments. In spite of everything, there were cabaret evenings, and they also gave us English lessons.

I'll expand on the topic by remarking that the *Dunera* song was probably written for one of these cabarets. Here are six of the eight stanzas:

> Deported on the *Dunera*
> With Australia our destination,
> Our bags have been broken into,
> O'Neill wearing our shirts.
>
> Strolling you have to run.
> The soldier shouts: "Hurry up!"
> And shopping in Cape Town
> They take our cash from us.
>
> Many thanks, dear cooks,
> Thanks for supper.
> If we had eaten,
> We'd have been long dead.
>
> My friend, why are you looking at the waves,
> Are you looking for a shark there?
> There's no need to go down there,
> Sharks are already on board.

In order to live in Australia,
Just become a kangaroo,
Learn to make large jumps—
Your bags are just as empty.

Unshaven and far from home,
Far from home unshaven,
We're going on the *Dunera*
Exported to Australia!

Let's return Georg Chodziesner's diary, portions of which are being cited for the very first time:

On August 21, the forty-second day at sea, the ship stopped suddenly at around ten in the morning. They said a man had gone overboard. Soldiers and Indians dashed to the railing and threw ropes with life preservers into the water. An Indian jumped into the water, and they got a rescue boat ready but didn't lower it. The ship manoeuvred back and forth, but no rescue was possible. After nearly two hours of fruitless searching, the *Dunera* looped around and continued on its way. We soon learned that it was Jacob Weiss from Vienna, a comrade from Kitchener Camp. That afternoon, we commemorated him in brief addresses on every deck. An investigation showed that Weiss, whose mother and brother were already in Buenos Aires, was granted a visa for Argentina shortly before his internment, but the internment prevented him from embarking on the journey. The visa in his passport, which they'd taken away from him and many others upon boarding the ship, ran out on the day of his suicide.

Another death took place a few days later. A patient died of a heart condition in hospital, and they lowered him into the sea.

The ship sailed into Australian territorial waters on the evening of August 26. The next morning, Fremantle and the Australian coast came into view during the deck walk. At about ten in the morning, Australian officials came to the ship in a launch. It had to do with medical and customs control. Before lunch, everyone had to line up by deck with his sleeves rolled up and, one by one, go past a civilian official who was standing at the top of the stairs. He looked everyone in the eye and examined their hands on both sides. As we learned, customs officials who had inspected the luggage in the wine cellar below were very upset that the suitcases had not been properly sealed, but broken into and only provisionally closed. . . .

In the early morning hours of September 3, the HMT *Dunera* entered Melbourne's smooth-as-glass bay. At around 10 A.M., the ship was at the quay, which had been sealed off by Australian troops, and a train was also waiting there to take away the internees. A number of Australian officers came on board, and they asked about our health. Although the constant presence of the liaison officer Lt. O'Neill made it impossible to speak freely, we were still able to give them an approximate picture of our voyage by way of our responses. The overcrowded decks spoke for themselves. Around 11 A.M., we began to disembark at the back of the ship, and we soon saw the first people making themselves at home in the train compartments. . . .

At seven in the morning on Wednesday, September 4, 1940, the ship put to sea again. . . . We were supposed to leave the *Dunera* for good on our final travel day, the fifty-seventh, and the morning began in dense fog. The sun broke through at around 10 A.M., and we could watch through the hatches as we came into marvellous Sydney Harbour with its numerous bays. At about 10:30, the harbour pilot came on board, and a tugboat pulled the ship beneath a wonderful bridge to the quay of the inner harbour where the ship moored. The voyage was over!

We had an early lunch and then began to disembark. At about 1 P.M., the first train departed, and the next one arrived immediately afterwards. Meanwhile, we opened the hatch covers on the decks, which had to be kept closed during the entire trip, opened them with force, because nothing more could happen now, and we wanted to get a better look at the disembarkation spectacle. At about 5 P.M., the last of us left the ship to board the fourth train. As we left Sydney, we managed to get a quick look at the city, then went out into the flat countryside. The ride was comfortable, the seats of the cars were well padded, and the Australian soldiers who accompanied us were very accommodating. When they heard about our experiences, they willingly distributed tobacco, chocolate, fruit, sandwiches, etc. After eight long weeks, we finally felt like human beings again. The journey continued on through the cold night. The last train arrived at Hay on September 7, 1940, at 11:30 A.M. Our accommodations consisted of two camps that were secured with triple barbed wire fences: each had thirty-six cabins, each of which could hold twenty-eight men. Lt. O'Neill visited the camp on September 10. We greeted his arrival with boos and calls of "Where is our luggage?" etc. He disappeared immediately, and the Aussies were amused.

The Australian military took all of our luggage from the ship to Sydney and, after thoroughly inspecting and assessing its condition, distributed it to us bit by bit. The ruined luggage with its contents largely missing was a dismal sight.

His typescript notes end here. There are no more notes regarding his stay at the camp near Hay on the Murrumbidgee River in Hay Shire, New South Wales.

The camp lay in a "flat, almost treeless, saltbush plain." Barbed wire fences, floodlights on poles, watchtowers. Continuous sandstorms.

Internees had no idea how long their detention would last, so the prisoners quickly began to organize the camp themselves. A banker introduced convertible camp money that paid for services, such as emptying the latrines. Architects provided beautification. Anyone who knew anything about agriculture organized fruit and vegetable cultivation, insofar as that was possible in this arid region. Merchants established a camp market that supplied more than just food. Orthodox Jews established a kosher kitchen. Sports enthusiasts created a soccer team. Musicians formed a symphony orchestra. Educators organized training courses and opened a so-called camp university.

The internees called themselves the "Dunera Boys," a compulsory community that later held a veterans' reunion. *The Dunera Boys* is also the title of an Australian film for television first broadcast in 1985 that is advertised as an entertaining DVD.

Georg was also a "Dunera Boy." What role did he play in organizing the community's self-help? Unfortunately, not a word about it has survived. Can we find any particulars at the Hay Prisoner of War and Internment Camp Interpretive Centre?

After the war, Chodziesner reported the following in a letter: "And so I was interned in Australia for two years, and all of my efforts to immigrate to North or South America or to any other country were in vain. In September 1942, I volunteered for the Australian Army and returned to civilian life in December 1945. My wife had died in Chile in the meantime and, after prolonged effort, I finally succeeded in bringing my son Wolfgang to Australia in May 1945."

| 103

In December 1939, the poet made a trip to Ludwigshafen to see Karl Josef Keller. This is doubly surprising, as she must have known by then that Keller was among the nationalist, "blood-and-soil" lyric poets. Did she not consider this relevant? Were her feelings stronger than her sense of reason?

As to the journey itself, it is almost unimaginable that she undertook such a journey by train, given that Jews had restricted freedom of movement. And she did so after the war had already begun, when people expected and feared the obstacles, hindrances, and harassment, particularly after the introduction of compulsory identification cards. Even for Aryans, train travel would have been difficult at the time. Many modes of transport were being used by the military, which was being moved from east to west in preparation for the campaign against France. I'd love to know how Gertrud Kolmar ultimately overcame those inevitable difficulties. Was she betting on her inconspicuous appearance? In any case, she showed great courage.

But it was all in vain. According to Johanna Woltmann, who corresponded with Keller: "She suddenly stood at the door of his apartment in the so-called Ruppelsche Villa on Industriestrasse, not far from the train station. Her entire visit lasted no longer than a quarter of an hour, then she made a quick getaway. She brought all of his letters and manuscripts back to him because they were no longer safe with her. He told me in 1978 that he felt quite helpless when she suddenly stood opposite him." Little wonder, as he'd been married since 1937 and, of course, never mentioned it to her.

Keller recounted in a letter:

When I saw her briefly for the second time, the thing I regretted most of all was the shocking and disturbing fact that, in a time which was dangerous for all of us, my esteemed poet stubbornly, if not to say intractably, refused to recognize the looming danger in the wake of *Kristallnacht*. I strongly urged her to leave the country as quickly as possible, whatever happened, and to get herself to safety in Switzerland where her sister was living. Even now, I still cannot fathom that she did not want to listen and thought my views were wildly exaggerated—even considered it possible that I was subject to some sort of persecution complex that could put me in the madhouse. I can still remember these words of hers particularly well.

She may well have been looking back on this experience when she wrote to her sister one year later:

Would you believe me if I put it this way: "I have never experienced a disappointment" and "Reality was always inconceivably more beautiful than any illusion"? Do you believe me? That's how it was for me. It's not as though I was never unhappy, as though I didn't experience any pain. No, I have been very, very unhappy. I've suffered great and deep pain, pain that I have also cherished in the way that an expectant mother is able to cherish the agonies with which her child blesses her. But I foresaw all of it, saw it coming, accepted it ahead of time. I knew it would cost me dearly, and there was no disappointment in that regard. From the outset, I have stricken the words "forever," "consistent," and "true" (insofar as they may apply to my partners) from my vocabulary. Circumstances have certainly led me to conclude that I was never "the one," was always "the other". . . You may well have thought me modest, but I wasn't. I had a low burning point and did not catch fire easily (a fire that quickly went out again). But on one (very rare!) occasion, it burned with a strong and lasting glow. My feelings then had the properties of King Midas, in whose hands everything he touched turned into gold. A great sun dawned immediately and gilded every spot, every pond, every puddle. And in the end, it was no longer so important what the sun did, how it behaved, or who was to thank for its rising, warmth, and radiance. The sun shines on the just and the unjust . . . Do you understand that, in this respect, I was never disappointed, could never be disappointed?

It's not as though I always experienced the great and the beautiful. I have also experienced the small, the petty, and the ugly, and I've had to wade through all kinds of filth. But afterwards, I always said and still say today that whatever was, was good . . .

| 104

Although not even one keyword is to be found about them in Kolmar's literary legacy, further events and developments require us to include other texts in this polyphonic biography.

I shall now continue with one of those accompanying voices, that of William L. Shirer. After the war, Shirer achieved renewed fame through his monumental work *The Rise and Fall of the Third Reich*.

He also evoked the ambience here: "Christmas Eve. Raining out, but it will turn to snow. The first war Christmas somehow has brought the war home to the people more than anything else. It was always the high point of the year for Germans but this year it's a bleak Christmas, with few presents, Spartan foods, the men folk away, the streets blacked out, the shutters and curtains drawn tight in accordance with police regulations" [*Berlin Diary*, 263].

And a cold spell came soon afterward: "Cold. Fifteen degrees below zero centigrade outside my window. Half the population freezing in their homes and offices and workshops because there's no coal. Pitiful to see in the streets yesterday people carrying a sack of coal home in a baby-carriage or on their shoulders. I'm surprised the Nazis are letting the situation become so serious. Everyone is grumbling" [*Berlin Diary*, 276].

Did father and daughter Chodziesner also grumble?

But the post office functioned no matter what! And that is why letters from Gertrud to her brother in Australia have survived, as have letters from Georg to Trude. Yet as a member of the British Commonwealth, Australia was an "enemy nation."

What didn't quite work, on the other hand, was the way that Hilde passed on global correspondence among family members. She only passed on shortened, typewritten transcripts of her correspondence with Georg. As a result, hardly anything more intimate was conveyed than in letters between Berlin and Zurich (and Ascona after that). Letters were also subject to dual censorship, so people would have been extra careful in expressing political opinions. So why did she shorten the texts? My assumption may seem a little unkind: Hilde wanted to go on record as the chief correspondent and therefore letters sent to her would obviously have to predominate.

Added to the overall family situation, Dorothea and her four-year-old son set off on the long trip to Chile at the end of 1939. They found a place to stay on the west coast in Concepción. Georg remained in the New South Wales internment camp for the time being. The couple was separated by the seemingly boundless expanse of the Pacific, more than a third of the earth's circumference. Their family had truly been torn apart. Dorothea would not live to see the end of the war, and it would take Georg a long time before he was able to bring his son from Chile to Australia.

And so when Gertrud wrote to her younger brother, obviously not for the first time, on January 28, 1940, she referred to him as "Dear Boy":

> It seems to me that I think as much about Thea and the little boy as I do about you. Yes, perhaps somewhat more about the little boy than Thea, since he was often in my care of late, as Thea was travelling most of the time. I have a flexible Japanese paper figurine that Hilde bought years ago at the Christmas market. It can do all sorts of tricks and people can do all kinds of things with it, which is why Wolfgang called it the *Grundstücksmann* [property man]. *Grundstück* [property] was more familiar to him than *Kunststück* [trick]. This *Grundstücksmann* took the place of a whole sack of toys, and we could amuse ourselves with it for hours. Papa claims that he never heard Wolfgang laugh as much as when we played this game. I wonder who plays with him now. And when I hear the mail slot bang each morning, I go expectantly to the door in hope of finding news, but thus far in vain . . .
>
> As Papa already said, there's nothing new with us here. It's doubly hard for me to be cooped up in a city flat nowadays. Time and again, I want to ride out to the open spaces, to our "previous neck of the woods," then walk in the forest and stomp around in the thick snow. But when I remember that I would have to return to the city anyway, I just forget about it. Apart from that, I still have ample work with household matters, and I'm not able to indulge in "personal pleasures" before nightfall.
>
> For your birthday, I wish you everything that you desire and all that you wished for Thea on her last birthday.

Hilde's transcript of the letter ends here. Also gone was the beginning of a letter of February 3, 1940, in which Gertrud reported on additional surprises via the mail, albeit through intermediaries, and recounted family news:

> Yesterday, two "pleasant surprises" at once: (1) a letter from Georg, and (2) an airmail letter from Thea, sent via Betty, who wrote to us that she also received letters for Thea's parents and Georg in the same envelope, and sent them off. It's evident from the content that Thea has already written us an ordinary letter from Chile, which is probably en route to us now. This one is dated 1/18. From it, we gather that various large groups of immigrants have been distributed among a number of provincial towns. Thea was housed in the city's best hotel up to now but at the time she wrote had just rented a room in a house whose owners were going to their "fundo" [small country estate] for three months. . . . Thea is going to share the housework with the lady, who is very nice, and someone will always be around to look after the little boy when she's out and about. Incidentally, he makes friends wherever he goes, with both children and adults, who amuse him and want to take walks with him. Concepción has lovely parks, and Thea takes morning and afternoon walks with the boy. He's grown a lot and thinks that Daddy won't recognise him because he's gotten so big and that he won't recognise Mommy, either, because she's gotten prettier. And did Mommy bring along the shaving soap from Berlin, because he will soon have to shave? . . .
>
> Thea's in very good health—which is surely why she's looking better. Her stomach is just fine, which accords with my opinion of her previous illness and, therefore, doesn't surprise me. The question of employment was the one dark albeit very significant point on this otherwise very bright canvas. She hasn't held a job up to now but confidently hopes to get one, all the more so since she found out that most of the *Augustus* passengers in other small towns have gotten jobs. In Concepción, people seem to make less of an effort to find work, but it will be all right . . . The cost of living is apparently low, so the room costs sixty pesos, that equals two dollars, per month . . . Thea's address is: Concepción, *en lista de correos* (general delivery). She doesn't seem to have gotten the airmail letter we sent to Concepción on January 2 or 3, but she got an earlier one that we sent to her girlfriend's address.—In the meantime, you have surely received our letter to you and the little one. Greetings from Papa and Trude.

Looking at Thea's airmail letter from Concepción here in Marbach, I again see the starting point of a wide-ranging family saga. Many best sellers are similarly conceived: Family members are scattered all over the world, so as to be on hand when events converge. And, to a more modest extent, events lend themselves to such a scenario here. Perhaps if Gertrud had survived the Shoah and Hilde had supplied her with enough material, she would have written a novel about her Jewish family in the style of the novel *Die jüdische Mutter* [*The Jewish Mother*]. Repeated reading of Thomas Mann's *Buddenbrooks* could have had a stimulating effect: "I want to go to bed now, but before falling asleep—and for the umpteenth time!—I'll read a little more of *Buddenbrooks*. The book is a classic in its own right."

| 105

Before I talk about a new beginning, I must again emphasize the fact that the poet was very busy with running the household. In addition, she spent a lot of time standing in line at shops during the scant periods in which Jews were permitted to shop at all. Helene Köpp, the housekeeper, still had close ties to the family. At the end of October 1939 she wrote, "I always go early to help Trudchen a bit. She certainly has to deal with the shopping, and one has to stand in line for so long."

Helene Köpp was involved in intrafamilial correspondence and wrote to Hilde and Sabine on many occasions. A small bundle of her letters resides in the Marbach Literaturarchiv, supplemented by letters from her illegitimate daughter, although the Chodziesner household passed her off as a niece.

What might the housekeeper have written on a shopping list at the time? Or did she know by heart the few articles that were demonstrably if only occasionally available?

It can't have been much. Konrad Kwiet wrote, "Step by step, the Nazi authorities prepared to deprive people of food. Jews had to give up eating meat and fish, white bread and rolls, whole milk and butter, eggs and fruit, chocolate and cakes, coffee and tea, wine and alcohol."

Max Plaut, an eyewitness, wrote, "The rations granted to Jews were grossly inadequate, and only mutual assistance and a large 'black market' prevented people from feeling exceedingly burdened by nutritional problems. Although offenses against the War Provisions Acts were severely punished (death penalty), there was still hardly anyone in the Jewish sector who would have hesitated to make use of the 'black market' establishment."

There would not have been a black market in Finkenkrug, nor would there have been one in Falkensee—we must assume that a certain anonymity was required. But I also can't imagine that Gertrud Chodziesner would have gone to a black market in Spandau or Charlottenburg. She would have continued to shop in the usual stores. What, then, could she still have gotten over the counter?

I'll relay a few of the items that Elsa Chotzen listed in her meticulously written household book: Fat? Rice? Jam? Vinegar? Bouillon cubes? Semolina?

Ammonia? Vitrolin [sulfuric acid]? Razor blades? Laundry soap? Lanolin soap? Dubbin? Yeast? Sultanas? Vanilla sugar? Baking powder? Baking oil? Lactoprotein? Smoked, salted herring? Red cabbage? Cheese? Toothpaste? Silk thread? Nivea Creme? Mothballs? And finally, birdseed for the canary? Yes, birdseed!

Shortly before Christmas 1939, Gertrud Kolmar began to write again, this time a longer work of fiction, *Susanna*. She wrote because she had to and because she could not live without it. Over the course of decades, she was consumed by a single passion: writing.

The text that she began on December 19 was completed on February 13, 1940. But the reprint, published by the Jüdischer Verlag, is not always accurate and contains small cuts and changes that don't make sense.

I am not going to retell or interpret the story here but simply provide a detailed sampling. I'm quoting from the typescript copy in the Marbach Literaturarchiv. Here is the opening:

> I AM NOT A POET, no. If I were a poet, I would write a story. I would write a beautiful tale that begins and ends with what I know. But I can't do it. I'm not an artist. Just an old governess with a greying head, worn-down forehead, and bags under her tired eyes. Her forehead was as smooth and shiny as a ball of ivory . . . But I'm only thinking about it now because she died several days ago: Therese Rubin, born Heppner, was seventy-two years of age. I read it the day before yesterday in the newspaper. A married daughter in Breslau announced her mother's death. Her name was not listed. Only a series of faraway cities: Shanghai, Tel Aviv, Hidalgo del Parral, San Francisco. Where will I be someday? Today, I'm sitting in this rented room with shabby green plush furniture, as I have for weeks, and my big suitcase waits in the corner beneath the ledge, hoping for the second affidavit from Plymouth, Massachusetts.
>
> It's been eleven years now . . . This may well have been the last one, this news item in the paper, and an ad in the paper was also the first. Sought: an experienced teacher to care for a slightly emotionally disturbed young girl. Good salary. I answered. A response arrived from the orphan's guardian, and letters were soon going back and forth. I was living in Moers at the time, and he, a lawyer, had no acquaintances in the Rhineland with whom I could have talked things over. But we came to an understanding. I packed up my things and travelled across Germany from west to east for an entire day.
>
> I remember . . .
>
> An old woman stood motionless in the middle of the train concourse, a sturdy peasant woman in a black cloth jacket, heavy skirt, and stout boots with a dark, floral scarf around her brown, hardened face, Slavic cheekbones. I waited near the ticket counters. An official closed and locked

the large, two-winged gate behind the travellers, and only the smaller door remained open. Then I took a step, still undecided, toward the old lady. "The young lady is here," she said, "good." She took my two handbags and stomped out.

It was getting on nine o'clock. Like so many others of its kind, the little town started out behind monument square in pitch blackness with pitifully shivering lights. But I don't think I saw much of it that evening because I just had to brace my umbrella against the wind, which swept patches of grainy snow, sharp as glass, in my direction. And I saw the sturdy back of the packhorse trotting steadily in front of me, never turning its head. Even later on, I heard scarcely a word out of her. Her name was Milda Morawe, and she was from Osterland.

I remember . . . She trudged through the front yard, then up a short flight of stairs, and pushed on the door. And while I shook off the whiteness at the threshold, someone stepped into the hall to greet me. It was Counsellor Fordon. But with his moustache, bushy white hair, and sage-coloured jacket, he looked more like an old forest ranger or a warrior.

His resemblance to Counselor Chodziesner was not coincidental: family members also occasionally compared him to a forest ranger. She has woven autobiographical details into the tale as a whole. There are only two main headings, "governess" and "borzoi." Here is a second excerpt that relates to the latter, the almost magical appearance of the greyhoundlike creature:

And I saw that it was thin and tall, wavy and silvery-white, slightly Isabelline, dappled here and there. It came and touched my hand with its long, cool snout and looked at me with gleaming, almond-shaped eyes. The old counsellor spoke from the shadow of a dog, and that's what it was, a dream of a dog, and I stroked him: "Beautiful boy . . ."

"You have to call her a beautiful girl," Susanna pointed out to me.

"Oh, she's a bitch . . ."

"Yes, she's a bitch and a princess, Empress of Byzantium."

Susanna lived in her own world with its own language, and these were very different from the governess's. Susanna had the following to say, for example: "And the Sea King comes and sees me and finds me beautiful. Do you know what the Sea King is like? His chest is covered in a bushy coat of black-green algae, and his polished head is as smooth and round as pebbles at the beach. And he wears a coronet of two silver fish that bite into each other's tails."

This girl should be brought to reason. But a symbiotic relationship between teacher and student develops that leads to disaster.

| 106

As if to say farewell, Gertrud went to Ahornallee again at the end of January 1940 in the wake of a visit to nearby Reichsstrasse.

She didn't recognize much of her childhood environment, for there were lots of new buildings. Despite the reintroduction of stately trees, the entire area would be completely foreign to her today. The villa has been torn down, and significant changes have been made to the surroundings, although much of this had already happened before the bombing:

Our house . . . looks older, dirtier, a bit neglected, yet otherwise appears unchanged. Even the thermometer outside the living room window is still hanging there. The fence, which was not the newest in those days to begin with, has become even shakier and completely rusty. The bell was missing from the old belfry, the door stood wide open, and a sign at the entrance read, POLICE STATION.

I went into the garden, trudged through the snow to the back of the house. No changes there either. A bird feeder hung on the railing of the veranda near the stairs. It looked to me as if it had gotten smaller. I didn't realise at first that the few trees right in front of my nose, the group in the middle of the lawn where the doe stood, which marked the contours of this strange, snow-covered thing right nearby, was our "pond." From where I was standing behind the house, I perceived all of this to be "farther away." It may be that I remembered the garden as larger. But it may also be that it looks smaller, first, because of the partition and development of the new plot, and second, because of the huge high-rise apartment block that looms directly over the old black wooden fence from where the Soorstrasse has been extended. In addition, the unswept snow made everything look alike, and you could no longer distinguish between lawns, flower beds, and paths. On the whole, the garden also seems to have remained much the same as the old one, even if the round flower bed is gone and there's no pavilion on the hill. The wine trellis is still there, as are the low apple trellis around the lawn and the acacia in front of the smoking room window.

Not having run into anyone, I went back to the gate when I realised that the rooms of the police station were open to the public, and I wanted to take a chance . . . At worst, they would show me the door. So I climbed the front steps and went through the little anteroom to our entrée with a bench and mirror. There, I was met by civil servant, who asked how he could help me. I told him and wanted to leave again straightaway. I was asked my name, the caretaker on duty said that he recognised it from the real estate papers on file, and they asked me to come in. The officer led me right into the hallway by the kitchen. In a nutshell, everything is apparently structurally unchanged, just freshly painted, bright, clean, and new-looking. I didn't go all the way up (probably not much to see up there anyway), but "peeked" into the living room, smoking room, and lounge instead. All offices now, no more wallpaper, but brightly whitewashed walls. . . . I hereupon expressed my thanks, took my leave, and headed back through Ahorn-Ulmen-Lindenallee toward Reichsstrasse.

. . . Today, I am a little surprised at myself because, although I was emotionally involved to some extent, I was not very deeply touched or moved by seeing it again. For some people, a trip such as this would have been a "pilgrimage" of sorts, a "return to a lost paradise." That was not the case for me, perhaps because no cloudless, blue skies hung over my childhood and youth . . .

This choice of words invites speculation about what it was that cast a shadow across her childhood and youth. Does her definition of youth also include the period of her relationship with the officer and the entire aftermath thereof? No clues have been passed down here that would provide a starting point for more concrete considerations. This statement must, therefore, continue to stand on its own.

| 107

We now come to May 1940 and another letter to Hilde in Switzerland: "Have I even written to you yet that I've been busy with conversational Hebrew since the beginning of April—because a suitable teacher conveniently happens to live right 'around the corner'? She told me that, because her previous students never got so far as to be able to carry on a real conversation, she's giving lessons like these for the first time in twenty years of practice. And success came yesterday, on May 14, when I 'cooked up' my first Hebrew poem after completing my fifth lesson."

A few days later, she wrote: "I continue to enjoy my language lessons and have recently written another poem, one that, for the first time, is not merely a curiosity and not merely the 'snow and dazzle and sunshine' of a certain famous poet (do you know her?). It's called *Ha Zwa, The Toad*. 'Of course,' said my teacher when I told her the title."

The fact that her teacher immediately pricked up her ears allows for two different conclusions: First of all, she immediately suspected that her grown-up yet modest, self-effacing, self-deprecating student identified with the poem. Even this one line of poetry would have proved her right: "I hop about like dark, unassuming desire." It could have seemed entirely appropriate to her, as well, that a toad would lie low during the day, would not want to be discovered. And by activating its vocal sac at night, it wanted to be heard but still not seen.

The second conclusion might be that the teacher already knew the title of the poem, perhaps from a public recitation. And did she then expect that her language student would, perhaps, write a Hebrew version of it?

Here are two verses of the oft-quoted poem from the collection *Das Wort der Stummen* [*The Word of the Voiceless*]. What comes up is a nondescript, crouching, thought-to-be-ugly apparition that ultimately wears a crown of gemstones:

> I am toad.
> And I love the stars at night.
> The thick evening's redness
> Simmering within purple ponds, barely lit.
> Under the rain barrel's
> Rotting wood I squat cringing and fat;
> And awaiting the demise of the sun
> My painful looks to the moon lie in wait.
>
> I breathe, swim
> In the deep, calming splendor,
> Humble voices
> Underneath the night's plumage of birds.
> Come then, and kill!
> May I be just loathsome vermin to you:
> I am toad.
> I wear a gem.

I must also highlight a sentence in a letter that references the toad poem: "I myself know that, as subject matter for writing my poems, I utilise the present and close at hand much less often than the past and far away."

| 108

Our poet creates the casual impression that she led her life solely within the extremely narrow confines of a close family circle and, indeed, lived in sublime, work-enhancing self-isolation. We can accept this interpretation only to a limited degree. Even from Finkenkrug, she went into central Berlin to participate in recitation evenings, and not only when her own poetry was being presented. And she took part in the "casual get-togethers" that followed. She acted in solidarity with her colleagues during the petition process. She participated in a Hebrew conversation class. And she joined a circle, a "very close circle that gets together every couple of weeks."

She listed the members of the group:

A painter and her husband, an independent scholar (philosopher), a recognised, important artist (and his wife, who is a nice person, also sometimes comes, but doesn't quite fit in with the rest of us), an Egyptologist (who has worked in Egypt and was previously a commissioner at the Egyptian Museum in Berlin), her sister, who teaches arts and crafts, and myself. When we're together, the conversation usually revolves around old-fashioned rather than contemporary things. I got there somewhat late one afternoon, and the men were already in the middle of an argument over the question, "Christ or the Buddha?" which proceeded in a friendly manner but with a fervour that, in the opinion of many people, "would" surely "have been worthy of a better cause." From time to time, we also read to one another from our own "collected works." I always tend to mistrust the awkward praise of friends, yet not all of us suffer from intellectual vanity and speak out when something doesn't appeal to us all that much. We tolerate opposition and are also protected from it to such an extent that we become what the now-deceased Marshall Lyautey called the French general staff, *une société mutuelle d'admiration* [a mutual admiration society].

Jerusalem at the North Pole: I've extracted these words from the novel *Die jüdische Mutter* [*The Jewish Mother*], in which this formulation is used to describe Martha Wolg's frame of mind. I use it freely here, however, and take it as a symbol of an ultimately, unreachable Jerusalem.

If this Jewish circle of friends discussed Christ and the Buddha, then we cannot rule out the possibility that they also discussed Yahweh and God. Would Gertrud Chodziesner, a Jewish woman, have been able to contribute to such a discussion? What was her Jerusalem?

Yerushalayim in Palestine, Jerusalem in the British mandated territory: Would it have occurred to her to undertake a fact-finding journey like Willy and Trudi Cohn did, and not only to formally prepare for emigration? Did she leave Jerusalem in limbo or place it at the North Pole?

I ask myself these questions: How seriously, how concretely did she profess her faith in Judaism? What effect did this profession of faith have on her standing in society, rather than in the relative freedom of poetry? Did she ever talk with Jews who were not family members or take part in discussions, debates, or conversations about Judaism, perhaps in this circle of friends? If people read from their "collected works," then did she ever recite this or that poem in which she professed her Jewish faith? And, if so, did people pick up on certain keywords?

Further questions that arise are: Did she ever try to make contact with the Jewish community in Schöneberg or did she remain a solitary Jew without specific ties or exchanges? And, having failed initially, did she lack the ongoing, serious intention of moving to the Promised Land in which Jews were gathering after nearly two thousand years of Diaspora, so as to finally cultivate their own land?

After making a rather noncommittal inquiry in Vermont, she ended up not wanting to go to North or South America. Her inner compass pointed in the opposite direction, eastward: "As when we pray, I have simply turned my face towards the east, and you know that this is no 'new fashion' in my case." The east of which she spoke was apparently the Far East: "I am really a kind of 'would-be Asian.'" Better Shanghai than Jerusalem? Her inner compass fluctuated: "My face looks to the east, to the southeast." Palestine was in the southeast. The following sentence may well confirm this: "I long to return home to a landscape that's farther south and east than Hellas."

If we take a closer look, what would the coordinates of her Jerusalem have been? Let us take Franz Werfel, who was among her most important fellow authors. He was also in Jerusalem during a trip to the Near East in 1925. Immediately after returning from the Promised Land, he began to learn Hebrew and to study the Bible and Talmud. But when it came to deciding where to immigrate in 1938, it seems that he'd forgotten Palestine and Jerusalem: "Whither shall I go? Where I am, I no longer belong. Where I belong, I do not love: it's not my dream, and I have no connexion with it in my heart."

Now what about his colleague Kolmar? Wasn't she at all curious? Her Judaism could have taken shape in Palestine, maybe even in Jerusalem. How would she have reacted to seeing people circle in front of the Wailing Wall, carrying the Torah scroll at a clip as cheering believers showered it with bonbons? Would she have also cheered and thrown bonbons or just silently walked on? She would have either had to commit herself to it or, like Else Lasker-Schüler, logically admit to herself that this was not the Jerusalem of her dreams.

Yes, Gertrud Chodziesner's Jerusalem was probably still at the North Pole, inaccessible, because she ultimately didn't want to reach it. Was it a highly personal Judaism that she cultivated? Sometimes I wonder if her profession of the Jewish faith and her solidarity with Jews was more rhetorical than concrete. Indeed, she convincingly transformed it into poetry, but no decisions or actions ever came out of it.

Is there a Judaism in which Jerusalem plays no central role? Like Islam without Mecca or Catholicism without Rome? Her Jerusalem apparently lay in a region without exchange, participation, or community. Whether real or unreal, it ultimately lay at the North Pole. So did it lie on polar ice?

| 109

The French campaign! What did father and daughter think of it, and how might they have expressed it?

In her father's case, this was now the third war he'd seen between Germany and France. As a child, Ludwig was certainly caught up in the patriotic enthusiasm of the Franco-Prussian War of 1870–71. He joined in the chauvinistic jubilation at the beginning of the First World War and also witnessed the dwindling of enthusiasm for the war, enthusiasm that finally turned to disillusionment. Along with the majority of the population, he probably had a skeptical attitude toward renewed war with France. Or was he also thinking of revenge for the *Schandfrieden* [shameful peace] of Versailles?

And his daughter? She had a particular fondness for France, had taken the state exam in French . . . the summer course in Dijon . . . France was the country of revered poets like Rimbaud and Valéry . . . She spoke of exhilarating experiences with the French language: "When I've had occasion to write a letter in French, then read it through afterwards, I've always been rather surprised to discover something fluid, easy, and even elegant in my writing style that I didn't realise was there. And the more successful I was with it, the more strange I seemed to myself, as it were."

And now we come to the bare facts! Did she follow events with alarm as Germany attacked Belgium, Luxembourg, the Netherlands, and rapidly advanced toward Paris(!)? Did the campaign become a topic of discussion at home?

Another kind of language began to dominate the press and radio. Here are several exemplary quotations from the 1940 edition of *Die Wehrmacht* [*Armed Forces*], a military magazine edited by the high command. It bore the subtitle *Der Freiheitskampf des grossdeutschen Volkes* [*The Freedom Struggle of the Greater German People*].

A sampling of language usage includes: "peaceful, destructive fire . . . the troops dug in . . . broke out of the woods . . . mortar fire . . . air explosions . . . they smoke the enemy out of their nests . . . break through the trenches . . . run over barbed wire barriers . . . take cover in ditches . . . beat back every counterattack . . . large-scale operation . . . full up with all sorts of bombs . . . fiercely defend . . . under fire from all types of weapons . . . in attack position . . . fireball . . . hellish barrage . . . on the double . . . bloodily fought position . . . collapsed in the fire . . . blood-soaked earth . . ."

The following is an unintentionally prophetic quotation from the same magazine: "From the beginning of the war and even thereafter, when the French army was already smashed and millions of refugees clogged the streets of France, the irresponsible leadership inoculated the people with a belief in final victory. Just as the Battles of the Marne changed France's fate twice during the world war, so, too, do people have faith that some miracle or other could save France."

This phrase would be broadcast verbatim throughout the remaining course of the Second World War until the turning point in 1944–45: "The irresponsible leadership inoculated the people with a belief in final victory."

| 110

In May 1940, several of Kolmar's verses were recited, not by the poet herself but by Leonhard-Feld. Once again, the occasion was an event for a Jewish audience: "Did I already mention the evening at the Cultural League—or rather, afternoon? 'Jewish words and tones'—songs and poems. Frau Feld brought me to the fore in a rather 'big' way: her best performance of the entire evening was the recitation of my two poems at the end. And yet there was so much else going around in my head and heart that all of it didn't register with me somehow."

Here is another excerpt about France from Willy Cohn's diary in the weeks after the *Blitzsieg* [lightning victory]:

> During the night of June 21 and 22, planes bombed Berlin for the first time. There were civilian casualties. I fear that the war will become more and more merciless. The English won't allow world domination to be wrested from them so easily.
>
> I listened to some of the führer's triumphant entry into Berlin on the radio. Was his triumph perhaps a bit premature?
>
> One hundred military vehicles drove through the city with the inscription, "From the Maginot Line to Opole." There is certainly something afoot with Russia, and perhaps we will soon be sitting in underground air-raid shelters.

| 111

A celebration of family feeling. According to a lengthy letter to her sister in Switzerland, Gertrud had formed an attachment to Sabine. Names were mentioned in it, and signs pointed the way to the lost world of Finkenkrug.

Back in the day: Helene, our cook, who used to bake little cakes for Sabine ... Back in the day: Wally, our maid, clever at tailoring ... Back in the day:

Flora, the "hind," and Jackie, the exotic bird . . . Back then: Frau Zerbe, a neighbor, took Flora and Jackie into her care when the house and property had to be sold off. Gertrud primarily wanted to know how Flora was doing, of course, and Helene Köpp was able to tell her after a visit to Finkenkrug.

In a child-appropriate way, Gertrud told the "little monster" about the situation in mid-July 1940. The western campaign had just ended, but immediate preparations were under way for Operation Sea Lion, the planned invasion of England. Here was a small island of safety in a world of destruction:

> For you, I'll make the lines a little farther apart. There will surely be words that you can't read yet, but perhaps you'll make out some of the letters. Thanks for the picture of the tree, which is really very beautiful. I won't write a poem about it, but a very long story instead. Only I don't have much time for it at the moment, and so it will be a good while before I finally complete the task. But I already know the beginning of the story: The trees are on an island in the middle of the ocean near Africa, and there are no people on the island, just plants and animals. I recently wrote a forty-page-long story that I really wanted to send to your mama, and Flora appeared in it. Do you remember Flora? Helene, who sends her greetings, has recently been to see Wally in the little house and also visited Frau Zerbe, the lady to whom we gave Flora and Jackie. Both are still alive: Jackie runs around with the chickens like she did with us, and Flora just injured her foot because she stepped on a shard.

The game of make-believe continued. It was triggered by a drawing of trees that "Püppi" had made for her aunt in Germany:

> Meanwhile, they've begun to sprout in my imagination, and as soon as I am self-sufficient with regard to writing, I'll have to forgo the poetic creations of other writers, which is only right. I've probably already written that I transplanted the trees from my imaginary island in the Indian Ocean (discovered in 1743 by the sailor I also created, Arlate du Moutier). But in the meantime, the island that I populated with all sorts of animals and plants has sunken into the sea once more. I only rescued the trees and am on the lookout for a new place to put them. I'm currently travelling back and forth between the countryside around Ebermergen (Nördlingen, Donauwörth) and the countryside around Bad Pyrmont (Hoexter, Hameln), so maybe I'll combine both areas into a future story. We'll see. I am a bit excited to see what will happen, almost as if I were not at all involved in the emergence of something new. And it really is something that "comes over you."

| 112

Writing would continue to take center stage. In a detailed letter from father and daughter to Hilde and Sabine Wenzel, the poet wrote:

> Incidentally, the nighttime and morning hours were always the most fruitful for me—but only if I didn't feel too worn out from the evening. The same can be said of winter afternoons, which are really like evenings. I've hardly ever been able to create anything in the daytime, not even when I have plenty of time, as on summer days in the fresh country air. Admittedly, I have never accomplished anything at all with a typewriter on my lap. I realise that, for many eminent writers, paper, pencils, pens, and the like—in short, the "tools of the trade"—play an important role. Those things are unimportant to me, and I can only use them if the actual creative work is behind me. Entirely the case with typewriters . . . They are the very last thing I use, and only for the final fair copy. That's why it's much harder for me to make significant changes to a typed text than it is for others. I think it would be impossible for me to sit down and type my work directly onto the page from memory. I haven't even been able to write letters this way up to now, assuming they're to be of any use, and must therefore always grab a pen.

In Kolmar's last letter, her last surviving letter at any rate, she comments to Hilde on the prerequisites for creating poems:

> I certainly never create from feelings of elation or strength but always from feelings of powerlessness. I allow myself to be lured to my desk in pursuit of sudden inspiration, a creative impulse, and thus cannot usually hang onto it: the fire dies down, the source dries up, and the poem remains fragmented. However, if I begin a new work the other way round, from a powerless, desperate place, I'm like someone who ascends from of the depths and prepares for a hike to the summit. At first, the goal is very far away, the view obstructed; yet as I march on, the vista gets ever wider and more beautiful. I do not tire during this gradual ascent, as often happens to me if I allow myself to get carried away by a flash of imagination. What I started gets finished, and the completed version does not peter out towards the end, as is often the case with poetry. (Herr Cohn even claimed at the time that my items would always get better towards the end.) I have to tell myself, "I can't do one more thing. My strength is drained. I won't accomplish another thing," then the right moment has arrived.

At the time, she was also engrossed in safeguarding her poems, which she felt were meant "for eternity." Once again, she addressed the following to Hilde: "Would you do me a small favour? It's really just a small one—assuming you haven't excessively mislaid *Worlds*. In rereading this collection of late, I found a stupid typo in the poem *Borzoi*, which doesn't appear so at first, and I'm asking you to please correct it." The word was *Hündin* [bitch] instead of *Hindin* [doe], and she'd like her sister to please correct it: "Otherwise, there would still be a major scholarly dispute several hundred years after my death as to whether the named spot in the Swiss manuscript or the existing, fragmented 'Berlin copy' could claim to be valid."

Now this was a veritable, productive obsession: sixteen printed lines of a letter sent abroad that solely concerned a necessary change in a single letter, "an 'i' instead of a 'ü.' " And right after that, she waxed a bit ironic by pointing to future Kolmar philologists who would compare the different versions.

Since the keyword "borzoi" has already come up, here is the poem of the same name from her cycle *Welten*. It brings to mind the part played by the white Russian wolfhound. It is both an ode to her dog and a poem that reveals a sometimes impassioned Kolmar:

> Lovely are you, and charming, with your narrow, elongated head,
>   your soft, brown, almond eyes shining,
> You're dreaming
> Of pale, northern birch trees in the marsh, of the monster burnt black,
>   the shovel-horned elk, ablaze;
> Your blood
> Still being hounded by the gray wolf through dark Russian pine forests,
> Still sensing herds of reindeer on the tundra, grazing on moss and lichen,
> Still hearing the anguished wailing, the polar hare's laments
> Before the hunter . . .
>
> The following day
> You rest quietly on the blanket and lift your womanly face to me
>   with the mildness of a doe, unlike a unicorn,
> Or you run, head down, sniffing and pawing
>   at the compost heap, shrubs and flower beds, like dogs do.
> On autumn nights,
> When the cooler stars flicker brightly,
> Every now and then the sound of droplets falling from trees,
> Since yellowing grass breathes freshness and moisture,

I pull my coat about my shoulders, open the iron door
Of the garden;
You hunt with giant leaps.
You fly, you scurry
Like a snowstorm over a carpet of faded, dripping leaves;
Silvery fluttering flame, your manelike tail blazing behind you.
Then I go, calling you with a muffled voice, and you wait,
    tall and light, extremely pale, a specter at the crossroads.
You stand and stare.

Other tenants in the same house, one floor up, kept a borzoi. Feelings of melancholy came up whenever she encountered her housemates and their Russian wolfhound: "People live right here in this house who have a dog that looks almost exactly like Flora, except that it's not pure white but has a few black spots on its coat. We would have gladly brought Flora along with us to Berlin, but it wasn't possible. If she had run across the boulevard, as was her wont, an automobile would surely have come along and run her over. We did not want this to happen, and that's why she stayed behind in Finkenkrug." This is how she presented it to her niece, yet the wish remained: "Flora! If only I could brush and comb you again . . ."

Upon closer examination, the longer poems divide into sections of free verse with very nearly predetermined breaks. This makes it easy to extract and single out sequences in which autobiographical elements shine through as on a palimpsest. Above all, there is the constant presence of the man she loved, both consciously and emotionally. Here is the last section of the poem "Der Engel im Walde" ["The Angel of the Forest"]. The poet intentionally inserted a blank line in the printed copy between the previous section and these final lines:

Come, my friend, with me, come.
The staircase in my father's house is dark, crooked and narrow,
    and the steps are worn down;
But now it is a house of orphans with strangers living in it.
Take me away.
In my weak hands the old rusty key fits heavily into the door.
Now it creaks shut.
Now look at me in the darkness, you, my home from this day on.
For me, your arms shall form sheltering walls,
And your heart shall be my room, your eyes my windows,
    so that morning can shine through.

And your forehead towers, when you walk.
You are my home on all the streets of the world, in every hollow,
    on every hill.
You my roof, you thirst with me, tired from midday's glow,
    shiver with me in lashing blizzards.
We'll get thirsty and hungry, suffer together,
Collapse together at dusty roadsides and weep . . .

And here is the closing sequence of the poem "Die alte Frau" ["The Old Woman"]. Once again, the poet intentionally inserted a blank line before it:

My eyes have become cloudy and can hardly bring yarn and needle eye
    together.
My eyes water wearily under their heavily wrinkled,
    red-rimmed lids.
Rarely
from their dull gaze dawns the weak,
    long-gone glow
Of a summer day,
When my light, rippling dress flowed through meadows of cardamine
And the longing of my lark call rose rejoicing to the heavens.

And here is another of Kolmar's sublime poetic endings, the final sequence from "Garten im Sommer" ["The Garden in Summer"]! In several poems, her lover is newly present in nearly leitmotif-like references to a hirsute chest. And the man is always by the sea.

Karl Josef Keller wrote after the war that "the relationship began when I familiarized her with a series of my works destroyed by war. She lavished a great deal of praise on them and first called me 'swan' in reference to Leda, then called me 'her swan.' In subsequent letters, I was her 'Aquarius.'"

Are you going now . . . should I follow?
Lead me, I'm freezing . . . I'm afraid . . .
I want to swim out to the cow lilies, the yellow lights.
Look, the fleece of your chest, overgrown like algae, and I know:
    that you are Aquarius.
And I know: you are piling up countless treasures, sea silver, mud gold
    deep within hidden chambers beneath the water, the earth.
Will you take my hands now, dive with me to the bottom, to the gate,
    guarded by a heavy, mustachioed catfish?

Shall I never see my sister or brother, or my aging father again,
   whom I love?
You, I tremble . . .
If I conceived, my child would have webbed fingers and toes,
   and seashells and duckweed oddly in increasingly dripping hair.
Return to shore . . . Mocker!

| 113

She created a fantasy game for Sabine in October 1940, a testament to her continued affection over time and space.

The game came about when her mother commented in a letter that six-year-old Sabine wanted to be a dancer. This keyword brought back memories: "Surely you know that I love the art of dance, and so I dug out my little collection of programmes and reminisced."

She then imagined that her little niece made a really big entrance as a dancer:

And the dance sequence? Right now, I don't quite see Püppi as "The Dying Swan" (Anna Pavlova) or "The Ancient Grave Scripture" (Charlotte Bara). But how about "The Dance of the White Kid," "Spring," or "Butterfly" to Edvard Grieg's music of the same name? I know of another dance with tambourine, ratchet, recorder, short, accompanied by a so-called children's orchestra—"The Little Monster" and another one, "Of a Sleeping Apple." I imagine (and could be wrong, of course) that Binelein may one day dance like Grete Wiesenthal, whom I admittedly know only from pictures and descriptions. Seems to me that there's something fresh, cheerful, carefree, and summer-holiday-like in her dancing . . . Which reminds me that Lucy Kieselhausen's dancing had something similar, and I've seen her more than once. I can very well imagine a slightly older Sabine in her charmingly grotesque, "Dimmy-Dommy" dance (I can still hear the melody).

So I've gone on about "frivolous matters" like dancing and female dancers for quite some time. But are they really "frivolities"? I hardly think so. Beautiful dancing is an art and, as such, great and eternal. But here's another question: Are you in the mood to read what I have to say about "Dimmy-Dommy" (which I just danced in my room, insofar as I could still remember it) and "The Dying Swan?"

Gertrud by herself, dancing to the accented rhythms of "Dimmy-Dommy" in a room of this Jewish household, humming or singing the melody . . . This image of the poet makes a lasting impression.

| 114

At the end of November 1940, Gertrud asked her sister a question: "Have I already written you that my teacher, the woman with whom I studied Hebrew for four months, has gone away?" "Gone away" was apparently some type of code: Was her teacher still able to leave the country or was she in a concentration camp? In this case, there is no response, no hint that would allow us to draw conclusions, just the following uninhibited, unencumbered report:

I was looking for a replacement and, one day, accompanied a housemate to her advanced course, which was set up by the Jewish community at the Lehrmann Schule (Joachimsthalerstrasse). I "freeloaded"; that is, attended the class as an "auditor" for an hour. But it was too beginner-like for me. After the class ended, the teacher spoke with me briefly and mentioned that, in contrast to my housemate, the teachers' course would presumably be best for me. There, the teachers only conversed among themselves, so that their language skills wouldn't get rusty. Perhaps the gentleman had an overly high opinion of my Hebrew, and I would not be able to keep up with such conversation. But, in any case, I want to try it—after the New Year. And now the teacher's suggestion has put big ideas in my head . . .

I've already reported from time to time that I've written a couple of poems in Hebrew and, following a number of improvements, my teacher declared them fit to print. Maybe this is true, maybe not. In any case, I know all too well that these poems were translated from the German, albeit not literally, but in a subtler sense even so, and real Hebrew poems would look and sound entirely different. Happily, it is not the case that a poet can or must speak solely in his mother tongue, else I would have no hope of ever versifying in the language of our forefathers. It is by no means so, and poets with foreign roots have often enriched the art in their new homelands with sounds and colours that would have never occurred to "natives." (As you probably know, Joseph Conrad was a Polish nobleman by birth.) And it must be added that Hebrew was not the first language of people anywhere in Europe until recently, but at most their second . . . in places where Yiddish was the first . . . But there is a difference between someone who speaks flawless German, French, or English and just makes it charming with a "tinge" or a "pinch" of foreignness, and someone who expresses himself quite clumsily in an entirely un-German, un-French, or un-English way. And my *Ivrit* still places me in the latter category. . . . I've recently learned what a Hebrew poem is not, how I may not versify, but now feel that I will soon know how I must write it. And this poem, which has not yet arrived ("the unborn"), is already taking shape within me. Maybe it will be months, even years, before I carry it to term. But it will come to light, and I hope it won't be a miscarriage, in spite of all its probable defects . . . Maybe that's why I haven't worked on anything more in the German language lately.

Did she still have a mind to immigrate to the Promised Land? Did she write poems to enhance new applications? Or had the study of Hebrew become an end in itself by this time? Did she seriously plan to replace her native German in her lyric work with the language of her Hebrew forefathers? In poems that remained disguised, as it were, from the society around her?

| 115

Siegfried Chodziesner, her father's youngest brother, immigrated to Italy back in 1938; he lived for a time in Florence, eventually moved to Uruguay, and resided in Montevideo. His brother Max, employed until 1938, also immigrated to Uruguay along with his son, Fritz. And so the three Chodziesners were lucky because the immigration quota was strictly limited to between one and two hundred refugees per year.

On November 24, 1940, Gertrud wrote to her sister in Switzerland that Aunt Rebecca, their father's sister, made a "farewell visit" before traveling to Montevideo

via Aachen, Paris, Irún, and San Sebastian to Lisbon, where they would put to sea on December 3. And I went through with them what I've gone through with other people I've said farewell to lately on many occasions. It seemed as though there was already distance between us, yet I didn't feel as if they were emigrating, but as if I myself had departed, and they had stayed on . . .
Uncle Alex was extremely surprised, almost indignant, and Aunt Lindenheim was really hurt when I made the truly heretical statement that I didn't long for Montevideo and not the least bit for America. . . . Just not America, if at all possible.

And what about Papa Ludwig, who was Rebecca's, Max's, and Siegfried's brother? Was he not at all moved to follow his family to Montevideo? Given their symbiotic relationship, Gertrud would have had no other choice than to follow him.

* * *

Uruguay! . . . Montevideo! . . . These topics may have come up fairly often in family discussions. And before each departure, they surely would have encouraged, even exhorted them repeatedly to join the family exodus to Uruguay.

And even as late as June 1941, Dr. Fritz Chodziesner, Montevideo, Feliciano Rodriguez 2668, would write to Hilde Wenzel: "I can neither procure entry to Brazil nor to another South American country at this time. The only option is entry to Uruguay which, for you and the child, would require a deposit of 5,000 Uruguayan pesos at the local state bank."

Even in October 1941, immigration to Uruguay was still on Gertrud's lips. Gertrud wrote the following in a letter to her friend Susanne Jung (we only have Hilde's cut version):

> Believe me, come what may, I will not be unhappy, will not despair, because I know that I am walking the path determined by my inner self . . . So many of us have wandered that path through the centuries—why should I want to take a different one? . . . In the past few days, my father has thought about moving to be with his brothers (the question is whether this would even still be possible). He wanted to do it for my sake because he considers his own life over—but I declined. This would be nothing but a forced migration based on outer circumstances, and I do not want to run away from what my inner self tells me. Until today, I never knew how strong I was. And this knowledge makes me happy.

But in 1939–40, family appeals were finally able to generate action: Ludwig, get a hold of yourself, this is your last chance! . . . Trude will surely be able to find something in Montevideo, either as a language teacher or as a housekeeper! This had the greatest potential in terms of the various options for emigration.

I'll emphasize once more that two uncles, an aunt, and a cousin would have been waiting for Gertrud and her father in Montevideo! If they'd only gotten the cash that one had to present to the immigration authorities, then Ludwig and Gertrud could also have done what the members of this anything-but-poor family had already accomplished.

I found help surprisingly close by regarding a means of saving Kolmar's life, at least in theory. I'd met J. Hellmut Freund, an elegant older gentleman and senior editor at S. Fischer Verlag, in the hallway and cafeteria at my publisher's offices on several occasions and spoken with him at length about Clara Schumann. I also conveyed my admiration for the works of Max Liebermann, who dictated a memoir, *Vor dem Zitronenbaum* [*Before the Lemon Tree*], that was published after his death.

Two chapters suggest the possibility that the poet could have survived, could have "Emigrated—Immigrated" to "Uruguay." This presented something in high definition that was previously terra incognita to me: how it was that people traveled to South America in the first half of 1939, and how an upper-middle-class family adapted to the situation there.

This would have been a viable alternative to remaining in Germany! She could have built a new life for herself. This is where she might have been able to write poems, short stories, or a second novel. And at least she would have survived the Shoah in Montevideo, might have returned to Germany later on, as did Hellmut Freund and his elderly parents in 1960.

Here is a sketch that recounts what Hellmut Freund experienced and what Gertrud Kolmar could have gone through under different circumstances and conditions that would have produced a different outcome.

The Freund household in Berlin also procrastinated before deciding to leave Germany. The father, a journalist, hoped to retain his German citizenship in the country where he had resided for so long, a country in which his mastery of the language was superior to that of his enemies. He stubbornly held onto the hope that, in the end, they would be spared an exodus.

But they subsequently prepared to emigrate. A primary concern was to obtain the required documents for Freund's parents, Julie and Georg Freund, and grandparents, Emil and Johanna Putzig:

> You had to stand in line for hours at the Karlstrasse office in order to get
> exit papers, as well as passports with the prescribed Jewish forenames. We
> showed up there in a group of five. It was a large office. Officials seated at
> a long table had to check everything. At the head sat the youngest official,
> a frail and red-faced man with possible heart trouble and a golden watch
> sitting in front of him. My grandparents were 79 and 70 years old, and
> Grandfather was still rather sprightly. A civil servant said, "Israel and Sara
> Putzig shall take a seat . . ." Their names were then called and, in a slightly
> intimidating way, the officials were . . . nice.
>
> I then moved on to the young man, who had to affix the most important
> signature. Eyeing the passport photo, he said, "You took this photo yourself."
> "Yes." "You must trim it more precisely."
>
> He reached for the scissors. It was so innocuous and so awful at the same
> time.

Then the packing began, and two officials were always present to inspect and record everything. Two giant boxes, so-called lift vans, were filled with belongings. People had to jointly draw up the required list, all the way down to the egg piercer. Two rooms were sealed by the authorities. People said their good-byes at home. The sobs were audible, even through the closed doors of their flats.

They took a taxi to the Hamburg Terminus. The stretch from Berlin to Hamburg was especially quick. The seats were reasonably comfortable, and there was even a phone room. Papa Freund had reserved two rooms at Streit's Hotel, and there was no problem, not even when he gave his name. Afterward, father and son were slightly amazed that they had set off at random in this regard. They arrived at the posh hotel on Jungfernstieg in the late evening. They were politely received, and there was no entry on the registration form under religious affiliation.

In a late-night conversation over a bottle of red wine, they spoke of emigration as emancipation. Taking leave of everything familiar was painful, to be sure, and they hadn't given any prior thought to their intensely painful departure. War would surely come, and they worried about their Aryan friends. While they dreamed of returning, they couldn't think about it seriously, for this presupposed the downfall of the Third Reich.

The next day, they embarked on the *Kerguelen,* a "semi-cargo" vessel belonging to the Chargeurs Réunis Shipping Company in Le Havre. The ship had gigantic cargo holds and several passenger cabins. There were fellow sufferers on board. The trip lasted for five weeks: The ship docked intermittently to load and unload in Antwerp, Le Havre, and Lisbon. After crossing the Atlantic, there were stopovers in Rio de Janeiro and Santos.

They finally drew closer to Montevideo. The captain, a man of distinction, summoned Papa Freund to the bridge and said, "Let me show you your new home." They felt uneasy as they sailed into the harbor, but an uncle was waiting at the quay. He had taken it on himself to provide the front money at his bank. Everyone's documents were scrupulously checked. A few fellow passengers had the wrong stamps and were not allowed to disembark.

Regarding Uruguay Freund observed:

A very American and highly European country. A country that believes absolutely in Western culture and also cultivates it. We can gain a foothold here.

Montevideo does not look friendly at first, a bit shabby. A sprawling city. Nothing but small houses with no upper floors and large families living in them for the most part. Mothers-in-law, aunts, and uncles are housed and fed in them.

We spent the first few weeks at a boardinghouse for emigrants that's owned by an insurance agent and his wife from Breslau. Their son succeeded in becoming a lawyer in Montevideo. We talked about job opportunities and exchanged life stories in a small common room at the boardinghouse. How did people feel after arriving in Uruguay as emigrants who were supposed to become immigrants? Everyone shared the feeling of having escaped. They were no longer subject to persecution, no longer in fear for their lives. The realization that terrible things were happening in Germany, all the terrible things they had witnessed directly or indirectly, had to see with their own eyes. What was happening in the concentration camps! . . .

Everyday life in Uruguay. The furniture was still in transit. The family (living in very cramped conditions) found an apartment for three of us from Berlin in the home of a Spanish woman. The rooms have primitive furnishings, but Mother Freund can cook there. Poorer emigrants come by and especially like to see schnitzels on their plates.

They live in one of the small, atrium-style houses. The street side has one or two rooms, *salitas*, then there's a corridor to a patio, a habitable inner courtyard, with a *claraboya corrediza*, a gabled glass roof that can be cranked open or shut.

One then moves around the corner, so to speak, to a somewhat more attractive house, even if it has no heat or basement. The front rooms are sublet—a small source of income. There are two bedrooms, for Hellmut, an *altillo*, a small room beneath the roof, originally intended for the maid. The first books were launched, purchased by a secondhand bookstore for German-language literature.

Uruguay: Not at all what one might expect, an exotic land . . . Temperate climate . . . A history shaped by the victorious struggle for freedom. So one could, should, and ought to settle down in Uruguay without giving up his mother tongue, roots, or nationality. And yet a person was still affiliated with the republic and its language. They referred to any naturalized person as *catalán*. The Prussian-looking old man was still *alemán* [German], yet was ultimately recognized as a citizen of Uruguay.

And so Ludwig and Gertrud missed their big chance! It would still not have been too late to flee Germany in 1940!

I am looking at a reproduction of an ad page from the May 1940 edition of the *Jüdisches Nachrichtenblatt*. An "officially approved" company was offering "support for Jewish immigrants" and providing "completion of all formalities, financial consulting, liquidation, administration, general power of attorney, trusteeship, annuity insurance (for remaining elderly members), correspondence with the authorities, and the like." Other Jewish companies offered "massive dry storage spaces" for furniture and transport of luggage abroad—even to Shanghai . . . About twenty-five thousand Jews fled, often by land, from Germany to Shanghai, where no visa was required.

The *Nachrichtenblatt* reported in 1940: "Since previously regular shipping routes for emigrants from the Mediterranean to the Far East, North and South America have been totally eliminated or become unreliable, the Emigration Department of the Reich Association of German Jews has immediately entered into negotiations with every possible authority on opening up land routes to the Far East and on combined land and sea routes via the Far East to North and South America."

The "new migration routes were: (1) land route to Shanghai via Manchuria; (2) combined land and sea routes to Shanghai via Vladivostok; (3) emigration to North America via the Far East; (4) emigration to South America (West Coast) and the West Indies via the Far East."

Ludwig and Gertrud Chodziesner remained in the Bayerisches Viertel in the Schöneberg section of Berlin. The urgent need to emigrate was a topic that had been sufficiently discussed! So why didn't they do anything about it in the end, and with all due resoluteness at that?

It's easier to understand why the daughter would have stayed than it is in the case of her father, who was once a successful, experienced lawyer. Like his brothers, nephew, son, and émigré daughters, he could have just as quickly and easily seen the handwriting on the wall. But he also stuck to his guns. Father and daughter settled into life in Schöneberg and, apart from taking walks, did not budge. Their lifestyles matched to such a degree that they hardly ever came into conflict, not even in the extremely tense situation in which they now found themselves.

I cannot provide insight, nor do I wish to come up with psychological concepts or commanding insights: I am simply stating the facts. In terms of the deaths that were imposed on them, it cannot possibly be said that they walked into the trap; rather, the trap drew inexorably closer to them.

| 116

The situation for the inhabitants of the Bayrisches Viertel had changed in the meantime: The *Gesetz über Mietverhältnisse mit Juden* [Act Regarding Jewish Tenancy] made it possible for local governments and municipal authorities to assign Jewish citizens to homes that were already inhabited by Jews. These "consolidations" facilitated checks by the police and secret police. Moreover, this measure, previously tested in Poland, facilitated "swift action," thus indirectly laying the groundwork for the deportations that would follow.

The Chodziesners were generally happy with their assigned subtenants, who tried to be considerate. However, the subtenants' need for communication was a problem for Gertrud:

Their generally real but sometimes imagined worries cause a kind of emotional narcissism to develop within them. This gives rise to the need to immediately unburden themselves of their worries or even just their experiences, as well as the worries and experiences of their relatives and friends. And the other one listening does exactly the same thing, simply waiting until Mr. X has finished his report about his son in Rio to then confirm, add to, or refute this by relating the fate of a niece who also lives in Rio, whereupon he immediately commences to talk for hours about his daughter in Buenos Aires. I sometimes have the impression of a "weak bladder"—people cannot keep their affairs to themselves. Pardon the less-than-polite term, but I believe it's true. Perhaps I am hard-hearted, too critical, when people are just trying to ease their burdens by talking to each other . . . If only that were true, but it isn't. Each of us is so burdened by his own baggage that he hardly sees the other person and is not thinking of easing the concerns of others at all. Both are speaking, but neither hears the other. I confess that I, too, often "cry with the pack," simply because it's quite pointless to strike a different tone. Afterwards I always get depressed and am happy to be alone again. We lived at a blessed, perceptible distance from all of that in Finkenkrug, but everyone sits around brooding here. I have a couple of good acquaintances, a quartet of two women and two men. When we get together, family matters disappear, as do private issues.

As soon as Gertrud sat down at the dining room table, a woman would come and keep her company. The dining room and kitchen became centers of communication. Even in her room, which she now had to share with her father, separated from him only by a curtain, she could not shield herself acoustically.

The constant comings and goings in the apartment, talking, talking (I talk, therefore I am!) became a strain: "There is something inimical to my nature that I must resist in all three of the renters. This irritates me every day, though I control myself in front of them." She must have had opportunities to remove herself, to insulate herself, but the margins were getting smaller.

It became evident right after the move that her father did not feel cramped: it seemed to revive him. The soon-to-be octogenarian changed, and the man who had often been stern and imperious became conciliatory. In Finkenkrug, the sort of life that seemed appropriate to him was going through the back gate of the property toward the woods with his dogs . . . Not seeing anyone, not speaking to anyone . . . But now he was glad when someone wanted company and came to visit them in their home. This astonished his daughter. What had been an intolerable burden to him was now a small relief. They found him to be a patient listener, and since his audience changed from time to time, he could relieve himself of his own stories and anecdotes repeatedly. His daughter felt as if all the benevolent spirits had left the apartment when these renters arrived. All I see or hear about is what's useless, foolish, disagreeable, or bad. Restlessness and irritability have come over Papa for months now, and I can't seem to come to terms with it. It's becoming hard for me to rekindle our old, hearty relationship, and with these final words, I must admit that it no longer exists. He has gotten closer and closer to our renters and our surroundings over time, and shut me out more and more in the process. His personality has changed in every way: he now embraces nonsense and gossip that he tolerated even less than I in Finkenkrug, and expresses sympathy for any stories from any persons that, to me, seem insignificant at best. . . . This state of affairs makes me sad, makes my heart heavy. I dearly wish things were different, and it's only recently that I've been making every effort to follow the advice of my Westend friends. They think that what doesn't please me about him is the result of the infirmities of old age and that instead of trying to be in peaceful harmony with him, only to have it fail repeatedly, I should begin to inwardly cut myself off from him. They think that I should see him as he once was and not grieve over the way that he appears to me now, but should accept it calmly and with more equanimity than I do at present.

And so it was that she "ceded the care of Papa largely to the tenants."
Gertrud's desire for verbal exchanges was, on the other hand, still quite low. She preferred to express herself in writing, and then in great detail. Father and daughter were thus estranged in this regard as well. And so, after decades of symbiosis, the daughter actually began to go through something akin to separation.

In reading Kolmar's letters, one sometimes gets the impression that, for the time being, they lived completely undisturbed in the house that had since become a "Jewish house." There were disagreements, irritations, nervousness, and clashes, but no serious problems.

But we should use caution in drawing conclusions about their living situation from these descriptions. A great deal was filtered out with a view to censorship. A person could not name incriminating facts, for doing so would have placed people at risk.

Here are two examples of omissions, of things that were kept secret. The first involved inspections to see if the curfew was being observed. An armed *Schupo* [policeman] stood in front of the apartment door. Tenants and subtenants were at the dinner table. Eyewitness Eppi Chotzen wrote: "At the head of the table, a civilian with a list interrogated everyone present in a very rude tone. In particular, they checked to see if all registered persons were present in accordance with the ordinance and, above all, that there were no additional persons staying with us. This was one of many depressing situations that I remember."

There was another, equally widespread type of incident that Gertrud would have never dared mention: the so-called *Kontrollgänge* [patrols], surprise raids by Gestapo officials. A report from Dresden should serve to illustrate this point: "The worst was the constant house searches. After a house search, the apartment looked like it had been robbed. I remember that they once overturned all of the furniture at my place. In addition, people absolutely were robbed. The Gestapo drove up in a car and left with suitcases full of stuff. People, old people in particular, were beaten frightfully and ordered to Gestapo headquarters the next day, where the harassment continued. They ordered old women to move a heap of coal from one side of the courtyard to the other by hand, and kept them doing so for the entire day with nothing to eat."

| 117

Aerial warfare is another important topic, although Gertrud Kolmar never mentioned it, at least not in her surviving letters. This does not mean, however, that the topic should be excluded simply because she failed to mention it. Nightly bombing raids on the Reich capital were becoming an increasing burden for father and daughter. Here, too, I must try to make their situation clear by means of analogy. William Shirer's diary again offers some examples. First, here is a retrospective in chronological order:

> Berlin, August 26, 1940: We had our first big air-raid of the war last night. The sirens sounded at twelve twenty A.M. and the all-clear came at three twenty-three A.M. For the first time British bombers came directly over the city, and they dropped bombs. The concentration of anti-aircraft fire was the greatest I've ever witnessed. It provided a magnificent, a terrible sight. And it was strangely ineffective. Not a plane was brought down; not one was even picked up by the searchlights, which flashed back and forth frantically across the skies throughout the night.
>
> The Berliners are stunned. They did not think it could happen. When this war began, Göring assured them it couldn't. . . . And then last night the guns all over the city suddenly began pounding and you could hear the British motors humming directly overhead, and from all reports there was a pell-mell, frightened rush to the cellars by the five million people who live in this town [*Berlin Diary*, 486–87].

Did this also happen at Speyerer Strasse 10? "In many Berlin cellars there is only one room. It is for the 'Aryans.' The Jews must take refuge on the ground floor, usually in the hall leading from the door of the flat to the elevator or stairs.

This is fairly safe if a bomb hits the roof, since the chances are that it will not penetrate to the ground floor. But experience so far has shown that it is the most dangerous place to be in the entire building if a bomb lands in the street outside. Here where the Jews are hovering, the force of the explosion is felt most; here in the entryway where the Jews are, you get most of the bomb splinters" [*Berlin Diary*, 520–21].

Did father and daughter, the poet and former *Notar*, sit behind the front door with their heads held down? "The British were cruising as they wished over the heart of the city and flying quite low, judging by the sound of their motors. The German *flak* was firing wildly, completely by sound. It was easy, from the firing, to follow a plane across the city as one battery after another picked up the sound of the motors and fired blindly into the sky" [*Berlin Diary*, 489].

If Gertrud and Ludwig Chodziesner had initially remained in the apartment, then they could have reported what Annemarie Seidel wrote about to her sister after this particular attack and after subsequent attacks: "At around one, just seconds before the sirens set in, my highly alert, hypervigilant unconscious awakened me. I then got dressed to the sound of barking small antiaircraft guns and nerve-shattering blasts from the big antiaircraft guns and, despite the curtains, the muzzle flashes lit up the dark flat like flaming electrical storms. The windows rattled, too, and shrapnel drummed on the tin roof. But the worst thing was that when the sirens woke you out of a deep sleep, they sounded like a huge fish in its death agony that suddenly got a voice and was screaming in unending torment."

She briefly described the "spectacle in the sky" as a "matrix of countless lights in the canopy of the heavens, where huge silent flares and oblique arcs of tracer bullets drew fantastic patterns."

She feared, as others did, that "this kind of warfare might readily continue indefinitely!" And so everyone was drawing up last wills and testaments, "to which too little thought was given in everyday life."

| 118

Gertrud Kolmar not only wrote detailed letters; she also continued to work on literary texts.

In a letter to Hilde describing circumstances, she wrote:

To me, every literary creation is like giving birth (and sometimes the pains are awful!). This currently takes place—in stages—at night. I go to bed early, and when the top tenants awaken me between 1 and 3 A.M. with their nightly, very noisy homecoming, I've already slept a few hours and my brain can begin working again. And by the time I have "moved the baby" a few centimetres, it's already 5 o'clock, and I can snooze a little. I write everything down immediately after dressing in the morning. And so I'm very tired, feel miserable, and probably have a headache: in short, all the signs of a "hangover" after a night of excess, which it certainly is. The next night, I thoroughly sleep off my intoxication. The noisy neighbours above me don't awaken me, and then the following night the whole routine starts all over again. I've sometimes tried to write during the day, as I did in Finkenkrug. But I don't have the necessary peace of mind to begin with and always feel guilty because I think I've neglected some sort of housework that's waiting for me. Second, Papa is sure to come to me right at that moment with some little concern of his or even just to tell me a story. And then, that's it—the spell is broken, and I can't find the thread again.

| 119

And Georg Benjamin? He was released from prison at Brandenburg-Görden in May 1941 but then transferred to Gestapo headquarters in Prinz Albrecht Strasse: "I request that the Jew Georg Benjamin be returned to the Central Gestapo Office in Berlin after his sentence has been served." It was customary in those days for the Gestapo to rearrest prisoners immediately after their official release.

Amazingly, there was no abuse at the infamous Prince Albrecht Palais, a building that also had prison cells and torture chambers in the cellar. Otherwise, the staunch anti-Fascist Hilde Benjamin would surely have brought it up in the biography she wrote about her husband. His detention was basically unjust, but he suffered no additional harassment, and this despite the fact that the following was noted in his discharge papers: "Benjamin is a committed Communist. The sentence served has not affected the Jew in any way. Even now, his political views must be regarded as negative." It sometimes happened that a uniformed officer, possibly a former patient of the prisoner, would write "do not mistreat" on the reverse side of an admission form. Did something similar, although exceptionally rare, happen in his case?

Georg was taken to the Wuhlheide Labor Camp, a barracks-style camp near Karlshorst. The prisoners were assigned to build new railroad lines in the area of the Wuhlheide train station. They were supervised by the police. Little bribes made it possible for Georg to occasionally see his wife and for her to slip him things. It was even possible for them to picnic together once in the sparse oak and pine forest of Heidewald.

Hilde Benjamin wrote:

I unpacked the potato salad, patties, and cherry pudding I had brought along, and we were happy. . . . Then I sat on the train platform, and he showed me his workmanship. He jumped from the running car and threw the switch. (I later thought that, had he fallen in the process, it might have saved his life.) He shunted a little electric locomotive back and forth. First, he waved from under the locomotive, then climbed into a freight car to take measurements. The cars were moving farther and farther away from the platform, and he climbed from one car to the next, farther and farther forward, away from me. A stormy afternoon haze still hung between the woods above the railroad embankment. I could hardly see him anymore when he took off his cap, stroked his hair, held his hands high in thanks. The train disappeared into the mist, and I could no longer see it.

What a heartbreaking picture of a farewell that would be their last.

| 120

The air raids on Berlin continued. Reports would come from another eyewitness, a journalist, who did not want to join the Reich Press Chamber in 1933 and therefore relinquished any and all opportunities for employment. His brother would provide him with housing and money from then on. Friedrich Kahl, whose pen name was Munding, wrote detailed letters from Berlin to his friend Fritz Scheffelt, a book dealer in Constance. Kahl had also lived and worked in Constance for a time.

Munding knew that any letter could be examined by the censors, so he had to outwit uninvited readers. A skilled writer, he made abundant use of sarcasm and irony, which the postal censors lacked the ability to sense.

As an example of this writing tactic, Munding reported on an antiaircraft barrage that, despite consuming an immense amount of ammunition, was totally ineffective. But he concealed this futile barrage in the guise of seemingly good news. After all, they managed to shoot down one plane.

So much for his disguised speech. I'll now move on to the first of his filtered reports about the mood in Berlin. These reports make clear what father and daughter must have also witnessed, although Gertrud, the former censor, didn't say a word about it in her letters to Switzerland. Did legitimate fear have the upper hand here, or did this indicate a considerable capacity for repression?

The English night pirates are now coming to Berlin quite irregularly. If you anticipate a visit, then they don't come. But if you think you can sleep undisturbed, then they are sure to come. Sometimes they come at ten, then again at midnight. Those are the general time frames. We sat in the cellar from midnight to six in the morning on Sunday. As you have probably read, only a few pilots get past our blockade. Recently, there were 150 planes, then there were 50, another time 30. Then we got a concert from hell, shooting like I've never heard, not even on the most frenzied days of the last war. There are antiaircraft batteries in every little spot: in the middle of the city, on houses and railway cars. Berlin is incredibly well defended. There must be many thousands of artillery guns, and they shoot salvos into the night sky at a wild pace. We've also managed to shoot down an airplane by now. The wreckage and mangled bodies of those who were in the plane, four men and a woman, are lying in Grunewald.

In the midst of this monstrous shooting, you can hear the humming of engines, as the planes do not usually fly very high at all. The ground shakes when the bombs hit, and fragments rain down on the houses and into the courtyards—it's a genuine aerial battle. Forty or fifty of us hunker down in the cellar. Children bawl and dogs howl in the apartments.

Munding and his style of commentary will lead us into the following year as well. In February 1941, he again takes up the topic of bunker building:

The amount of construction on an underground city here in Berlin is truly outrageous. In addition, they're building mysterious towerlike structures, but no one knows their significance. These are situated at the zoo, and lamps are even being used to work on them at night. In addition, they're building autobahns and a new Reichsmarschallpalast, and part of the Esplanade Hotel is being cleared to make room for it.

All of this is incredibly urgent, and they call from Berchtesgaden time and again to see how things are progressing.

Since we have pressed millions of subjugated peoples into slavery, all sorts of things can get done. . . . The large concrete blocks they are building in the city are antiaircraft towers. They may be as high as ten storeys, may serve as a kind of citadel, just in case.

It must be emphasized that Munding wrote this before the Wehrmacht invaded Russia, and the nonaggression pact between Germany and the Soviet Union was still in force! But Munding accurately diagnosed megalomania and dreams of conquest four years before the end of the war: "The rumours will not go away that we will march through Russia to restore order in Iran, Iraq, and Syria." Given the degree of hubris, it was to be expected that bunkers within the city limits would be used for ground combat.

| 121

Gertrud in the city . . . The reality of that period was more heightened in Berlin: more information, more participation, whether voluntary or forced. Yet this heightened reality was rather secondary for her:

> What happens to me now is unreal and remote. If I don't actually dream, then I don't awaken either. I wander through an intermediate world that is not a part of me and in which I have no part. During a visit last year, one of my friends remarked that when I spoke of Finkenkrug, I called it home, as though Berlin were not a home to me. I was quite unaware that I spoke this way, but I knew this was how I felt . . . In any event, I've written to you often that I am torn out of my native soil by the roots since we moved here. And I long for soil in which I'd be able to take root . . . When I read so many foreign letters, whether handwritten or in newsprint, what strikes me as sad and strange is the fact that the authors are leading a sort of "aerial life."

| 122

In the summer of 1941, Gertrud Chodziesner was also called up for compulsory labor within the framework of measures being implemented throughout the Reich. This mainly concerned the elderly, as younger people comprised the majority of those who had left the country.

As early as December 1940, the Reichanstalt für Arbeitsvermittlung [Reich Institute for Labor Placement] ordered the *Geschlossener Arbeitseinsatz* [segregated labor deployment] of all Jews who were unemployed and living on welfare. "Segregated labor deployment" meant "warehoused Jews," forced laborers who were quartered in barracks, fenced in, and monitored by the plant management at the respective industrial sites. In Berlin alone, this was the method used to conscript about two-thirds of the approximately thirty thousand Jewish forced laborers to work in armaments factories. The others were assigned to work gangs or employed in roadwork, street cleaning, garbage collection, institutional kitchens and laundries, and harvesting potatoes and beets.

In April 1941, labor deployment was expanded to include all Jewish men under the age of fifty-five and all Jewish women under fifty, so Gertrud Kolmar was also included in the regulation.

She had to register and travel to the Zentrale Dienstelle für Juden [Central Jewish Service Department] of the Berliner Arbeitsverwaltung [Berlin Employment Administration] in Kreuzberg. She most certainly experienced a very unfriendly reception in this building with a baroque facade. Eyewitness Marie

Simon said, "The overture was horrendous. I was ordered to the employment office in Fontanepromenade, widely called the 'harassment promenade,' and the notorious Jew hater and persecutor Eschhaus was its director. Before anyone communicated with us, they had us wait in a very dark, narrow hallway for hours out of sheer spite. We shifted from one foot to the other. It was very depressing for the simple reason that we were very fearful about what was coming. You didn't know how long it would take, and you certainly felt that they'd orchestrated this unpleasant situation deliberately." When someone made an inquiry, it sparked a torrent of abuse with cries of "Impertinent Jewish rabble!"—and so it continued.

In order for someone's "workbook" to be issued, he or she first had to fill out forms in claustrophobic office spaces. He or she had to answer questions about his or her education and qualifications. But regardless of what he or she wrote down, he or she was classified as an "unskilled worker."

After taking care of the formalities, the conscripts had to listen to an address from Eschhaus, an excerpt of which has survived:

Ladies, you are now entering a factory and that is where you must work. You can be glad that you will finally become acquainted with sensible, purposeful work in your lives. You know full well how much better off you are than those who have recently taken to working in Poland.

The most important thing you have to remember is the term "workplace sabotage." And when are you guilty of workplace sabotage? When you avoid work, when you do poor work, or not enough, and so forth. I have ordered that every case of workplace sabotage be reported to me personally, and you will see just how much these reports interest me. I will personally come to talk to you about it, but I will also bring two people from the Gestapo along, who will take the person in question to a concentration camp.

Yes, and then there's the question of your many illnesses! Everyone knows that all Jews are sick, dying, and not suitable for work. And yes, you also have all of your medical practitioners, nice gentlemen who can further prove your claims. Your medical practitioners are all gentlemen who write medical certificates and perform miracles of health for their dear patients. Not anymore! I am proud that I have already put three of these worthy people behind bars. It would give me the greatest pleasure to increase their numbers in the concentration camps a bit!

Forced laborer Chodziesner received a "*Verpflichtungsbescheid* [obligatory enlistment notice] by virtue of the order of the authorised representative of the four-year plan to secure manpower needs for jobs of special political importance to the state, and by the *Dienstpflicht-Durchführungsverordnung* [Regulation for the Implementation of Compulsory Service] of March 2, 1939." Accordingly, she had to report to the central office once again for the purpose of "starting work."

She received a notice of assignment to a cardboard box factory that also listed an appointment for a job interview. She had to hand over her papers at the payroll office, including her workbook, disability, and tax cards. She had to fill out a company form with information about her person and status, had to agree to the terms of the job (for example, giving notice: standard; vacation: standard), and also had to confirm that she had received and acknowledged the work rules. Gertrud Chodziesner also received an assigned company number, a plant ID card, and a yellow badge. (Aryan employees wore a blue one.)

The forced laborer was registered with the local branch of the national health insurance plan. A payroll sheet was created for her. The standard starting salary for Jewish forced laborers was around 70 reichspfennigs per hour. Depending on the working conditions, another 3 reichspfennigs were paid as a bonus for dirty work. But it was up to the firm to decide whether or not to pay the bonus. Wages varied widely on the whole, and many Jews received an hourly wage of about 40 reichspfennigs, sometimes even less. The average starting salary of between 70 and 75 reichspfennigs was comparable to the "hourly wage rate" of an Aryan mason. In terms of today's purchasing power, that would be around 7 euros or the approximate hourly wage of workers hired by labor contractors.

According to the regulation on forced labor, salary reductions were possible because people assumed "that the performance of Jewish labor was significantly lower than that of our other employees." But Jewish forced laborers could still bring complaints, including wage issues, before the legal aid office of the district administration of the Deutsche Arbeitsfront [German Labor Front] in Berlin. They could even bring an action before the Labor Court, and "pending" proceedings were, in fact, documented.

Regular, legally established wage deductions included a so-called head tax, plus health, employment, and disability insurance. The total deductions amounted to around 25 percent.

The workers were often plagued by "Jewish regulations," and the Gestapo monitored compliance with them. The historian Konrad Kwiet wrote:

Even the smallest violations could be interpreted as sabotage and resulted in draconian penalties—immediate deportation as of the end of 1941. Company personnel were instructed to report any incident. A few were only too happy to make use of this obligation to report on fellow workers. They monitored Jewish forced labourers' every movement, even checked their sandwiches during the lunch break to see if they were eating forbidden foods. Besides the accusations and denunciations, there were the little nasty taunts or insults, as well as the bellowed orders, the snarling and incitement to work. This tone was nearly ubiquitous, and company personnel chimed in almost everywhere, even if they didn't necessarily feel bound by National Socialism or antisemitism.

The poet was a forced laborer—and this in the armament industry, no less, which I've been reading about in the meantime. And so I envisioned her mounting detonators on grenades at Siemens and Halske, and thought I could now imagine how they pestered and harassed her there. After all, there were numerous reports that confirmed the worst suspicions. Here are just three voices.

One conscript who was also assigned to a cardboard factory had this to say: "I first worked at a labelling machine, and then I had to work on a large expander. It punched out very heavy cardboard. It was a heavy machine that could not be kept inside the factory building, because the (floor) boards were rotten. So they put the expander in the middle of the courtyard and built wooden housing around it. We called it the witch's hut. Horrible accidents occurred there. One woman got her finger caught in the machine, and one got scalped when her hair got caught in it."

Inge Deutschkron, who I at least saw at a reading in Berlin, wrote about forced labor in a spinning mill that produced parachute silk: "For ten hours, we had to make sure that the thread on the rotating spindles didn't get tangled or break off and that the spindles didn't run empty. The room was hot, the work hard and arduous. The noise rendered all conversation with colleagues impossible. During the break in the breakfast room there was only one topic: 'How do we get out of here?' Women who had been working there for quite some time reported that they had been subject to harassment."

Another forced laborer, Ilse Rewald, wrote: "They stuck me in an armaments factory in Bergmannstrasse. Ten hours of hard physical labour can be incredibly long . . . separate toilets for Jews, forbidden to enter the canteen, a 'J' on your smock, the star. In the summertime, Jewish colleagues sat in the yard amongst the garbage cans and ate their bread, spread with a paste of semolina or lard . . . Sometimes I left the shop to run cold water over my wrists, because I thought I would fall over before long."

When putting together a biography, I find that my earlier expectations are seldom met. Many times, I am surprised by details that don't fit my preconceived notions or match my original concept. But that's also what makes the work so exciting, and this is probably true for the reader as well.

Yes, Kolmar had to work in a factory. But she neither turned grenade shells nor mounted detonators. They sent her to the Epeco Cardboard Box Factory on Herzbergstrasse in the Berlin borough of Lichtenberg. Just what she did there cannot be inferred from her letters, for she only mentioned working on a "big machine."

I tried to learn about cardboard production on the Internet but found the results rather confusing. Did she work on a cartoning machine? Or on a collapsible cardboard box machine? Or on a horizontal cartoning machine, assuming there was such a thing in those days? She would most likely have worked with corrugated cardboard equipment. Packing materials were mainly produced for the armaments industry, and corrugated cardboard was constantly in demand there. This was also the most common type of delivery packing in the production of consumer goods. Anyway, single-layer or double-layer corrugated cardboard was used. The inside cover . . . corrugated rolls and steam formed the "ripple" on it . . . preheat cylinder, spray dampening device . . . The ripple was fastened to the inner cover with starch glue . . . and fastened to the outer cover . . .

Gertrud Sara Chodziesner was placed in a group with other Jewish women. The work was not particularly strenuous for her, or so she said in her letters.

What most disturbed the poet was the constant talking during work, the constant yak-yakking of the group in her ears:

> I longed to get away from the rubbish, gossip, and tittle-tattle that are
> apparently indispensable accompaniments to a women's section. I longed
> for a "silent existence," and since the men were one short, I jumped in
> of my own accord, and the manager later approved it after the fact. So it
> was blessedly peaceful around me for a few weeks until I realised that the
> work was really too heavy for me in the long run. And so I regretfully
> had to go back to the women's group. Incidentally, I'm on good terms
> with all the other women but do not have any close contacts amongst
> them. The men, on the other hand, have welcomed me into their circle,
> to which I "belong."

And then the very thing happened that she could not have previously imagined: though she clearly didn't love it, she began to approve of her work because she could get away from the much-frequented apartment during the day. Even the ride in the subway was a relief, as she could read or ruminate. If work was more than seven kilometers away or an hour's travel time from home, then the employment offices granted a special pass to both men and women who were legally required to do forced labor. These permits were good for just one form of transport on just one line, however, and transfers were not allowed. Most of the conductors examined the passes very carefully. But there were some conductors who, as one forced laborer reported, simply waved them on "if you held the yellow ID in front of their noses."

She could breathe a sigh of relief when she arrived at the firm: "Yes, I realised that I was gradually starting to feel at home there, a feeling I no longer have here in the flat. And I know that, come Monday morning, I will walk those dark halls and sense that I am 'home again.'"

Even three months later, she wrote:

> This journey at the crack of dawn, the daily grind, the effort it takes (for it does) . . . I ought to see all of this as an imposition, as drudgery, as repellent to me, and inwardly beat against it like a wall until I bloody my head. Instead—instead I feel that by the time that I have walked through both courtyards and forced my way through the narrow plank door into the workshop with the big machines, dark and sparsely lit, with heaps of cardboard waste and an automobile in the way, I am "home again." "Home." It's a fact. More at home than at 10 Speyerer Strasse, for that's where my tenants dwell, strangers who have taken possession of my—our—things, and nothing belongs to me anymore. Well, maybe my room is still mine. But only when everyone's out.

She was subsequently relieved that she was not, as people put it at the time, "hounded" or "given a hard time." She liked her work. Apart from any assurances, here's a clue: After a minor accident at work, an injury to her finger, she would have had every right to a two-week medical leave. But she did not want that, so she just let the doctor treat her and went back to work. And she was proud of the fact that, among Jewish and non-Jewish workers alike, she missed the least amount of work.

| 123

Kaddish for Georg Benjamin: His apparently relatively light imprisonment in Görden and Wuhlheide ended abruptly. On August 10, 1941, he was relocated to the Mauthausen Concentration Camp in Austria, which was feared for its literally murderous forced labor in the quarry.

The brutality intensified in the month of August, when SS administrators divided concentration camps into categories. Mauthausen was classified as a "Stage III Camp" for the liquidation of dissidents. Prisoners sent to Mauthausen were mainly those "who were considered incorrigible or unruly." This is what I read in the *Encyclopedia of the Holocaust*.

Moreover: "Across from the main gate there was a meeting plaza. Prisoners had to line up there for roll call in the morning and evening, and sometimes prisoners were killed right there in front of everyone. A kitchen, washroom, and laundry were housed in three stone buildings to the side of the parade ground. The third building housed the 'Bunker' (the prison) and the gas chamber disguised as a shower room. Prisoners were shot in an adjoining cell."

Furthermore: "Mauthausen became the concentration camp and extermination center for 'undesirable political elements' within the German Reich and for dissidents in occupied countries. . . . Since the camp was overcrowded, the sanitary conditions worsened; typhoid and dysentery epidemics broke out, and the death rate rose markedly."

Georg Benjamin arrived at Mauthausen in the middle of August after traveling for several days. By August 26, his wife received a letter from the commandant's office, informing her that the Jew Georg Israel Benjamin had died: "Cause of death: suicide by touching a power line." The death certificate issued by the registry office at Mauthausen II gave the hour of death (1:30 A.M.), but it did not specify the cause of death.

Georg Benjamin was not among the prisoners who were shot, gassed, or "annihilated" by working in the quarries; he was driven into the camp's high-voltage barbed wire fence. A prisoner at the camp said, "Clothed only in shirts and underpants, the Jews from the transport were chased into the barbed wire. And they hung there until morning. After the work details had left the camp, the electricity was turned off, and the corpse carriers had to take them away."

| 124

Gertrud gladly, almost hastily, left the apartment in the morning. She described the domestic situation in a detailed letter to Hilde. And she also conveyed the atmosphere and mood on this occasion in September 1941:

You can spot my "sisterly affection" and joy over your letter in the fact that I could have stayed in bed today, Sunday, but was "already" up at 7 A.M. and "already" starting to read these lines before I got dressed. "Already" is in quotation marks because the time is late enough for my present circumstances, and I usually crawl out of the down comforter three hours earlier. I don't even need to, could easily sleep 'til four thirty or a quarter to five. But I always have to take care of all sorts of things before leaving in the morning that I am too tired to do when I come home in the evening. Shine shoes, make sandwiches, and, above all, darn my stockings, which get tiny new holes in them day after day. There's usually some sewing in the evening, as well as various household chores, so I'm afraid I don't get to read, to sit quietly and think anymore (or, if you will, to dream), and not just for lack of time. (I often plan to stay awake, to lie awake and reflect a bit after going to bed, tenish. Yet despite the best of intentions, I fall asleep as soon as I pull the covers over me.) Since my bed is in the dining room, I don't really have a "haven" anymore, no room for myself. I've always had a feeling of homelessness here, and now it's gotten more intense. It's certainly gratifying that the tenants feel completely at home here, as they've said themselves. But this has resulted in their constantly going to and from our rooms, or so it seems to me. When the mother brings my food, for example, she often sits at the table and chats with Papa during my brief meal. Then her daughter usually arrives, remarking that it tastes better in the company of friends and likewise takes a seat. Of course, I can't say that I've had more than enough company all day long and a little peace, quiet, and solitude would do me good at this point. Now there are beings that radiate silence and tranquillity, but our tenants are not among them. They are decidedly social beings, and even their preferences, of which there are many, are mainly of a gregarious, sociable nature. . . . With everything that's going on, I'm amazed at the lightness with which these people resign themselves to the present day, which surely must oppress them more than me. I've already praised their tremendously obliging nature, and it's wonderful for Papa that he can tell them his stories, youthful adventures, and professional experiences "for hours." They love to listen, and he forgets his sorrow while he's talking.

I mostly feel superfluous during conversations like these, and not just because I already know Papa's stories, and not just when he is talking. The tenants' conversations also strike me as strange. Ever since I've been gone during the day, I've "lived away" from home, so to speak. It's a bit the same for me as what I sensed with soldiers who came back from the battlefields in the last war. Without being very aware of it, they and the ones who stayed at home spoke different languages and no longer understood one another. And all good intentions to be close to one another didn't change a thing. Perhaps it's similar for those who stayed here and those who emigrated . . .

Time and again, Hilde Benjamin came from Steglitz to visit Uncle Ludwig and his daughter in Speyerer Strasse. The visitor later wrote of this period:

I was met by a new, friendly, and seemingly outgoing woman. We found common ground in our discussions—which were not removed from worldly things but concerned many issues of the day, from the most substantive to the politically stressful. We were together for only a few short hours in which even silence did not get us down. Gertrud also witnessed the final weeks of my illegal meetings with my husband and the news of his murder. . . . I witnessed her way of working and her unspoken anticipation of the end. . . . If I were to try to explain Gertrud's nature, I would say that the wall behind which Gertrud lived was not just inconspicuous and peculiar; she exuded both great calm and inner disquiet. She seemed dark but not gloomy. The colours surrounding her were dark and warm. She was severe but only mildly bitter. She made a cool but never cold impression. Perhaps you can only intuit what she was like from the nuances of these disparities.

| 125

Jews in Berlin and Jews in the Reich as a whole felt the effects of the war more directly than Aryans did. Just as soon as the war began, Jews got no ration cards for meat, milk, or tobacco. They were no longer entitled to butter, eggs, rolls, white bread, marmalade, chocolate, coffee, tea, or alcohol. They had to purchase all-too-scarce staples in "Jewish shops" or in regular shops at prescribed hours with food ration cards marked with a *J*. Then, in 1941, they were forbidden to buy shoes or to have shoes resoled. They could not buy soap or shaving cream. They got no more firewood or coal.

And they were no longer allowed to enter restaurants, ride tour boats, use train station waiting rooms, or—assuming they were even permitted to purchase a ticket—use dining cars or sleepers; they were not even allowed to use public transportation in the city or to keep pets.

The *Judenstern* [literally, "Jewish star," patterned after the Star of David] was introduced in the fall of 1941. Gertrud Chodziesner also had to sign a form that served as a certificate of receipt:

> I hereby acknowledge receipt of one Jewish star. I am aware of the statutory provisions concerning the wearing of the Jewish star and of the prohibition against wearing medals, decorations, and other insignias.
>
> I also know that I may not leave my residence without carrying written permission with me from the local police authority.
>
> I agree to treat the badge with great care and to turn down the edges of the fabric when sewing it onto a piece of clothing.
>
> A copy of this receipt is in my possession.

And the *Judenhaus* [Jewish house] on Speyerer Strasse also had to be "labelled," to wit, "with a paper Jewish star that corresponds in a size and shape to the label mandated in Section 1, paragraph 2 of the Police Regulation on the Marking of Jews of 9/1/1941, and must be kept white, however, so that it stands out better against the mostly brown doors."

Renewed hate propaganda accompanied the introduction of the Star of David, made of paper or cloth. There was a Star of David on a Nazi Party wall newspaper with the caption, "Whoever wears this badge is an enemy of our *Volk*."

How did Gertrud feel when she walked in front of the branded house, wearing a yellow star on the left side of her chest?

There's a blank space in the written record, so I will again draw new analogies, based on statements that may roughly apply.

Martha Haarburger: "It was torture for us to wear the yellow star with which they branded us as criminals from 1941 on. I had to fight daily to remain calm and composed when I went out on the street."

However, there were also Jews who saw the star as a sign of their creed, and a slogan reflected this view: "Wear it with pride—the yellow patch!" Anyone who was still a bit of a joker saw it as a "sheriff's badge" and felt distinguished.

Jacob Jacobson, former head of the Archive of German Jews in Berlin, reported:

> I must confess that, when I first left my apartment in Charlottenburg wearing the Star of David, I was prepared for attacks, scorn, and derision from the ginned up public sentiment, but nothing of the sort happened. The first person I met, a lady who was a complete stranger to me, was also wearing the star. I instinctively tipped my hat to her and, by doing so, broke the spell once and for all. Yet this does not mean that very unpleasant confrontations did not come about later in connection with the "Jewish star." On the first day, it got me secretly procured cigarettes, and many fellow sufferers could also recount similar experiences. And much later—like others—I got smuggled bread and meat cards from friends and strangers.

The following could have happened on the authorized journey home from work: "As I stood in the subway—Jews weren't allowed to sit—I suddenly felt a hand in my coat pocket. And when I automatically took hold of it, I felt someone tapping very soothingly on my fingers. I didn't know whether it was a man or woman, for they got out at the next stop. I got off soon thereafter, and when I took a peek, there were meat ration cards in it."

But the pressure increased, as did the stress. A woman wrote: "My mother had lived in this house for twenty-eight years; everyone knew her, but from the moment we wore the Star of David, they cut us dead. No one would talk to us. We were just air."

| 126

Another attempt to induce Gertrud and her father to emigrate came shortly before the general ban on emigration (October 23, 1941). Once again, Peter Wenzel—probably not by himself—visited his sister-in-law and father-in-law to pick up more typescripts for safekeeping. Surely they talked about the touchy subject on everyone's minds. Nearly every way out was blocked in the meantime—did that include the escape hatch to Switzerland?

Wenzel would hardly have spoken openly to his wife about his final attempt, but what he did write suggests that his overtures were again rejected: "Both of them are in good health. Both have demonstrated such great fortitude these last months that one can only hope they will survive the coming physical and mental woes. Their lovely housemate takes good care of them, and she will continue to look after Papa, should Trude be drafted to work in one of the newly acquired eastern territories. Not much more is known about this as yet."

Was the Jewish woman's obligation to serve in the eastern territories a surprising new development or camouflage? Does this really mean that Gertrud was about to be deported to the east, and Papa would remain at home alone, looked after by subtenants?

The recipient of this letter was apparently alarmed. Hilde made contact with the writer Mary Lavater-Sloman, who moved from Hamburg to St. Petersburg, lived in Moscow, moved to Greece in 1919, and finally wound up in Switzerland. This author was not someone whom Gertrud particularly admired. A few of her characteristic titles include: *The Bright Shadow, Mistress of the Seas, Genius of the Heart, The Forgotten Prince,* and *Triumph of Humility.* The wife of a Swiss engineer, Lavater-Sloman expressed good intentions, but more seemed hardly possible:

Dear Mrs. Wenzel, it's really terrible that you have received such alarming news from Germany! You poor thing, I can only imagine how much this must upset you. Of course, we will immediately do everything possible to bring your sister to us here in Switzerland. In fact, we've already gotten started. We know virtually every path that one must take, for this is now our eighth attempt . . . But it will sadden and disappoint you to learn that we've tried in vain thus far, and my husband has little hope that we'll succeed this time. The authorities here and in Germany are putting up resistance. But we still want to try anything and everything.

In January 1942, Hilde would write the following to her sister-in-law Thea in Chile:

> The director of the carton factory where she works claimed that Trude was
> once very reliable and conscientious, which I can well imagine. This man
> then seems to have felt sympathy for Papa, which was certainly humane
> and decent of him, for Trude is absolutely not the kind of person who can
> somehow ask someone for sympathy. But, of course, you never know how
> long it will last. A lot of people are gone. Papa said he'd be able to stay, that
> he didn't want to leave Trude alone. But she took the view that she would
> survive and, at his age, he should stay.

| 127

The robbery continued! At the beginning of 1942, Jews had to hand over even more items: heaters and sunlamps, heating pads, stoves, irons, hot plates, vacuum cleaners, toasters, pots, hair dryers, records, record players, typewriters, and bicycles.

And this happened during a very cold winter in which they had permafrost from January through March, with temperatures hovering repeatedly at around minus twenty degrees.* Eyewitness Joel König, who was training for a Zionist model farm, wrote:

> We had already gotten used to a lot of things. Jews were not allowed to
> own bicycles or to use electrical appliances. Jews were no longer allowed
> to use public telephones. The business with the woollens and furs was the
> most rotten and spiteful thing we had seen in print, yet there it was in black
> and white. Everyone on the farm went to his wardrobe and picked out the
> woollen garments that were best to keep, so as to give all the rest away. . . .
> This new regulation was no trivial matter. It forced us to wear our best and
> only warm clothing, even for the dirtiest jobs. But the most annoying thing
> was that, while we were in the mood for much more serious matters, we had
> to discuss the issue of how the regulation was to be interpreted. More and
> more members of our *chaverim* (comrades) were being deported. Whose
> turn was it to be relocated with his parents? Were insoles made of rabbit fur
> within the meaning of the regulation or not? Was it true that we were no
> longer allowed to send food parcels to deportees? Were we allowed to keep
> just one pair of wool socks?

* Minus twenty degrees Celsius is about four degrees below zero Fahrenheit.

| 128

As 1941 ended and 1942 began, a love story took shape, a factory romance that began chastely at any rate.

Gertrud told her sister about it for the first time in a letter that went on for four pages. She wrote most of her subsequent letters at around four or five in the morning before leaving the house.

A twenty-one-year-old Jewish medical student fell in love with forty-seven-year-old Gertrud. We know so little about her relationship with the officer during the First World War or about her subsequent relationship with the chemist and Nazi poet Keller. In this instance, however, her detailed accounts have been passed down. I'm going according to her letters. I will not summarize what went on over a period of months—developing, inhibiting, unfolding, fading—but have instead chosen characteristic sequences from the letters and arranged them in chronological order.

To begin with, she didn't even mention the young man's name to her sister. Was she afraid of the censors? They could have been reported. A love affair between forced laborers would not have looked right. Forced laborers had to slave away until they were completely spent and were not supposed to have any time or strength for new passions.

The tale that Gertrud had to tell could fit into the category of "bittersweet love stories," or so she thought. And she posed the question, "Is it a love story at all or just bittersweet? I don't know . . ."

The hero of my story is the "youngest and nicest" worker at the factory. The whole thing started very conventionally, you see. But I can't do a thing about it, for he really is the nicest and youngest: dark-haired, tall, slim, but sinewy and very physically strong, though you wouldn't know it by looking at him. He's a very spirited, handsome Jewish guy with an intelligent face and symmetrical features, whose lively facial expressions admittedly often turn to a grimace . . . As a matter of fact, it was merely his taciturn manner that first caught my attention in the breakfast room. He sat off by himself, rather than at the "men's table," and read books after the meal. My language skills were the starting point. Then, one afternoon, he saw me do a job that obviously made me very cross. But it's easier for me now because I have more experience. Since it was already quitting time for him, he rather tersely and briskly offered to do my job for me. I initially refused, but he would not back down. . . . When people "shuffled around" in the breakfast room, I came to sit at his table through no effort of my own, and we then often chatted during meals. But he'd already started to tell me very personal things in private and to honour me, an almost total stranger, with confidences that took me by surprise in light of his usual reserve. I told him how amazed I was. He explained that he was completely sure I was trustworthy because he'd been watching me for a long time. He then told me a few things about myself that actually proved he'd been a keen observer.

So it went for weeks. She asked herself if this was a happy time and preferred to describe it as "delightful." There are further signs of her infatuation in her description of the young man:

I rejoiced when I saw him walking through the factory every morning in his abundantly tattered and grimy blue linen suit, but slim, handsome, vibrant, and lively nevertheless—and I am still happy about it now—I felt happy whenever he greeted me with a smile, and yet . . . The "and yet" lies in the fact that I never knew what I should call him, and our relationship seemed to perpetually continue as it began. Given the difference in age (but did he know how old I was?), I could not allow myself to think of anything that remotely had to do with the word "love." So should we speak of friendship instead? This characterisation would not have hit the mark either. And companionship? Companionship was never my thing. I don't have the slightest talent for it where men are concerned, and it goes against my nature . . . So what was it anyway? I've since discovered many of my own character traits in him. From the standpoint of age, I could have been his mother, and I've sometimes thought, "My son . . ." And so I tried to be a "maternal friend" to him, but to no avail. He always treated me like a peer and, whenever he spoke to me, acted "the man" through and through: very certain, very determined, assertive. And this did not displease me . . .

But she was also not displeased when the relationship seemed to have ended after a quarrel. She pictured him with a younger woman. A relationship? He seems to have dealt with her rather abruptly, "like someone newly engaged who energetically and decisively turns away from his previous beloved, so as to be deemed a tabula rasa for his bride." And how did she respond? "Finally! This was, indeed, the dash of the erotic, the drop of love that I felt was missing in our relationship."

And she saw the moment as a time for reflection: "I am now rather proud. It's such an honour for a twenty-one-year-old to fancy a forty-seven-year-old! . . . To expect manners from young people instead of a show of indifferent friendliness towards an 'old grandmother' (as I could certainly be by now)! . . . I can no longer see him these days without smiling secretly and thinking: Look at it however you like! You were still mine once. There was truly something between us, and not even with the best will in the world can you make it go away. And I still do the favour that I did for him in the good old days: I sweep out his workshop after work. Will things remain this way? . . ."

Here are a few lines from back then about aging and a woman's age. Just a few years earlier, Kolmar wrote one or two poems about old women, or rather, poems in which she assumed the role of aging and older women. She was just over forty at the time. Was this a form of anticipation? Or rather flirtation? Playful association with her imagined older self?

A woman who was forty in the 1930s would have felt vastly older than a twenty-first-century woman of the same age. A woman was old at forty back then, and that's how women saw themselves after forty. Assuming she was married, a woman of that age thought only in terms of stable married life. A woman of forty in an open relationship with a possibly even younger lover would have been regarded with suspicion rather than envy. Many women that age would hardly have trusted themselves to express erotic and sexual feelings.

| 129

After a long hiatus, she began to write again and even surprised herself:

> As recently as a few months ago, I would not have thought myself capable
> of such physically demanding work. But lo and behold, I can do it! . . .
> This story I am writing is admittedly "only" prose and not verse. Even
> so, the ability to practise my craft again after a long break has come as an
> unexpected gift. How very slowly this little work is growing and progressing.
> But it's growing and progressing all the same, mainly when I get up and
> dress in the morning and during the subway ride. I also scribble on a slip
> of paper in the breakfast break. And if I've been able to nurse this oh-so-
> little piece along and think that what I've done is good and beautiful, then
> I am occasionally very happy . . . And methinks it must be real, genuine
> art that doesn't rely on hours of leisure, a writing desk with armchair, the
> tranquillity of a workroom, or all kinds of comfort and repose, but is capable
> of overcoming every limitation of time and space . . . This is a sign not only
> that I have a bit of talent (I knew it anyway, but this is a welcome affirmation
> of that knowledge), but also that it has deep roots which cannot be torn out
> and, despite all the trimming and pruning, it always germinates and shoots
> up again.

In mid-April 1942, she finished the "little work": "About twenty-six closely written pages in a notebook, in three months' time, at a snail's pace, and yet I'm glad it worked at all!" Apart from its size, nothing is known about the story, which has been lost, along with another story that she began even later.

The author concluded that she had to be highly motivated if she were to continue writing, given the restrictions of constant fatigue and the bustle of living with subtenants. A keyword surfaces here that had already appeared in Horst Lange's report in the *Rabenpresse* about a meeting with Kolmar, which said she looked and was "obsessed." This was not merely a skill or proficiency she possessed but something that held sway over her. She simply had to write, even under the most cramped, harried circumstances, and only a lack of sleep, peace, or time could hinder her in the end. In addition, there was no space that protected her from disturbances at that time. Furthermore, she had no prospects of publication and the acceptance that went with it. With whom could she communicate in lyric code or narrative? Did she read new texts to her father? Save for him, there was apparently no audience at home. Added to that was the likelihood that her typescript (and maybe a carbon copy) would go missing, especially during this time of persecution and liquidation. Not everything was safely deposited in Switzerland.

But she probably put aside these questions. The process of writing was primary. In this case, the main force that motivated her was stronger than any fatigue, exhaustion, sadness, or fear; in this case, something asserted itself and prevailed. The general situation admittedly did not allow her to critically proof the new text or to revise it, condensing, intensifying, and it remained in its original form. But the crucial factor was that she wrote.

Spring came. She still traveled to Lichtenberg, never tiring of the long journey, and she rather enjoyed what was, for others, just a waste of time, an annoyance. Forced laborer Chodziesner tried to make the best of everything, all the more so in the month of May, even if 1942 was a war year:

> I always look forward to the morning ride (which is still coming up for me today), to the bright green honeysuckle all around the old Lichtenberg Church, to the small pink almond tree in the front yard of an almost rural cottage—there are still a good many farmhouses surrounding the old manor—and to a few blossoming plum trees in the community gardens. The trees are blooming late this year; they usually flower by the end of April . . .
>
> Apart from this, I am enjoying the *Duino Elegies* and, to understand them better, I'm again reading the *Letters from Muzot* in between.

A forced laborer reading Rilke. . .

Looking back and looking ahead: On July 19, 1942, she again found time to write a detailed letter to her sister in Switzerland. Here more than ever, I feel the poet should speak for herself:

> I have worked at this job for a year now, have never been absent due to illness, and even got through my accident without vacation time. I believe I hold the record among all male and female, Aryan and Jewish workers at our factory. . . . When I think about the fact that I found women's work extremely difficult when I started to work at the factory, and I now work with the men as a fully qualified replacement for a couple of other men who were terminated for unsatisfactory performance . . . I recently worked with the women for three or four days, and the work itself was very relaxing—as compared to my "men's" work. But the women's chattering and screaming got to me, and I was happy when the men's foreman showed up and declared that they couldn't do without me for long. Four of the five labourers living in our building do the same job at the factory, day in, day out. I am the only one with more interesting work, although I began with a rather monotonous job, just like the others. But I soon reached the point where I looked at factory work as not merely a grim, compulsory necessity but as a kind of instruction, and I wanted to learn as much as possible . . . Little by little, I'm definitely noticing that I get a feeling of home there, a feeling I no longer have here. And I know that tomorrow morning, Monday, I will walk the rather dark halls with the sense that I'm "home again." As I already wrote you before, it is really so that I've told my destiny that "I will not leave you, for you bless me." And Friedrich von Schiller's words surely also hold true for me: "If thou tak'st the Godhead in thy will, It no longer sits upon its throne."
>
> Alas, alas, and that's what weighs me down so: wherever my opinions, my views find expression, they hardly ever evoke a response. And that's why they seldom find expression. I cannot surrender any of the spiritual strength that I indeed possess to other companions in distress. If I got more deeply involved with them, they would only diminish me without my having anything to gain. They don't understand me, perhaps think me arrogant . . . I dare not tell them what I am telling you, what is surely not news to you: Although there were earlier decades when things went "really well" for us, that's not what they were for me. They mainly called for qualities of a sociable or social nature, qualities I lacked for the most part. But I'm equal to and have in spades what these times demand. As a child, I would gladly have been a Spartan. Be that as it may, I wanted to be a hero later on.

| 130

We now have some news from the family, beginning with Hilde: she changed residences several times in Zurich, changed her domicile in Switzerland.

Sabina Wenzel said the following in her letter, though she didn't provide time frames: She lived with her mother "in sublet rooms until we moved into a studio flat in a modern housing development on a hill. It was a large room, partitioned by wardrobes, and one side looked onto the street, while the other had a balcony with a gorgeous view over all of Lake Zurich."

Then they changed locations: "An old Ticino house in a village above Locarno ... Orselina after that ... Then we were short of money, and my mother got to know a woman living in Centovalli, who told her that one could live there very cheaply. We rented a little old granite house that had no lights or water at first. In the early morning, we heard smugglers passing by on their way into the valley. Two months later, we moved into another house farther down, where we had running water."

Despite various changes of address, Hilde was the central coordinator for intercontinental correspondence. As I already stressed, most letters reached their addressees, albeit postal censorship caused delays. The envelope of each airmail letter from sister-in-law Dorothea contained a "Wehrmacht High Command" stamp and adhesive tape with "opened" printed on it. And so the German Ministry of Propaganda had entered neutral Switzerland by way of censoring mail from South America! Letters from a sister or brother in Australia sometimes showed a double adhesive strip that read, "Opened by examiner ... OK ..."

Hilde and Peter divorced in 1942. As we've already seen, he tried in vain to immigrate to South America. His son reported to me from Rio de Janeiro that he subsequently refused to do military service, was then employed as a paramedic and interpreter in occupied France, after which he worked as a businessman near Berlin at Zeuch-Generatoren in Wannsee, a firm that was classified as crucial to the war effort. Gertrud said he told her that "the marriage would probably not have fallen apart so completely if he and his wife had stayed together in the same location. I didn't dare tell him that I sincerely doubted it ..."

And now to Margot in Australia ... As expected, the ornithologist had no opportunity to work in the science field, so she got herself hired on a poultry farm.

She reported the following in 1941:

The farm that I wrote to you about turned out to be a complete disaster, because the people there were utterly impossible. Apart from that, it could have been so wonderful. You have no idea what their family life was like: nothing but "scolding, bickering, and terrible outbursts" from morning to night. And they happened to be orthodox Jews! The woman was morbidly stingy and had no idea about cooking and housekeeping. I lost ten pounds in four weeks. The man, who was otherwise quite alright, thought his main role was to talk, and it was generally expected that, given this arrangement, it fell to me to take care of the work. It was not even possible to get proper work done due to this dawdling, not a single punctual meal, etc. And so, several pounds lighter, with a few pounds in my pocket, I gave up the job posthaste and moved in with an acquaintance who lives very close to my old residence near Liverpool. I help out on her poultry farm and earn some nice money in the bargain. . . . For the time being, I've put off my dream of operating my own farm and have absolutely no intention of ever throwing in my lot with Jewish emigrants again.

In mid-June 1942 Georg (Camp Futura, Victoria) had to inform his sister in Switzerland that "Margot got very ill again and died on June 5. Her old heart condition, combined with the sorrows of recent times, particularly her concern for Papa, undermined her resilience. Your big brother Georg."

| 131

Contrary to expectations, the factory romance that Gertrud believed had ended was still not over that spring of 1942. In a sequel to her account, she tried to distance herself from events by styling them into a bad novel by a bad author:

Perhaps because he was not satisfied unless it had a happy ending, it pleased him to see the ending of his story as something temporary, a kind of intermediate stage, and to dispatch a sequel afterwards. The title is bad and consists of two juxtaposed quotations: "I will not leave you, but don't greet me under the linden tree!" That is, the hero and heroine openly persisted in their mode of hostile silence. This silent animosity came expressly from the hero, and the heroine attuned her behaviour to his. "Openly" even held true in the presence of a single third party. And if the woman "reported officially" to the young man before witnesses, then he looked at her sternly, almost angrily, when she opened her mouth, as if to say, "Don't you dare carry on a private conversation with me!" And his features visibly brightened just as soon as he heard, "Come over to Frau Langner's machine: the belt slipped off again when she switched it on." Yet if the two happened to meet while sweeping out the workshop, then he was always the one to start off the conversation rather awkwardly with banalities, such as, "So, we've managed to get through another day," or "If you lend out your tools, then they're sure to get broken," and the like. The heroine let him carry on a little monologue at first and interrupted only if he got more personal. In the end, they would usually get around to talking, "just like in the old days." He parted company with his comrades at the streetcar stop one afternoon and went up to her at the back of the platform (she almost never ran into him there because he always finished later than she did). But he acted as if he were surprised by the encounter . . . Don't you find the whole business implausible, the writer a rank amateur? . . . Such things only happen in bad novels and not in real life . . . Will there be a third book? I believe the author is capable of it . . .

I've quoted her en bloc, as Kolmar proved to be witty and ironic once again. But she outdid herself in a subsequent letter: "Did I already write you that I've occasionally seen a picture of a 'male hermaphrodite with secondary female characteristics' in a textbook on anatomy? Well, we have a sort of 'hermaphroditic comradeship with secondary erotic characteristics.'"

By early May, she wanted to end this stalled relationship with the former medical student. In a letter to her sister, she tried to motivate herself to do it. Here again, she would say it in her own words, which makes her much more fully present to us:

When at home, I always intend to break up with him or, less forcefully put, to loosen the ties. I am no longer the one looking for him, and he is the one who comes to my work station, actually has to come, because he is responsible for keeping the machines in good order, and mine is frequently unpredictable. But when he's right in front of me, when his handsome, intelligent, sooty, poorly shaven face lights up visibly when he greets me in the morning, then—then I lack the courage to say anything about splitting up. But tomorrow is Monday, and I want do it tomorrow for sure. . . . I'm certainly not the kind of woman to grasp at straws, and the idea that I, an older woman, would be looking for younger men is spiritually abhorrent to me. I would gladly have struck up a real friendship. But this strange, quasi-romantic situation is distressing in the long run . . . Incidentally, it seems strange to me that he, like nearly every man who's been close to me, is engaged to someone else. But he's not really all that close to me . . .

| 132

Factition [Ludwig might have written . . .]: Dear Brother in Montevideo, I'm pulling myself together to write this letter in hopes that it will overcome the monstrous distance between our cities. I've known your address by heart for a long time: Calle P.P. de la Sierra 3220. Why the high number? Irrespective of street names, are houses in Montevideo numbered as we were accustomed to in earlier centuries, when our cities were still towns, rather than constantly reshuffled heaps of rubble that stretch for miles? And not only houses have been (and are still being) destroyed to their foundations, but also trees have been mangled as well—even Berlin's Grunewald must look bad. There's a lot of shredded, splintered wood in the little city park here in Schöneberg, too. Full-grown trees have snapped like proverbial matchsticks. The evil Tommies did this by indiscriminately dropping high-explosive bombs and land mines that have only spared industrial areas for the most part. It's almost a blessing that our sort are not allowed in the park any longer, so I don't have to see the destruction up close. But I cannot forgo looking at bushes and trees, especially not at this time of year when everything is greening up again. So I sneak along the quiet street directly above the long stretch of park and look down into the greening hollow. At least I am not forbidden to do this. I no longer dare to dream of going into parks or forests; never again will I be able to take a stroll through the Brieslang Forest, breathing deeply, occasionally calling to the dog at my side. So I pad around Berlin W 30 without Gertrud because her new duties haven't allowed her to accompany me for ages. And I've never before felt so intensely comforted by things that sprout and come up green again every year, even in this year of war. Standing pensively on "Am Volkspark" Strasse and looking down into the valley, I can only wonder at nature's unending patience and tenacity. If anyone besides you were listening to me right now, I would make a great speech on behalf of Mother Nature, though my voice is not nearly as powerful as it was at the beginning of this horrific, cruel century. Perhaps it's nature's sedative that I don't see as clearly as I used to, an injustice that cannot be remedied at present, and so my view of the valley that turns green again every year remains gently blurred.

I take this image with me through Salzburger Strasse to Speyerer Strasse, an image that no one can take away from me, an image that can only be erased upon my death. When I am standing motionless above the hollows on occasion, rooted to the spot, you might say, I wish that I could hide myself down there in the roots of a gigantic tree until it's all over. And then, each year, I could marvel and offer praise: You're greening and blooming again, still greening and blooming, continuing to green and bloom, and when I am long gone, you will green and bloom. When my grown, scattered children are gone, you will green and bloom. When my two grandchildren no longer exist, you will green and bloom, if and when mankind succeeds in destroying all life on earth. This will be the consolation that I will take with me, only I still don't know where I am going.

| 133

Fear and terror were on the rise among Jews in Berlin. In the early autumn of 1942, Gestapo officials from Vienna took over the direction of the *Judenreferat* [Jewish Section] of the central office of the Gestapo in Berlin.

The practices of Gestapo officials in Berlin were considered "flabby" and corrupt as compared to those of the Viennese Gestapo—corrupt, above all, and not just in isolated cases. As reported, Jewish homes were attacked and looted, and Jews were robbed within the framework of deportation. They caught the head of the Jewish Section with an "entire warehouse" and another high official with a "little box of gold." Ten Gestapo officers were arrested, and more were added over time.

SS *Hauptsturmführer* [Captain] Alois Brunner implemented the infamous "Viennese methods" in Berlin. Houses were surrounded, streets blocked off, and moving vans drove up. One woman reported: "Everything was accompanied by the most extreme violence: they bashed in doors and broke into homes.... SS *Scharführer* [Sergeant] Slawick stood in the courtyard with his riding crop. (This man, Slawick, was like a beast. I do not know any name for it.) The raiders ran through the house. Get ready to evacuate. The terror was indescribable. Around one hundred dear, good people (we all liked each other in the house) had to pack instantly.... I got into bed and cried, cried like never before in my life. My boy was gone, and now so was my daughter."

| 134

At the beginning of September 1942, Ludwig Chodziesner had to hand in an eight-page questionnaire on which he declared his assets. Along with other expropriation records, the document has survived in the archive of the Berlin Regional Tax Office. As his former solicitor colleague Bruno Blau noted in his memoirs, not all of which have been published, the Berlin Gestapo destroyed all deportation documents and "dejudification records" in the final weeks of the war but, in the mad rush, may have overlooked or forgotten to inform the tax authorities.

The document was reproduced in the catalog of the Kolmar exhibition in Marbach. The old man filled out the questionnaire with a shaky hand. He answered "Yes" to the question, "Are you a Jew?" and placed an exclamation point after it.

The declaration of assets was a prelude to total dispossession. This act of plunder, which impacted the daughter along with her father, was disguised in bureaucratic garb: *Sicherstellung der zurückgelassenen Vermögenswerte*

[confiscation of abandoned assets] . . . In this regard, Jews were no longer entitled to dispose of . . . listing, holding in trust, and utilization of Jewish property
. . . estate . . . liquidation of abandoned assets . . . allocate to a blocked account
set up for that purpose . . . deportation and administrative costs . . . to be paid
into a general expense account . . . scale of fees . . .

A marauding and murderous state emerges from behind all these bureaucratic phrases and pseudo-legislative paragraphs to send this brutally simple
message: The old man belongs to a segment of the population that we hate, so
we are taking everything away from him, and then we will send him away and
kill him.

"My last will" . . . these were the first words of his last will and testament that
Gertrud's father drew up in July 1942:

> My legal heirs, namely, my son Georg, and my two daughters, Margot and
> Hilde, emigrated some time ago and reside in foreign countries, such that,
> according to Section 4 of the Eleventh Ordinance to the Reich Citizenship
> Act of November 25, 1941, neither they nor their children can inherit
> anything from me on account of my death. I therefore appoint my eldest
> daughter, Gertrud Sara, born on 12/10/1894, in their place. She shall
> receive my entire estate as sole heir. I name as her substitute Frau Hilde
> Lange-Benjamin, Düntherstr. 7, Berlin-Steglitz. To her son, I bequeath a
> legacy of 1,000 (one thousand) reichsmarks.
>   Written in my own hand and legally signed, Ludwig Israel Chodziesner,
> *Justizrat.*

As executor, Hilde Benjamin, resolute woman that she was, even visited her
in-laws at the "Jewish house." So Gertrud received encouragement and consolation from "Hilde Benjamin, who comes here often."

The deportation of Berlin Jews came in the very cold month of January 1942.
Hermann Samter, an active member of the Jewish community, reported the following in a letter:

> Transports have been leaving again (all of them for Riga) since January,
> such that ten thousand people are already gone from Berlin. As of late, all
> evacuees under sixty (or "migrants," the only thing we're allowed to call
> them nowadays) have to walk the route on foot from Levetzowstrasse to
> the Grunewald train station. Can you imagine what that means in this
> cold? The people who left yesterday rode in cattle cars. There were very
> many old people among them, and some as old as seventy-five were taken

out of nursing homes. And a great many of those old people will not even survive the trip! And we have no idea what happens afterwards, as there has been no more news from Litzmannstadt [Łodz, Poland] since the war began. Mail sent there comes back with a note that there's no postal delivery on the street in question. People suspect typhus, but they don't really know the reason.

Papa Chodziesner's imminent deportation meant renewed robbery, and this time it would be total.

This was the procedure: A senior bailiff presented Chodziesner with an "asset seizure order" via a certificate of delivery. The form from the central office of the Berlin Gestapo was riddled with section marks and said: "Based on Section 1 of the Act on the Seizure of Communist Assets . . . in conjunction with the Act on the Seizure of Assets of Enemies of the People and State . . . shall, in conjunction with the Führer's and Reich Chancellor's decree on the utilisation of the confiscated property of enemies of the Reich . . . the entire assets of Ludwig Isr. Chodziesner, born on 8/28/61 in Obersitzko, most recently living in Berlin, Schbg., Speyerer Strasse 10, be confiscated in favour of the German Reich."

After immediately effecting and subsequently filing confirmation, the Gestapo Office for the Utilization of Assets in Moabit sent the following statement: "I am sending the attached transport list of those Jews whose assets have been forfeited to the Reich through seizure within the framework of deportation."

And so the prevailing injustice was codified in three ways: Point number one is that, by means of an official form, Chodziesner was presumed to be a Communist and an enemy of the Reich, and his assets would be confiscated on these grounds.

Point number two is that his assets were not "subversive to the people or state." Total expropriation was actually linked to denaturalization, but this was not the case here: they did not even make a pretense of it, nor did they go to any further trouble.

Point number three is that Ludwig Chodziesner had to pay Reich Flight Tax for his imminent deportation to the Theresienstadt Concentration Camp! And so Theresienstadt in the occupied territory of the General Government of Bohemia and Moravia was defined by decree as a foreign country, and the mass shipment of people to the camp was declared a "change of residence"—that is, emigration. What brutal cynicism!

Chodziesner also had to "furnish collateral," and the property in Steglitz was mortgaged for that purpose. A letter from the tax office in Schöneberg to the Office for the Utilization of Assets in Moabit read: "Chodziesner has put up security for Reich Flight Tax by taking out a collateral mortgage of 37,250.00

reichsmarks against the property at Fregestr. 30, corner Holsteinische Str. 30. A *Löschungsbewilligung* [consent to cancellation of the mortgage in the land register] is attached."

"Confiscation of Assets" appears at the bottom. The Reich Ministry of Finance was a pseudo-legitimate authority for robbery and expropriation.

An official form notified the tax office in Berlin-Schöneberg: "The assets of the Jew (name and address followed) have been confiscated to the benefit of the Reich by order of the Gestapo Office."

As if he hadn't already suffered enough injustice, Ludwig Chodziesner was obligated to conclude a *Heimeinkaufsvertrag* [home purchase contract]. What sheer fraud!

It included the following pretense: "With the conclusion of this contract, the obligation is assumed to grant the party to the contract room and board for life, to have laundry done, to see to it that he/she has necessary medical attention and medicines, and to provide for necessary hospitalisation."

The Reich Association of Jews was forced to conclude such bogus contracts. And this ensued on the specious grounds that "since it is incumbent upon the Reich Association to raise funds for the entire community to be housed (in Theresienstadt), including needy persons, it is the duty of all persons who have assets at their disposal to not only cover their own housing costs through the purchase amount to be paid to the Reich Association but also, above and beyond that, to also provide funds to support the needy to the extent possible."

Friedenberger Martin commented:

By means of this passage, they deliberately covered up the real motives behind the campaign, namely, forced deportation and expropriation. They fabricated transporting people to Theresienstadt as state-sponsored housing in an old age home and disguised the skimming off of liquid assets, which in a few cases generated a great deal of money and bore no relation to the actual cost of a retirement home of any kind, as a supportive contribution to the community for the benefit of the less well-off members. German Jews to whom this applied had to transfer their entire personal assets to the Reich Association. This included cash, bank balances, securities, asset backed receivables (mortgages and land charges), and other monetary claims, such as life insurance policies with cash surrender values. . . . The Reich Association wired the purchase amounts received to a Special H account at the Bankhaus Heinz, Tecklenburg and Co., which was under sole control of the Reich Main Security Office.

In other words, it went to the SS.

* * *

And so, shortly before his deportation, the former lawyer and *Notar* was completely disenfranchised and robbed of everything.

His daughter Gertrud, son-in-law Peter, and visitor Hilde Benjamin "tied up the meagre bundle for the eighty-one-year-old" (according to Benjamin). Did they accompany the old man to the collection point? It was probably the demolished synagogue complex on Levetzowstrasse.

Whether it was the Levetzowstrasse or the Oranienburgerstrasse or the Grosse Hamburger Strasse transit camp ... the radical detachment of the Vienna Gestapo first made sure that all of the chairs, tables, beds, and closets had been removed, "such that only the bare floor remained in the houses. Only mattresses without blankets or sheets were allowed to be placed on the floor in the sleeping quarters." This is where Chodziesner would have to wait for about three weeks to be carried off.

Prior to that, he had to sign the following statement for the Gestapo: "I have been informed that my entire assets, as well as those of my family members, have been confiscated. I must refrain from any disposition of the assets. The state police shall use the harshest possible measures to punish violators. I am aware that verification of the declaration of assets shall be carried out prior to transport and that I cannot count on any leniency in the event of a violation of this decree."

This confirmed that Gertrud, the closest family member, had been robbed as well. Added to this were indirect threats and intimidation.

Later on, the following sentence was printed on a form: "The Jew was deported to Theresienstadt."

Of course, Gertrud could only use code to inform her sister that their father had been deported. On September 14, she wrote: "This morning I was at Käthe's, and she seemed truly grateful for my visit, because she's been very lonely since divorcing her husband. After they lived together for so many years ... The breakup has clearly hit her harder than it has him, and her only comfort is that it was for his own good, and that he is doing well, or so she hopes."

She took to using her middle name, Käthe, which she otherwise never used, and the deportation became a divorce. She hinted at a sense of loss.

Using coded language again, she reported on September 27 that Gertrud Fuchs, who had lived in the same apartment as a subtenant up to then, had also been deported, apparently to the same destination as their father, to whom she referred as "Herr Kolmar":

I'm in the midst of an "insecure life" right now, because Frau F. has
apparently parted company with her children and given up her room here
to run her widowed brother-in-law's household from now on. She's moving

to his place on October 1. This brother-in-law, a certain Herr Kolmar, was with us recently. He sends you his best and is the father of Gertrud Kolmar, a former friend of yours. Since Frau F. is cooking for all of us, I still don't know what will become of the entire thing, whether they will keep the apartment, move out, or rent it. These days, I want to go to the community to gain clarity.—Forgive these thrown-together lines: they're merely supposed to show signs of life.

Ludwig Chodziesner, along with about a thousand other Jewish men and women, was transported or escorted from the collection point to the Moabit freight station on Putlitzstrasse. Train Da 523, the third "great elders transport," left from there on October 3, 1942.

A report of every transport was sent by telex to the Reich Security Main Office ("attention: SS Sturmbannführer Eichmann"), usually by a Gestapo captain: "Urgent, for immediate delivery. Concerning: the evacuation of Jews. Procedure: standard."

Klaus Scheurenburg, an eyewitness, reported about a later transport to Theresienstadt that could also apply to this "elder transport" of October 3:

> The train ride lasted forever. It was the kind of slow train that made regular stops. Although it was only 350 km from Berlin to Theresienstadt, it took until late evening. We had to get out on a short stretch of track alongside a large open field. I thought about running away. But then I saw that the train was surrounded by SS men with machine guns and dogs. On this day, they turned us from civilians into concentration camp prisoners. When we all got on, they were still shouting, "Everyone on, please." But now they said, "All Jewish swine out, but make it quick, or we'll get you packing—this way, you swine!" A German shepherd almost got me: the dog was obviously trained to bite people's heels. We were driven with whips into casemates that made an eerie impression. There was constant yelling, kicking, beating, and shooting. The men were immediately separated from the women. . . . After about forty minutes of marching in almost total darkness, we stumbled into a large building, apparently a barracks. We had to stop, go on, then stop again. . . . I went to my quarters, a former horse stable with hundreds of men sleeping in it. Daylight never came in: just a few small windows on the front side let a bit of grey twilight into the room.

Theresienstadt was a fortress city of the kind that the Austrians established in the eighteenth century. Despite subsequent sieges, you can still see the basic structure of the Longwy fortress in France, to cite one example. The city was a huge fortress with artillery-resistant walls and headed bastions. Within the chessboard street plan were the barracks of the garrison, the main square, the garrison church, town houses, and businesses, including the food trade in particular.

At the Wannsee Conference of January 1942, Nazi leaders declared Theresienstadt the "old-age ghetto" of the "Protectorate of Bohemia and Moravia." Jews "over sixty-five or over fifty-five and infirm" were to be incarcerated there, as were Jews "who were severely disabled veterans or had received medals for bravery (The Iron Cross, Golden Medal for Bravery, etc.)."

The fortifications made it easy to defend the city. And so people could move freely within the walls, but space was extremely tight. Theresienstadt was designed to house about four thousand to seven thousand residents, but there were sometimes more than fifty thousand prisoners penned up there. This military installation was about one hundred thousand square meters in size, such that there were only about two square meters per inmate. Housing consisted of three-level bunk beds in the former garrison barracks, in village houses, and in warehouses. Under such crowded conditions, the sanitary facilities were totally inadequate and epidemics correspondingly frequent. Ruth Klüger emphasized that the term "old-age ghetto" was a euphemism and characterized the fortressed camp as a "stall in front of a slaughterhouse."

Theresienstadt was a transit camp. The prisoners laid a branch line toward Bohušovice/Eger, a stop on the Dresden-Prague rail line. For each train that arrived at the camp with about a thousand prisoners, a corresponding number of other prisoners had to be deported "to the East." By war's end, a total of sixty-three deportations had taken place. Forty-six thousand were deported to Auschwitz, only about twenty-seven hundred of whom survived; more than twenty thousand prisoners were sent to Poland, only about fifty of whom survived; of the ten thousand prisoners sent to White Russia [Belarus], only ten survived.

Theresienstadt was a kind of purgatory where everything, including cultural life, was on call or on recall. Works composed and performed at Theresienstadt are well known, including music by outstanding composers like Gideon Klein and Victor Ullmann. Composers and performing artists were also gradually deported, and Gideon Klein was twenty-two when they sent him to Auschwitz.

The Nazis undertook a notorious beautification program at the fortress city prior to the 1944 visit by a delegation from the International Red Cross, which was permitted to inspect the camp for the first time. They shot a propaganda film called *Der Führer schenkt den Juden eine Stadt* [*The Führer Gives the Jews a City*]. Ludwig Chodziesner was long since dead by then. He either died in Theresienstadt or was murdered in an eastern camp.

* * *

What did people in Berlin-Schöneberg know of Theresienstadt? What could they have known? The purpose of deportation was by no means kept under wraps. Considering all the rumors that circulated about the concentration camps and the Gestapo's conscious representations of them, it almost seemed like a privilege to be deported to Theresienstadt, also called *Theresienbad* (i.e., a spa) by the propaganda machine.

Those who still held out any hope had their hopes dashed upon arriving at Theresienstadt. Peter Utitz, a survivor, wrote:

> The first impressions were so bad, so shattering, that nearly every single person said release would have to come soon or no one would survive. In this place of misery, all ten plagues of Egypt seemed to have been unleashed here in spades. An unimaginable plague of flies, water shortages, a foul stench, and the smell of decaying corpses—that was our welcome. On average, 130 people died each day. The food was wretched, the bread mouldy. Huge queues formed in front of the food distribution points at so-called mealtimes. The nutritional value of the food was not even sufficient to compensate for lost energy. We were billeted in a ground-floor barracks that had three-storey bunks and previously served as an ammunition depot. A nail or even a place to sit became precious possessions that were carefully protected against theft.

| 135

Taking stock and evaluating the situation . . . On November 4 at 6 P.M., Gertrud Chodziesner had a visit from an official of the Reich Finance Administration. He filled out two forms and, a few days later, the stamp of the *Oberfinanzpräsident* [chief finance president] in Berlin confirmed receipt and forwarding of same:

> According to the daughter Gertrud Sara Chodziesner, the daughter lived in 1 apartment with the evacuee. The apartment consists of 4 1/2 rooms. Of these, 3 1/2 rooms are rented to Jewish tenants, while the daughter occupies 1 room. The furniture and other furnishings in the rented rooms, which are valued at 1,000 to 1,500 reichsmarks, have allegedly been transferred to the daughter as property inherited in part from the mother and in part from the father for assistance rendered. . . . The daughter declared that, insofar as she did not already own the items, the items were transferred to her by her father as property in 1939, and she has furnished proof thereof by submission of a letter dated July 29, 1942. She furthermore declared that,

above and beyond her work income, she provided for herself by renting the furnishings as furnished rooms for 200 reichsmarks per month.

As was usual after deportation, they apparently wanted to confiscate the furniture, but Gertrud was able to prevent this by providing reasons and proof. And so there were no valuation charges or cost estimates, just an hourly charge of one half hour.

The estimation sheet confirmed, indirectly, that the daughter would have to figure on future scarcity. The two hundred reichsmarks that came in from the tenants each month would contribute little to her overall livelihood, as she would have to pay a very high rental tax for a "luxury flat" from then on.

Gertrud Kolmar could and must have counted on being deported herself, possibly even "liquidated." What must have been going on inside her at the time?

We can draw inferences from a letter. On December 15, 1942, she wrote to Hilde:

> And so I will suffer my fate, be it tall as a tower, be it black and oppressive as a cloud. Even if I haven't yet seen it, I've affirmed it in advance, faced up to it in advance, and so I know that it will not crush me, will not find me too weak. How many who simply folded at the mere sight of a fate far too big for them have asked themselves whether they'd earned some kind of punishment, whether they had to atone in some way? I was no worse in my conduct and pursuits than other women. But I knew that I did not live as I ought to and was always willing to atone. And I will take all the suffering that has come upon me and may yet come upon me as my penance, and it shall be just.

In January 1943, she reckoned "to have learnt a lot. One thing above all: *amor fati,* love of one's fate. The seeds have probably always lain within me, maybe even in the form of a green stalk. But only now has the bud opened to become a flower . . ."

Amor fati: "The seeds have probably always lain within me." We can interpret this to mean that she had already accepted her senseless, unnecessary self-sacrifice in her literary practice and thus created deep insight into the mythical. This sacrifice was more or less foreordained in the selfless consent of an Ischta to offer herself to—or, more precisely, to allow herself to be killed by—Tiberius, which turned out to be unnecessary, as her killer finally admitted. This self-sacrifice was in turn related to Jephthah's daughter's consent to allow herself to be killed by her father—as a random victim, no less, and without any meaning whatsoever. And did the line connecting Jephthah's daughter and Ischta now extend to include Gertrud herself? Was she willing to honor with her life what she'd pursued literarily?

The behavioral pattern, the agreement to offer up their lives, even though they did not know or understand the meaning of the sacrifice, remained unchanged. Jephthah's daughter–Ischta–Gertrud: an eerily consistent progression of ongoing identification, a story explained by a preceding one and influencing a subsequent one. It would soon be her turn, and she seemed to see it that way. She was resigned to it from the outset. *Amor fati:* not just accepting one's fate but even loving it!

This succession of letters contains other terms like "expiation . . . repentance . . . punishment"! Expiation, repentance, punishment—but for what? Was it because she was not allowed to bring her child into the world? Or because she could not start a family? Or because she did not follow repeated advice and feel compelled to immigrate to Uruguay, for instance, so that her father would have been saved from deportation and murder? However she may have reproached herself, how could she have considered the threat of her imminent deportation just?

She had denounced Nazi terror nearly ten years earlier in her poems and, in the intervening years, would have heard many things that validated her condemnation of the ruling powers. Now her father had lost everything, and the eighty-one-year-old had been sent to the transfer ghetto called Theresienstadt. They could have found out what happened to Georg Benjamin and what went on in concentration camps years ago! This woman in her late forties knew full well that they would come for her one day and send her to a camp, so why didn't she protest vehemently? On the contrary, she rehearsed her role as willing victim!

How was it possible for such a sense of guilt to develop in this woman with an underdeveloped ego, who practiced altruism her whole life long, especially in her caretaker role at home? The life she had led was not a pious one, to be sure, but largely selfless to the point of self-sacrifice. Was this the kind of life that one must "do penance" for, and in a concentration camp, no less? Was she prepared to accept it obediently, to even feel that it was justified?

How did she develop such a victim mentality, even though she knew that there was no cosmic "judge" who presided over guilt and penance; even though she knew, in fact, that a murderous leadership with not the slightest interest in guilt and atonement had taken wholesale action against the old, men, women, and children? And are we to believe that she wanted to be dragged meekly into the machinery of destruction? In the final analysis, did she not justify an unjust system when she said to herself, yes, I have earned this punishment, even if it should be the death penalty, for I have not lived rightly?

In the face of impending death, she was apparently trying to give her life symbolic meaning. As has been proved biographically and autobiographically, she gave personal meaning to the senseless, the nonsensical, the sense averse . . . And now the apparent meaning extended to sacrificing her life, to martyrdom . . .

This model can hardly be adopted, because it was collectively decreed. Individual characteristics no longer played a role, and whatever was inherent in her, whatever she may have been "predestined" for, did not come to pass.

Nevertheless, she made a desperate attempt to give meaning to it. How can I explain this to myself, let alone to others? As the result of Jewish thought patterns?

In Gertrud Kolmar's first play, the old Jew says, "I must have sin in my hair, something unclean that I don't see, and I haven't been baptised. Why else am I being punished? On Friday evening at the dinner table . . . My wife Débora had already arranged the cup and Sabbath bread in the red embroidered cloth for me and lit the lights. I wanted to recite kiddush, to bless the wine, but then there was a thundering at the door. And they invaded the room like Haman's soldiers, and took me away." The important phrase here is, "and I haven't even been baptised. Why else am I being punished?"

I found it hard to empathize or resonate with this thinking. But then I had a conversation with Jews my own age in Berlin, all of them from assimilated and secular families. They survived because their parents emigrated in time. A possible explanation emerges here: Even if Gertrud Kolmar grew up in a secularized environment, she would still have known people "who practiced their faith." And for those people, a tradition was relevant that "held a people together for over two thousand years" through persecution, expulsion, and killing. For a person to have assimilated in spite of an identity that was shaped by a history of suffering could, in itself, have awakened feelings of guilt.

But she clearly, even decisively, resisted assimilation and professed her Judaism, at least in her poetry. However, her profession of faith appears to have remained poetic, and she never undertook to join a Jewish congregation. Gertrud Chodziesner apparently never set foot in a synagogue, never attended a service, never showed solidarity with a community. She remained an isolated, solitary Jew. Was she aware of this? Was it painful?

| 136

At the end of October, Gertrud told "little monster" Sabine in Switzerland:

I had a very guilty conscience this morning at around 5:15, because I couldn't write you a nice, long letter like I have every other year. I don't lack the love and desire, just the time. Three new tenants, three ladies, are moving in here tomorrow. They will get the two front rooms, one large and

the other small, and I am in my former room again, the one I had given
to Frau Fuchs. So I had to clear out all of the closets in both front rooms,
mainly books from two libraries, and put them in with me, and that was a
nice piece of work. So you've got to make do this time with a birthday card.

She wrote to Hilde a week later:

I hope the "monster" will not be angry with me because she has to make do
with a mere birthday card, while Mama gets a letter. But today I have a
bit of mental and physical peace in which to write, and I didn't have that
eight days ago. (The doorbell just rang, and I had a little chat with the
landlady.)

And before I started, one of the new tenants called me in to show me
that her heater was leaking, so I had to first look for a small container
to place underneath it. On this occasion, I entered the room for the first
time since I handed it over to her—and was horrified. The tenant is a
good-natured but somewhat silly and infantile creature. She's a Christian
and, although already in her thirties, a member of some pious young girls'
group. In spite of the fact that she's at home until one in the afternoon, her
room is an indescribable disaster ("her comb was lying in the butter").* I
really shouldn't rebuke her since I am not "free of blame or flaws" myself.
But . . . the wall decorations! There are white postcards with verses and Bible
passages in black and red lettering on the wallpaper, on the mirror, and in
the picture frames, plus a wooden pokerwork, a white cardboard cross with
a silver print of Jesus, and an artificial rose bouquet in a glass jar on the
dresser . . . ghastly!

| 137

After her father was deported and the family's assets had been confiscated,
Gertrud, like many Jews in Berlin, had to rely on forced labor as a source of
income. With the introduction of the new *Verordnung über die Erhebung einer
Sozialausgleichsabgabe* [Regulation on the Levying of a Social Equalization
Tax], standard wages were reduced by an additional 15 percent. And here's a
supplementary keyword: the wage-lowering *Minderleistungsklausel* [underper-
formance clause]. After these new cuts, the poet must have lived on a pittance.

* * *

---

* "Her comb was lying in the butter" [*da liegt der Kamm auf der Butter*] is a German expression that
means "everything was a mess."

Gertrud Kolmar changed workplaces shortly before Christmas 1942 and worked on Wilmersdorfer Strasse in Charlottenburg from then on. Since the new workplace was less than seven kilometers from her apartment, she was no longer allowed use public transportation and had to walk about forty minutes. But that didn't bother her. The work was decidedly easier, and she felt like she had "advanced from a blacksmith to a watchmaker."

Gertrud also wrote about it to her brother in Australia. Her sister Hilde again later whittled down the front and back portions of the letter.

For starters, Gertrud thanked him: "Your monthly letters 'trundle' over to me in fairly quick succession these days. In September, for example, I got three in the same delivery." She then talked about her work in the cardboard factory and very discreetly indicated a new relationship:

> When I worked for weeks at a time "with the men" in the summertime, I had the chance to visit a small overgrown lot during breaks. I lay down in the grass between mulleins and nettles and was really happy about the little bit of green and sunshine . . . Incidentally, I worked with the men of my own volition, would almost like to say, on my own authority. I longed to get away from the rubbish, gossip, and tittle-tattle that are apparently indispensable accompaniments to a women's section. I longed for a "silent existence," and since the men were one short, I jumped in of my own accord, and the manager later approved it after the fact. So it was blessedly peaceful around me for a few weeks until I realised that the work was really too heavy for me in the long run. And so I regretfully had to go back to the women's group. Incidentally, I'm on good terms with all the other women but do not have any close contacts among them. The men, on the other hand, have welcomed me into their circle, to which I "belong." One of them grew into a collegial relationship that developed into a friendship. (It occurs to me that you might believe what isn't so—this comrade is all of twenty-two years old, though unusually mature for his age.)
>
> In a few days, I'll be forty-eight! As the saying goes, "Time goes by, the light fades." And yet it doesn't strike me that I'm all that old.

With the change in workplace, her factory romance seemed over for good. She believed she could now look back coolly and evaluate:

> Saying good-bye was difficult, which is little wonder. But I was surprised and must say also moved that his voice faltered slightly during those last words in the workshop. In the end, I meant more to him than I thought, than I had allowed myself to believe. A forty-eight-year-old woman and a twenty-two-year-old man make a strange pair. It's astonishing that things

trotted along so well. . . . At my age I am happy and thankful to have gotten this gift, a much greater rarity than love between an eighteen- and a twenty-four-year-old. Be that as it may, it was indeed very beautiful! And perhaps . . .

Gertrud sent her sister another encrypted message on January 5, 1943, about Hilde Benjamin's Christmas visit and another visit from "Käthe" at her place:

Apart from Hilde B's. visit on the 26th and my visit to Käthe's, I was quiet and "solitary, not lonely" within my four walls during the holidays. Käthe is always happy when someone comes over to whom she can talk about her ex-husband, as he's always in her thoughts. He doesn't write to her (probably in order not to make their separation more difficult for her), and since you were friends with him, she asked me if you were still corresponding with him. This was the avenue through which she wanted to hear from him, no doubt. But, needless to say, I had no information to give her in response . . .

However, a message supposedly came in February about the man who was constantly on her mind: her father had died on the thirteenth of that month. It was still the norm to notify people of concentration camp deaths, either by telegram or form letter. The cause of death as stated on these forms was, without exception, fictitious.

Kolmar's letters admittedly contain no reaction to this event. This annoys me. Is it possible that the news never reached her?

| 138

In a letter of February 20, 1943, Gertrud told her sister about the recent reappearance of her young man:

"Man proposes, God disposes." In my last letter, I declared that I absolutely opposed writing sequels to finished novels and that my own was finished for good. But then, on the afternoon of February 7, most probably while you were writing to me, the doorbell rang, and my hero appeared on the scene once again. It was such a surprise because he woke me from my afternoon nap, and I didn't even have time to change out of my old work dress (from my chambermaid days) into a more suitable outfit. I was just as unprepared when he visited me again last Sunday. My whole theory about being offended, and so on, was erroneous, as many theories are.

Well, I was happy, but . . . "But" means that, after these little appetizers, I am feeling doubly hungry for a good meal. Strangely enough, so long as I believed that we had parted forever, it was not so difficult for me to be without him every day. But these short visits, in which we had to part company before the conversation turned from formalities to deeper subjects, only served to whet my appetite, so to speak, without being able to satisfy it.

Her last surviving letter came a day later, on February 21, 1943. The letter hinted at an incipient prospect for the future, namely, that she wanted to write again: "You say that from time to time, you're 'strongly of a mind to write.' So am I. I sometimes think that, regardless of work, time pressures, anxiety, and fatigue, I can get started. Yet in the past few days, anything that seems ready to take shape always flutters away. I wrote my last little work, a story, exactly one year ago, and now I think that if it's able to take shape, it will presumably become another piece of fiction."

Future prospects . . . But they would be brutally cut off scarcely a week later.

In the cobblestones at the front entrance to the Berlin house where I worked on this book for a long period is a recessed "stumbling block," a little concrete cube with a square brass plate the size of your hand. The name Bertha Solomon is stamped into it, accompanied by the remark that she was deported to Auschwitz in 1943.

The house in which she had lived, the house in which I was living, is on the Landwehr Canal but has since been cleaned up and thoroughly renovated. Even so, the staircase is in the same style and the front door in the same place as back then. So the fiftyish Bertha Solomon was led out of this house, and she had to climb onto or was lifted onto the truck bed. Then she was driven to a transit camp.

| 139

The possibility of escape . . . Another air raid on Berlin, and Schöneberg is in the hot seat again. Jews are not allowed in the air-raid shelters, so she makes final preparations in the apartment, reinforcing the windows with cardboard squares. She has sewn two blankets together in sack line fashion and filled them with essential clothing and provisions. She doesn't need to hurry all that much since, as a rule, there's a window of several hours between the sounding of the alarm and the all clear. Thus, she sets off at a time when hardly anyone is on the streets, and even checkpoints are rare. She walks the streets, her heart beating faster, but not frantically. If bombs were to strike near her, she would soon be covered in dust and debris, which would make it plausible for her to state upon questioning that she'd been bombed out.

With a Star of David sewn correctly onto her coat, this little woman has disguised herself in the simplest manner possible: she has tied the blankets with a rope that hangs over her shoulder, one part of the sack in front, the other in back, so that the "Jewish star" is unavoidably hidden.

She marches through the city in a northwesterly direction at first, a cloth covering her mouth, maybe with sunglasses on as protection from the corrosive smoke. The continuous sound of the all clear has still not been heard, so she speaks to no one. The farther she marches, the greater her sense of inner peace. Sometime in the very early morning hours after the all clear signal finally sounds, she reaches a train stop, and one of the first trains is actually going toward Westend. The old conductor is far too sleepy to do a proper check; he motions to her, then rests his head and closes his eyes.

The Jewish woman keeps hers open. Is the huge hospital building burned out or just blacked out? Villas with windows, villas without windows. And now a stop: her stop. She walks down the street for a bit, turns onto a path that leads through the allotment gardens to the so-called Grünfelde Colony. A coffee garden lies fallow. The glass of a battered BLITTERS EDEN sign, briefly illuminated by her dynamo flashlight, is almost completely plastered over. The outer planks of a skeletonized bowling alley have been torn out and used for firewood. No more flags. Barren fruit trees. Chicken wire fences.

One of the fences is fairly rugged. The little Jewish lady immediately realizes that there are chickens in one of the many allotment gardener's houses with garden beds adjoining it. The stable is barricaded. But the little woman has planned ahead, has tools with her so that she can gain entry to the property and stall. She listens with bated breath. Did she hear someone? Owners who had either been bombed out or were looking for shelter near the city limits had even nested in the community gardener's colony. But nothing stirred. Dogs had become extremely scarce, for how could people feed them in the midst of famine?

Breathing a sigh of relief, she pushes on the door in its frame, even if it no longer closes.

She inspects the paltry furnishings with her flashlight. The little Jewish woman doesn't sit on either of the two chairs but squats on the floor, resting on her blankets. After all the fear, excitement, effort, and exertion, she falls asleep. Deep sleep. She awakens with a start. In the first light of morning, she's but the black outline of a seated woman. The star, the yellow star, is not covered:

"Well, lit'l falling star, has tho' flown away?"

"I nearly froze to death."

"I've been peeping at you th' entire time, a little heap of misery, eh? Well then, shall w' make a cup o' kiddie coffee?"

Chickens cluck. Maybe a keyword, "kiddie coffee," could carry us a bit farther along?

"A stable by th' hut? . . ."

Aye—and heavily fortified. You ought to have a watchman for the chickens: good neighbors just ebbing away, can't even count on fellow gardeners anymore.

The woman is older. Works in a textile factory that makes army coats. But "coats won't help n'more, what with how cold it's gonna get 'cross the board." Taking turns at night on fire watch. She zooms out of there to feed the chickens between the night shift and early duty: "D'you know somethin' of chickens?"

They had a garden in Havelland, kept ducks and chickens.

"Can ya kill 'em, too? Gut 'em?"

"Th'whole t'ing . . ."

"Looks like a right proper working community." Pragmatic decision. Plus a bit of superstition is the only protection against bomb attacks: "So long as you's here, nottin's gonna happen t'us."

(So much for an alternative ending.)

| 140

Farewell to life: she foresaw this in her poems early on. This poem from *Das Wort der Stummen* [*The Word of the Voiceless*] testifies to homesickness in a metaphysical sense:

> Why shouldn't I want to die today?
> I've got to pass away sometime.
> My days, my years roll
> Downhill to the lakes,
> Where gray fish sing of silence,
> Cow lilies speak, soft and golden,
> Vipers cradling in scaly rings
> Their silent flute breaking.
>
> There's breath yet at my cheeks,
> Another song on my lips,
> If my eyes have already gone the way,
> That leads me from this life,
> From the city with curved lights which
> Plows sharply through the darkness,
> With contorted, raging faces
> Reviling every little message.

I would like to keep my own face,
Which overflows with words,
Would like to tilt it so, folding it silently,
Like a goblet enclosing a flower,
Until it no longer hears the stone's mockery,
or the drivel of garbage,
Only the dew, the tender crying of children,
Floating and glimmering through the flowers.

Age totters with his begging bowl
Shivering over barren pasture;
Deep inside the red tones of a copper butterfly,
In the grass's green lettering
I want to sink down and rest, forsaken threshold,
Where a temple on the banks disappeared:
Dust. And sometimes to shy from the wave
Beneath my head like a hand.

And she anticipated her own farewell even earlier, which is to say, in the period between 1927 and 1932. We must remain philologically strict here, because the lyric *I* bids farewell to itself and is not identical to the poet herself. But such boundaries seem permeable in her poem "Die Begrabene" ["The Buried"]. In 1927, her year of new beginnings, Berlin-style humor again comes through in this, of all places: "Decay is happy in the land of light . . . it dyes its dress indigo." Or in the form eschatological slapstick: "It romps through the world in a coffin". . . A joke with a macabre note, a coffin searching for a grave:

We all pursued a single goal,
And what kept us going, was pleasure and play,
And what drove us, was worry and need,
And our reward, was death.

Now, peacefully stretched out
I lie covered with earth;
"I need and have" were never mine,
"I must and will" left me alone.

Decay is happy in the land of light;
It dyes its dress indigo,
Wears it smooth today and fuzzy tomorrow
And builds the Tower of Babel.

It rushes its likeness onto canvas,
It stakes it to fences and newsstands,
Its empty yaw grins and grabs
And is called success and science.

With a crude factory of madness, rampant murder
It smashes the hundredth record,
It romps through the world in a coffin—
When will it find the burial ground?

It's victorious in screaming, jumping, running;
When the grave finally awakens,
And has stretched itself, yawning
And covered it with earth.

At around the same time as this rather burlesque poem, she emphatically changed key in "Die Sinnende" ["The Pensive"]:

When I am dead, my name will hover
For a little while above the world.
When I am dead, may I still
Be found somewhere along fences behind fields.
Yet soon I will be lost,
Like water flowing from a scarred pitcher,
Like fairies' secretly forfeited bounty
A little cloud of smoke from a speeding train.

When I am dead, heart and loins fade,
what held me and kept me moving steps aside,
And only my open, quiet hands,
Alien, are placed beside me.
And around my forehead it will be
Like before daybreak, when the mouth of a cave catches the stars
And out of the canopy of light's stone shadow
Giant pleats hang a gray scarf.

When I die, I just want to rest,
My face turned inward,
If the child has seen too much,
And then to sleep well and deeply,
When, shaking, I present myself,

What I was: a waxy light
To guard the second world.

| 141

The Schutzstaffel, which was primarily responsible for guarding and transporting deportees, supported the Gestapo during the so-called factory action. They carried out these operations in more the one hundred forced labor camps, companies, and businesses in Berlin and, as previously mentioned, more than eight thousand Jews were taken into custody. Yet around four thousand managed to flee in time and to go into hiding. A third of them were on Gestapo lists throughout the Reich! The dictum that all Jews went like sheep to the slaughter did not apply here: many responded quickly and acted decisively. It must also be pointed out that there were many suicides in those days. According to documents from a single police station, twelve people committed suicide in Schöneberg alone! Most of them took an overdose of Veronal, a barbiturate.

Forced laborer Gertrud Sara Chodziesner was not one of the four thousand who were able to abscond in a timely fashion. Did she fall into the trap unawares? Didn't she listen to the warnings? Is it possible that she didn't even want to escape their clutches because of guilty feelings?

They obviously valued her at work as willing, reliable, and helpful, so was there no one to at least warn the woman by dropping hints? Mind you, an attempted escape could easily have failed. Police roundups took place on the streets and on public transportation, and riot squads broke into houses.

A Jewish forced laborer named Siegfried Cohn reported on the factory campaign and will serve as a stand-in:

> This is February 27, 1942. A clear, mild winter day. . . . Early that morning, my boss gave me the task of procuring several large sheets of paper in the corrugated cardboard manufacturing area to fix problems in the blackout system. Since they couldn't hand me the paper right away, I stood next to the large corrugated cardboard machine.
>
> Suddenly, an Aryan worker came up to me and whispered to me, "Hey, the Gestapo is on the premises, and you're all being picked up!" I replied that he shouldn't talk such nonsense and, after getting the paper I needed, went back to my floor, where particularly large numbers of forced labourers were at work.
>
> When I got upstairs, I noticed a lot of agitated people running to and fro, and when I asked a colleague what was up, he told me that all Jews were to

gather their personal belongings and assemble in the casino on the ground floor. I took my jacket, cap, and briefcase, which also had my breakfast in it, and went to the aforementioned area. There were several men (Gestapo officials) sitting at a table, and a number of SS men were running back and forth. After all Jewish forced labourers, both male and female, had gathered in the casino, each was called up and searched by the Gestapo. If memory serves, the number of people came to between one hundred fifty and two hundred. They used the opportunity to take away my pocketknife and brought us to two large trucks that were waiting in the courtyard. The fully loaded trucks then drove to a barracks in Moabit, and we had to stand so close together in them that we were unable to move at all.

Gertrud Chodziesner was probably taken by truck to a Berlin transit camp, a barracks or Jewish community center, maybe even the centrally located Konzerthaus Clou which, like most entertainment venues, had been closed in the meantime.

Regardless of where they housed her, the rooms would have been overcrowded, the sanitary conditions utterly inadequate. She would have been in fear for her life because a heavy bombing raid on Berlin took place on the night between her abduction and deportation. A total of 250 RAF bombers dropped incendiary bombs, high-explosive bombs, and air mines (blockbusters) over the entire metropolitan area. There was no protection for these sequestered Jews who, even in this instance, were denied access to cellars or bunkers.

Records provide detailed information about the transport to which Gertrud Kolmar was assigned: It was the third major transport from Berlin to Auschwitz, and the thirty-second *Osttransport** from Reich territory ... Approximately fifteen hundred men, women, and children ... departed from Moabit freight station on March 2 ... in covered freight cars ... scheduled travel time: seventeen hours ... arrival at Auschwitz on the morning of March 3 ...

Gertrud Kolmar was now in the death mill. It is often assumed that she was immediately headed for *Sonderbehandlung*† ["special treatment"] upon arrival in Auschwitz. But internal reports reveal that, even among the women, only a small percentage got assigned to work details, and this was not only true at the Buna Works. So we must not rule out the possibility that Gertrud Kolmar was

---

* *Osttransport* [transport to the east] meant deportation, usually to the death camp at Auschwitz or one of the other *Vernichtungslager* [extermination camps] that were set up as part of the Nazis' "Final Solution" to the Jewish question.

† *Sonderbehandlung* [special handling] was a Nazi euphemism for killing.

sent to the queue of those being admitted to the camp as prisoners. Perhaps an examining physician saw that she was accustomed to manual labor. As a condemned person, she would have been in store for hellish, murderous work.

It's more likely, however, that her fate was decided with the flick of a hand during the selection process: too small, too old, then *Sonderbehandlung*.

The poet in the gas chamber . . . should I even attempt to visualize this? In many of her poems, Gertrud Kolmar reproachfully depicted the way the men of the SA abused human beings, so she would have had little patience for ignoring the facts in this instance as well. I'll leave it to eyewitnesses, members of the Jewish *Sonderkommando** that was charged with removing the corpses, to tell the story. These are their accounts: "The arriving victims had to go down twenty steps. Women and children were the first to undress. The Germans brought them from the stairs into a large room—the *Entkleidungsraum*.† There were numbered hangers and hooks on which they were to hang their clothing. So they hung up their clothes and moved along until they entered a hallway. From there, they turned left and were at the entrance to the gas chamber."

Another conscripted member of the *Sonderkommando* wrote: "After a while, I heard piercing screams coming from the gas chamber, banging against the door, but whining and moaning as well. People began to cough, and their coughing became stronger by the minute. This indicated that the gas had begun to take effect. The noise became unmistakably louder at first, then subsided by the minute, and soon turned into a dull, many-voiced wheezing."

| 142

I don't wish to end the book with these accounts and would rather point out that they've named a newly laid out street in Central Berlin after Gertrud Kolmar. There could hardly be a more symbolic route.

This cul-de-sac lies in a block where history congregates. To the east is Wilhelmstrasse, the location of governmental ministries for decades, now dominated by upscale, GDR prefabricated concrete buildings. Parallel to Wilhelmstrasse is Ebertstrasse, formerly Hermann Göring Strasse, accompanied by offshoots of the zoo to the west. These two axes are tied together by Vossstrasse to the south and Behrensstrasse to the north. The gardens of various

---

* *Sonderkommando* [special command unit] was a work detail of death camp prisoners, mostly Jews, who helped dispose of gas-chamber victims.

† The *Entkleidungsraum* [undressing room] was where victims removed their clothing before entering the gas chamber.

governmental buildings used to lie within this square configuration of streets. Today, many representatives of German states have "In den Ministergärten" addresses.

Gertrud Kolmar Strasse begins at Vossstrasse. In those days, it would have been flanked by a gigantic complex of buildings, the new Reichskanzlei [Reich Chancellery], which was built under the direction of Albert Speer and extended from Wilhelmstrasse to Hermann Göring Strasse. In 1949, the Soviet military administration blew up the ruins, stately even then.

Gertrud Kolmar Strasse now leads straight through the site of the former Reich Chancellery. In fact, the street lies in rather close proximity to Hitler's oversized *Arbeitsraum* [workroom]. It passes the western edge of Hitler's bunker and may well go over the place where Hitler's body was burned.

The street has thus become a symbol: it crosses the area where Nazi power unfolded and leads closely by the sector of its downfall. And I say to myself that Gertrud Kolmar has the floor again. Meanwhile, her poems are even available in translation. [The following poem was assembled from English, French, and Italian translations of her poems. Non-German lines are italicized.]

> *And we, we have proceeded through the gallows and the rack . . .*
>> When I die, I just want to rest,
>> My face turned inward.
> *Vers l'Orient j'envoie mon visage*
> [I turn my face to the East]
>> When I am dead, my name will hover
>> For a little while above the world.
> *Il crepuscolo azzurro scende denso d'umidità*
> [The blue twilight descends heavy with moisture]
>> Then I flew into your nest of mane
>> Held on tightly with my mouth and claws
>> And could no longer sing.
> *Those who walk about here are but bodies . . .*
>> When I am dead, may I still
>> Be found somewhere along fences behind fields.
> *La nuit, je veux l'enrouler autour de moi comme un drap chaud*
> [I wrap the night around me like a warm sheet]
>> When I am dead, heart and loins fade,
>> what held me and kept me moving steps aside,
> *É solo la notte in ascolto: ti amo, ti amo popolo mio . . .*
> [And only the night listening: I love you, I love you, my people]
>> The table, bed, wardrobe, and whatever is there,
>> day, the forest, love, all that was.

I have quoted poems and sequences from the three-volume edition of *Das lyrische Werk* [*Lyric Works*], edited with commentary by Regina Nörtemann, who is also responsible for the volume *Die Dramen* [*The Dramas*].

I would like to add my thanks to Frau Nörtemann for many helpful leads and, above all, for putting me in touch with Sabina Wenzel, Ben Chodziesner, and the owner of the hitherto unpublished letters of Gertrud Kolmar. (It is his wish to remain anonymous.)

I would also like to express my thanks to those who contributed important material. I had email correspondence with Sabina Wenzel about her "poet aunt" and, most notably, about her own mother.

My communication with the poet's Australian nephew, Wolfgang Ben (W. B.) Chodziesner, was particularly gratifying.

* * *

My long-standing preoccupation with the Third Reich informed my approach to Gertrud Kolmar. This book is structured around the dual investigation of her oeuvre and times. Here are just a few of the titles:

Die Juden in Deutschland 1933–1945, Leben unter nationalsozialistischer Herrschaft [*Life Under Nazi Rule: Jews in Germany, 1933–1945*] practically became my handbook. Edited by Wolfgang Benz and coauthored by Volker Dahm, Konrad Kwiet, Günter Plum, Clemens Vollhas, and Juliane Wetzel, the work served as my main source of quotations from eyewitnesses.

Simone Ladwig-Winters's *Anwalt ohne Recht, Das Schicksal jüdischer Rechtsanwälte in Berlin nach 1933* [*Lawyers Without Rights: The Fate of Jewish Lawyers in Berlin After 1933*] was important with an eye to Kolmar's father. Ditto Klaus Luig's *Jüdische Juristen in Köln während der NS-Zeit* [*Jewish Lawyers in Cologne During the Nazi Era*] . . . particularly because he is not of Aryan descent.

I found documentation of oral histories in the volume *Die verheissene Stadt, Deutsch-jüdische Emigranten in New York* [*City of Promise: German-Jewish Immigrants in New York*], edited by Thomas Hartweg and Achim Roscher.

The tale of two alternative lives is modeled on Helga Cazas's *Auf Wiedersehen in Paris, Als jüdische Immigrantin in Frankreich 1938–1945* [*Au Revoir à Paris: Life as a Jewish Immigrant in France, 1938–1945*] and J. Hellmut Freund's *Vor dem Zitronenbaum, Autobiographische Abschweifungen eines Zurückgekehrten* [*Before the Lemon Tree: Autobiographical Digressions from One Who Returned*].

I have also quoted from Friedrich Munding's *Dass ich nur noch selten schreibe: Briefe aus Berlin 1940–1943* [*Since I Write Only Rarely: Berlin Letters from 1940–1943*], edited by Werner Trapp.

Das Exil der kleinen Leute: Alltagserfahrung deutscher Juden in der Emigration [*Exile of the Little People: Everyday Experiences of German Jews Who Emigrated*], edited by Wolfgang Benz, proved frequently instructive.

Gorch Pieken and Cornelia Kruse's *Das Haushaltsbuch der Elsa Chotzen: Schicksal einer jüdischen Familie 1937–1946* [*The Household Book of Elsa Chotzen: Fate of a Jewish Family, 1937–1946*] offers a host of details.

Jan-Pieter Barbian's *Literaturpolitik im Dritten Reich: Institutionen, Kompetenzen, Betätigungsfelder* [*Literary Politics in the Third Reich: Institutions, Authority (Powers), Fields of Activity*].

And the most recent among listed publications, Martin Friedenberger's *Fiskalische Ausplünderung: Die Berliner Steuer- und Finanzverwaltung und die jüdische Bevölkerung 1933–1945* [*Fiscal Plundering: The Berlin Tax and Fiscal Authorities and the Jewish Population in the Period, 1933–1945*]. This monograph exposes the many injustices that lawyer Chodziesner and his daughter had to endure.

* * *

Pictures usually play an integral role in a biography. But in this instance, sifting through the surviving photos proved very disappointing. We have so few photos of the poet that she may well be the least photographed of all twentieth-century poets. There is only one portrait photo, taken sometime in the mid to late 1920s by an unknown photographer, and it has become iconic in the meantime. There are only two or three other group photos in which Gertrud Kolmar literally appears on the periphery, and these photos quite clearly emphasize her inconspicuousness. She apparently had no interest in being photographed and, on that score, never placed herself in the foreground. It seems as though she wanted to leave no trace of her earthly life. If her sister and brother-in-law had not collected her writings and passed them on, then Gertrud Kolmar would have disappeared, save for very few published works.

As for photos, there are only a few options—pictures of her father, her siblings, and the house—and these can be reproduced with only limited results. It would seem natural, of course, to show her father on his trusty steed, in his lawn chair, or at the window. And it would, of course, be tempting to show the house in the country and to, perhaps, be confronted with a photo of the house as a modern-day sports complex. But such a sampling would only serve to push the poet even further into the background, would it not? [Translator's note: We have not included photos of Gertrud Kolmar and her family in this edition. Anyone who is interested may consult the book *Gertrud Kolmar: Leben und Werk in Texten und Bildern* by Beatrice Eichmann-Leutenegger (Frankfurt, Ger.: Jüdischer Verlag, 1995).]

So it's better to have no photos at all than to have a paltry assortment from which the poet is largely absent anyway. In a macabre way, it confirms what her lifestyle amounted to: please don't stand in the foreground, but stay humbly on the sidelines, preferably remaining invisible. By dispensing with a photo section, I am also making an indirect statement about the poet who, along with the family that meant so much to her, is decidedly at the center of this biography. Only within the framework of her family history would she have been able to give her blessing to her life story. Her wishes shall now be carried out posthumously.

—*Dieter Kühn*

Führer [leader] refers to Adolf Hitler, who gave himself the title *Führer des deutschen Reiches und Volkes* (leader of the German Reich and people).

GDR or German Democratic Republic (Deutsche Demokratische Republik) was a socialist state established in 1949 in the Soviet-occupied zone of Germany. It existed until 1990.

Hauptsturmführer [head assault leader] was a rank equivalent to captain in several Nazi Party organizations, including the SS.

Justizrat [counselor] is an honorific title granted to lawyers.

Machtantritt [accession to power], *Machtergreifung* [seizure of power], and *Machtübernahme* [takeover of power] refer to the Nazi takeover of the democratic Weimar republic in 1933.

Notar is a lawyer who specializes in property law, corporate law, family law, or estate planning. There is no equivalent in the U.S. legal system. Although *Notar* is often translated as "notary" or "notary public," that is actually a misnomer.

Reich can be translated "empire," "government," or "state." Reichkanzlei (Reich Chancellery) was the office of the Reichskanzler (chancellor of Germany), the position Hitler gained in 1933.

SA or *Sturmabteilung* [Assault Division] was the military wing of the Nazi Party.

Sonderbehandlung [special treatment] was a Nazi euphemism for killing.

Sonderkommando [special command] was a work unit of prisoners, mostly Jews, who helped dispose of gas-chamber victims.

SS or *Schutzstaffel* [Protection Squad] was the special police force of the Nazi Party.

Sturmbannführer [assault unit leader] was a rank equivalent to major in several Nazi party organizations, including the SA and SS.

Sturmführer [assault leader] was the lowest rank of commissioned officer in several Nazi party organizations.

Tag is the word for "day," but it can also mean "assembly"—as in *Reichstag* [parliament]—or "rally"—as in *Parteitag* [party rally].

Volk [people, nation, or race] refers to the German people, especially as the carriers of the customs, beliefs, and art that make up German culture. The term also conveys a sense of superiority and the idea of a universal mission for the German people.

"Abandoned, The," 155–56, 223
"Abused, The," 120–21
"Angel of the Forest, The," 300–301
"Anno Domini 1933," 121–22
"Astray," 65–66
"Beautiful Miracles of the Seven
    Kingdoms, The," 79–80
"Blessed, The," 989
"Borzoi," 299–300
"Brüssow Coat of Arms," 144–45
"Buried, The," 355–56
"Candle, The," 148
"Castaway, The," 102
"City, The," 204–5
"Clown, The," 93–94, 185–86
"Dancer 2, The," 69–71
"Daughter, The," 167–68
"Dedication," 200–201
"Embroiderer, The," 33–34
"End/Ending," 54
"Fish King," 184
"Forgive," 52
"For the Prisoners," 125–26
"Friedland Coat of Arms," 145–46
"From Westend," 39–40
"Fruitless," 98
"Garden in Summer, The," 300–301
"Governess, The," 72–73, 223
"Grandmother," 100–102
"Homesick," 354–55
"Humorous Poem," 69
"Idol, The," 184–85

"I Know," 41–42
"In the Camp," 124
"Invalid, The," 98–99
"Jewess, The," 170
"Jewish Mother, The," 128–29
"Kingfisher," 113
"Lassen Coat of Arms," 81–82
"Marching Song," 41
"Mine," 39
"Moses in the Basket," 185
"My Son," 52–53
"Old Woman, The," 301
"Pensive, The," 200, 356–57
"Poetess, The," 225–26
"Poultry Park," 171–72
"Rag-and-Bone Woman, The," 185
"Robespierre," 143
"Rose of the Condor, The," 80
"Sea Miracle," 153–54
"Self-Sacrifice," 52
"Silver Lovebirds!" 46–47
"Single Ticket," 71–72
"Stroll," 99–100
"Swan, The," 186
"Toad, The," 292
"Traveler, The," 113–14
"Undeveloped, The," 102–3, 184
"Waiting On," 201–3
"Watch," 156–57
"Wild Boar," 113
"Zechlin Coat of Arms," 146–47

"alte Frau, Die," 301
"An die Gefangenen," 125–26
"Anno Domini 1933," 121–22
"Aus Westend," 39–40
"Begrabene, Die," 355–56
"Borzoi," 299–300
"Dichterin, Die," 225–26
"Dienen," 201–3
"Einheitsschein, Der," 71–72
"Eisvogel," 113
"Ende," 54
"Engel im Walde, Der," 300–301
"Erzieherin, Die," 72–73, 223
"Fahrende, Die," 113–14
"Fischkönig," 184
"Fruchtlos," 98
"Garten im Sommer," 300–301
"Gauklerin, Die," 93–94, 185–86
"Geflügelpark," 171–72
"Gesegnete, Die," 99
"Götzenbild, Das," 184–85
"Grossmutter," 100–102
"Heimweh," 354–55
"Ich weiss es," 41–42
"Im Lager," 124
"Irre, Die," 65–66
"Jüdin, Die," 170
"jüdische Mutter, Die," 128–29
"Kerze, Die," 148
"Kranke, Die," 98–99
"Kröte, Die," 292
"Liebes Silberpaar!" 46–47

"Lumpensammlerin, Die," 185
"Marschlied," 41
"Meerwunder," 153–54
"Meins," 39
"Mein Sohn," 52–53
"Misshandelte, Der," 120–21
"Mose im Kästchen," 185
"Opfergang," 52
"Robespierre," 143
"Rose des Kondors, Die," 80
"Scherzgedichte," 69
"schönen Wunder aus den sieben
    Reichen, Die," 79–80
"Schwan, Der," 186
"Schwarzwild," 113
"Sinnende, Die," 356–57
"Spaziergang," 99–100
"Stadt, Die," 204–5
"Sticklerin, Die," 33
"Tänzerin 2, Die," 69–71
"Tochter, Die," 167–68
"Unerschlossene, Die," 102–3, 184
"Vergib," 52
"Verlassene, Die," 155–56, 223
"Verworfene, Die," 102
"Wacht," 156–57
"Wappen von Brüssow," 144–45
"Wappen von Friedland," 145–46
"Wappen von Lassen," 81–82
"Wappen von Zechlin," 146–47
"Zueignung," 200–201

Dieter Kühn has received numerous awards for his novels, short stories, biographies, and radio plays, including the Hermann Hesse Prize and the Literature Prize of the Bavarian Academy of Fine Arts.

Linda Marianiello is a literary and arts translator from German to English. She has participated in Helen and Kurt Wolff Translator's Prize seminars and translation workshops at the Goethe Institute in Chicago. She is a member of the American Translators Association and has served on the board of the New Mexico Translators and Interpreters Association. Marianiello is also a classical flutist who has performed with symphony and opera orchestras, including the Bavarian State Opera and Munich Radio Orchestra in Germany.

Franz Vote is a literary, arts, and medical translator from German to English. He is a member of the German Language Division of the American Translators Association. He is also an orchestra conductor who has led orchestras at opera houses in Gelsenkirchen, Aachen, and Munich, and at the Bayreuth Wagner Festival. In the United States, he held positions on the conducting staff of the Metropolitan Opera and as music director of the Seattle Opera production of the Ring cycle in 2000–2001. He now serves as music director of the New Mexico Bach Society.